MEXICO

WESTVIEW PROFILES · NATIONS OF CONTEMPORARY LATIN AMERICA
Ronald Schneider, Series Editor

†Available in hardcover and paperback.

ABOUT THE BOOK AND AUTHORS

In the four years since the first edition was published, Mexico's political system—exceptional among Latin American nations—has been severely tested. The administration has been struggling to cope with the effects of a depressed market for oil, the demands of an increasingly vocal opposition, and the foreign policy challenges posed by violence in Central America. In this timely second edition of a work that has received favorable attention in the United States and in Mexico, the authors extend their analysis of Mexico's current and future prospects to cover the dramatic developments of the past few years.

Throughout, the authors have updated their discussion to assess the social and political impact of the latest elections, the recent earthquakes, and the continuing cycle of economic crisis, recovery, and renewed crisis. They also pay special attention to Mexico's initiatives for peace in Central America and to recent shifts in Mexican-U.S. relations.

Appropriate for courses in Mexican studies, Latin American politics, and Third World development, this text also will be of value to anyone interested in Mexico's political and economic affairs.

Daniel Levy is associate professor of Latin American studies and of educational administration and policy studies at SUNY-Albany; faculty fellow, Nelson A. Rockefeller Institute of Government, SUNY; and research affiliate, Yale University. **Gabriel Székely** is a professor at the Center of International Studies, El Colegio de México, and acting associate director at the Center for U.S.-Mexican Studies, University of California–San Diego.

MEXICO

Paradoxes of
Stability and Change

SECOND EDITION, REVISED AND UPDATED

Daniel Levy
and
Gabriel Székely

Westview Press / Boulder and London

Westview Profiles/Nations of Contemporary Latin America

Paperback cover photo: Mexico City's famous Plaza de las Tres Culturas (Plaza of the Three Cultures) at Tlatelolco (Photo courtesy of Bud Lewis)

Published in 1987 in the United States of America by Westview Press, Inc.; Frederick A. Praeger, Publisher; 5500 Central Avenue, Boulder, Colorado 80301

Library of Congress Cataloging-in-Publication Data
Levy, Daniel C.
  Mexico: paradoxes of stability and change.
  (Westview profiles. Nations of contemporary Latin
America)
  Includes index.
  1. Mexico—Politics and government—20th century.
I. Székely, Gabriel, 1953–   . II. Title.
III. Series.
F1234.L65 1987   972.08   86-11003
ISBN 0-8133-0349-4
ISBN 0-8133-0350-8 (pbk.)

Printed and bound in the United States of America

The paper used in this publication meets the requirements of the American National Standard for Permanence of Paper for Printed Library Materials Z39.48-1984.

10   9   8   7   6   5   4   3   2   1

TO APRIL AND PAMELA

Contents

Tables

Illustrations

Foreword

The predictably regular election of presidents every six years underscores Mexico's remarkable political stability, institutionalized for half a century now after two decades of revolution and civil war. At the same time, Mexico once again has fallen into a severe economic crisis, and this crisis has serious political implications. Mexico's foreign debt, for example, has soared over $100 billion—nearly the highest in the world whether in per capita terms, as a percentage of gross national product, or as a proportion of export earnings. Moreover, Mexico has repeatedly had to seek rescheduling of its debt, accompanied in each case by additional austerity measures and a significant increase in its total foreign debt burden.

Against such a background, dissatisfaction was sure to increase and was expressed eventually at the ballot box. Accustomed to a near monopoly over elected as well as appointive offices, the ponderous governing party chose to increase its manipulation of state electoral results—apparently unwilling to admit the extent of erosion of its popular base and the growth of the opposition. One price has been, as is inevitable in such circumstances, a contribution to the undermining of regime legitimacy and to further alienation of important societal groups.

Beyond and behind the present serious malaise and its implications for the conduct of Mexican national affairs lies another set of considerations that lend urgency to the quest for a broader and deeper understanding in the rest of the Western world of Latin America's second most populous nation—one destined to join the exclusive club of lands with over 100 million inhabitants by the middle of the 1990s. First, there is the highly ambivalent relationship between Mexico and its northern neighbor, the United States, plagued by the former's memories of virtual rape in the mid-1800s and subsequent domination and by the latter's ingrained attitude of inherent superiority. Indeed, it can be said with considerable justification that Mexican immigrants ceased being "wetbacks" only when the post-1973 energy crisis forced the United States to turn toward Mexico as a source of gas and petroleum. Although most people in the United States believe that they know more about Mexico than about any other Latin American country, their perceptions of Mexican society and culture are far too often a mix of Tijuana and Acapulco plus the residue of any personal contact with Chicanos in this country. As a result, real understanding of this developing middle power remains sorely lacking, except, perhaps, in the bordering areas of the Southwest where contact between the two peoples is most intense and continuous.

The existing literature on Mexico is extensive and on many subjects highly informative. Yet the best is essentially monographic, going deeply into some rather narrow topic and rarely escaping the limitations of a single academic discipline. Once in a generation there have been books that successfully explained the essence of Mexico, at least from the perspective of the time. In this category fall John Reed's coverage of the Revolution, Frank Tannenbaum's explanation of the Cárdenas era, and Howard Cline's portrayal of Mexico on the verge of industrialization. The Mexico of the end of the twentieth century is far more complex and marked by contradictions than even that of the 1950s; therefore a fresh and more systematic inter-pretation is badly needed. To this end Daniel Levy and Gabriel Székely have combined their talents and differing backgrounds to produce a superb synthesis that captures both the drama and tragedy of today's Mexico. Politics are at the center of their analysis, yet the Mexico that emerges from the pages of this book is a whole, not compartmentalized into society, economy, and culture with some assumed relationship to political life. Moreover, by examining the alternative policy prescriptions put forth by Mexico's major political-intellectual currents, they provide an added di-mension for those interested not only in what Mexico is and how this came to be but also with where it is going and how it might get there.

Ronald Schneider

Preface

Prefaces to second editions tend to be dull. Authors take pride in the first edition's success, claim that their basic arguments are holding up against the tests of time and scholarly scrutiny, humbly allow that those arguments nonetheless could have been improved, and emphasize that the new edition adds significant information. Admittedly, this preface follows that pattern. If it assumes interest—and, much more importantly, if the second edition itself assumes interest—it is less because of changes in our basic perspectives than because the analysis has been extended to take account of the enormous changes that have occurred in Mexico itself over the four years between the two editions.

The September 1985 earthquakes that ravaged parts of Mexico City could be seen as a cruel metaphor for the beleaguered nation: Major struggles involving great sacrifice have been required just for survival amid further uncertainty. Mexico has been a nation under siege. Economic collapse, social suffering, and political dissatisfaction have characterized recent developments. The Mexican political system has been severely challenged in the past four years. And the developments and challenges have attracted increased attention from the United States, ranging from the thoughtful to the hysterical. But despite crisis, pain, frustration, and a degree of political delegitimation, the Mexican political system has maintained its remarkable stability, and outright civil disruption remains rare.

We wish that the first edition had more fully foreseen the deep changes that have been occurring. We wish we had devoted more space to certain ongoing concerns like the rise of relatively "technocratic" leaders and the implications for Mexico of violent conflict in Central America. Such concerns are highlighted in the second edition. So is the cycle of economic crisis, partial recovery, and renewed crisis. And so are the elections of 1985 and 1986 with their lessons about government and democracy in Mexico.

We reiterate our gratitude to Levy's university, the State University of New York at Albany, and extend it to two institutions with which Székely has been associated in the past four years: El Colegio de México and the Center for U.S.-Mexican Studies at the University of California–San Diego.

On a more personal note, we reiterate our gratitude to April Levy and extend it to Pamela Székely, both of whom have been wonderfully supportive and to both of whom this edition is dedicated.

Daniel Levy
Delmar, New York

Gabriel Székely
La Jolla, California

Preface to First Edition

The common problems involved in coauthorship are especially challenging for those who try to bridge national boundaries. We are therefore happy, perhaps even surprised, to find ourselves far closer friends at the end of this book than when we began it. It has been a rewarding experience for both of us. Yet, it has not come easily. The continual struggle for mutually acceptable, compatible content and style has been as time-consuming as it has been trying.

It is only natural that the authors differ on many issues concerning Mexican politics. We have grown up in different nations, under different social and personal influences. Moreover, Levy has drawn predominantly on U.S. bibliographical sources and Székely predominantly on Mexican ones. All this does not mean that Levy represents "the U.S. view" and Székely "the Mexican view." It does mean that we have brought different sensitivities, different insensitivities, and different educational and research experiences and resources to the task. We believe that it is important for those U.S. citizens interested in Mexican politics to hear not just from U.S. but also from Mexican authors.

We have resolved our political differences in a few ways. First, we have divided responsibility. We have each written four chapters, shaping them to our own tastes: Levy wrote chapters 1, 2, 4, and 6; Székely wrote chapters 3, 5, 7, and 8. Nonetheless, we have both criticized and strongly influenced each other's chapters. Second, we have compromised. Where disagreement could be reduced, the chapter author adjusted his work. In those few cases where disagreement proved intractable, we chose to delete specific thoughts rather than to risk a schizoid product. Third, we have restricted the scope of our work. We have not attempted to develop and elaborate our own normative preferences. Instead, we have tried to analyze the principal realities of Mexican politics. In doing so, we have focused on how Mexico has managed to achieve a degree of political stability unmatched in Latin America and on what Mexico has and has not reaped, politically, economically, and socially, from this stability. However obvious and compelling the degree of political stability, it has manifested itself amid complex, sometimes subtle, paradoxes of development. We happen to agree a bit more substantially in our analysis of Mexican reality—the stability and the paradoxes—than in our normative preferences. We each strove to be as objective as possible, but we recognize that our political views inevitably influenced the content and structure of every chapter.

In the process of writing this book, we have interacted with many scholars, from both sides of the border. Their insights have contributed significantly, although we naturally assume responsibility for the final product. We wish to thank Juan M. del Aguila and Rose Spalding for their chapter-by-chapter comments on the entire manuscript. Several other colleagues also offered valuable comments, usually sharing their special expertise on one or two individual chapters. We thank Silvia Arrom, Bruce Bagley, Roderic Camp, Arturo Cruz Sequeira, Cynthia Hewitt de Alcántara, Lorenzo Meyer, Cynthia McClintock, Kevin Middlebrook, Dale Story, and Gustavo Vega. April Levy deserves our gratitude for her editing and for originating the idea of binational coauthorship. Ron Schneider and Lynne Rienner, academic and editorial engineers of Westview's Nations of Contemporary Latin America series, have been generous in their support, advice, and encouragement; we particularly thank Lynne Rienner for her vote of confidence in approving a significant increase in the length of this study. Finally, we thank photographers Rodolfo Romo de Vivar and James P. Brochin for taking and providing most of the photographs we use and Rosa María Casas and her staff for facilitating access to the library of the Mexican Embassy in Washington, D.C.

For varied sorts of support we thank the following institutions with which we have been associated during the writing of the book: Yale University, the State University of New York at Albany, the National Autonomous University of Mexico, the George Washington University, and the Overseas Development Council.

Daniel Levy
New Haven, Connecticut

Gabriel Székely
Mexico City

MEXICO

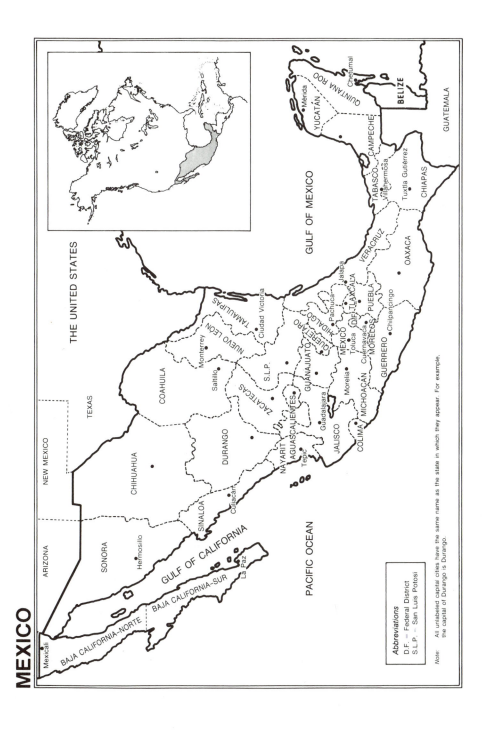

Abbreviations

D.F. = Federal District
S.L.P. = San Luis Potosi

Note: All unlabeled capital cities have the same name as the state in which they appear. For example, the capital of Durango is Durango.

1

Introduction

POLITICAL STABILITY AND DEVELOPMENT

A Model of Political Stability?

Mexican politics has been notable for its stability—indeed, the Mexican regime has been uniquely stable within Latin America. Since 1973 alone, Argentina has swung from military to civilian rule twice, Chile from liberal reformist to Marxist to rightist authoritarian rule, Peru from leftist military to rightist military to civilian rule, and Uruguay from civilian to military and back to civilian rule. Similarly, we need go back only to 1964 to record two major regime transformations in Brazil; to go back a half century would be to include multiple transformations in most major Latin American nations, as well as the notoriously unstable smaller ones such as Bolivia. Not only most of Latin America but also much of the Third World beyond has found political stability an elusive goal.

Mexico has been different: Mexico has maintained the same basic political regime for well over fifty years.[1] It is the only major Latin American nation not to have had a military coup in the post–World War II period. Every president selected since 1934 has survived his six-year term and then peacefully relinquished office to his successor. Since the 1940s (or even earlier), despite leadership changes, the regime has almost always held close to a basic mode of national development emphasizing political stability with economic growth. However shaken Mexico has been by the economic disasters of the 1980s, it has usually been strikingly successful in achieving these two goals. Consequently, those interested in such development, from political scientists to politicians to foreign governments to bankers, have frequently pointed to Mexico as a model, a model to be assessed and even emulated.[2]

What, then, does Mexico look like after its extended period of political stability? To agree that Mexico has been uniquely stable is not necessarily to agree on whether stability has been a blessing or a problem. Those who disapprove of the present situation and favor fundamental changes may well regard political stability as either a neutral fact or an obstacle to desired change. Much depends on the relationships one sees between political stability and other components of development. Some see political devel-

1

opment in terms of a combination including regime stability, institution building, and widespread inclusion of the citizenry. Others find this definition morally bankrupt and conceive of development in terms of meaningfully independent participation or of democracy. Still others emphasize economic development, either in terms of production, industrialization, and per capita income, or very differently, in terms of resource distribution. An emphasis on resource distribution overlaps various concepts of social development, focusing on such issues as the distribution and quality of education, health care, and other services.[3] Many works have attempted to explore the relationships among some of these criteria of development. Here we focus on the relationship between political stability and other development criteria. Specifically, we ask how various factors have contributed to political stability and, even more important, what political, economic, and social realities have characterized stable Mexico.

Stability amid Deep
and Intensifying Problems

Political stability should not imply the absence of political (or economic and social) change and flexibility, examples of which are found throughout the book. Political stability, as used here, refers to the maintenance of the regime and its basic development model. Nor does the stability of the regime guarantee the passivity (let alone the well-being) of its citizens. There have been many protests in Mexico, including violent ones, and the regime has continually faced numerous and serious threats. That the Mexican regime is now in crisis is debatable; that Mexico itself is in crisis, in the broader sense of facing huge and recently aggravated economic and social problems, is not debatable. Mexico's crisis demands our attention, partly because of the threat it may pose to the regime's stability, but principally because the crisis itself stems from underlying problems that begin to tell us what a stable Mexico has and has not accomplished.

Chapter 2 briefly highlights the dimensions of the deep economic crisis that surfaced in the 1980s, while Chapter 5 analyzes in much greater depth the sources as well as the dimensions of Mexico's ongoing economic and social problems. Our purpose in this introduction is to give a feel for the immediacy of some of these problems in everyday Mexican life. Decades of political stability and economic growth have surely alleviated some of the terrible social and economic problems that have historically plagued Mexico. But they have just as surely not alleviated others. And this very contrast may sharpen the threat to the system's survival. For whether the result is called a revolution of rising expectations, frustrated aspirations, or relative deprivation, it is less a people's abject circumstances that tempt them to rebel than their perception that these circumstances are unnecessary and unjustified. The subjective view of what is unjustified is often made in comparison to the visible privileges enjoyed by others and to hopes dashed in times of crisis.[4] We will look briefly at both long-standing problems, made keener by their juxtaposition to increasing privilege, and at new

Modernity and wealth live side by side with extreme poverty in one of the central paradoxes of Mexican development. (The sign reads "expropriated lands" and gives a file number.) (Photo courtesy of Rodolfo Romo de Vivar)

problems caused perhaps by the forward motion of development itself and aggravated by recent economic troubles.

Poverty, malnutrition, disease, unemployment, underemployment, illiteracy, and inadequate education are examples of old problems that still endure, now alongside increased wealth and opportunity. Income distribution is one of the most unequal in the world, and it is becoming even more unequal (see Chapter 5). In medicine, modern facilities have expanded while many still rely on folk cures and herbs. Even according to official data, perhaps 20 percent of the population older than fourteen is illiterate, and perhaps double that figure received fewer than four years of primary education—these figures are typical of Third World nations—whereas nearly 15 percent of the population (compared to roughly 2 percent in 1960) has access to higher education, a figure close to that for much of Europe.[5] Transportation offers another case of increasing contrasts. In urban settings, developed Mexico uses automobiles, taxis, or modern buses that take only as many passengers as there are seats; less developed Mexico must rely more on older buses, often packed tightly. Between cities, developed Mexico travels by plane, car, or first-class bus equipped with air-conditioning, stereo music, toilets, assigned seats, and sometimes complimentary soft drinks. The second-class buses are rarely equipped with any of these features and pack in as many passengers, often carrying fruit, fowl, and other market wares, as can be made to fit.

We have looked briefly at cases in which development has produced results for almost all to see but for only some to share. We now turn to cases in which the quality of life has actually diminished for most Mexicans, though again mostly for the less privileged. Population growth, both a product of development and a contributor to many chronic problems, illustrates the point. Mexico's population may not have been substantially larger in 1872 than it had been during the Spanish conquest three and a half centuries earlier; but, in the twentieth century, as political stability replaced revolutionary violence, the population began to soar. Additionally, development has furthered population growth by extending life expectancy. The population grew at about 1 percent per year early in this century, 1.7 percent per year in the 1930s, and 3.4 percent per year in the 1960s. Indeed, Mexico came to have one of the fastest population growth rates in the world. The population climbed to over 75 million, and roughly one in two Mexicans was under fifteen (meaning largely, although not fully, unproductive).[6] As population soars, more food has to be produced, more health care and education provided, more land distributed, just to stay even. And much more employment must be created.

Perceiving the dangers of unbridled population growth, the government began to act. As "candidate" for president in 1970, Luis Echeverría boasted of his opposition to population control, eagerly presenting himself as the proud father of eight children; as president (1970–1976), Echeverría helped initiate a governmental family planning program. The birthrate has slackened impressively, from a peak of roughly 3.7 percent per year in 1977 to little over 2 percent by 1986 (with the average age finally rising), earning Mexico's National Population Council the UN's 1986 population award. President Miguel de la Madrid (1982–1988) pushed a 1 percent goal for the turn of the century.[7] Nonetheless, most projections would put Mexico's population over the 100 million mark by that point.

Mexico's urbanization is another phenomenon that can be identified simultaneously with lack of development and development itself. Mexico's cities do not have industrial bases that provide sufficient employment, income, and opportunity for their citizens, yet cities grow as population grows and as frustrated but aspiring villagers leave their more traditional settings. The uprooting social effects of migration often bring special problems for the migrants themselves and for increasingly overcrowded cities.[8]

Mexico City, which has grown very rapidly, already has roughly 18 million people, with estimates for the year 2000 running to 26 million and more. Government efforts to reverse the trend through decentralization policies have made notoriously little headway. Not the first to push decentralization, President de la Madrid announced that no new industry would be authorized in the capital, and he advocated industrial, educational, and governmental decentralization. But centralization often builds on itself and involves not just population but economic, intellectual, and political networks. Few are willing to surrender the services and opportunities of Mexico City for the provinces. Furthermore, the economic crisis has robbed the government of the means to offer incentives and to absorb the costs of decentralization. And so life continues to worsen for Mexico City's residents. These problems have become a major theme for young Mexican writers.

Although most urban difficulties, like limited access to good water supplies, increasing drug use, and crime, affect the poor more than the privileged, many other difficulties affect all. For example, Mexico City has perhaps the worst air pollution in the world. In 1984, the U.S. State Department labeled Mexico City an unhealthy post for its employees and awarded them extra benefits for working there. A product of development— the automobile—has been a major contributor to this pollution.

Nor is pollution the only way in which the automobile makes Mexican life increasingly difficult. Mexico City's traffic jams have become unbearable; they have worsened drastically in the last decade. Residents who drive to work may spend up to four hours daily in transit. Estimates of work hours lost are staggering. The city's traffic, crowded into a few main streets, is worse than in any U.S. city, and its rush hours are far longer. Yet, despite the automobile's problems, public transportation is not a satisfactory alternative. Mexico City's *metro* (subway) does carry over 4 million passengers daily (more than New York City's does), and it is clean, quiet, and efficient. It expanded its routes in the 1980s. But the increased passenger load is such that for a few hours each morning and again each evening the metro is a battleground, again much worse than the subway system in any U.S. city. For their own protection in the crunch hours, women and children are literally separated from men and funneled toward different sections of the train platforms.

Amid such troubles, major oil discoveries in the 1970s offered hope. Chapter 7 will analyze how different observers have viewed the different impacts of oil on Mexican problems. For now we note that some see oil as a blessing allowing Mexico to cope with many of its chronic problems better than it otherwise could, whereas others see oil perpetuating or even aggravating these problems, as the benefits oil produces go to a few and the debt and inflation it aggravates affect all. Some evidence for both perspectives on oil's impact can be found in the economic crisis that received so much attention in the mid-1970s. It is true that oil drove economic growth from its nadir in the mid-1970s back to and even above its characteristic post–World War II rates. But it also helped to drive inflation to a new postwar high of 30 percent in 1980, a rate that had become much higher by 1982, by which time even the renewed growth halted. As we will see, oil's impact on today's economy is multifaceted.

Moreover, oil-based growth has symbolized how Mexican development has favored big industry over agriculture, especially subsistence agriculture. In fact, Mexico at present is threatened by the loss of its traditional self-sufficiency in many basic foods. Examples include corn (basic to the ubiquitous *tortilla*, or flat corncake), sugar, rice, beans, and other vegetables and fruits, as well as coffee and cotton. "Crude for food" is an exchange many Mexicans fear as they see themselves forced to rely on the oil-importing United States

Mexico's suffering was symbolized and aggravated by the 1985 earthquakes. (Photo courtesy of Phyllis Duffy)

to feed themselves. Thus, in 1980, Mexico declared self-sufficiency in basic grains to be a major national *goal*. This declaration was an implicit admission of the failure of the "rural modernization" policies (e.g., new techniques to overcome production problems) pursued since 1940 as part of the growth-stability development model. Rural modernization never led to concomitant "rural development" (defined as progress in the way people live). In fact, rural modernization was really aimed not so much at rural but at urban development, accepting rural misery in the hope of inexpensively feeding the growing urban population.[9] Despite its own suffering, rural Mexico had succeeded in feeding Mexico. Now, the regime acknowledged, new policies would be required in order to prevent even that achievement from slipping away (see Chapter 5 on the new food programs).

Cruelly, Mexico's woes were aggravated by devastating earthquakes (centered around Mexico City) in September 1985. The major quake registered roughly 8 on the Richter scale and killed perhaps 20,000 people. The quake destroyed about a thousand buildings and damaged thousands more. Many were left homeless, and Mexico was saddled with yet further human and financial burdens.[10]

However serious and worsening many of Mexico's social and economic problems have been, they have not, at least not yet, transformed Mexican politics. Political stability has persisted. And it has persisted despite continual assertions that a house divided against itself cannot stand, that the development/nondevelopment contradictions are too deep, that the status quo is untenable, that fundamental change is inevitable. Most works written in the 1950s and 1960s argued optimistically that political, economic, and social development criteria usually—perhaps naturally—complement and even promote one another. This had supposedly been the experience of U.S. and West European development. Because Mexico had already achieved both political stability and economic growth, many observers assumed that meaningful political participation, as well as more equitable distribution of the wealth and improved social-welfare indicators, were likely to follow. Others believed that the negative side of the development ledger would pull down the positive side, tearing political stability asunder. Many commentaries emphasized either-or propositions: Frustrated aspirations would have to be *either* satisfied, probably through a democratic, reformist, or socialist option, *or* more directly repressed, probably through a right-wing, authoritarian, or fascist option. Unless something was done—soon—the system would be undone.[11]

Increased guerrilla activity in the late 1960s and early 1970s seemed to support the either-or interpretations. In those years, guerrillas polarized politics, or made latent polarization overt, and the regime bolstered its repressive apparatus. Guerrilla activity has had a rich history in Mexico, and its intensity increased in both urban and rural areas. Even the government and the press came to refer to a crisis of political terrorism, no longer dismissing guerrilla activity as common banditry. A rash of political kidnappings shook Mexico in the early 1970s. Senator Rubén Figueroa, leading Monterrey industrialist Eugenio Garza Sada, and the president's own father-in-law were among the victims. Some, like Garza Sada, were assassinated. Others, like Figueroa, were released, probably after the government secretly acquiesced in guerrilla demands. A perception of government weakness enhanced the guerrillas' image. Combined with the economic crisis (flight of capital out of Mexico, inflation, devaluation of the *peso*) and with controversial land seizures, this perception of government weakness contributed to somewhat rash speculation about possible military intervention in Mexico's proudly civilian system. But the guerrilla threat peaked and declined, and the regime was still intact. One of the best-known guerrilla defeats was the 1974 killing of Lucío Cabañas, a former primary school teacher, who had for seven years led guerrilla operations in the mountains and who was probably involved in the Figueroa kidnapping.

The single most dramatic recent political crisis peaked in 1968. Students opposing the regime's authoritarian and conservative policies went beyond the usual bounds permitted for dissent in Mexico and were violently repressed. By its harsh action, the regime "solved" the problem of open and organized political dissent, but it left a deep problem of political legitimacy.

The legitimacy problem is less dramatic than the guerrilla or student protests, but it is a deep and difficult one. The official party has shown weaknesses in most recent elections, raising serious doubts about the regime's popular support. Abstention rates have become much higher than the regime would like. Some observers have even remarked that the "party of abstention" could be viewed as the regime's toughest electoral opponent. Chapter 3

considers this challenge to legitimacy and the new party challenges that
have consequently been engendered. It also considers the regime's responses
to the challenges and highlights its closely watched and controversial electoral
victories of 1985 and 1986.

Despite varied challenges, whether manifestly political or rooted in
deep and perceptibly aggravated socioeconomic problems, Mexico (at least
up until now) has remained politically stable. Stability has been shaken
but not undone. The predictions that have proven most accurate are those
that emphasized the viability of Mexico's political regime and the flexibility
of that regime to meet otherwise destabilizing problems (see Chapter 4).
Indeed, at a pinnacle of the perceived threat to its stability, just a few years
after crises had toppled many other Latin American regimes, the Mexican
regime peacefully transferred power from one administration to the next.
This shift from President Luis Echeverría to President José López Portillo
(1976–1982) will therefore be analyzed from various political, economic,
and foreign policy perspectives in subsequent chapters. The new administration proudly proclaimed the regime's viability. Its minister of programming and budget and the subsequent president of Mexico, Miguel de la
Madrid, expressed the regime's optimism this way: "We have history, we
have ideology, we have the system, and we have the leaders." Nor was all
this propaganda or the wishful thinking of biased sources. Foreign investors,
for example, generally saw in Mexico a favorable environment, stable into
the future. Compared to the 1976 Echeverría-López Portillo transition, the
1982 López Portillo-de la Madrid transition, despite Mexico's seriously
mounting economic problems, was not surrounded by speculation about
imminent regime collapse. Instead, many domestic and foreign news commentaries initially stressed the regime's remarkable and revitalized stability.
Naturally, such commentaries were hedged as Mexico slumped into a terrible
economic crisis in 1982 and again by mid-decade. One could point out that
severe economic crises inevitably pose threats to political stability; in fact,
this book repeatedly stresses that Mexico's political stability has been
fundamentally tied to economic growth. Or one could emphasize how
remarkable Mexico's political stability must be to have survived economic
problems that would have toppled other Third World regimes.

Yet the future of Mexico's political stability is by no means certain.
A key factor is economic growth, because although the regime has survived
sporadic growth crises, it has not faced sustained growth problems comparable
to the ongoing social problems. But the growth problems of the 1980s have
been more sustained than any in recent Mexican history. In any case, one's
forecasts, hopes, and proposals depend largely on which of many contrasting
factors are emphasized, as Chapter 8 suggests. Just as the crises of the
recent past have not resulted in instability, so the persistence of stability
to the present does not guarantee its continuation. Mexico's vaunted stability
could conceivably be undone even in the near future.

By now it should be obvious that this text avoids predictions. Instead,
it will seek to understand the logic of Mexican politics. But such logic does

not imply inevitability. Although we cannot hope to explain fully Mexico's extraordinary political stability, we can try to come as close as possible to that goal. Should stability lose its hold tomorrow, all the best explanations of how it once functioned might suddenly seem to have been at least partially inadequate.[12] What is clear is that the much-discussed "contradictions" of Mexican development have not (yet?) resolved themselves, that either-or propositions have not (yet?) materialized. This does not mean that we avoid considering alternatives to contemporary political patterns. It does mean that we look hardest at what continues to be Mexico's reality.

LAND AND POPULATION

This book is about Mexico's politics in the broadest sense, including its economics, sociology, and history. It is not truly an introduction to Mexico in general because it does not deal with those areas that fall primarily outside the political sphere. Still, we need some background on the land and population to understand the context in which Mexican politics operate. One need not believe that geography, natural resources, regionalism, culture, ethnicity, and demography determine politics to believe that they affect politics, presenting different opportunities and challenges. And surely it is mostly the people whom we ultimately care about when we study politics, just as it is the people whom politics affect.

The Land

Geographically, Mexico is both large and varied. Its 760,000 square miles (1,968,000 square kilometers) make it the third largest nation in Latin America, after only Brazil and Argentina, and one of the ten largest in the world. A profound geopolitical aspect is the 2,000-mile (3,200-kilometer) northern border with the United States. Also important, although less so, is the 600-mile (960-kilometer) border with Guatemala and the 160-mile (260-kilometer) border with newly independent (1981) Belize. Beyond these southern borders lies the rest of Central America.

Apart from the issues of Mexico's sheer size and borders, two geographical factors that deserve mention in the political context are natural resources and regional diversity. Mexico is neither unusually unfortunate nor—except as oil may change this—unusually fortunate in its natural resources. There is, however, a myth of special richness. Historian Daniel Cosío Villegas has traced the roots of that myth to the early colonists.[13] Spanish conquerors succumbed to a combination of calculated exaggeration (aimed at securing greater support from Spain) and enthusiastic miscalculation. Subsequently, both Mexicans and foreigners have perpetuated the myth, sometimes in order to blame those in power for Mexico's failures, sometimes to stereotype Mexicans as lazy, undisciplined, or ignorant, thereby perhaps seeking to justify foreign involvement.

On the positive side, Mexico is rich in minerals. Justly famous for its gold and silver since colonial times, Mexico has remained a leading producer of silver. Other important minerals have included lead, zinc, copper, and sulfur. Mexico also has some good ranching and timber lands, as well as fishing waters. Oil, of course, has now become the foremost natural resource.

Realists must also appreciate the harsher economic side of Mexican geography. Mexico lost much of its best agricultural land in nineteenth-century warfare with the United States. Today most of Mexico's land is mediocre agriculturally, and much of the rest is on the coasts; unfortunately, Mexico's climate is very varied, not just by latitude and longitude but by height above sea level, and the coastal climate is not generally favorable. Indeed, the climate tends to be hot from sea level to 2,000 feet (600 meters), before becoming more temperate to 8,000 feet (2,400 meters) and cooler above that height. Rainfall is also a problem, insufficient in some regions, excessive in others. More than half of Mexico is dry; about one-fourth, mostly mountainous area, is rainy and temperate; and the rest is tropically rainy.

Mexico also suffers from rugged topography. Its mountains hinder not only large-scale agriculture but also transportation and communication. They impede national homogeneity by dividing Mexico into regions. It is not difficult to appreciate the divisions. Mexico City is 7,000 feet (2,100 meters) above sea level and still lies in a valley. If the air pollution level permitted, a person in Mexico City could see himself surrounded by mountains. If he then journeyed overland to the east or west, the descent would come only when nearing the coast, a dramatic descent demonstrating at once Mexico's physical beauty and its challenging topography.

Different commentators have suggested different but related regional divisions. The government itself has divided Mexico into five regions.[14] The North Pacific, with the states of Baja California, Sonora, and Sinaloa, is the second largest in land. But because much of the land is desert, the region has a relatively small population. The North stretches from the Sierra Madre Occidental (mountains connected with the Sierra Nevada in the United States) to the Gulf. Comprising San Luis Potosí, Zacatecas, Chihuahua, and Coahuila, it has roughly 40 percent of the land, including plains and the Sierra Madre Oriental (connected to the Rocky Mountains). It has about 20 percent of Mexico's population. So the main geographical features of the northern half of Mexico are the two Sierra Madre ranges, with the plateaus in between. Central Mexico, surrounding the Federal District, is the third largest region in area but includes roughly half the population. This region is itself a valley ensconced in high volcanic terrain. The Gulf Coast, including Veracruz, Tabasco, and the Yucatán, is a flat lowland region, relatively small in size and population. Finally, the South Pacific is the most rural region, resembling parts of Central America more than it does much of Mexico.

Mexico's topography and regionalism make the nation effectively larger in terms of achieving political or cultural homogeneity than sheer size would indicate. They have a good deal to do with Mexico's ethnic, cultural, social, and occupational divisions.

The Population

As Mexico is large and diverse in geography, so it is large and diverse in population. Its population of some 80 million puts it among the world's eleven most populous nations.[15] Mexico has the largest population in the Spanish-speaking world, trailed far behind by Argentina and Colombia, the two next largest in Latin America, as well as by Spain itself, the region's mother country.

Most Mexicans are the product of two very different ethnic groups, native Indians and colonizing Spaniards. Few Spanish women came to the New World, making miscegenation between Spanish males and Indian females inevitable. Some of the political ramifications of the Indian-European mixing are explored in Chapter 2. *Mestizos* (mixed Indian and Spanish) vary from mostly Indian to mostly Spanish, but in general the balance inclines more toward the Indian side than it does in most other major Latin American countries. Within Mexico, the balance is different in different regions, as what may be typical skin color or height in one region would not be typical in another.

Estimates vary on how many relatively pure Indians live in Mexico. Definitions themselves vary. Some anthropologists rely more on physical traits, others more on cultural habits, others on whether people are bound to their land rather than mobile or on whether they have greater ties to their villages than to the nation. Some rely on people's self-perceptions. Most definitions lead to an estimate that there are a few million Indians. For example, probably around 5 percent but possibly up to 10 percent of all Mexicans speak only or primarily an Indian language, although there has been a trend away from such monolinguism since 1930, just as other distinctive traits have been diminishing.[16] Diversity is reflected in the many Indian languages, of which Maya and Nahuatl are merely the most common. Different Indian groups concentrate in different regions, mostly in southern and central Mexico. The people, as well as the land, in certain areas of southern Mexico have more in common with Central America than with the rest of Mexico. Thus, culturally and economically, as well as geographically, many Mexicans are a long way from Mexico City. Descendents of the Mayas are concentrated in the south and the Yucatán, Zapotecs and Mixtecs in Oaxaca, Tarascans in Michoacán, fiercely independent Yaquis in Sonora, and Aztec descendents in various parts of Mexico. Different groups have their own languages, customs, dances, music, and clothing; they may also have their own economic systems, often based on maize and home industries, such as pottery and textiles, or on collective labor, concentrating on one key product to trade with other villages. In short, Mexico is fragmented not just by divisions between Indians and others, but even by differences among the Indians themselves.

We cannot describe Indian worlds without soon describing mestizo worlds. It is less important to fix the exact number of Indians than to appreciate how much the Indian presence has affected social norms, cultural relations, and political habits in the larger society. *Compadrazgo* (a godparent relationship), for example, is an Indian custom but also a Mexican custom.[17] Most Mexicans, not just Indians, eat corn and beans and tortillas, even though Mexicans rely increasingly on packaged, canned, and processed products. Indian culture fuses with Spanish Catholicism to produce special hybrids. Mexico is therefore not as religiously homogeneous as one might infer from the fact that well over 90 percent of the people are Catholics (most of the rest are Protestants, and roughly 50,000 are Jewish). The Virgin Mary is a central symbol for many, but the dark-skinned Virgin of Guadalupe is a central symbol for more. Many Mexicans, especially in rural areas, observe the Day of the Dead, while Catholics in much of the world observe All Souls' Day. Although the Day of the Dead borrows some customs from All Souls' Day practices, it also adds particularly Indian aspects. This is not to say that the Catholic Church has been unimportant in Mexico's political history (see Chapter 2) but that Indian influences are part of the religious experiences of many Mexicans. Additionally, many Indian words have made their way into the "Mexican" language. Even the very name "Mexico" may come from an Indian root such as Mexica, one of the Aztec tribes, or Mexitl, an Aztec epithet for God. And it is not by chance that Mexico's most famous museum is the Anthropological Museum. The plaque dedicating the museum (in 1964) acknowledges Mexico's debt to its Indian heritage: "Mexico today pays homage to indigenous Mexico, in whose example it recognizes essential characteristics of its national origins."

Ethnic diversity goes beyond all the degrees of the Indian-Spanish mix. Blacks were brought to Mexico as slaves in colonial times. Just as Indians tend to be clustered in certain regions, so blacks, or more commonly, Mexicans of mixed black-mestizo origin, are clustered along the coasts. Veracruz, for example, resembles a Caribbean as much as an inland Mexican city in many ways. Additionally, ethnic regionalism is naturally accompanied by cultural regionalism. In music alone, what is typical changes from mariachi bands to *zapateados* (rapid step dancing characteristic of Veracruz and the north) to Caribbean *salsa*.

For all its diversity, however, Mexico is one nation. Indeed, the degree of homogeneity is increasing. Indian enclaves are receding, although slowly. Spanish is increasingly the pervasive language. Modern transportation and communication have played a unifying role, and expanding educational facilities have played a socializing role. Urbanization also diminishes the intensity of some regional differences; by 1980, nearly three-fourths of the population lived in urban areas (the figure varies depending on the definition of "urban area"). Most Mexicans living outside the major cities live in villages, not in rural isolation, and migration from villages to cities continues at a rapid pace.

Most important to our study is the centralization of political life in Mexico City. Political centralization itself has been a great source of national integration. Despite regional, topographical, ethnic, and cultural cleavages, unified political power is concentrated in Mexico City, in the government, in the executive branch, in the presidency. All Mexico, although in different degrees, falls under this authority. Most political roads lead to the capital. This political centralization seems especially remarkable when one considers the centrifugal forces, geographical and cultural, with which Mexican politics must cope. In the ensuing chapters (especially 3 and 4), we explore the regime's relative success in establishing its political authority.

MEXICO'S IMPORTANCE FOR THE UNITED STATES

Along with Mexico's sheer size and extraordinary political stability, geographical, cultural, and economic interactions provide obvious reasons for U.S. readers to be interested in Mexican politics. For example, several of the largest U.S. banks found themselves with up to half their primary capital at risk in Mexico's precarious economy in the 1980s. Whereas analysis of many key economic and other Mexico-U.S. interactions is left for Chapters 5 and 6, we focus here on the increased U.S. interest in and need for knowledge about Mexico.

Brazil is the only Latin American nation that can be considered more important than Mexico in terms of population and economic production, but for the United States there is little question about Mexico's preeminence. Yet U.S. interest in Mexican politics traditionally has been minimal. Ever since the 1973 announcement of Mexico's great oil resources was taken seriously, however, there has been an upsurge of U.S. news coverage.[18] President Carter established a major presidential commission on Mexico, a rare indicator of special U.S. attention to one nation, and the United States and Mexico established a consultative commission that went beyond any of its bilateral predecessors reaching back to 1960. The commission was reorganized in 1979 into eight policy-oriented groups (e.g., trade). In 1981, López Portillo, one of the few heads of state to have met with president-elect Reagan, became one of the first to meet with the newly inaugurated U.S. president. Amid keen U.S. interest and fear concerning Mexico's economic crisis, drug traffic, and Central America, Reagan, de la Madrid, and their top aides met several times.

Unfortunately, this growth of interest comes up against long-standing barriers to understanding. Mexico's renowned poet-essayist Octavio Paz posed the problem this way:

> When I was in India, witnessing the never-ending quarrels between Hindus and Muslims, I asked myself more than once this question: What accident or misfortune of history caused two religions so obviously irreconcilable as Hinduism and Muhammadanism to coexist in the same society? . . . How could I forget that I myself, as a Mexican, was (and am) part of a no less singular paradox—that of Mexico and the United States? . . . In general, Americans have not looked for Mexico in Mexico; they have looked for their obsessions, enthusiasms, phobias, hopes, interests—and these are what they have found. In short, the history of our relationship is the history of mutual and stubborn deceit, usually involuntary though not always so.[19]

At their worst, U.S. views of Mexicans, and therefore, indirectly, of Mexican politics, still revolve around the stereotypes of indolence and immaturity nurtured in Hollywood and in the advertising media. A prominent weekly like *Time* has imprinted such stereotypes onto its analysis of Mexican policymaking, entitling a cover story on Mexico-U.S. relations, "Mexico's Macho Mood" (October 8, 1979). U.S. views are frequently colored by biases induced by its own preoccupations, especially with anticommunism.

Observers may differ on the degree to which geographical proximity naturally breeds understanding or resentment between Mexicans and their northern neighbors. They may also differ on the degree to which greater knowledge would reduce bilateral tensions. But most believe that this knowledge could make for more intelligent handling of Mexico–United States affairs. On the positive side, the growth of scholarly centers and publications on both sides of the border has been impressive in the last decade.[20] Also, many U.S. citizens showed neighborly concern when they helped aid victims of the 1985 earthquakes.

Another incentive for U.S. readers to learn more about Mexico is that the United States *domestically* is greatly influenced by its southern neighbor. One reason that Mexico's influence on U.S. life sometimes fails to attract greater attention is that U.S. influence on Mexican life is even more obvious and pervasive. In fact, we cannot understand contemporary Mexico without appreciating the enormous extent of U.S. cultural as well as economic penetration. Thousands of U.S. citizens have retired in Mexico, and thousands of others have bought vacation homes there. More important, many Mexicans come to live by behavioral norms exported by the United States. The Castro family in Oscar Lewis' anthropological classic *Five Families* illustrates the point: Pancake mix breakfasts substitute for tortillas, fried beans, and chili; U.S. cosmetics and toys become "necessities."[21] Processed food reshapes the diet, and "burgers," Shakey's Pizza, and Kentucky Fried Chicken are found in Mexican cities. English words creep into Mexican speech, especially as the majority of films and much of the television and music in Mexico come from the United States. Mexico's most widely read magazines are adaptations of *Reader's Digest* and *T.V. Guide*. Mexico has opened a huge U.S.-style amusement park ("Adventure Kingdom"). And, although soccer remains the number one sport, U.S.-style football is more popular than in any other Latin American country, baseball more popular than in all but a few.

But cultural penetration is very much—and increasingly so—a two-way phenomenon. Hispanics may soon surpass blacks as the biggest minority in the United States, and Mexican-Americans, or Chicanos, are the largest Hispanic subgroup. The Chicano presence is especially large if we consider the term broadly, including all those of Mexican descent, whether U.S. citizens or not. In fact, the United States is now perhaps the fifth-largest Spanish-speaking nation in the world. Continuing migration is one major root of the Chicano population in the United States, but another is simply the population inhabiting the land taken from Mexico by the United States in the nineteenth century; thus there are now wry jokes about a Mexican reconquest via population growth. Catering to the Mexican-American and other Hispanic populations, dozens of Spanish news periodicals and hundreds of Spanish radio and television stations have arisen in the United States. Television from Mexico comes via cable to major U.S. cities such as Los Angeles, New York, and Washington and reaches perhaps 12 million viewers.[22] Food, music, and language provide further manifestations of Mexican culture in the United States. Even the U.S. "national pastime" has felt a Mexican influence, most notably with Fernando Valenzuela's status as one of baseball's top box-office attractions. Education provides a good example of an important Mexican influence on the United States, even though the U.S. influence on Mexico is greater. True, U.S. money and academic models have helped shape some of Mexico's universities, especially private ones, and many of Mexico's ablest students attend U.S. graduate schools. But the Autonomous University of Guadalajara has more U.S. medical students than does any school in the United States, and there are more and more Chicanos in U.S. schools, from primary school through university. Half the kindergarten pupils in Los Angeles have Spanish surnames. Bilingual education and Chicano-relevant curriculum are prominent in some locales. Finally, there are many institutional interchanges between Mexican and U.S. universities.

Although political muscle has been building less rapidly than cultural influence, "Chicano consciousness" has grown. The political impact is naturally strongest in the Southwest, where most Chicanos live, but it is also significant in major urban centers, such as Chicago. Recognition of this power was evident in the 1980 presidential election, when Reagan and Carter both focused their campaigns on the Mexican-American vote more than any major party candidates had ever done. Candidate Reagan unabashedly tried to enhance his image in the Mexican-American community by traveling to Mexico, just as Senator Edward Kennedy had done during his losing quest for the Democratic nomination. In 1984, Republicans hoped that Reagan's relative success in attracting Chicanos away from the Democrats could establish for the long term a vibrant two-party competition for the Chicano vote. Additionally, Mexico has voiced concern for persons of Mexican descent living in the United States. President López Portillo (on a September 1979 visit to the United States) boldly addressed Hispanics on the need to give a political voice to the cultural consciousness they share with Mexico. "We would like to deal with an organized community," the president declared, adding that "we are proud that you proudly maintain an identity with us." However, President de la Madrid, whether because of his less assertive style or because his hand was weakened by economic crisis and consequent dependence on U.S. aid, was not vocal about such a shared consciousness. Besides, the interests of Chicanos and Mexican citizens (let alone the Mexican government) often do not coincide.[23]

Nowhere are the fates of Mexico and the United States more obviously intertwined and two-directional than at the border.[24] Millions live within a short distance of the extensive border and the border population is growing rapidly. The politics, economies, and cultures on each side are shaped by those on the other side. One can think of influences ranging from party affiliation, to labor-capital interchanges, to language and family ties. The degree of interchange is reflected by the fact that this is the world's busiest border. Already by 1972 the number of yearly crossings at the San Isidro–Tijuana point alone reached the 25 million figure. Since 1982, the effects of sharp peso devaluation have been perhaps most vividly illustrated on the border, as increasing numbers of Mexicans have crossed northward to seek work, or at least to convert pesos to dollars, while U.S. citizens crossed southward to take advantage of suddenly lower prices.

And yet, despite the volume of border interaction, and even some important homogenizing effects, nowhere is it more obvious how utterly different the two nations are. Where else does a border juxtapose two societies so ethnically, culturally, socially, economically, and politically different? One might think of Israel and its Arab neighbors. Beyond that case one could point to political divisions in Germany and Korea, or to religious divisions in Ireland and in India-Pakistan, but not to such accumulated differences. Moreover, this accumulation of Mexico-U.S. differences, far from being random, describes a critical division between the less developed and the more developed world. Focusing just on the division between wealth and poverty, per-capita income in the United States is roughly six times that in Mexico.[25] Entrance and exit lines at the border also symbolize the Mexico-U.S. development gap. Entrance into Mexico is usually immediate, no lines, virtually no inspections, no wait. Exit from Mexico into the United States frequently is an ordeal, involving long lines, careful and tedious inspections (including indignities for Chicanos reentering the United States, who may be suspected of seeking illegal entry), and delays sometimes lasting for hours.

Despite bilateral influences and interdependency, any study of Mexican politics must appreciate the enormous underlying differences between the two nations. It will not then be surprising that Mexican politics generally are very different from U.S. politics, or that Mexican political stability has a different legacy and contemporary meaning from U.S. political stability. The challenge for us is to understand Mexican politics on its own terms.

CHAPTER PREVIEWS

The following brief outline indicates the major concerns of each chapter. Chapter 2 provides a historical overview of how the bases of contemporary stability have developed. A central question is how stability could be forged against a historical background often characterized by instability. By analyzing the degree to which certain political, economic, and social goals were achieved in previous periods, the chapter helps provide a historical context within which to evaluate contemporary Mexico. Chapter 3 analyzes the major actors in Mexican politics and the principal processes and structures through which they participate in the political system. A central challenge here is to understand how a developed network for citizen participation coexists with the regime's strong control over participatory structures. Political parties and elections receive special attention. Chapter 4 provides a broad view of the political system. It analyzes how well political stability is reconciled with other political goals: political freedom, political equality, political change. The chapter tries to show how extraordinary stability has been consistent with mixed achievements in these other areas.

Chapter 5 turns to the economic model that has at once benefited from and buttressed Mexico's political stability. Here we discuss how some enviable economic achievements have coexisted with a terribly unequal distribution of wealth and its consequent social problems. This chapter also analyzes the economic crisis of the mid-1970s and how its apparent resolution failed to remove its fundamental causes, thus not averting the renewed and aggravated economic crises of the 1980s. The relationship between Mexico's domestic and foreign policies is discussed in Chapter 6. We try to show how Mexico's own conservative development model has been compatible with a seemingly leftist foreign policy and how Mexico's traditional dependence on the United States has squared with Mexico's increased assertiveness in foreign policy. Special attention is given to Mexican relations with Central America and to critical Mexico-U.S. policy problems (migration, trade, drugs, tourism). Chapter 7 focuses on a major contemporary policy issue in Mexican domestic and international politics: oil. The chapter serves as a case study exemplifying key tendencies analyzed in preceding chapters, including some different ways in which oil may affect the major characteristics of Mexican development. The debate surrounding the best ways to spend oil revenues raises issues concerning alternative futures in Mexico. The relationship between these futures and contemporary reality is pursued in Chapter 8.

NOTES

1. We use *regime* to refer to a type of government; we use *government* both interchangeably with regime and to refer to a particular administration.

2. Probably the best-known modern work on development that focuses on political stability is Samuel P. Huntington's *Political Order in Changing Societies* (New Haven, Conn.: Yale University Press, 1968). Huntington regards Mexico as "highly successful in political development," attributes the nation's economic growth to its political stability, and accords Mexico special attention as a model of stability. The quotation is from p. 324; also see pp. 315–324 and passim.

3. From 1954 to 1970, Mexico followed a pattern known as *desarrollo estabilizador* (stabilizing development), which involved such policies as stable domestic prices and a stable foreign exchange rate. Dissatisfied with the results of desarrollo estabilizador, President Luis Echeverría (1970–1976) tried to introduce *desarrollo compartido* (shared development). President López Portillo then tried to revitalize the basic development model, and President de la Madrid tried to alter and modernize it (Chapter 5).

4. One such classic analysis of the causes of revolt is found in Alexis de Tocqueville's *The Old Regime and the French Revolution*, trans. Stuart Gilbert (New

York: Doubleday, 1955). One more modern, empirical affirmation is Ted Robert Gurr's *Why Men Rebel* (Princeton, N.J.: Princeton University Press, 1970).

5. On the educational problems see Jorge Padua, *Educación, industrialización y progreso técnico en México* (Mexico City: El Colegio de México, 1984), p. 84. On higher education, United Nations Educational, Scientific and Cultural Organization, *Statistical Yearbook 1977* (Paris: UNESCO, 1978), p. 151, indicated 6 percent for 1970 and 10 percent for 1975; expansion has continued at a fast pace.

6. The datum on historical stagnation comes from Frank Tannenbaum, *The Struggle for Peace and Bread* (New York: Columbia University Press, 1950), p. 10. On the growth, see Thomas E. Weil et al., *Area Handbook for Mexico* (Washington, D.C.: Government Printing Office, 1975), pp. 36–38, 44. A 75 million figure for 1983 is given in World Bank, *World Development Report, 1985* (Washington, D.C.: World Bank, 1985), Annex, p. 175.

7. See Francisco Javier Alejo, "Demographic Patterns and Labor Market Trends in Mexico" in *Mexico's Economic Crisis: Challenges and Opportunities*, ed. Donald Wyman (La Jolla, Calif.: Center for U.S.-Mexican Studies, University of California, San Diego, 1983), p. 83; Alan Riding, *Distant Neighbors: Portrait of the Mexicans* (New York: Knopf, 1985) p. 226. On de la Madrid's goal, see his "Fourth State of the Nation Address," *Excélsior*, September 2, 1986, where a figure of 2.1 percent for 1986 is compared to 2.6 percent for 1982.

8. For relevant discussions see Clifford Kaufman, "Urbanization, Material Satisfaction and Mass Political Involvement: The Poor in Mexico City," *Comparative Political Studies* 4, no. 3 (1971):295–320; Wayne A. Cornelius, "Urbanization as an Agent of Latin American Political Stability: The Case of Mexico," *American Political Science Review* 63, no. 3 (1969):833–857.

9. The "modernization-development" contrast is elaborated in Cynthia Hewitt de Alcántara, *La modernización de la agricultura mexicana 1940–1970* (Mexico City: Siglo XXI, 1978), p. 283 and passim. For an analysis of the food crisis that stresses how export, not urban, interests have been favored, see Steven E. Sanderson, *The Transformation of Mexican Agriculture: International Structure and the Politics of Rural Change* (Princeton, N.J.: Princeton University Press, 1986).

10. Jorge Luis Sierra Guzmán, "After the Earthquake, The City Rebuilds," *Voices of Mexico* (June–August 1986):12–14. By late 1986 the government's rebuilding efforts showed some improvement.

11. See, for example, Octavio Paz, *The Other Mexico: Critique of the Pyramid*, trans. Lysander Kemp (New York: Grove Press, 1972), p. 45: "Here is the dilemma: either the developed Mexico will absorb and integrate the other, or the underdeveloped Mexico . . . will end up by strangling the developed Mexico." One of the widest-read "either-or" formulations can be found in Pablo-González Casanova, *Democracy in Mexico*, trans. Danielle Salti (London: Oxford University Press, 1970), pp. 158–197.

12. The issue need not be seen as continued stability versus regime dissolution. Intermediate solutions are possible. Historians who look back on Mexico in the 1980s and 1990s may disagree as to how much the regime persisted, with deft accommodation to heightened challenge, or fundamentally changed.

13. Daniel Cosío Villegas, *American Extremes*, trans. Américo Paredes (Austin: University of Texas Press, 1964) pp. 7, 162–171.

14. Weil et al., *Area Handbook for Mexico*, p. 14.

15. For an analysis of Mexico's population see Francisco Alba's *The Population of Mexico: Trends, Issues, and Policies*, trans. Marjory Mattingly Urquidi (New Brunswick, N.J.: Transaction Press, 1982). The World Bank gave a mid-1984 figure of 76.8

million. See World Bank, *World Development Report* (Washington, D.C.: World Bank, 1986), p. 181.

16. Peter Coy, "The Indians of Mexico," in *Latin America and the Caribbean: A Handbook*, ed. Claudio Véliz (New York: Praeger Publishers, 1986), pp. 705–706.

17. Compadrazgo relationships may bind a community together and make it more self-sufficient by imposing reciprocal obligations. Where compadrazgo ties rich and poor, for example, the poor may receive material help and security in return for which the rich may receive labor, a sense of community identity amid their wider "modern" interactions, and firmer support for political stability.

18. For an analysis of this coverage see Thomas Michael Laichas, "Mexico in the U.S. Press: A Quantitative Study, 1972–1978," in *Statistical Abstract of Latin America*, Vol. 20, ed. James W. Wilkie (Los Angeles: UCLA Latin American Center Publications, 1980), pp. 582–594. See also Roberta Lajous de Solana and Jesús Velasco Márquez, "Visión de México en la prensa de Estados Unidos: 1984," in *México–Estados Unidos, 1984*, ed. Manuel García y Griego and Gustavo Vega (Mexico City: El Colegio de México, 1985), pp. 31–42.

19. Paz forcefully added that Mexican views of the United States are equally ill informed. "The idea that Mexican people have of the United States is contradictory, emotional, and impervious to criticism; it is a mythical image." "Reflections: Mexico and the United States," trans. Rachel Phillips, *The New Yorker*, September 17, 1979, p. 136. Cosío Villegas, *American Extremes* (p. 29), made similar two-way points. In fact, because the United States must divide its attention among so many nations and regions, while Mexico is so tied to the United States, the imperative to "know thy neighbor" should be especially clear for Mexicans.

20. A prime example is the Center for U.S.-Mexican Studies at the University of California, San Diego, which has produced a formidable series of studies, and the University of California system overall has established a vibrant network of activities related to Mexico. Additionally, one could cite, among others, the U.S.-Mexico project at the Overseas Development Council in Washington, D.C. Moreover, Mexican interest in studying the United States has taken great strides, as El Colegio de México has shown with its Mexico-U.S. program.

21. Oscar Lewis, *Five Families* (New York: Basic Books, 1959).

22. On the 12 million see José Roldán Acosta, "La adquisición de satélites," *Gaceta-UNAM*, February 10, 1983. For further sources dealing with influences upon the U.S. side see Linda B. Hall, "The United States–Mexican Border: Historical, Political, and Cultural Perspectives," *Latin American Research Review* 20, no.2 (1985):223–229.

23. Rodolfo O. de la Garza and Karl Schmitt, "Texas Land Grants and Chicano-Mexican Relations: A Case Study," *Latin American Research Review* 21, no. 1 (1986):123–138.

24. For an overview of some major border issues, including environmental and economic ones, see Edward J. Williams, "The Implications of the Border for Mexican Policy and Mexican–United States Relations," in *Mexico's Political Stability: The Next Five Years*, ed. Roderic A. Camp (Boulder, Colo.: Westview Press, 1986), pp. 211–234.

25. World Bank, *World Development Indicators* (Washington, D.C.: World Bank, 1985), Annex, p. 175.

2

A Brief Political History

I repeat that we are nothing except a relationship: something that can be defined only as a part of a history.

Mexico has a plurality of pasts, all present and at war within every Mexican's soul.

—Octavio Paz¹

To understand contemporary Mexico, one must understand its past or, more accurately, its pasts, for Mexican history is rich in conflicts and cataclysmic changes. Many of these changes seemingly brought victories for certain principles, but the victories often proved ephemeral. Probably few countries celebrate so many holidays, partly because victories were so frequently followed by defeats, necessitating future victories. We focus here on five continually glorified principles or goals: *political stability, political liberty, economic growth, increased economic equality,* and *national independence.* Special attention is given to the epic twentieth-century struggle for stability, seen against a historical backdrop in which extraordinary instability was the norm. Obviously, not all the ostensible goals have in fact been pursued by all those who have shaped Mexican history. Mexicans have disagreed sharply—and still do disagree—citing different victories and defeats, heroes and villains. Nonetheless, these goals represent recurrent themes in Mexican history. They also still command wide support among Mexicans, despite a lack of consensus on their exact meaning or priority. The exploration of these goals in different eras should therefore help provide conceptual coherence for our chronological overview. (A summary of the U.S role in Mexican history is left for Chapter 6.)

PRECOLONIAL AND COLONIAL ERAS

The Indians who inhabited Mexico in the precolonial period form an integral part of contemporary Mexico. They were not driven into historical oblivion by their European conquerors; instead, they mixed with them. As Octavio Paz wrote: "The historical memory of [U.S.] America is European, not American. . . . Exactly the opposite is true of Mexico, land of superimposed pasts."[2]

Mystery surrounds much of the early history of Mexico's Indians, but it seems likely that they were attracted to the region by such favorable factors as the warm climate and available water. With the shift from hunting to agriculture and more permanent settlement came higher civilizations of Olmecs, Mayas, Toltecs, and Teotihuacanos. In the twelfth century, the Aztecs abandoned the arid north for the fertile central valley, built Tenochtitlan (later Mexico City), conquered their enemies, and established an empire complete with governors of the provinces, tax collectors, courts, and ruling military-religious castes. Aztec rule has been compared to contemporary Mexican rule—both forged a centralized stable system of a markedly authoritarian and hierarchical nature. But Aztec rule is also remembered as a symbol of *Mexican* independence, violated but never fully vanquished by the foreign conquerors who would establish "New Spain."

Only a few hundred Spaniards under Hernán Cortés conquered Mexico in 1519. They were aided by superior weaponry and by fortuitous native religious beliefs that white gods would one day appear. Most of all, they were aided by the lack of unity among Mexico's Indians. The Aztecs ruled over other tribes, and some of these saw in the commotion surrounding the Spanish arrival an attractive opportunity to rebel. Images of a simple, harmonious, peaceful society succumbing to the warlike invaders are misleading. Precolumbian Mexican society was quite politically complex and conflictual. Some Indians defied Cortés; others were unsure, submissive, or even supportive. Leading the defiant ones—current allusions by gastronomically stricken tourists to "Moctezuma's revenge" notwithstanding—was not the Aztec emperor Moctezuma, but his defiant nephew, Cuauhtémoc. It is Cuauhtémoc who is today memorialized in Mexican books, monuments, and street names as the early symbol of independence.

Some contemporary Mexicans, particularly conservatives, emphasize positive features of Spain's three-century colonial rule. Most important was the introduction of Christianity. For those who believe that Christianity offers the route to godliness and salvation, this event can hardly be overemphasized. Care was taken to protect the Indian, while hoping to convert and assimilate him. How different this was from the English settlers' efforts to push aside or kill the natives. A degree of political integration and stability was achieved, and Mexico City became one of the two central poles of development (Lima was the other) for all of Spanish America. Even some limited degree of self-government could be found. Finally, something can be said for the sheer courage and perseverance of the early conquerors.

Most Mexicans, however, have a more mixed or even negative image of the colonial era. To the extent that the Spaniards sought assimilation, they did so on the basis of paternalistic imposition of their own religion, values, and privileges. Even the Spanish who settled in Mexico were themselves exploited by Spain's mercantile economic system. The system robbed Mexico of its mineral riches while prohibiting free trade with any but the mother country. Certainly most Mexicans were not favorably affected by the colonization; a rigidly unequal social hierarchy insured that. At the top were the Spaniards, or *peninsulares*, followed by *criollos*, who were of Spanish descent but born in Mexico, followed much further down by mestizos, and still further down by the Indian masses. The Indians' plight probably worsened, in fact, as settlers carved out large estates at the expense of traditional communal landholdings. Overall, Spanish rule was paternalistic, elitist, and authoritarian. Crown and church together saw to that. Stability was probably the goal that fared best in the colonial era.

A contrast of Mexican and U.S. colonial experiences provides fascinating insights into contemporary differences. One major contrast involved the mother countries themselves. Spain had an absolute monarchy, strong church-state ties, and a still largely feudal economic system. At least by comparison, England appeared to have a more limited monarchy, a more vibrant parliament, more self-government, greater church-state separation, and leadership in the capitalist industrial revolution. Spain's organic, holistic, corporatist, conservative tendencies contrasted with England's more individualist, pluralist, liberal ones.

Another key contrast involved the native populations themselves. Whereas the English confronted nomadic tribes, the Spanish confronted relatively developed civilizations. The first would be swept out of the way; the second could not be. Thus the English transplanted their relatively liberal politics and culture largely intact, while Spain mixed its more conservative culture with those of a hierarchical native society. Within Spanish America itself, an interesting contrast emerged. Those countries (e.g., Mexico and Peru) with the most highly developed Indian civilizations naturally attracted the colonizers' greatest interest; whether one emphasizes the colonizers' oppression of the native civilizations or the blend of two hierarchical civilizations, these countries became very inegalitarian in their political, economic, and social affairs. Those countries (e.g., Argentina and Uruguay) with less developed Indian civilizations attracted less colonial interest; then, in the nineteenth century, European immigrants, with their liberalism, found fresher terrain on which to establish themselves. In a sense, therefore, countries with the most formidable Indian and colonial heritages were handicapped in pursuing many of the goals often subsequently associated with "development."

THE FIRST CENTURY OF INDEPENDENCE

Mexico's eventual political independence (1821) resulted from a combination of weakened rule in the wake of Napoleon's conquest of Spain and accumulated Mexican grievances—especially when socioeconomic gains achieved through reforms were followed by setbacks and frustrated rising expectations. Criollos and privileged mestizos battled the peninsulares and their Spanish establishment. But the revolt was no struggle for the deprived masses. In this configuration, Mexico resembled most of Spain's rebellious colonies.

The most interesting Mexican twist was the involvement, albeit aborted, of many Indians. Their leader was Miguel Hidalgo, priest (for Indians had become Christians), champion of the oppressed, nationalist (whose leadership role in the independence struggle is still recalled in annual ritual by Mexico's president on the night of September 15), "Captain-General of America"— and failure. It was not Hidalgo's brutal methods that sealed his fate; it was his utter lack of military skill and criollo desertion. His successor, although more successful, was also to be betrayed by wealthy criollos. The relatively privileged had never forgotten that they had more to fear from the aspiring masses than from unyielding elites. Like the revolution of a century later, the War for Independence (1810–1821) was complicated, meandering, protracted, decentralized, and ultimately unfulfilling for the masses. In fact, independence came only when the Mexican upper class finally turned against Spain, partly because Spain itself had now adopted a liberal constitution!

Not surprisingly, then, the War for Independence did not produce an egalitarian revolution. Nor did it bring political stability. And the lack of stability went hand in hand with economic problems. In turn, these political and economic failures made Mexico's new national independence very fragile. The early independence period is especially interesting for its illuminating political-economic contrasts to contemporary Mexico. Indeed, it has been called the "era of anarchy."

Independent Mexico inherited an economy in dreadful shape.[3] Mexico was in debt, its treasury was bankrupt, and the nation lacked strong commercial ties to European markets. In short, a crippled economy desperately needed a great deal of capital. This view was shared by those who would become "liberals" and those who would become "conservatives." Differences emerged when, for example, liberals wanted to promote private enterprise at the expense of a strong church and state, two institutions that conservatives wanted to uphold. Yet many conservatives were not simply harking back toward a bygone or feudal age; they favored powerful banking institutions and foreign investment.

Unfortunately, the Mexican state could not attract the needed capital without first establishing political stability—and this it could not do. Only two presidents completed their four-year terms during the thirty-five year span from 1821 to 1856. Part of the problem was regional. Centralists wanted to build power in Mexico City, federalists in the provinces. Most of the problem was economic. Governments did not have the resources to meet basic legitimizing needs, to make it worthwhile *not* to revolt. In reality, this economic problem was tied to the regional problem. Central governments could not extract more resources from society without engendering provincial challenges. Without those resources they could not even pay the army, thus provoking military coups. So just as Mexico could not get needed economic capital without stability, it could not establish stability without needed capital. Understanding the relationship between political instability and economic stagnation during much of the nineteenth century will help us to appreciate, by contrast, the stability-growth relationship in much of the twentieth century.

Only against this backdrop of deeply rooted political and economic problems can one begin to imagine the spectacular personal successes that notoriously irresponsible or incompetent leaders often achieved over responsible ones. Soon after Mexico freed itself from Spain, Augustín de Iturbide appointed himself emperor; thus far the main result of independence was criollo royalty. As governments rose and fell quickly in the ensuing decades, a perverse continuity was the incredible tenacity of Antonio López de Santa Anna, Mexico's most despised, traitorous, duplicitous native son, who in 1848 presided over the loss of roughly half Mexico's territory in war with the United States. Santa Anna's most consistent preoccupation was self-interest. Among his favorite self-designations were Most Serene Highness, Father of the Country, Savior, and Perpetual Victor. It is a sad commentary on Mexico's political instability from the 1820s to the 1850s that the last title had some validity. Almost no one could establish a viable government and a viable economic base.

Mexico's problems were greatly aggravated by foreign intervention. France, Great Britain, and Spain all demanded reparations for losses suffered during Mexico's turmoil. In 1864, France named Austrian Archduke Maximilian to rule Mexico. As in the war with the United States two decades earlier, Mexican independence suffered as domestic strife and instability weakened the nation's ability to defend itself. This time, however, Mexico eventually defeated the foreigners, and liberals regained power.

Although they did not achieve sustained political stability, liberals held the upper hand for much of the third quarter of the century, era of the reform (La Reforma). Their accomplishments were numerous. They permitted many political liberties, including elections, although with limited suffrage. They attacked the church's enormous privileges, reducing its large tracts of (untaxable) lands, its immunity before the law, and its control over social affairs such as education and marriage. They expanded public educational facilities. Mestizos and a growing bourgeoisie captured some privileges previously reserved for a small elite. And the reform's great leader, Benito Juárez, was himself an Indian from the poor state of Oaxaca. Historian Daniel Cosío Villegas called the liberals a "group of men without equal in our history, men with the virile optimism of those who feel a nation being born from their own hands, and for whom liberalism was a new religious faith."[4] Yet a less flattering evaluation also exists. Classic nineteenth-century advocates of individualism, the liberals opposed traditionalism and communitarianism, whether oriented toward the church or the Indian. The liberals worshipped liberty, not equality.

However one evaluates the liberals' ideology, their reform's reach exceeded its grasp. It had greater success in limiting church privileges than in establishing a new liberal order. Regional oligarchs took advantage of formal democratic structures to thwart progressive change, so that both Juárez and his liberal successor had to rule largely through specially invoked executive authority. Ultimately, the liberals fell in 1876 to a military coup headed by Porfirio Díaz, who had been a general in Mexico's successful effort to end the French intervention.

Even when the liberals lost power, the traditional conservatives could not regain control. Instead, with Díaz as Mexico's supreme leader, a new political philosophy reigned. This was the era of positivism, which stressed that progress derives from science and order. Like liberalism, positivism was imported from Europe by most Latin American nations, but few felt its impact as strongly as Mexico. Like liberalism, positivism based itself mostly on "progressive" Europe and was generally indifferent or hostile to both tradition and egalitarianism. Unlike liberalism, positivism did not characteristically embrace individual liberty.

The achievements of the *porfiriato* (1876–1910) were substantial. Foremost were political stability and economic growth. Stability must be appreciated against the new nation's background of instability. Governments had come and gone so often that the military had become a very desirable career for upwardly mobile mestizos, one offering good chances to reach positions of power and corruption. Instability had frustrated Mexican efforts to attract waves of European emigrants, who instead took their skills to Argentina, Uruguay, or the United States. Most important, political instability had doomed the more significant efforts to attract foreign capital and technology. Now, finally, Mexico had an extended period of political stability. This stability, in turn, contributed to dramatic economic growth. Thus the porfiriato reversed the vicious cycle of economic weakness and political instability that had characterized the early independence period. Foreigners gave Mexico high credit ratings and made secure, profitable investments. Railroads, oil, electricity, steel, and sugar mills led the way. "Rails and Progress" boasted one prominent slogan. The strong porfiriato regime also succeeded in extracting increased tax revenues from the domestic population. National income soared, along with exports and imports.

Order and growth were achieved, however, with disdain for liberty and equality. Divisions of power between the national and state governments and separation of powers within the national government were bypassed as Díaz centralized political might into his own dictatorial hands. The reform's free elections, speech, and press were lost. The government co-opted peasants, gunmen, and bandits by offering good salaries, uniforms, and power and turned these *rurales* loose to repress dissent in the countryside. And considerable repression was necessary in order to implement policies that were not just dictatorial but economically harsh for the masses. Mexico's development model required cheap peasant and urban labor and no strikes.

Positivism provided the handy rationale that the intellectually fittest must forge a necessary, natural path to progress. Neither ignorance nor short-sighted humanitarianism should impede that progress. Thus, the government did not need to worry that it was providing, for example, terrible education in rural areas. Economic growth was expected to help the rich, the small middle class, and—through trickle-down economics—even the poor. In fact, only the first two expectations were fulfilled. Large landholders increasingly pushed peasants off their land into laborer status, which often culminated in debtor status. Conditions worsened at the turn of the century,

"Before the Revolution." Porfirio Díaz and *los científicos* (wise men). The cabinet (1909) represents the old guard. (Photo courtesy of Juan M. Casasola)

when world depression hit hardest at the masses. After decades of "order and progress," wages and living standards were deteriorating for many, and probably more than four in five Mexicans remained illiterate.[5]

While most Mexicans suffered, foreigners prospered. The porfiriato encouraged foreign penetration of major sectors of Mexico's economy. Independence took a giant step backward.

Parallels to contemporary Mexican politics (since 1940) are striking. Leadership for both regimes emerged from the ruins of movements (the reform, the revolution) to change society. Underprivileged masses do not benefit, at least not nearly in proportion to economic growth, and dissent is repressed. Yet the stick is combined with a carrot of co-optation, as expanding economies and bureaucracies offer jobs, and money from corruption is available. Both regimes are also enlightened enough to couple repression with intelligence, promoting scientific and professional pursuits, whether for the sake of "positivism" under the porfiriato or "modernization" in the contemporary system. Both use the trappings of democratic liberalism to obscure authoritarian behavior. (Díaz showed rare candor when he referred to Congress as "my herd of tame horses.") Notwithstanding the economic crisis of the 1980s, both have generally molded strong, positive relationships between political stability and economic growth. And both could reasonably claim that, whatever their shortcomings, the real alternative in Mexican history has not been democratic and widely shared prosperity, but destructive

political instability, a crippled economy, and consequent vulnerability to
foreign intervention.

In fairness, however, there are also important differences between the
past and present regimes. Today's uses a smaller stick and a larger carrot
than the porfiriato did. Repression and exclusion are less extensive. Peasants,
and especially organized workers, fare better than before. The middle class
has grown significantly, partaking of a measure of liberty and an expanded
measure of economic opportunity. Finally, both social and political mobility
are greater.

REVOLUTION

The marked lack of social and political mobility under the porfiriato
contributed to its fall. Aging regimes that do not let in rising groups or
circulate elites risk overthrow by those excluded. Economic growth had
spawned new interests that felt thwarted by the porfiriato dictatorship.
Intellectual foundations for rebellion were established by a reborn liberal
movement that demanded, at a minimum, free elections, a free press, and
a return to the reform's 1857 constitution. The regime reacted with repression.
The economic situation made matters worse. In response to a depression,
the government adopted harsh policies (e.g., calling in loans) and thereby
alienated even some of the elites. Politically, Díaz fumbled his one major
show of flexibility, an announcement of his personal retirement, by retreating
into typically rigged reelection. This about-face was the match that ignited
a flammable accumulation of grievances. So, almost a hundred years after
the start of the War of Independence, an equally protracted and far bloodier
revolution began.

Like many revolutions, Mexico's started with a moderate stage. So
brittle had Díaz's dictatorship become that it collapsed without any revolutionary push. Mexico's new president, Francisco Madero, was a young
foreign-educated idealist from a wealthy landowning family. His slogan,
"effective suffrage, no reelection," tells us as much about what he did not
champion (fundamental socioeconomic change) as what he did (political
reform). Madero was no fiery revolutionary. He restored the reform's basic
tenets, including a free press and individual property rights. He also restored
free elections, but, as earlier, suffrage was really limited to only part of the
population. A form of political liberty, not political equality, and certainly
not economic equality, was Madero's abiding principle. Courageous as he
was, Madero ultimately failed because he neither smashed the old regime
(its politicians, civil service, army, church, and entrenched economic interests)
nor controlled the revolutionaries bent on so doing. The first—and, according
to some, the last—really competitively elected president of Mexico in the
twentieth century was murdered in a 1913 coup, covertly aided by the
United States. The coup installed dictator Victoriano Huerta, destroyed
political freedom, and inaugurated the revolution's most violent epoch. Like
the democrat Madero, the dictator Huerta did not thoroughly overhaul the

porfiriato's governing elite.[6] Had either Madero or Huerta consolidated his power, the events of 1910 to 1913 might, in retrospect, hardly be seen as revolutionary.

At least three major armies were pitted against the new dictatorship. They were by no means united among themselves, however. Emiliano Zapata led peasant forces from the south. Their chief demand was clear: land. When Madero urged moderation, Zapata withdrew his support, effected land reform in his home state of Morelos, and pressed to spread the revolution. Zapata's forces had a coherent revolutionary program but were perhaps essentially conservative socially. Even their cry for land was an attempt to preserve their communal, insulated traditions. The second army, Pancho Villa's forces, lacked a similarly coherent program but displayed the violent revolutionary zeal popularly attributed to them.[7]

The third army, the constitutionalists, was led by Venustiano Carranza. This group was the least revolutionary of the three. It was composed largely of ranchers and self-made men. If it did not represent society's established elite, neither did it represent primarily the masses. Perhaps the key factor was that the group included many of those excluded from the Díaz regime's ruling elite. The porfiriato had proved itself incapable of sufficient personnel turnover, incapable of sufficient incorporation of young elites, and therefore vulnerable to rebellion from frustrated aspirants. By 1915 the constitutionalists were rising to political supremacy. Allied with the powerful "Northwest Group," Carranza defeated the zapatistas and villistas after these groups had abandoned Mexico City and returned to their regional strongholds. (The revolutionary legacy of the northwest has led some observers to look with special interest on the contemporary regime's electoral weaknesses, and even losses, in that region.)

More revolutionary turmoil than revolutionary change came in the next few years. Carranza himself had been a landlord, a senator during the Díaz regime, a governor during the Madero regime, and a cacique (regional strongman with his own army) before leading the constitutionalists to power. Reform was thus limited in part by Carranza's rather nonrevolutionary values; but it was promoted by his keen political sense. Carranza understood that a degree of reform was necessary to consolidate the new regime. Thus he would have to support the 1917 Constitutional Convention. The convention probably went well beyond Carranza's own wishes and certainly promulgated a truly revolutionary doctrine. The Constitution is a strongly nationalistic proclamation, asserting Mexico's control over its natural resources. It pledges land reform. It pledges labor rights, such as a minimum wage, an eight-hour day, improved working conditions, workmen's compensation, maternity leave laws, freedom to shop at other than company stores, and even some employer responsibility for health, housing, and educational opportunities. It has been called the first modern socialist constitution, preceding the Soviet Union's. At the same time, however, like Mexico's earlier reform, it replicates many U.S. concepts meant to guarantee political freedom: federalism, separation of powers, a bicameral congress, an elaborate Bill of Rights. The

"The Revolution Peaks." Pancho Villa in the presidential chair, with Emiliano Zapata on his right (1914). Their revolutionary forces did not long occupy the capital, the focus of political power. (Photo courtesy of Juan M. Casasola)

framers of Mexico's constitution attempted to include what they perceived as the best of both worlds.

Carranza's effort in 1920 to circumvent free elections by installing a puppet successor led to his own murder and a coup by the Northwest Group. The group installed its leader, Alvaro Obregón, as president. From 1920 to 1924, Obregón pushed beyond Carranza's restrained reform, particularly in labor and educational policies. Mexico built schools and launched a literacy campaign. Whereas Carranza, the politician, did what he thought the circumstances dictated, Obregón, the statesman, more actively pressed for reform in keeping with his own vision of a new society. If Díaz had represented repression of demands for socioeconomic change and Madero a gentlemanly ignorance or indifference, Carranza represented political acquiescence and Obregón active partnership.

Plutarco Elías Calles, another leader of the Northwest Group, peacefully took over the presidency in 1924, but his plot to circumvent the no-reelection rule by reinstalling Obregón in 1928 was abruptly foiled by Obregón's murder. Calles nonetheless remained the supreme power behind the throne until 1934. He was revolutionary in his attack on the church but failed to push many promised social reforms. His major accomplishment, without

"The Revolution Fails." By 1920, after Zapata's death, some of his generals allied themselves with Obregón. This alliance may symbolize the defeat of a true peasant revolution and the peasants' subsequent incorporation into the regime's highly inegalitarian system. (Photo courtesy of Juan M. Casasola)

doubt, was to forge Mexico's uniquely successful one-party system. Although his successor pursued a more revolutionary course, Calles pointed Mexican politics in its present direction: political stability (with substantial limits on liberty) and economic modernization (centralized banking, improved tax collection, financial stability, agricultural credits, infrastructural development, and increased U.S. economic penetration of the Mexican economy), without effective redistribution of the newly generated wealth.

If Calles thought he had appointed yet another subservient successor in Lázaro Cárdenas (1934–1940), he soon learned otherwise. Cárdenas's strength derived from the strong bond he established with Mexico's masses. Never before or since has the revolution produced such a revered figure. Contemporary reverence for Cárdenas is reverence for the major absent but not forgotten goal of the revolution: greater equality. If the porfiriato provides a historical parallel to contemporary policy, Cárdenas's administration provides the great symbolic alternative.

As governor of Michoacán in the 1920s, Cárdenas had established his commitment to agrarian reform. He dramatically demonstrated this commitment, while deepening his mass support, by campaigning for president throughout the country for one and a half years. As president, he distributed more land than had all his revolutionary predecessors combined, even though there had been significant distribution since 1920. Ironically, this distribution may not have reduced income inequality or improved real wages for the masses. Peasants got land, but in the form of small plots, without the adequate capital, irrigation, or skills to develop them. Yet Cárdenas cut through the usual cynicism of Mexican politics. Undoubtedly, much of his reform represented a pragmatic response to the worldwide depression, but Cárdenas also acted out of his own reformist convictions. He established mutually warm, trustful feeling with the masses. He also placed reins on official luxury. That Mexico underwent only a small shift from rural to urban areas in the 1930s is an indication of the hope that Cárdenas gave the peasants on the land.[8] Finally, Cárdenas was revered for nationalizing the oil industry in 1938. Mexico's masses had reason to feel that Cárdenas was *their* president.

Cárdenas's conception of an activist state at the service of the people had little in common with democratic notions about political liberty. Reforms would be initiated more from the top down, "for the people," than from the bottom up, "by the people." Peasant and worker demands were carefully handled through the official party. Labor should restrain itself, Cárdenas could argue, because it was properly integrated into a progressive state, which was, after all, one of its major employers. Educational policy tried to elevate socialist solidarity above the free interchange of conflicting ideas. Like his predecessors, from whom he differed notably in socioeconomic approaches, Cárdenas directly pursued political stability much more than political liberty or bourgeois freedoms. Cárdenas's first major step to guarantee the strength of the presidency was, ironically, to expel Calles, the man who had originally appointed him but who then persisted in trying to undermine him. Cárdenas proceeded to assert his central authority over regional as well as labor caciques whenever he felt them to be threatening that authority. At the end of his term, by bypassing leftist leaders within the party to appoint a moderate as his successor, Cárdenas in effect chose to institutionalize rather than to intensify the revolution.

AFTER THE REVOLUTION

Some observers have questioned the degree to which a revolution really occurred. They point out that Mexico merely switched one elite for another, that the plight of the masses was not substantially improved. A pertinent cartoon shows one peasant asking another, "Who finally won the revolution, the zapatistas or the villistas?" Answer: "Neither one; the Revolutionary Family governs us."[9] Leaders like Cárdenas emerge less often, while those like novelist Carlos Fuentes's Artemio Cruz appear.[10] For Cruz, revolutionary goals are quickly subordinated to material goals. He becomes preoccupied more with Paris or New York than with Mexico. He uses the power of the state to repress rather than to help the less privileged.

Upheavals need not change everything to be revolutions, however. Many important changes were achieved. A fossilized oligarchy was replaced by a much broader ruling elite. Peasant participation guaranteed that certain policy consequences, such as land distribution, would flow from the regime change. Labor became a major institutionalized political factor. A new political order, based on a strong civilian party structure, was born. And if violence is any criterion of revolution, Mexico's upheaval more than qualifies.

Mexico's transformation also included a cultural revolution. Nationalism was a key factor, although foreign influences remained strong in education and some related cultural fields.[11] The revolution weakened the explicitly European orientation of the Díaz regime and focused on Mexico's indigenous roots. The Indian was increasingly depicted not as an exotic savage, but as a mature person—even the source of all that was good in Mexico—in literary works such as Gregorio López y Fuentes's *El Indio* (The Indian). Pedro Lamicq's *Piedad para el Indio* (Mercy for the Indian) called for the integration of the Indian into Mexican life. José Vasconcelos wrote of the mission of the cosmic, Ibero-American race as a fortuitous blend of Indian, European, and African roots. Composers such as Carlos Chávez and Silvestre Revueltas would work repeatedly with folk themes. Writers such as Samuel Ramos, Jesús Silva Herzog, Octavio Paz, and Leopold Zea would explore the essence of Mexicanism. Archeologists would pursue their unique exploration of Mexico's roots. Architects associated ornament with bourgeois decadence and strove instead to transmit revolutionary values. But it was the painters who made the greatest impact, particularly with their grand murals depicting indigenous and revolutionary themes. Among the most famous were Diego Rivera, David Alfaro Siqueiros, José Clemente Orozco, and Rufino Tamayo. One could speak of a distinctly Mexican style. Cultural independence had taken great strides, even if one could argue that U.S. media have significantly changed the situation in recent decades. Added to all this one should consider the popular nationalistic culture, epitomized by the revolutionary ballads, like *La Cucaracha*, which, with considerable folkloric embellishment, hark back to distinctly Mexican themes. Importantly, folk music and dance are prominently and proudly featured at official government gatherings.

Political-economic consequences of the revolution for the post-1940 system will of course by analyzed throughout the rest of this book. Suffice it here to offer a very brief chronological overview. President Manuel Avila Camacho (1940–1946) concentrated on taming revolutionary fervor, whether directed against the church or against the United States. A positive accomplishment was the creation of Mexico's social security system. His successor, Miguel Alemán (1946–1952) became at least a symbolic antithesis to Cárdenas, the antihero of leftist historical interpretations. Alemán strongly favored industrialization, business interests, and the trickle-down approach to distributing wealth, explicitly pursuing economic growth while hoping that all might eventually benefit from the bigger pie. Agriculture, notably communal agriculture, plunged into low-priority status, which the regime would maintain for decades. Nevertheless—and this is crucial to the institutionalization and stability of the Mexican regime—Alemán did not specifically undo all of

Cárdenas's reforms or declare them illegitimate. Alemán's successor, Adolfo Ruiz Cortines (1952–1958), then proclaimed a "balanced revolution," that is, one balanced between the *alemanista* and *cardenista* approaches. His moderation, integrity, popularity, and relative inactivity made him something of a Mexican Eisenhower.

Next, López Mateos (1958–1964) declared himself a leftist "within the revolution." But nearly all administrations since 1940 have really inclined more to the alemanista pole. By the mid-1950s the state role in the economy had diminished, leaving more leeway to the private sector, and still greater emphasis was given to industry over agriculture. López Mateos readily repressed labor, particularly the rebellious railroad workers, in order to protect the sanctity of the growth-stability model. Gustavo Díaz Ordaz (1964–1970) went still farther, repressing even middle-class university students when he perceived a possible challenge to the regime. His administration's strong inclination toward the alemanista pole was unquestioned.

Luis Echeverría (1970–1976) showed once again that "leftist" presidents are not above authoritarian repression. Although he granted a greater degree of freedom than his predecessor, he also clamped down on governors, the press, and peasants. In socioeconomic affairs, Echeverría made a major attempt to deviate from the alemanista model, but he achieved only mixed results. He managed some success in subsidizing food and housing and increased the government's control over certain economic sectors, including communications, commerce, industry, and foreign investment. But he failed dismally in other attempts, such as tax reform. His overall effort to alter the development model, to fortify the public and domestic sectors, and to redistribute wealth a bit earned him the enmity of foreign economic interests and of Mexico's middle and upper classes. Mexico's economy plunged deeper into disaster, culminating in the 1976 peso devaluation. It is important to understand that Echeverría deviated from the alemanista model fundamentally not because he was an irresponsible radical adventurer, as many of his detractors would have it, or because he was a dedicated revolutionary, as many of his ardent supporters would have it; he acted mostly because he saw serious crises within the development model.

Until 1981, José López Portillo (1976–1982) successfully restored the confidence of those who were sympathetic to Mexico's basic development model. Political stability seemed surer, the economy once again grew at enviable rates, and the middle and upper classes and foreign and domestic investors were pleased. Political reform was extended. Mexico maintained its progressive hue in foreign policy, notwithstanding some moderation of strident rhetoric. During most of López Portillo's administration, political liberty probably flourished more than it had for at least several administrations. On the other hand, corruption expanded well beyond its usual proportions, and the presidency itself was widely implicated. Moreover, government policies retreated from Echeverría's banner of fundamental socioeconomic reform. Austerity measures were imposed, and wage increases were held far below the rate of inflation. The regime acknowledged that no new grants of land to peasants would be undertaken. Overall, there was an effort to move away from heady populist politics in favor of more rationalized, technocratic policies. We will explore signs that some important modifications in the basic development model did in fact continue under López Portillo, but the overriding point is that economic growth, not increased economic equality, was once again viewed as political stability's most critical partner.

But economic policy was in turmoil as the worst crisis in decades enveloped Mexico in López Portillo's last year. Data showing the proportions of the crisis are provided in Chapter 5. Capital flight accelerated; the government seriously cut its spending, its subsidization of basic goods to consumers, and its public works projects (while helping to bail Mexico's largest private concern out of its own deep crisis); and government, business, and labor clashed over wage and price policies. In September 1982, the government announced a dramatic move: It was taking over all domestic private banks. Amid such deep crisis, Mexico was forced to count on foreign interests for a multi-billion-dollar rescue package. More than US$4 billion would come from International Monetary Fund credits, an almost equal amount from combined U.S. sources, and additional aid from Japanese and European banks. Naturally, such aid flows largely on donor terms, as with increased U.S. oil purchases at preferential prices. Although the international impact of oil prices and interest rates had contributed to Mexico's economic crisis, López Portillo's return to the basic tenets of Mexico's vaunted stability-growth model seemed either less complete or less desirable than many had previously thought.

Thus, Miguel de la Madrid (1982–1988) assumed office amid great crisis and uncertainty. Hoping to restore confidence at home and abroad, he launched a "moral renovation" campaign to attack corruption, and he moved away from the erratic, populist, and even demagogic tendencies of his two predecessors toward a leadership style of prudence, pragmatism, and tolerance. (In fact, de la Madrid was repeatedly criticized for being too uncharismatic, too restrained, and too technocratic.) The range of political liberties and respect for dissent expanded. Despite increased constraints on its freedom of action, Mexico upheld basic tenets of its progressive foreign policy. But de la Madrid's major policy arena was the economy. Chapter 5 provides details and explanations; here we merely highlight basic trends. De la Madrid pushed significant economic reforms, including opening the economy to more foreign investment and competition, decreasing public subsidies, selling off many unprofitable government enterprises, and dismissing thousands of bureaucrats, including high-level ones. The economy initially rebounded strongly, and, by 1984 and into 1985, improvements were manifest in massive debt restructurings, economic growth, private investments, private-sector imports, trade accounts, non-oil exports, and reductions in inflation. Compared to such 1982-83 shocks as falling private investment, negative growth rates, and equally unusual inflation rates—and compared to the continued economic woes plaguing most of Latin America—

The PRI's candidate, Miguel de la Madrid, on the campaign trail, Mexico City, November 1981. (Photo courtesy of Rodolfo Romo de Vivar)

the turnaround seemed impressive. Some analysts began showcasing Mexico as a political-economic model again. And the apparent turnaround occurred despite falling international prices for oil.

But the picture was mixed even during the upsurge. Economic rationalization meant unemployment, austerity, and suffering for many, with real wages falling rapidly. Falling oil prices and high U.S. interest rates took their toll. By mid-decade, the depth of economic crisis became painfully clear. Inflation and the public deficit did not decrease as planned. Nor, despite Mexico's enormous sacrifices, did its debt burden decrease. What decreased were business confidence and Mexico's independence from U.S. and multinational financial agencies. Capital flight came to be accompanied by an emigration of not just laborers but more privileged Mexicans. Consequently, progressive social reform seemed indefinitely postponed; the social question was how much intense suffering would be exacerbated. Politically, basic reforms also slipped on the policy agenda, elections were tainted, and even many observers who had emphasized the Mexican regime's extraordinary ability to maintain stability amid hardship wondered how much deterioration could be tolerated. Overall, considerable political uncertainty gripped a system commonly identified by stable bases crafted long ago.

INSTITUTIONALIZATION

The question is continually asked and never adequately answered: How can a revolution be institutionalized? Most observers agree that the revolution has died, probably around 1940, although the date has been debated.[12] Contemporary Mexico has followed a model of stable development, not revolutionary change. By institutionalizing its revolution, Mexico has simultaneously cemented certain changes already achieved by the revolution and shielded the system from further revolutionary change. The story is revealed through the political histories of certain key societal institutions.

The Party

Development of Mexico's official political party was the linchpin of institutionalization. Calles was the party's principal architect. Having failed to restore Obregón to the presidency in 1928, Calles sought a mechanism by which to perpetuate the regime after he himself left office. He ably persuaded most regional and labor caciques that a centralization of political power was in their interests. This centralization was especially important because the early revolutionary period had been characterized by centrifugal forces. Calles proposed that caciques band together through a central party to perpetuate certain privileges, as all would be lost if the existing disorder continued. Recent events spoke loudly for Calles: Madero, Zapata, Carranza, Villa, and Obregón had all met unnatural deaths. Violence continued to surround most local as well as national elections. Three contenders were killed in the 1928 presidential campaign. Religious warfare continued with violent intensity (see below). Moreover, Mexico was now headed into the worldwide Great Depression, which was bound to exacerbate worker discontent. Mexico's power-holders needed political order.

Calles was remarkably successful. Enough power-holders bought the message (some allowing themselves to be bought out of politics with lucrative business opportunities) for the new party to take on considerable power. From the nineteenth century on, parties had lacked cohesiveness, often rising and falling with their leaders. Furthermore, the party "system" had been highly fragmented, with many weak parties. But from fifty-one registered parties in 1929, Mexico was down to four by 1933.[13] And the more ex-president Calles ruled and dispensed favors through the party, the stronger that party became. Thus the regime overcame the regional dispersion of political power that had often contributed to instability. The party was a mechanism to centralize political power in Mexico City.

Yet the party might have faded early. Institutionalization of the regime was one reason that Calles built the party; perpetuation of his own political power was another. But any possibility that the party would be merely a personal vehicle for Calles ended when Cárdenas, as president, cut Calles loose from the party.[14] More significant, Cárdenas did not try to extend his control over the party after his own term. Given his enormous popularity, this was a considerable victory indeed for the cause of institutionalization. Instead, Cárdenas used his popularity to strengthen the party. He reorganized it from a regional basis, so important initially to bring in the local caciques, to a functional basis, so important now to incorporate the masses. The hero of land distribution organized local peasant leagues into an official agrarian sector. He similarly backed the organization of a giant central labor union.

Those who failed to join up soon found themselves powerless. Influence and benefits, after all, now came through the party. So Mexico had successfully created a party that brought into the system the peasant and working masses whose rising expectations may otherwise have created further revolutionary pressures. Cárdenas was neither the first nor the only leader to favor such incorporation, but he was the most successful. Calles had brought the elites together into a common forum, and Cárdenas completed the picture by bringing in the masses.

Given the plight of peasants and workers in recent decades, Cárdenas's incorporation of them into the official party may be seen as ultimately producing greater gains for political stability than for equality or liberty. By not excluding peasants and workers from the formal political structure, the regime would not allow them to develop *independently*. Serious attempts to pressure the regime for fundamental socioeconomic reform in contemporary Mexico often receive neither support nor even indifference but damaging opposition from official peasant and worker representatives. Additionally, the party's nonrevolutionary nature was reinforced by the 1942 inclusion of a "popular sector" composed of diverse groups (small industrialists, professionals, youth, women's groups), mostly of middle-class background, with little revolutionary heritage or outlook. In 1946 the party, originally the National Revolutionary Party, then the Party of the Mexican Revolution, assumed its present and poignant name: Institutionalized Revolutionary party (PRI). As we will discuss in the next chapter, it has dominated Mexico's party system ever since.

The Military

The rise of a strong party contributed greatly to taming Mexico's military. Cárdenas actually brought the military into the party structure. He reasoned that the military was involved de facto in politics already— better to integrate it into an institution controlled by others.

The significance of taming the military can be grasped by looking at historical experience. Nineteenth-century Mexico had one of the "worst" records of military intervention in politics of any Latin American nation.[15] Local armies loyal to given caciques were decisive political forces. Military might most often determined who ruled Mexico. The armed forces served as prime vehicles of social mobility: Soldiers might rise through the ranks, but power-seekers could also realize their dreams by toppling existing governments. Although Juárez, and especially Díaz, made some progress in curbing the military, the military remained active even after the revolution. Obregón and his successors took matters more in hand with a carrot-and-stick approach. They put all generals on the federal payroll, eventually provided social security for soldiers, and allowed ample opportunities for corruption; they also purged disloyal generals, shifted others away from their power bases, and slashed military expenditures.

The results have been startling. Mexico boasts steady civilian rule. This loss of power by the military was not sudden, however. Even after the military's dominant and direct role in politics ended and even after the military as an institution was excluded from the formal party structure, army generals headed the party until 1964.[16] No civilian was elected president until Alemán in 1946. Nonetheless, the military's decline was sure. Generals within the PRI increasingly made room for civilian domination. In reality, several of Alemán's immediate predecessors had been warriors only by loose, image-inflated definition anyway, but every president since Alemán has clearly been a civilian. Eight military officers held cabinet positions unrelated to defense between 1929 and 1946; only one has done so since 1946. Officers held fifteen governorships in 1940; there has been, at most, only one serving as governor at any time since 1964. There have been military challenges, such as rebellion in 1938 and a general's electoral campaign in 1940, but the ease with which the civilian regime turned back these challenges showed the regime's strength rather than its vulnerability. Besides, even such limited challenges have been less frequent since 1940 than previously.

The taming of the military has been startling by comparison not only with Mexican history, but also with almost all of contemporary Latin America. It has been common for the military to topple governments and, particularly in the 1970s, to rule directly for extended periods. Even in countries where civilians ostensibly rule, they often must share considerable power with the military. Not in Mexico. The Mexican government has been in the hands of a professional civilian elite, not just soldiers in mufti or soldiers newly turned civilian.[17] Compared to its regional counterparts, Mexico's military has had much less power to veto or influence civilian policy, or to demand big payoffs for nonintervention. As one indicator, Mexico spends much less of its budget on the military than do most Latin American countries.

This does not mean that Mexico's military lacks functions. It means that these functions mostly *serve rather than threaten* the civilian system. The military watches for potential threats to stability. It is an arm of repression against those—rural guerrillas, peasants, workers, and, exceptionally, students—who mount significant challenges to the regime. The military also engages in certain infrastructural development projects. Its allegiance to the civilian rulership is a source of legitimacy for both groups.

Mexico's military may appear unique, but it is really the civilian political system that is unique. The civilian system determines the military role. Unlike the situation in much of Latin America, conservative interests have been able to count on Mexico's civilian structure to maintain political order and economic privilege. Were this structure to fail in the future, the military role could well change. In fact, interesting signs of change have recently appeared and will be examined in the next chapter. For decades, however, Mexico's military has been uniquely institutionalized within the civilian-dominated political structure, and we do not see a fundamental transformation in progress.

The Church

As with peaceful military-regime relations, the importance of peaceful church-regime relations must be seen against a turbulent historical background. In precolumbian and even colonial Mexico, dominant religions and political institutions were generally tightly bound, but church influence often constituted a powerful counterweight to the newly independent government. Church ownership of perhaps one-third of Mexico's land gave it extraordinary resources.[18] Together with other large landholders, the church significantly shaped conservative Mexican politics. Political liberals and many capitalists seeking a more open economic system therefore challenged the church. The reform's 1857 constitution seriously eroded church power. Although liberal ideology was clearly a force, the reform's attack on the church must also be seen in the context of the governmental instability, rooted in inability to raise adequate revenues, that had characterized newly independent Mexico. The church's land was nontaxable, depriving the state of badly needed revenue.

Despite positivism's antireligious bias, church influence recovered somewhat during the porfiriato. So the revolutionaries felt it necessary to attack church privileges again. The Constitution of 1917 prohibits property ownership by religious institutions or personnel, forbids church participation in politics, limits participation in education, denies voting rights to the clergy, and gives government the authority to designate places of worship and to fix a maximum number of ministers for each state. Church-state tensions peaked under Calles. Until 1926 there had been only limited enforcement of anticlerical constitutional provisions, although there were certain stiff measures, such as the drafting of priests. Calles then launched a virulent antichurch crusade, provoking armed rebellion from many Catholics (the cristero rebellion). Calles's crusade must be understood in terms of his unyielding attempts to centralize political power and the potential threat to Mexico's revolution still posed by the church. The regime would accept the church only after the regime itself became more secure and the church in turn retreated from political affairs. Cárdenas relaxed the crusade, although his neo-Marxism guaranteed anticlerical politics. His successor displayed no such negative posture toward the church: "I am a believer," he declared. The period in which revolution had preempted Catholicism as Mexico's only sanctioned religion was over.

Today, the church's presence mocks harsh constitutional restrictions. There are seminaries, church-run schools, religiously inspired universities, priests walking about in clerical garb. Government employees receive "spring vacations," which could just as accurately be called vacations for Holy Week (the week between Palm Sunday and Easter). All this is possible because the church no longer threatens the regime. It is, in fact, functional to it. Church activities offer living proof of a degree of political liberty. Also, in Karl Marx's terms, religion may be a flower on the chains of repression, a flower that deflects the masses' attention from their material plight (although it is not held fundamentally responsible for constructing those chains). And the church may be a useful counterweight to forces pushing the regime in more leftist directions.[19]

This is not to say that the church's principal aims are political rather than spiritual. Nor is it to say there are no church-state tensions. Many Catholics resent the government's antichurch posturing. The government, for its part, wants to keep church influence minimal. Strong mass allegiance to the church, contrasted to increasingly manifest apathy or cynicism about the government, is embarrassing, to say the least. The outpouring of enthusiasm by perhaps 20 million Mexicans for Pope John Paul's 1979 visit was uncomfortably similar to the preference shown by the Poles for their pope over their premier. The regime is also wary of the prominent role reform-minded priests have recently played in much of Latin America, opposing authoritarian regimes in Brazil, Chile, and Central America. The era of inevitable church allegiance to Latin America's conservative forces is over. Mexico's church now has an active minority, spearheaded by the likes of the progressive bishop of San Cristóbal de las Casas, who argue that the masses deserve a better material fate in *this* life. Some priests at the grassroots level have assumed a mission to raise the political consciousness of peasants and Central American refugees living in Mexico. For the most part, however, the church lacks the independent political power it previously had in Mexico or the independent power it still has in certain other Latin American countries.

The University

Few, if any, major institutions lend themselves as readily to dissent and disorder as the university. Although rarely capable of unilaterally destroying regimes, universities in less developed nations often initiate and then help lead potentially destabilizing conditions. And Mexico's university had a history of turmoil to rival that of the military or the church.

Porfirio Díaz's positivists had no sooner opened their National University (1910) dedicated to progress and order than the revolution ripped it apart. Sheer revolutionary turmoil was one factor. Beyond this, the university became a special target of revolutionary assault. It was indicted for challenging the revolutionary regime's authority, with serving the elite and esoteric ends, rather than the masses and practical problem-solving. Many in Congress wanted to cut all ties to the university, and indeed, subsidies ceased in 1934. Calles was especially harsh, as he was against the church. "The state should control education at all levels, from elementary to university. . . . Unfortunately, university youth is 80 percent or more reactionary and tries to . . . dislodge the revolutionaries from power and thus keep them from combating . . . capital and the clergy."[20] Nor did Cárdenas's victory suggest much relief. He strongly supported a socialist constitutional reform. Although it was implemented only sporadically, it was used by the likes of labor boss Vicente Lombardo Toledano to battle defenders of pluralist academic freedom. Cárdenas made it clear that there would be no government subsidies until the university joined actively in the "social program of the revolution." Many professors resigned in protest.

The university, divided but mostly antagonistic to the government, remained the scene of considerable disorder. Between 1933 and 1944 not one of its rectors (presidents) lasted more than two years. Nor was the revolutionary fight restricted to higher education; many teachers were assassinated in the countryside. Yet while both Calles and Cárdenas wanted revolutionary control, they also wanted order, as their party-building efforts suggest. So in 1929 the government granted partial autonomy to the university and in 1933, full autonomy. One idea behind these grants was to placate university opposition. Another was that the autonomous university, without government funds, would soon perish, opening the way for creation of a truly revolutionary or "proletarian" institution. Meanwhile, Cárdenas proceeded to establish a government-run National Polytechnic Institute, geared to serve the revolution as the university would not.

As expected, the university simply could not survive without government funds and therefore increasingly pledged its loyalty to the revolution. A new statute passed in 1944 limited student and faculty power, establishing instead a strong rectorship and what many considered to be a U.S.-style governing board. Such a board, and its appointed rector, were far less likely than students and professors to engage in disorder or to challenge the regime. The university itself became much more stable. Whereas the rectorship had changed hands twenty-three times in the thirty-five years between the revolution's inception and the new statute, it changed hands only nine times in the next thirty-five years. Rarely since 1944 has disorder at the National University seriously threatened the regime. When it does, as in 1968, the government is likely to resort to repression. The situation varies regarding Mexico's now extensive network of public universities in individual states, but rarely is there a dire threat to state governments, and even such threats do not necessarily endanger the national regime.

On balance, however, the institutionalized regime went even further than the university to reach a modus vivendi. It resumed its subsidies to and greatly reduced its ideological assaults on the university. It invited faculty, alumni, and administrators into government positions. Most of all, it ceased to insist that the university be revolutionary, instead allowing it considerable autonomy. Indeed, this autonomy has not characteristically been used to promote revolutionary ends, such as fundamentally changing Mexico's social structure. The regime no longer pressed for a revolutionary university *once the regime itself was no longer revolutionary.* Early in 1946 the regime changed the socialist amendment on education, replacing the doctrine of class struggle with the doctrine of national unity. In fact, the regime has developed good relations with several elite private universities that are conservatively oriented and serve regime interests well.

Like the army and church, even the university performs many functions that reinforce the regime's position. One good example is the training and recruitment of political elites. Mostly, the government merely tries to guarantee that the public university not be a significant destabilizing force. The government still has great trouble with the public university—more than with the church—but for decades neither institution has seriously threatened the regime, nor been forced into revolutionary lockstep with it.

REPRISE

With its unusually inclusive official party, civilian control over the military, and modus vivendi with the church and university, Mexico's contemporary regime has protected itself from many of the traditional threats faced by other Latin American regimes. As Samuel Huntington has written, a weak political system in which different social forces competed with each other amid feeble political institutions transformed itself into a system in which these social forces have been largely subordinated to strong political institutions.[21] Probably the major autonomous domestic center limiting the Mexican regime's power today is business. But business has generally reinforced, not diluted, the institutionalization just described. It has usually supported the regime's basic development model, based on political stability and economic growth. Business-regime tensions have sharpened since the early 1970s, but, for the most part, the regime has tamed the forces it has had to in order to guarantee its stability, leaving a degree of autonomy only where such autonomy could be afforded. (The contemporary relationship between regime stability and group freedom and power is pursued in Chapter 4.)

It would be more charitable to compare the results of such institutionalization to the realities of Mexican history than to any standard elaboration of revolutionary goals. Where the postrevolutionary regime has failed to fulfill historical aspirations, it has hardly been unique in Mexican history. Where the regime has had more success, there is more, but hardly uniform, historical precedent. Greater individual political liberty has rarely been achieved in Mexico; the principal precedent might be the reform period. Rarer still has been any sustained effort to decrease economic inequality. The key symbolic precedent here would be the Cárdenas years. In the struggle for national independence, the war against Spanish colonial rule and the revolution emerge as the two most notable victories, although neither prevented significant economic and cultural dependency on foreign powers. Finally, the contemporary regime's clearest success lies in its achievement of political stability and, until the 1980s, economic growth along with it. Although the porfiriato provides one strong historical precedent, the frequent turbulence in Mexican history makes the contemporary regime's achievements in this regard seem considerable indeed.

We close this chapter with a brief schematic summary of how Mexico has historically approached the interrelationships among political stability, political liberty, economic growth, decreased economic inequality, and national independence.

The Spanish crown stressed, quite successfully, colonial political stability combined with economic gain for the mother country. It obviously did not consider offering much more than the modicum of democratic liberties it granted to its own citizens in Spain, and it even more obviously opposed independence for the colonies. It delegated the inequality issue to the church, insuring that it would be approached far more as a spiritual than an economic issue.

Clearly, the criollos of the early nineteenth century pursued national independence as their prime goal, hoping that independence would subsequently underpin their own political and economic control. As those Indians who joined in the independence struggle soon discovered, the criollos were staunchly opposed to spreading economic resources. Nor did the criollo movement, like that of the privileged classes in the United States, begin to establish a democratic system. Such a system did, however, emerge as a chief preoccupation of many of Mexico's nineteenth-century liberals, whose crowning success came with the reform and 1857 constitution. Democracy was deemed compatible with both political stability and economic growth. The new order would naturally benefit the masses, it was argued, but opinions were more mixed as to the degree of *direct* effort that should be made on their behalf. The liberals proved their commitment to independence by opposing perpetuation of colonial customs and by fighting to oust the French occupation forces. Conservatives were generally more sympathetic to Mexico's inherited colonial culture and less sympathetic to liberal democracy. Nonetheless, they generally shared the liberals' frustrated concern for political stability and economic growth, and neither group raised the banner of economic equality. As the reform gave way to the porfiriato, the latter ushered in a ruling creed that displayed unusually clear priorities. Political stability and economic growth were the twin idols. As strong national independence would be incompatible with economic growth, foreign investment was encouraged. And as, allegedly, neither stability nor growth could be intelligently guided if the system betrayed itself by pandering to principles of political democracy or economic equality, progress was entrusted to "survival of the fittest," not to the popular will.

The porfiriato's vaunted political stability exploded early in the twentieth century. Francisco Madero, Mexico's first leader of the revolutionary period, broke sharply with the positivists' political beliefs, although not so sharply from their economic beliefs. Among the grassroots movements, both the zapatistas and villistas struggled to decrease inequality and to promote independence, while remaining relatively indifferent to Madero's brand of liberal democracy; the zapatistas were especially concerned to achieve a political order that would allow them to return to peaceful agricultural pursuits. Carranza's constitutionalists began to point Mexico away from both the *maderista* emphasis on political democracy and the zapatista and villista emphasis on economic redistribution, moving instead toward contemporary priorities of stability and growth. Calles intensified these tendencies.

Under Cárdenas the Mexican Revolution was recalled to its goals of national independence and egalitarianism, although the revolution's emphasis on political stability rather than liberal or bourgeois democracy was maintained. In Cárdenas's view, greater national independence and more equal distribution of wealth were not just compatible with but were necessary to political stability; without them, Mexico would be an unstable pawn of powers from without and a time bomb to be detonated by its own deprived masses from within. Alemán's followers, on the other hand, would see direct efforts to redistribute wealth as obstacles to economic growth; the two economic goals could be compatible only when growth expanded opportunities and the overall size of the economic pie. Alemanistas basically felt that foreign investment, credit, and trade lead to growth and therefore stability. Interestingly, there has been no major, consistent split between cardenistas and alemanistas regarding political liberty; such liberty may be accepted, even encouraged, but only insofar as it does not endanger political stability or economic growth. As the contemporary regime (since 1940) has inclined decidedly toward the alemanista position, the pursuit of political stability has been consciously tied to the pursuit of economic growth.[22]

We can find reflections of indigenous, colonial, liberal, conservative, positivist, and revolutionary pasts all present today. But neither all these pasts nor the various principles they have promoted are *equally* represented in contemporary Mexican politics. In general, the institutionalized regime has been most successful in attaining the historical goals of economic growth and, especially, political stability, less successful in attaining the goals of national independence and political liberty, and least successful in attaining the goal of increased economic equality.

NOTES

1. The quotes are from, respectively, Octavio Paz, *The Other Mexico: Critique of the Pyramid*, trans. Lysander Kemp (New York: Grove Press, 1972), p. x; and idem, "Reflections: Mexico and the United States," trans. Rachel Phillips, *New Yorker*, September 17, 1979, p. 148.

2. Paz, "Reflections," p. 140.

3. Political liberty increased, mostly for the criollos, but not for most Mexicans. The following two paragraphs in the text derive largely from Frank Safford, "Bases of Political Alignment in Early Republican Spanish America," in *New Approaches to Latin American History*, ed. Richard Graham and Peter H. Smith (Austin: University of Texas Press, 1974), especially pp. 72, 91–92; and Barbara H. Tenenbaum, "Straightening Out Some of the Lumpen in the Development," *Latin American Perspectives* 2, no. 2 (1975):7–9.

4. Daniel Cosío Villegas, *American Extremes*, trans. Américo Paredes (Austin: University of Texas Press, 1964), p. 10.

5. Frank Tannenbaum, *Mexico: The Struggle for Peace and Bread* (New York: Columbia University Press, 1950), p. 154.

6. Peter Smith, *The Labyrinths of Power: Political Recruitment in Twentieth Century Mexico* (Princeton, N.J.: Princeton University Press, 1979), p. 163.

7. Hollywood has produced a number of colorful movies about the Mexican revolution and its leading personalities. Unfortunately, most tell us more about Hollywood than Mexico. One of the finest and most intimate scholarly books, unusually well written, is John Womack's *Zapata and the Mexican Revolution* (New York: Knopf, 1969).

8. James Wilkie, *The Mexican Revolution: Federal Expenditures and Social Change Since 1910* (Berkeley: University of California Press, 1967), p. 256.

9. *Los Supermachos*, January 23, 1975.

10. Carlos Fuentes, *The Death of Artemio Cruz*, trans. Sam Hileman (New York: Farrar, Straus, 1964).

11. See Frederick C. Turner's account of revolutionary nationalism and even xenophobia, *The Dynamic of Mexican Nationalism* (Chapel Hill: University of North Carolina Press, 1968). Also see Mary Kay Vaughan's account of persistent dependence on foreign thought, *The State, Education, and Social Class in Mexico, 1880–1928* (DeKalb, Ill.: Northern University Press, 1982).

12. Standard reading on this issue includes Stanley Ross, ed., *Is the Mexican Revolution Dead?* (New York: Knopf, 1966). Even more skeptical in tone is Peter Calvert, "The Mexican Revolution: Theory or Fact," *Journal of Latin American Studies* 1, no. 1 (1969):51–68. For a review essay covering recent historical research on institutionalization, see Thomas Benjamin, "The Leviathan on the Zócalo: Recent Historiography of the Postrevolutionary Mexican State," *Latin American Research Review* 20, no. 3 (1985):195–217. Revisionists stress that the revolution's legacy has generally been to consolidate (not destroy) the inegalitarian, capitalist, politically centralized structure that emerged in the porfiriato.

13. Pablo González Casanova, *Democracy in Mexico*, trans. Danielle Salti (London: Oxford University Press, 1970), p. 34.

14. For a detailed account of Cárdenas's efforts at party institutionalization, see Wayne A. Cornelius, "Nation-Building, Participation and Distribution: The Politics of Social Reform Under Cárdenas," in *Crisis, Choice and Change: Historical Studies of Political Development*, ed. Gabriel A. Almond, Scott C. Flanagan, and Robert J. Mundt (Boston: Little, Brown and Co., 1973), pp. 392–498. Naturally, we do not mean to imply that the revolution's preoccupation with institutionalization and stability began only in 1929. It is embodied, for example, in the ideology and efforts of Alberto J. Pani, who served in high policy positions under seven consecutive constitutionally elected presidents from 1910 to 1933. Keith Allen Haynes, "Orden y Progreso: The Revolutionary Ideology of Alberto J. Pani," paper presented at the Sixth Conference of Mexican and U.S. Historians, Chicago, September 1981.

15. Samuel P. Huntington has called Mexico "the worst." *Political Order in Changing Societies* (New Haven, Conn.: Yale University Press, 1968), p. 256.

16. Robert K. Furtak, *El partido de la revolución y la estabilidad política en México* (Mexico City: UNAM, 1978), pp. 217–218. For further accounts of the institutionalization of the military, see Edwin Lieuwen, *Mexican Militarism: The Political Rise and Fall of the Revolutionary Army, 1910–1940* (Albuquerque: University of New Mexico Press, 1968); and Jorge Alberto Loyoza, *El ejército mexicano (1911–1965)* (Mexico City: El Colegio de México, 1970). See also Chapter 3, fn. 6.

17. John Conklin has given supporting data for 1940–1965 and starkly contrasted Mexico to other Latin American nations. "Elite Studies: The Case of the Mexican Presidency," *Journal of Latin American Studies* 5, no. 2 (1973):247–269.

18. Frank Brandenburg, *The Making of Modern Mexico* (Englewood Cliffs, N.J.: Prentice-Hall, 1964), p. 188. For a detailed account of the struggle to institutionalize the church, see Nicolás Larin, *La rebelión de los cristeros (1926–1929)*, trans. Angel C. Tomás (Mexico City: Ediciones Era, 1968). For an English-language source on the state-church issue, see David C. Bailey, *¡Viva Cristo Rey!* (Austin: University of Texas Press, 1973).

19. Thus, for example, the church has deplored the violent means of Mexican guerrillas and Castroites. President Echeverría, in inimitable style, turned the tables

a bit by using progressive religious ideals to attack conservatives. Monterrey industrialists, he declared, were bad Christians because of their selfish pursuit of wealth rather than social justice.

20. Quoted in Sebastian Mayo, *La educación en México* (Rosario, Argentina: Editorial BEAR, 1964), pp. 261–262. Our account of the struggle to reach an accommodation with the public university is drawn from Daniel Levy, "University Autonomy Versus Government Control: The Case of Mexico," Ph.D. dissertation, University of North Carolina, 1977, pp. 66–151.

21. Huntington, *Political Order in Changing Societies*, p. 318.

22. For a lengthy yet readable single-volume overview of Mexican history the reader is referred to Michael C. Meyer and William L. Sherman, *The Course of Mexican History* (New York: Oxford University Press, 1979). A comprehensive source on Mexican history is the series of volumes entitled *Historia General de México* and published by El Colegio de México.

3

Political Institutions, Processes, and Actors

Political participation is the process in which individuals, groups, or classes in a society articulate their material interests, their ideological preferences, or their particular conception of the public interest. The first section of this chapter identifies the formal state and societal institutions through which Mexican political participation takes place. Special consideration is given to the roles of the president, the heads of key ministries, and those in other federal positions as well as to the ruling party (PRI), labor, the peasants, and the business community. Nonelectoral forms of political participation by actors such as the media, intellectuals, and what sociologists have referred to as *marginados* (including slum inhabitants and many Indians and unorganized workers) are left for Chapter 4.

In the second section, our discussion of the political parties and political reform focuses on elections, one potentially important form of political participation, considering such questions as: What are the ideologies and constituencies of the opposition parties, as compared to the PRI? Is a more truly multiparty system evolving in Mexico? What is the significance of the recent political and electoral reforms and of Mexico's electoral experiences in the 1980s?

STATE INSTITUTIONS

A critical characteristic of the Mexican state is the unusually strong position of the president relative to that of any other political figure. Authority is highly centralized and checks and balances are minimal, even though Mexico is nominally a federal republic modeled after the U.S. system of government. Congress, notwithstanding recent reforms, has been practically a rubber stamp, passing nearly all laws proposed by the president without effecting major modifications; the judicial branch of government has exhibited only a slightly greater degree of autonomy.[1]

As most important legislation is initiated and carried through to approval by the president, hardly any opportunity exists for effective

Mexico's National Palace, built in the sixteenth century (although remodeled and enlarged several times), remains a powerful architectural reminder of Spanish colonial influence. But it also represents the seat of centralized political power in Mexico and in the presidency. (Photo courtesy of Rodolfo Romo de Vivar)

interaction between citizens and their representatives during the lawmaking process. However, groups and individuals may occasionally influence the way in which laws and policies are actually implemented. A common element of day-to-day politics in Mexico is the presentation of demands to local and state governments, to departments of the federal bureaucracy, and even directly to the president. As the ultimate authority, the president can overrule an interpretation of the law made by any other government authority; the practice of reinterpreting written law also occurs at lower levels of government. This mechanism for managing demands provides some welcome flexibility in a system generally characterized by rigidity and a lack of efficiency, but it also contributes to widespread corruption. (Groups or individuals with good contacts and resources are most likely to attain a favorable interpretation of a law or policy.)

The president has broad powers to choose his close associates. He selects the ministers of defense and navy after consideration of the merit system prevailing in their respective bureaucratic structures. The new president usually appoints other ministers from his group of long-time friends and collaborators. In addition, although every new president has to negotiate with some powerful groups about certain positions in his initial cabinet, as time goes on he progressively replaces those ministers who pose problems and eventually attains full control of his cabinet. In the end, all ministers try to be as loyal as possible to him, partly because the outgoing president chooses his successor from among the members of his cabinet (see Chapter 4). The president, who is elected every six years for only one term, has very broad dismissal as well as appointive powers, and his actions in this respect need not be sanctioned by any other authority.

Juxtaposed to the weakness of the Congress and the courts, the strong presidency confers very broad powers upon the members of the cabinet. The eighteen ministers and the holders of cabinet-level positions, such as the directorships of the state oil monopoly (Petróleos Mexicanos—PEMEX) and the Central Bank and the mayoralty of Mexico City, specialize in a number of tasks in which they enjoy formal autonomy from other officials. Generally, the major intragovernmental constraints on ministerial activities are imposed by the president himself, who personally approves most of his ministers' important proposals.

One can identify a certain hierarchy of influence among ministries according to the command over resources each enjoys. A few examples illustrate this point. In the area of domestic politics, the minister of the interior (Gobernación)—with functions overlapping those of the U.S. F.B.I. and Interior and Justice departments—is chiefly responsible for the state's internal security. This broad responsibility gives the minister far-reaching powers. He should be aware of every major political event in the country, in particular of all legal and extralegal actions with political implications. He is also the chairman of the Federal Electoral Commission. His position allows him to know better than any other cabinet member the critical details about how the Mexican political system works and to extend his contacts and exercise his authority throughout the nation. Naturally, every president chooses a man he trusts to be his minister of the interior. For such reasons, this minister has often become president in the subsequent administration.

The heads of the Ministry of Finance and of the Central Bank make most major decisions in the fields of fiscal and monetary policies. These institutions have usually favored policies geared to attaining the maximum possible rates of economic growth, even at the expense of lower-income groups. The Ministry of Commerce and Industrial Development elaborates more specific policies affecting the interests of the business community, and the Ministry of Energy, Mines, and State Enterprises heads the public sector of the economy, which is very large by U.S. standards.

Other important roles are played by the Ministry of Agrarian Reform, which deals with demands from the peasantry; the Ministry of Agriculture and Water Resources, which is in closer contact with large farmers; the Ministry of Labor, which deals with labor disputes and with working conditions in general; and the Ministry of Programming and Budget (previously Presidencia), which was reorganized by López Portillo to coordinate the actions of all other governmental agencies wherever possible, supervise the budget, and draw up a national development plan. Although it was not intended as a super-ministry, Programming and Budget has assumed great influence. (In 1980, López Portillo appointed his son as undersecretary.)

Programming and Budget has also been a source of well-organized and, in some cases, previously undisclosed information and statistics. This constitutes a welcome improvement over the long-standing lack of information on many subjects. With the appointment in September 1981 of the minister of programming and budget, Miguel de la Madrid Hurtado, as president of Mexico, the role of this agency took on additional significance.[2] Subsequently (1982), the Office of the Comptroller General, with ministerial rank, was established to support President de la Madrid's efforts to reduce corruption within the public sector.

There is much to be learned about the influence of the minister of defense in the political process, and this matter is intimately linked to the broader question of military participation in politics. In Chapter 2 we argued that such participation changed from near-dominance in the revolutionary period to much more limited functions in support of the emerging civilian regime years later. However, four qualifications to our earlier statement are in order. First, there are no empirical studies concerning the many middle- and lower-level positions that are apparently occupied by members of the armed forces in practically all agencies of the federal government. Such information is necessary in order to have a more complete picture of the military's role. Second, although in the 1980s the army has played a visible role helping the government suppress challenges from the left (Juchitán, Oaxaca) and from the right (Piedras Negras, Coahuila), military leaders expressed their frustration following the 1985 earthquakes. Instead of implementing a previously approved plan whereby the military would exercise its authority and use its technical resources and expertise in case of a natural disaster, the president decided that the mayor of the capital should lead the rescue efforts. The mayor's lack of experience and the magnitude of the task combined to produce a series of coordination and policy flaws, and he was the subject of widespread criticism. The army reluctantly limited itself to "maintaining order." At the same time, thousands of individuals spontaneously provided assistance to the devastated areas of the city in a show of generous but probably inefficient social solidarity.[3] What is noteworthy is that many saw this affair as proof of an unwarranted lack of trust by civilian leaders in the armed forces. Third, an emerging change in perceptions about how national security interests are best served may provide the rationale for a more visible role by the military. López Portillo's minister of defense, Félix Galván, who was the most outspoken minister of defense in many years, defined the term "national security" very broadly as "maintaining a socio-economic and political equilibrium which is guaranteed by the armed forces."[4] This is a perspective on national security shared by most Latin American military leaders—including many who have assumed the reins of government by force. However, it also reflects the fact that, as a neighbor of the superpower United States, Mexico has not worried for a long time about threats from the north to national security. Moreover, the Central American republics have been far too weak to pose a direct threat from the south.

This does not mean that the military is unconcerned about the defense of the country from external threats. In fact, our fourth qualification refers to recent changes in traditional perceptions about the meaning and the needs of national security. The external dimension is now a matter of concern to policymakers in Mexico City. This change was initially promoted by a Defense Ministry that sought, just as many other governmental agencies did, to legitimize its competition for the financial resources available from oil exports. In addition, the ongoing political turmoil and generalized instability in Central America and the Caribbean, as well as tensions along the Mexico-Guatemala border, led to unusual public discussions of national security. Debate has been accompanied by governmental decisions to shore up the equipment and the visibility of the armed forces. For example, during two weeks in December 1980, the Mexican Army conducted maneuvers before López Portillo and a number of guests of the Guatemalan high military command. More than 40,000 soldiers (including parachutists) participated (in the southern states of Chiapas and Tabasco), along with several air force T-33 jets, tanks for delivery of medium-range rockets, and helicopters.[5] These maneuvers were explained on the grounds that Mexico must be ready to protect its oil fields.

Defense Minister Galván shopped around for some time for supersonic jets to add to Mexico's combat capabilities. In 1977, a request was made to the United States, following a similar request by Guatemala, to buy twenty-six Northrop F5-E fighters for more than US$150 million. Later, U.S. Tiger planes and Israeli Kfir jets (following Galván's visit to Israel in 1981) were considered for purchase. Following approval by the Reagan administration, Mexico decided to buy more than a dozen F5-E fighters, and it bought fifty-seven modern Swiss Pilatus transportation planes. Mexico is producing G-3 automatic rifles under West German license and medium-range rockets and armored personnel carriers. In addition, the navy produces patrol boats (Olmeca class), and it has imported destroyers from the United States (Gearing class) and frigates from Spain (Halcón class).[6]

The concept of national security was incorporated into the development plans of both López Portillo and de la Madrid. In substantive terms, a thirty-sixth military command zone was established in the border state of Chiapas, and special development plans have been drawn to channel greater government resources into that region. The Mexican government thus has responded to increasing social and political tensions that have resulted from the establishment of extensive refugee camps, as well as Guatemalan guerrilla attempts to use those camps as sanctuaries.[7] Although the election of President Vinicio Cerezo in the mid-1980s accelerated an improvement in relations with Guatemala, the Mexican government remained concerned that conflicts south of the border might impose the need for a more comprehensive (and expensive) defense policy and a greater role for the military.[8] The incursions of Guatemalan army units into Mexican territory in 1983 and 1984 had aggravated these concerns. Given that Mexico's extraordinary stability for several decades has been based in large part on the limited role of the military, any long-term change could be critical indeed.

Supersonic F5-E fighters bought from the United States in 1981 symbolize the growing modernization and visibility of Mexico's military. (Photo courtesy of the Northrop Corporation)

SOCIETAL INSTITUTIONS AND ACTORS

The second set of institutions to be discussed are those that are not part of the state but that make demands on state institutions. These include labor, the peasantry, and the business community. Organized labor and the peasantry constitute special case studies in that they are formally incorporated into the ruling political party, the PRI. The "popular sector" (middle classes) is the third group included in the party, whose multiple tasks will be analyzed below.

Observers who see such incorporation as a mechanism for the subordination of independent action by these groups stress the "corporatist" nature of Mexican politics. Corporatism refers to "a system of interest representation linking . . . associations of civil society with decisional structures of the state," and "state corporatism" refers to the dominance of the state over these associations.[9] In this respect, the successful corporative control of even a limited number of working-class organizations has been enough to maintain political stability. (Only unionized labor is incorporated in the workers' sector of the party.) For example, it has been estimated that of 8 million wage earners in urban areas in 1970, only 26 percent were unionized. A majority of labor unions are located in key industries in the production process and in the most urban-industrial states of México, Nuevo León, and Jalisco and in the Federal District. These four geographical areas account for more than 50 percent of all unionized workers.[10] Thus, political stability has been maintained by exercising corporative control over only one-quarter of the working people in urban areas. Moreover, these workers, compared to nonunionized workers, receive disproportionate amounts of the benefits of social programs sponsored by the state. Such programs include education, health insurance, and credits for housing.

A similar situation exists in the countryside. Although the benefits of the agrarian reform program have not been extended to all, the government has provided some organized peasants with land and other resources for the production process. The fact that much less has been done for unorganized peasants has not visibly and critically undermined political stability. A central question, therefore, is just what explains why the majority of *unorganized* workers and peasants—who have benefited little from the revolution—have not stood up again (as they did in the revolution) for their rights. Frankly, this question has been inadequately explored by students of Mexican politics. Some common explanations are that background and political culture may lead to a lack of effective effort in influencing policy; that provision of material benefits to some groups creates for others the illusion that they might eventually become recipients; and mostly, that fear of repression prevents the unorganized poor from actively seeking to improve their lot. More substantive research is necessary before reaching conclusions. What follows, therefore, will focus on relations between the state and *organized* labor and peasants, relations that have been studied more systematically.

The Role of Organized Labor

The foundation in 1912 of the Casa del Obrero Mundial, the headquarters of Mexico's emerging labor movement, represented one of labor's first organizational efforts. At the outset, it was met with an unfriendly attitude and even repression by Francisco Madero's government and later by Victoriano Huerta's government. In 1914, a year after Huerta's coup, Huerta himself was overthrown and the Casa was able to resume its activities in a new building provided by Venustiano Carranza's closest ally, General Alvaro Obregón. This was the beginning of what turned out to be a pattern of a very strong association between the labor movement and the emerging political regime. In 1915, after months of internal divisions and debate, the Casa decided to stand on the side of Carranza and Obregón in their struggle against the revolutionary peasant leaders! A formal pact was signed in Orizaba, near Veracruz, where Carranza's government was then located. The pact included a commitment on the part of the Casa's leaders to send a number of brigades to the military front. These brigades participated in battles at El Ebano and Celaya against Pancho Villa's forces, and in Veracruz they helped to crush some of Zapata's battalions. So labor provided brigades to defeat what many would consider the most truly revolutionary armies of the people.

In spite of its contribution to his victory, however, labor's relations with Carranza were always precarious. In fact, had it not been for the efforts and vision of General Obregón, labor might have been much more severely repressed and left out of the political process. The peak confrontation with Carranza came on July 31, 1916, when the leader of the Electrical Workers Union called for a general strike. The main demand was that wages be paid in gold instead of paper money, which had a constantly changing value and was not always honored. Following Carranza's repression of the strike, Obregón approached some of the more moderate leaders to suggest that they close the Casa for good and instead form a study group to propose legislation favorable to labor during the upcoming Constitutional Convention in early 1917. He committed himself to furthering labor's cause. The outcome was perhaps the most progressive social and labor legislation in the world at the time, contained in Article 123 of the new Constitution of February 5, 1917. Another outcome, crucial to the stability of the emerging regime, was the formulation of an alliance between labor leaders and the victorious military leaders. By 1918, the alliance was formalized by the establishment of a national labor confederation—the Mexican Regional Labor Confederation (CROM)—with assistance provided by the state.

The following year CROM's leader, Luis Morones, participated in the formation of a labor party to support Obregón's candidacy for the presidency. CROM played a similar role in 1924, in support of General Plutarco Elías Calles. By 1928, however, CROM's relations with the state started to deteriorate as Morones himself sought to become president. The confederation suffered a split in the early 1930s. In 1936, President Lázaro Cárdenas threw his support behind Vicente Lombardo Toledano, who became the first leader of the newly created Confederation of Mexican Workers (CTM). Its membership reached about 700,000 by 1938, when it was incorporated by Cárdenas into the official party (at the time called the Party of the Mexican Revolution)—a step consistent with the regime's objective of developing close ties with organized labor.

Some of labor's leaders were drawn into the Chamber of Deputies over the years, while others participated in the policymaking process, together with representatives of the government and business. In addition to these co-optation mechanisms, some unions were granted special privileges to secure their loyalty to the regime. However, this strategy did not always work as expected because of the complex nature of labor's organizational structure. Although the CTM progressively became the dominant labor organization (estimates of its current membership range from 1.5 to 3.5 million), several very important unions fall outside CTM's control—even though they may belong to the PRI. One such union, the Federation of Unions of State Workers (FSTSE), which is part of the PRI's popular sector, includes the powerful governmental bureaucracy and those employed in the low-cost, state-sponsored national educational system (with a total of about 1 million members). Other very important unions include the railroad, electrical, and telephone workers' unions. Totaling more than 400,000 members, these unions are noteworthy not only for their relative strength, stemming from their critical position in the economy, but also because some of them have at times posed the most serious challenges to corruption and state control over the labor movement. For example, the Electrical Workers Union has remained an independent-minded organization in spite of repression against it on several occasions. The Railroad Workers Union conducted a series of strikes leading to the nationalization of railroads in the mid-1930s; in 1958 and 1959, the union demanded an increase in salaries, participation in management, and labor's autonomy from the state. Before 1968, no other massive independent political action had been met with such repression as that faced by the railroad workers in the late 1950s. The regime forcefully reminded organized labor of the importance attached to close and smooth relations between them. In much less dramatic fashion, the point was made again when the Telephone Workers Union's efforts at democratization in the late 1970s receded only after the army's outright repression of its strike.

In the 1980s, government-labor relations came under stress as the country plunged into severe economic crisis and as President de la Madrid sought to curb corruption and to impose guidelines of technical efficiency on some long-standing patterns of political dealings. To be sure, such stress has not completely dominated those relations. De la Madrid initially granted significant concessions to attract the support of official labor leaders. The latter had expressed strong reservations (which they have since substantially confirmed) when de la Madrid's appointment as the PRI's presidential candidate became public. Perhaps the most relevant concession involved a new provision included in the constitution in early 1983, which established that in addition to the public and business sectors of the economy, a "social sector" would operate under labor's responsibility. Unions could expand their control of productive enterprises, purportedly to enhance the financial resources of all their members.[11] Business leaders complained about the special privileges granted to labor leaders, who would most probably become the main beneficiaries of the new law.

Overall, however, government-labor tensions increased in the 1980s. The case of the Telephone Workers Union exemplifies the defiance of certain union leaders regarding government austerity policies and controls on wages. In sharp contrast to the discipline shown by the CTM in the midst of economic crisis, telephone workers pressed for higher wages until the government took direct control of the firm in September 1984 and then threatened the union with massive layoffs.[12] Furthermore, thousands of independent union activists marched in Mexico City on several occasions demanding that the government unilaterally refuse to pay the nation's huge foreign debt. Some violence occurred, as during the 1985 and 1986 May first Labor Day parades, but was quickly put down by government security forces.[13]

In fact, more significant challenges to the government have come from official rather than independent or leftist unions, and not necessarily as a result of protests against the hardship imposed on workers due to Mexico's deteriorating economic situation. Under de la Madrid, the government mounted some comparatively sophisticated and comprehensive attacks on union corruption, principally involving the oil and teachers unions. In the first case, some government measures were aimed at undermining the capacity of union leaders to pocket financial resources illegally. In 1984, for example, a new regulation at the Ministry of Programming and Budget required that public agencies either manage construction works directly or conduct an open bidding process and grant a contract to the party that presents the best project proposal in technical and financial terms. In the case of direct management, public agencies should under no circumstances resort to third parties to carry out these construction works. When contracts have been awarded (say, to labor unions), the beneficiary is not allowed to subcontract or to retain the services of a third party to perform the job.[14] In the past, the unions gained several million pesos for these kinds of contracts.

As far as the teachers are concerned, Secretary of Education Jesús Reyes Heroles tried to weaken their organization by engaging in a nationwide effort to decentralize the administration of public education programs (although the effort had other educational goals as well). Local governments would have gained control over the budget and other resources, and local unions would have had to negotiate with them on a case-by-case basis. The union resisted government pressures, and when Reyes Heroles passed away, his successor did not show the same resolve in pursuing decentralization.

It is fair to say that de la Madrid tried to check union corruption and even attained some progress, thus going beyond the mere rhetoric of previous administrations. It was perhaps for this reason that when de la Madrid later resigned himself to conciliatory gestures with some of these unions, he lost credibility with sectors of public opinion that are critical of the special privileges that are given to certain unions. Moreover, when oil labor leaders went on the offensive, publicly criticizing the president, perceptions about de la Madrid's weak leadership and lessening determination gathered momentum. The head of the oil union, José Sosa, in quite unusual terms, responded publicly to the president's criticism of his organization and instead blamed management for a series of problems in the oil industry: "As a consequence of poor administration, PEMEX is about to sink and, if it does, you, the country and all of us will sink together."[15]

Such examples illustrate that state-labor relations in Mexico are not without serious conflict. In fact, the potential for conflict is always present, given the fact that labor's leaders do not simply stand by and do nothing for their constituencies or themselves. If the official political party itself does little to foster labor demands, affiliated mass organizations may indeed do something on their own. Of course, this does not mean that labor is best characterized as a strong and independent participant in the Mexican political process; corporatism is still the modal pattern in state-labor relations in Mexico. What it does mean is that sectors of the labor movement have demonstrated some capacity to act independently from the state and the official party in order to pursue their own interests. Continued high levels of inflation and unemployment could make control over suffering unions increasingly difficult—as the upsûrge in strikes and mobilization favoring autonomy from the state already indicates. And government attempts in the 1980s to cut down the privileges of corrupt union leaders illustrate the increasing costs the state must be ready to pay to secure control over the labor movement. But as long as organized labor remains a political actor strongly allied with the state, political participation probably will be kept within limits. Moreover, the unorganized majority will be kept marginal. Finally, those unions that have recently declared their independence from state control are still too small to represent a fundamental change in state-labor relations.[16]

Peasant Participation and Land Reform

Analysis of peasant participation in politics often focuses on the struggle over land ownership. There has generally been a substantial gap between peasants' demands for land and the effective actions of the various governments. Bureaucratic red tape, the pace of population growth, and the inability of industry to absorb all of the labor freed by the agricultural sector are among the factors explaining this continuing gap between demand for and supply of land. Another pertinent consideration is the limited availability of land for cultivation, given Mexico's geographical profile. In this respect, the ongoing resistance of many landowners to granting their lands to the state, and the state's own policies favoring large agricultural holdings at the expense of peasant claims for land, are rooted in the belief that many small plots can be dangerously inefficient. Some experts have presented evidence to support this argument; others have refuted it wholeheartedly. The record shows that the regime sided with the proponents of a land reform program, but only a moderate one.

The pace of the land distribution program slowed following President Miguel Alemán's introduction in 1946 of two legal provisions to protect large landowners from expropriation measures. The first was the increased size of land exempted from public expropriation, set at 100 hectares (247 acres). The other was the introduction of the judicial procedure known as *juicio de amparo*, which gave landowners the right to contest in court expropriation orders by the Ministry of Agrarian Reform. Most of these legal processes lasted for decades, much to the disadvantage of frustrated peasants. Thus, 37 million hectares (91 million acres) were distributed between 1916 and 1946, but the amount for the period 1947 to 1976 was substantially lower, roughly 20 million hectares (49 million acres).[17]

About 2 million heads of family have benefited from the agrarian reform program, and a similar number are still claiming their right to land. Land reform has been one of the most effective tools used by the regime to maintain political control over the peasantry. President López Portillo, however, committed his administration to end the distributive phase of the agrarian reform, and President de la Madrid followed suit. No more land would be expropriated. Still, all past presidential orders were supposed to be effectively implemented. Even this proved to be a formidable if not impossible task: It has been estimated that more than 50 percent of lands legally distributed—more than 27 million hectares (66 million acres)—have never reached peasant hands.[18] And viewed from a historical perspective, the struggle for land is unlikely to come to an end as a result of an executive order, even though peasant participation has been largely controlled by the state.

Ever since President Cárdenas incorporated the peasantry into the official party, efforts at achieving independence from the state have generally been either repressed or co-opted. For example, Rubén Jaramillo led a movement in Zapata's region, pursuing some old land claims, but he and his family were killed by soldiers in 1962. Notably, some peasants formed the Independent Peasant Confederation (CCI), in 1963, but the organization was soon divided, and by 1974 it had joined the state-controlled peasant movement. The CCI formalized its alliance with the National Peasant Confederation (CNC) during signing ceremonies at Ocampo. But in spite of the political stability that has resulted from the effective control and co-optation of the peasantry, and from continual repression, land invasions are still a common feature of life in rural Mexico. Usually, landless peasants conduct these invasions. But on other occasions, cattle raisers and large landowners illegally occupy peasant property. The issue of landownership, therefore, remains unsolved.

Peasants will continue to leave the countryside because of the lack of opportunities there. They will continue to migrate to urban areas or to the United States, the political consequences of which are discussed in subsequent chapters. As long as these channels for social mobility remain open as a safety valve, they can be counted (more than satisfaction of the peasants' material demands) among the factors that have contributed to the overall stability of rural Mexico. Of course, one last option exists, given the long struggle of the peasantry for its own survival, that should not be discounted. Mexican peasants could organize themselves independently from the regime in order to bargain from a position of greater strength for their desired role in society. The ongoing unrest in rural Mexico is a signal that difficult years lie ahead for everyone involved. But just as in the case of labor, the establishment of an independent powerful peasant organization at the national level remains an unfulfilled objective.

We have argued that effective political participation by workers and peasants has generally been limited. More decisive, though often less visible, participation comes from another actor—the business community.

The Business Community

Despite many legal provisions and much rhetoric to the contrary, the Mexican economy has remained essentially capitalist. Confusion among foreign observers in this respect has stemmed partly from the fact that the constitution reserves for the state the exclusive rights of ownership and exploitation of underground natural resources. This places an important constraint on private property, a constraint pointedly uncharacteristic of many capitalist nations. In addition, a very large public sector exists in Mexico. The state controls oil, electric power, communication systems, railroads, fertilizers, much of steel output, a large share of credit sources, and other strategic inputs for production. And yet, state control has been used more in support of than in competition with the private sector. For example, oil has been provided abundantly and at subsidized prices to the private sector ever since the 1938 nationalization of the industry. The strong state that grew out of the revolution has played a crucial role in the process of economic growth while it has maintained political stability. The private sector, nonetheless, has often been critical of state policy.

What are the origins and evolution of the participatory organizations representing the private sector? How do these relate to the state? One of the first acts of the new constitutional regime of 1917 was to encourage businessmen to organize themselves and to participate in the process of economic reconstruction. On November 3, 1917, the Confederation of Chambers of Commerce of Mexico, today known as CONCANACO, was born. Less than a year later, industrial producers formed the Confederation of Industrial Chambers (CONCAMIN). These institutions, together with the National Chamber of Manufacturing Industry (CANACINTRA), which was founded in 1941, received initial support from the state. However, CON-CANACO and CONCAMIN became relatively autonomous and critical of governmental policies over time. Other organizations came to life independently of state actions and have always been critical of the government when they have considered their interests injured by government action. The Mexican Bankers Association, the Confederation of Employers of the Mexican Republic (COPARMEX), the Mexican Council of Businessmen, and the Association of Insurance Institutions have all fit into this important category, although the first association lost its power following the 1982 government takeover of private banking.

Another channel through which the private sector expresses itself has emerged as the economy has grown more complex. We refer to the combinations of industrial, commercial, financing, and investment firms resulting from the concentration of capital in fewer hands. The origins of the proliferation of what have been labeled *grupos* date back several decades in some cases. For example, the oldest and strongest of these grupos is based in the northern city of Monterrey. It has grown from a beer industry in the nineteenth century into an economic empire including steel, electronics, mass media, banks (until 1982), and many other enterprises controlled by the four grupos into which the original one has been divided. One of them, the Grupo Alfa, controls steel production and a television channel (eight) among its properties. Grupo Visa controls a large share of the national beer exporting industry (Cervecería Cuauhtémoc) and, again until 1982, the Banco de Londres y México. In 1985, Grupo Visa acquired control of the Mexico City–based Grupo Cremi's beer industry (Cervecería Moctezuma) to save it from bankruptcy.[19] This is but one example of the many links that exist among Mexican business conglomerates.

Finally, some foreign investors have been able to exercise influence on domestic politics affecting their interests. They do so by negotiating the terms under which new foreign investment comes into Mexico or the terms on which to continue investing within Mexico. A celebrated case concerns the role played by the U.S. Chamber of Commerce in Mexico City. By incorporating Mexican businessmen into its ranks, this association has been able to present the views of its mainly U.S. investors publicly and on a continual basis.[20]

Of course, the private sector is not homogeneous. There are competing interests among organizations, and the government exploits this competition to its advantage. In general, however, the private sector is the actor that has best organized itself independently of the regime. Its interests have been favored by the regime to a greater extent than those of labor, peasants, or sectors of the middle class—even though each of these three is a formal constituency of the official political party! There is also considerable inter-action between government agencies and the various representatives of the business community, both during meetings of business organizations and within the framework provided by formal structures set up by the government to discuss certain economic policies. To be sure, there have been some conflicts, such as business skepticism in regard to the nationalization of the electric industry in 1960 and business opposition to the support given leftist governments in Cuba, Chile, and Nicaragua. But never in the previous few decades had relations between the private sector and the regime been so severely strained as they were during Echeverría's administration. Both in rhetoric and in practice, each attacked the other to a point unknown in recent Mexican history. Because of its implications for the relations between the state and the business community, particularly as those relations remained tense in the 1980s, a brief account of this conflict follows.

Carlos Arriola has written a well-documented analysis of the confrontation from 1973 to 1975 over labor and fiscal policies and over the central issue of the limits on public intervention in the economy.[21] In a context of rising inflation, the leaders of all major labor organizations, represented by their Congress of Labor, presented Echeverría with a series of demands in early 1973. These included a proposal for price controls, wage increases, and a forty-hour working week. Following months of unsuccessful bargaining with business organizations, labor announced that it would resort to a general strike in support of a 33 percent increase in salaries by October 1. Echeverría supported labor. To further complicate the picture, the coup d'etat in Chile on September 11 had led to massive leftist demonstrations, which were wholeheartedly disliked by the business community. In addition, Eugenio Garza Sada, the leading figure of the Monterrey Group, was killed on September 17, allegedly by an extremist organization of the left. According to Arriola, Echeverría assured himself of the army's support, took the offensive, and called for a "popular alliance" to face mounting pressures on his government by the business community, which only then cooled down its rhetoric. Tensions eased further in the aftermath of a huge demonstration organized by the PRI in Mexico City. It led some weeks later to an agreement to raise wages by 20 percent, thus ending the threat of a general strike. Politicians who become in some measure alienated from the private sector apparently need to rely increasingly on the army and on mass-based working-class organizations (within the PRI) to legitimize their rule. This last resort, however, has been generally unnecessary because of the formal and informal ties that most politicians have with the business community.

Even after the 1973 crisis eased somewhat, tensions continued during the next few years. In 1975, all business organizations (with the exception of CANACINTRA, which withdrew from the conflict) formed a common front to face what they perceived as "a threat to the free enterprise system," establishing the Coordinating Business Council (CCE). The CCE delivered a document to the president expressing its positions on several critical matters. For example, it declared private property to be a natural right, called on the state to sell some of its enterprises to the private sector, and claimed that direct foreign investment with a majority interest should be permitted in some cases. (By law, any firm must have at least 51 percent Mexican capital.) These positions were so opposed to principles commonly accepted in Mexican society that the document was condemned even by such traditional allies of the private sector as sectors of the Catholic Church and the rightist National Action party (PAN).

Toward the end of Echeverría's term (1976), events led to a renewed crisis. The president announced, during his State of the Union address on September 1, that the government had decided to devalue the peso. This measure had last been taken in 1954. A capital flight ensued, facilitated by the impossibility of implementing foreign exchange controls in a country with such a long border with the United States. Further, inflation was rampant, at more than 20 percent for 1976, and the gross domestic product grew by only 2.1 percent over the previous year. The overall crisis confused large sectors of the population as well as domestic and foreign observers of Mexican politics. There were wild rumors of a coup d'etat planned for the twentieth of November.[22] Perhaps the most interesting aspect of the confrontation was that as the economic growth model became strained, different perspectives held by several groups within the PRI and the private sector, and those in control of state institutions, on the proper course for Mexico to follow came to light.

Although lessened government-business tensions in the late 1970s and at the onset of the new decade led many observers to conclude that bad relations under Echeverría had marked a deviant period, subsequent developments indicated that the earlier confrontations reflected deep, difficult, and persistent differences. In fact, in the 1980s several events cast doubt on the degree to which government and business actually maintain a working relationship. Although private investors reaped a substantial share of the benefits associated with the oil boom years, López Portillo's decision to expropriate the banks caused government-business relations in his administration to end on a sour note. Furthermore, speculation regarding business satisfaction with the election of Miguel de la Madrid as president of Mexico in 1982 proved ill-founded. However conservative or technically sound most of his economic policies were, they usually failed to elicit even a mildly enthusiastic response from the business community. Low investments at home and huge capital flight were among the negative indicators of business response (Chapter 5). What concerns us here, however, is the deterioration of government-business relations in the political realm. Under de la Madrid, tension prevailed even though there was not an open conflict of the kind witnessed during the Echeverría years.

Business leaders tended to regard de la Madrid's pro-business policies as too little, too late, accompanied by an impulse to retreat too quickly when problems showed signs of abating, as in 1984. Many complained that de la Madrid's reassertion of planning and the leading or "rectorship" role of the state in the economy, as well as the formalization of the "social sector" of the economy in the hands of labor, constituted unfair encroachments on their own sphere of activities. And when the government expropriated a large number of urban properties in the aftermath of the 1985 earthquakes to provide housing for the homeless, many initially feared that the stage was set for a new round of regime-sponsored "assaults on private property."[23] Additionally, some businesses saw themselves as losers in de la Madrid's economic opening to more foreign penetration.

Many businessmen, breaking with tradition, became involved in publicly supporting an opposition party (PAN) at a time when the U.S. press was, to the Mexican regime's discomfort, focusing attention on the Mexican electoral process. Allegedly, businessmen were subject to government harrassment and threats that were denounced in the national press and that elicited a public denial from the interior minister Manuel Bartlett.[24] Business leaders persisted in expressing their political views in public to the chagrin of government officials. For example, in 1986 the head of COPARMEX stated that "in the political arena, the vicious cycle of elections-fraud-violence, characteristic of certain regions, causes enormous damage to the nation's spirit."[25]

Such disputes on political-economic issues led observers like John J. Bailey to warn that "the rupture of the government-business pact is so severe that it will require several years, certainly beyond this *sexenio*, to repair."[26] On the other hand, until recently, flexibility and compromise have generally characterized relations between the state and the business community because they have shared some basic goals for Mexican society. Most important, they have shared an interest in self-preservation; this is why their competition for power has been kept within limits.

We have argued that government relations with key social actors are undergoing important although as yet indeterminate transformations. In the following section we will analyze the changes that have taken place in the electoral arena.

THE ELECTORAL AND PARTY SYSTEMS

One distinctive form of political participation involves the competition of political parties for power through elections. Because in Mexico the official party has rarely faced a serious challenge at the polls, many analysts have downgraded the importance of electoral participation. But, recently intensified challenges stimulated in part by reforms providing a freer political environment and encouraging a larger sector of the population to vote make it necessary to include elections in our discussion of political participation. The major provisions of the most pertinent laws governing elections will be discussed first. Then, because political parties are principal actors in the electoral arena, we will provide a brief sketch of their background, key principles, strategic objectives, and constituencies.

Evolving Rules

One should see the present party system in historical perspective. Once the revolutionary warfare was over, a comprehensive federal electoral law was passed by the new Congress in 1918. Voting rights were restricted to literate, married males at least eighteen years old and to literate, unmarried males at least twenty-one years old. Political parties could be formed easily, with only minimal requirements, such as holding a constitutive assembly of at least one hundred people. Also, political parties were forbidden from affiliating with religious denominations. When a new federal electoral law was approved in 1946, it reflected some of the important changes that the Mexican political process had undergone during the preceding three decades. In particular, the official political party had been formed in 1929. The party was bent on monopolizing the electoral process, so the new law tried to avoid challenges by independent candidates to the party's presidential nominee, as had occurred in 1940 and in 1946. It included provisions giving the government and the party absolute control over the electoral process. For example, the Federal Electoral Commission could hardly be considered an impartial body. It has always been headed by the minister of the interior and has included a representative of the Chamber of Deputies and a representative of the Senate; such provisions have given the regime practical control over the commission. Furthermore, the formal confirmation of electoral results is reserved to both chambers of Congress, where the PRI is not seriously challenged. This phenomenon of self-certification, which has precedents dating back to colonial times, hardly guarantees impartiality in reviews of the electoral results. Finally, the 1946 law made it difficult for new political parties to emerge, requiring certified registration of at least 30,000 members nationwide, with 1,000 or more distributed in at least two-thirds of the total federal entities in Mexico at the time.[27] Until recently, the minister of the interior also had the right to decide whether or not a political party would enjoy legal status.

During the thirty years following the 1946 law, electoral reform was sporadic and limited. Three of the more telling openings were the 1954 law that granted women the right to vote, the 1963 law that guaranteed the opposition minimum representation in Congress, and the 1969 law that lowered the minimum voting age to eighteen years, irrespective of gender and marital status. The new age requirement is particularly relevant in a country where most of the population is young.

In 1977, a substantial political and electoral reform was enacted. From the electoral standpoint, its main thrust was the establishment of a mixed voting system in the Chamber of Deputies, which is more powerful than the Senate. The latter, composed of 64 members elected for a single six-year term, has been left untouched. There are 300 seats in the Chamber corresponding to the electoral districts into which the country is divided. All candidates who win a simple majority in these single-member districts win the election for a single three-year term. In addition, 100 seats are assigned on the basis of complex mathematical formulas of proportional representation. All parties that win fewer than 60 seats under the majority system and that have run candidates in at least one-third of the districts under this system are entitled to a share of these 100 seats. This allows even small opposition parties a place in the federal Congress. The Federal Electoral Commission—still dominated by the government—decides on the legal status of political parties. The commission is headed by the minister of the interior. It includes one representative of the Chamber and one of the Senate, as well as a notary public who, amazingly, rather than holding a disinterested position, has been granted voting rights. Opposition parties that have been granted full legal recognition also have voting rights on the commission, so it is conceivable that government control of this body could diminish in the future if the opposition takes unified positions. The government, however, has so far been successful in keeping control of a majority of the votes in all commission proceedings. In addition to the votes of representatives that are directly related to the PRI and the government, three opposition parties usually allied with the PRI provide their loyal support on the commission.

There are currently two procedures available for parties seeking legal status. One is to apply for *conditional registration*, which allows any party to participate in elections. Such registration would become "permanent" upon attainment of at least 1.5 percent of the total votes cast nationally; failure to attain that minimum in any single national election results in the loss of legal status. All parties that chose this option reached their minimum during the 1979 elections, although their fate would probably have been different had the abstention rate been lower. In the 1982 presidential elections, the Social Democratic party (PSD) failed to attain this minimum 1.5 percent of the total vote and thus lost the opportunity to be granted legal status on a permanent basis. The older Authentic Party of the Mexican Revolution (PARM) also failed to attain that minimum and consequently lost its legal status. By contrast, the new Revolutionary Party of the Workers (PRT) attained permanent registration by gaining 1.8 percent of the presidential vote.

The second option involves presenting the Federal Electoral Commission an official copy of the party's statutes and principles and proof of a minimum of 65,000 members distributed as follows: either 3,000 or more in at least one-half of Mexico's states, or 300 or more in at least one-half of the 300 electoral districts. Upon fulfillment of these requisites, the commission is supposed to decide within 120 days on the application. Only one party, the Mexican Workers party (PMT)—which did not participate in the 1979 and 1982 elections—has sought legal status under this provision. In 1984, the PMT was granted a conditional registration that became permanent when that party obtained in the 1985 elections a share of the national vote above the minimum 1.5 percent. The PARM followed a similar course to recover its legal status. But the application of the PSD and of nine political associations for legal status was rejected by the Federal Electoral Commission in 1984.

Finally, the 1977 reform guarantees all legally recognized parties free radio and television time every month to broadcast their programs and activities. This may have encouraged many voters to become involved in the 1982 elections by supporting the parties that appeal to them, although it is well known that participation increases during presidential electoral contests.

It has been argued that the 1977 reform was launched partly as a response to the apathy and abstentionism plaguing the regime in the 1970s and partly as a way to bolster the left as a counterweight to the right, thereby portraying the PRI in the responsible middle. If so, the outcomes of three consecutive federal elections since 1979 have been mixed at best in terms of the regime's objectives. For example, the abstention rate recorded in 1979, over 50 percent of registered voters, was unexpectedly high. Although the rate fell to about 30 percent during the 1982 presidential elections, it bounced back to 49.5 percent in the 1985 federal elections for the Chamber of Deputies.

Furthermore, the PAN has been the chief beneficiary of the 1977 reform. The PAN's benefits have not been counterbalanced by notable gains on the left. It will be shown below that the PAN has filled easily the largest share of the seats reserved for opposition parties in various elections. Thus, in the 1983 local elections, the PAN took 8 of 118 municipal positions (the PRI took 106), and its success was highlighted by victories in several state capitals in the north. In the arena of competitive local politics, this was the PAN's most impressive showing at the polls since the 1967 elections. As for presidential elections, the PAN obtained in 1982 its largest share of the vote after abstaining from participating in the 1976 elections.

The 1977 reform lasted roughly ten years before a new law modified it. The chamber was expanded to 500 seats with 200 instead of 100 chosen by proportional representation. Although the majority party can win a share of the 200, it cannot exceed 350 seats total. However, the PRI's majority appeared to be further guaranteed as it could hold more than half the seats even were it to win less than half the vote. Other provisions included abolition of the conditional registration procedure; creation of an electoral tribunal named by Congress; election every three years for half the Senate; and prompter announcement of electoral results. Would the new reform promote democratization, as the regime claimed? Supporters and skeptics alike found evidence for their views in the regime's recent record in managing electoral reform.

How Much Electoral Reform?

To evaluate the extent of political reform in the electoral arena, we must look closely at the nonpresidential elections of 1985 and 1986 in which the regime's commitment to reform was at stake. De la Madrid had pledged in the first few years of his presidency to honor true electoral results as part of a general pledge of honesty in government. Indeed, de la Madrid had accepted some opposition victories in 1983 (although one could as easily point to the dubiously extensive legislative majorities the PRI nonetheless grabbed); more broadly, the president had accepted with dignity a considerable range of criticism. Middle-class sectors were particularly attentive to de la Madrid's words about the forthcoming elections as they critically assessed the regime's performance and respect for democracy.[28] Moreover, uncommon international (especially U.S.) attention concentrated on these elections as tests of reform, especially in light of the coverage given to recent controversial elections in Central America and to redemocratizing elections in much of South America.

The important northern states of Sonora and Nuevo León were among seven states with governorships at stake in 1985. These two races overshadowed those for the Chamber as many believed that a vulnerable and scrutinized PRI might for the first time acknowledge a gubernatorial loss, thereby increasing interest in the fourteen 1986 gubernatorial races—including the PAN stronghold of Chihuahua.[29] Additionally, the 1986 campaign involved many state legislatures and well over a thousand municipalities, among which were the major ones of Chihuahua city and Ciudad Juárez in the state of Chihuahua.

In the end, however, the elections represented continuities much more than reform; they were in fact blows to reform. The regime claimed all the governorships in both years, refusing even to acknowledge that the most important of those contests were close. Instead, it *added* to its dominance among municipalities in Chihuahua and the nation and retook from the PAN both Chihuahua city and Ciudad Juárez. As the data on individual parties will illustrate shortly, the regime merely continued to yield a few more seats in the Chamber. Further continuities were evident in voting fraud: missing ballot boxes, duplication of names, "votes" by citizens who never went to the ballot box, and last-minute disqualifications of opposition party poll watchers.

Several considerations probably help explain the regime's stubbornness regarding electoral reform. To begin with, even a genuine disposition for change cannot easily brush aside deep-seated structural factors that perpetuate certain practices. Whatever the president's declarations, many bureaucrats did not believe that Mexico should open the political process, at least not while dealing with the dangers of economic crisis and social austerity. Many national and local PRI leaders feared for their careers if they lost to the opposition. The interior would not want to preside over an unprecedented government defeat. Moreover, although some believed that Mexico's limited federalism would render an opposition governorship impotent, the danger loomed that a governorship could bolster otherwise more isolated PAN municipalities in key states. (Of course, strong and specific directives from the president could not have been easily ignored, but these were lacking.)

Most important, elections have still not become the test many have expected or hoped of them. They have provided a test of the regime's priority on democratization or its handling of the tradeoffs between independent political participation and its own control. But Mexico's elections are not fundamental tests of popular opinion or citizen reaction to the president's handling of economic challenges. Crucially, the regime and its official party continue to regard power-sharing with other parties as a foreign model, alien to the bases of Mexico's enviable stability. (The true functions that elections have served for the regime are discussed in the following chapter.)

More broadly, the 1985 and 1986 elections reveal important continuities in the general political arena, where we still find not only weakly organized opposition to the regime, but also a shortage of political information needed for democratic choice. The public does not know whether the reported vote count is accurate or, perhaps, does not know how inaccurate it is. Furthermore, in general the public has been shielded from the electoral process by the national media's inattention; typically, Mexico City's residents know more about events outside Mexico than about events in Nuevo León, Sonora, or Chihuahua. The PRI's campaign hardly provided specifics on the basis of which people could evaluate its performance in office. Nor was information available on such aspects of the campaign as the extent or source of PRI funds (tied to the government). Just as typically, however, the PAN did little or no better. It denounced the PRI as a long-standing failure and called for change. It blamed the PRI for corruption and economic difficulties, but it did not tell citizens what alternatives it had.

Such continuities in the face of calls for further reform do not, of course, signify the absence of change. The strength officially credited to the opposition, and its augmented representation in the Chamber, could not have been assumed just a few years back. PRI weaknesses in large cities and with the middle class and professionals have been increasingly exposed. The clamoring for change, combined with intensified international and domestic protest over apparent fraud in both 1985 and 1986, may illustrate the regime's difficulties in carefully circumscribing the rate of reform. Indeed, the opposition's more insistent protests against fraud and the lack of reform, alongside its still more pro forma protests, are worth watching. In particular, the forty-day hunger strike staged by opposition leaders in Chihuahua following the 1986 elections served as a rallying point for numerous political forces demanding respect for electoral results. For the first time in Mexico's contemporary political history, the national leaders of the PAN and of several independent leftist parties, as well as intellectuals and businessmen, joined forces announcing a "national march for democracy" to take place during the 1988 presidential elections. This was followed by a public proclamation by leading PRI figures, such as Porfirio Muñoz Ledo and Cuauhtémoc Cárdenas, calling for reform and democratization within the official party itself. Variously promoted and obstructed, electoral reform faced an unpredictable but intriguing future.

*　*　*

Analysis of the PRI and other electoral contenders will form the remaining pages of this chapter. Which are the major political parties of contemporary Mexico? For what do they stand? From whom do they draw their support? How have they reacted to and fared under the political reform?

Institutionalized Revolutionary Party (PRI)

The background of the official party was discussed in Chapter 2. Here we will discuss only the PRI's electoral and current political role. The PRI is headed by a president and a secretary-general, who are directly responsible to the party's national executive committee. Members of this committee are elected by the national assembly, which provides a meeting point for representatives of labor, the peasantry, and the "popular sector." Although a very strong and direct link exists between the PRI and the regime, they are different. The party is in charge of insuring support and legitimizing the regime. The party's most important tasks concern socialization, mobilization, recruitment, conflict resolution, and the provision of an ideological base for official policy; the party in general does not press the demands of its formal constituencies on the regime. On the other hand, this does not prevent the party's individual mass organizations from making demands. Furthermore, the group of politicians in control of official institutions at any given time—as opposed to the politicians in control of the party—is in charge of substantive policymaking; the party has little voice in the formulation of policy. Also, party personnel and regime personnel are not the same, although ministers may come from the party ranks, and government officials remain active in using their positions to promote PRI candidates.

In recent years, the PRI's standing has been challenged in several respects and has eroded (not just in the electoral arena). For example, the rise of technocrats (Chapter 4) has led to a diminished role for the PRI in political recruitment. The party has suffered severe conflicts among its constituent sectors. None of this is to argue that the PRI has become insignificant. On the contrary, whatever his identification with technocratic rather than traditional political approaches, President de la Madrid recognized the PRI's importance and took some steps to arrest its decline. At the same time, the PRI helped build support for the president on such crucial and sensitive matters as economic, electoral, and anticorruption policies.[30]

Although critics have argued that the PRI needs to democratize itself to prevent a further decline, the party has not moved far in that direction. Most candidates continue to be chosen in traditional, restrictive fashion, which means that only a few of the 16 million members claimed by the PRI have a say in selecting their representatives. Those who have advocated reforms to make their party more independent of the regime and more representative of party constituencies have been largely frustrated. Recent intraparty struggles have resulted in further losses in the influence of the peasant and labor sectors. Then, too, the PRI's twelfth national assembly (1984), rather than issuing a modest but a true reform program, produced a series of typically unintelligible pronouncements: "In Mexico there is no longer room for personalistic nor for boastful leaders," declared President de la Madrid. And the head of the party warned the delegates that "the political schemes of the nineteenth century will not be allowed to take hold in Mexico."

In the electoral arena, the PRI continues to play a central if increasingly challenged role. During presidential elections, the selected candidate appoints a close associate to coordinate all activities related to his actual campaign, which usually lasts about ten months. The campaign's chief oversees the organization of mass meetings throughout the country to support and legitimize the candidate. In addition, the Institute of Political, Economic, and Social Studies (IEPES), the PRI's planning branch, organizes endless seminars involving professionals, intellectuals, and other groups. The purpose of these meetings, the PRI declares, is to provide the candidate with some sense of what different sectors of society consider to be the major problems the new administration should address. An occasional outcome of these meetings has been the establishment of the party's electoral platform and plans. Such plans, however, have been shelved once the candidate has been elected.

The PRI has exercised such a monopoly over the electoral process that its candidates have seldom lost an election, as is indicated in Tables 3.1 and 3.2. When they have, the government, through its control of electoral bodies, frequently has seen to it that the PRI would fill the positions anyway. That many of the electoral results have been based on fraud is almost uncontestable, although we may never know the specifics of each case. At the same time, it seems that the PRI would have retained an overwhelming majority in most cases even if elections had always been fair. For example, the results of the 1979 and 1982 federal elections, although plagued with many shortcomings, probably were among the cleanest of Mexican history, with representatives of the opposition participating in overseeing the voting. The PRI nonetheless got more than two-thirds of the national vote in both years, even though its share diminished significantly (from 80 percent in 1976 to slightly under 70 percent in 1979 and 1982 and to 65 percent in

TABLE 3.1
Presidential Electoral Results, 1934–1982

Year	Percentage of Votes Cast			Total Votes Cast
	PRI	PAN	Others	
1934	98.19	—	1.81	2,265,971
1940	93.89	—	6.11[a]	2,637,582
1946	77.90	—	21.80[b]	2,293,547
1952	74.31	7.82	17.85[c]	3,651,201
1958	90.43	9.42	0.13	7,483,403
1964	88.81	10.97	0.20	9,422,185
1970	85.82	14.00	0.17	13,892,624
1976	98.69	—	1.31[d]	16,925,880
1982	68.40	15.70	15.90	22,539,272

[a]The main opposition candidate was General Almazán (5.72 percent of the vote), whose Revolutionary Party of National Unity was short-lived. Some claim he really won the election.

[b]Ezequiel Padilla's Democratic party got 19.33 percent of the vote.

[c]This challenge by General Henríquez was better organized than Padilla's was, but it failed too. Henríquez was supported by the Federation of Mexican People's Parties (15.87 percent of the vote).

[d]López Portillo ran an uncontested election. The then legally unrecognized Communist party nominated labor leader Valentín Campa; it claimed one million votes.

Note: PRI = Institutionalized Revolutionary Party; PAN = National Action party. Total percentages may not add to 100.00 because of nullified votes.

Sources: Pablo González Casanova, *Democracy in Mexico* (London: Oxford University Press, 1970); Robert Furtak, *El partido de la revolución y la estabilidad política en México,* 2nd ed. (Mexico City: Universidad Nacional Autónoma de México, 1978); and Comisión Federal Electoral.

1985) in the elections for the Chamber of Deputies. And the PRI still attained 72 percent of the 1982 presidential votes; this might appear to be a significant decline from 1976, until we remember that abstentionism, itself a rejection of the PRI, also declined from 1976 to 1982. While the PRI's de la Madrid received over 16 million ballots in capturing more than seven of every ten presidential votes cast in 1982, his closest competitor, the PAN's Pablo Emilio Madero, trailed far behind, receiving only 3.7 million votes, or 16.4 percent of the total. The only other presidential candidate to garner a sizable share of the vote, with roughly 1 million ballots, was Arnoldo Martínez Verdugo of Mexico's Unified Socialist party (PSUM). But even PSUM's 4 percent of the vote represented a disappointing showing for this new leftist coalition challenging the PRI. While the PAN did

TABLE 3.2
Electoral Results for the Chamber of Deputies, 1961–1985 (in percentages)[a]

Year	PRI	PAN	PPS	PARM	PCM/PSUM[b]	PST	PDM	PRT	PMT
1961	90.2	7.6	0.9	0.5	—	—	—	—	—
1964	86.3	11.5	1.4	0.7	—	—	—	—	—
1967	83.3	12.4	2.8	1.3	—	—	—	—	—
1970	80.1	13.9	1.4	0.8	—	—	—	—	—
1973	69.7	14.7	3.6	1.9	—	—	—	—	—
1976	80.1	8.5	3.0	2.5	—	—	—	—	—
1979	69.7	10.8	2.6	1.8	4.9	2.1	2.1	—	—
1982	69.3	17.5	1.9	1.4	4.4	1.8	2.3	1.3	—
1985	64.8	15.6	2.0	1.6	3.2	2.5	2.7	1.3	1.6

[a]Total votes for certain years may not equal 100.0 because some were declared invalid or void.

[b]In 1981, the PCM merged with other small parties and a faction of the PPS to become the new PSUM.

Note: PRI = Institutionalized Revolutionary party; PAN = National Action party; PPS = Popular Socialist party; PARM = Authentic Party of the Mexican Revolution; PCM = Mexican Communist party; PSUM = Mexico's Unified Socialist party; PST = Socialist Workers party; PDM = Democratic Mexican party; PRT = Revolutionary Party of the Workers; PMT = Mexican Workers party.

Sources: Comisión Federal Electoral; Diario Oficial, various issues.

considerably better, these two parties still looked very much like also-rans next to the PRI's continued dominance.

The PRI has also dominated all elections for the Chamber of Deputies. Table 3.2 shows that its share of the total vote diminished significantly following the 1977 political reform but also that the opposition is still too divided to mount a serious challenge to the PRI. The PAN's 11 percent and the Communist party's 5 percent are unimpressive compared to the PRI's 69 percent of the vote in the 1979 elections. In the 1982 elections for the Chamber of Deputies, the PAN increased its share, but the new Unified Socialist party and other smaller parties registered some losses, while the PRI held its own. In the more controversial 1985 elections, the PRI's share of the vote fell to a still commanding 65 percent.

A close look at the 1985 electoral results reported in Tables 3.2 and 3.3 reveals that parties allied with the PRI were rewarded while those in the opposition suffered setbacks.[31] First, questions were raised about the Socialist Workers party (PST) vote increase to 2.5 percent of the total and, more importantly, about the twelve seats allocated to it under the proportional representation system. The PSUM, which gained 3.2 percent of the vote, was awarded the same number of seats as the PST and five fewer than in 1982. Meanwhile, the PRT, another small party on the left, was awarded

TABLE 3.3
Party Affiliation of the 400 Deputies, 1979, 1982, and 1985 Elections

Elected Under the Simple Majority System				Elected Under the System of Proportional Representation		
	1979	1982	1985		1979	1982	1985
PRI	296	299	289	PAN	39	50	32
PAN	4	1	9	PCM/PSUMa	18	17	12
PARM	—	—	2	PARM	12	—	9
				PPS	11	10	11
Total	300	300	300	PST	10	11	12
				PDM	10	12	12
				PRT	—	—	6
				PMT	—	—	6
				Total	100	100	100

aSee Table 3.2, note b.

Source: México, Secretaría de Gobernación, Diario Oficial (Mexico City, various issues).

six seats even though it did not qualify for any given its poor electoral showing (1.3 percent), which was below the minimum established by the 1977 reform law. The regime seemed to prefer a divided and thereby a weaker left.

Additionally, while the regime conceded nine victories by the PAN in simple majority districts, it punished that party severely in terms of the seats awarded to it under the proportional representation system. Thus, a drop of two percentage points in the PAN's voting strength in 1985 compared to 1982 translated into a sharp reduction of seats in the Chamber under the proportional system from fifty to only thirty-two.

Moreover, the PARM—an ally of the PRI—garnered only 1.6 percent of the 1985 vote but was given 11 seats in the Chamber. Interestingly, it has been argued that the two seats in simple majority districts won by the PARM resulted from internal divisions within the PRI in the state of Tamaulipas, which has been a traditional stronghold of the PARM. Many PRI sympathizers, so the argument goes, disenchanted with the dominant role played in local politics by many corrupt oil union leaders, crossed party lines and dealt their former party, the PRI, a surprising electoral blow.[32]

The elections in Mexico in the 1980s reaffirm (as does Table 3.2) that the official party's most consistent challenger at the polls has been the National Action party, to which we now turn our attention.

National Action Party (PAN)

The PAN was formed in 1939 with initial support from the Catholic Church, some businessmen, and other groups that felt alienated by the

As the legitimizing machine for the "revolutionary" regime, the PRI promotes mass participation. The banners represent the PRI's official peasant, youth, popular, middle-class, and bureaucratic constituencies. (Photo courtesy of Rodolfo Romo de Vivar)

radical reforms of President Cárdenas. In effect, the PAN has assisted the PRI to legitimize the electoral process. Except in 1940 and 1976, it has nominated its own presidential candidate every six years. In the presidential elections in 1976, it abstained from nominating a candidate (following a very divisive and acrimonious national convention). As a result of that decision, it lost 40 percent of its voting strength, which had been at its peak—2.2 million votes—in the 1973 elections for the Chamber of Deputies. The results of two consecutive elections since 1979 (shown in Tables 3.2 and 3.3), however, confirmed the PAN's status as the principal party of opposition. In 1979, the PAN won more than 1.5 million votes (11 percent of the total), four Chamber seats under the system of the simple majority, and thirty-nine seats on the basis of the new system of proportional representation. Results for the 1982 elections again showed the PAN to have been the major opposition winner. It increased its share of the vote to 17.5 percent and the number of its deputies elected under the proportional representation system to fifty, mostly at the expense of the PARM. The other four opposition parties maintained roughly the same number of deputies they had attained in the 1979 elections under this system.

The PAN is particularly strong in Nuevo León, the Federal District, Chihuahua, Sonora, Puebla, and Jalisco—most of Mexico's wealthiest areas. Regionally, the PAN's greatest appeal is in the north. The party's supporters

are mostly from cities within these strongholds and from the middle class. In fact, this relatively privileged class composition is one of the most significant aspects of this party. It has failed to gain the backing of large labor unions and other working-class organizations. Nor, despite some interesting electoral victories in rural districts, has the PAN had formidable rural support. Nearly two-thirds of its votes in 1979 came from urban areas. In comparison, the PRI got only one-third of its total from the 128 urban electoral districts in Mexico.[33]

Like the PAN, the Communist party also got more than 60 percent of its votes from urban areas; thus, the major challenge to the PRI's electoral strength is found in the cities, especially the big cities. Ironically, even though the regime has done less for rural than for urban areas, it has been least vulnerable in the countryside. This is probably because the official party has exercised greater control over the peasantry, a sector of the population that has had less access to independent political organizations. Another problem faced by the PAN is that despite its conservative bent, it has not done well with the upper class, which long ago realized that its best bet is to work with the PRI in order to influence public policy.

In general, the PAN has reacted positively to the strengthening of other opposition parties, with which it can now join forces against the PRI.[34] Issue-oriented coalition politics were previously unknown in the Mexican party system, but recently the PAN has found itself voting together with other parties—even with the Communists! More important, it seems increasingly unlikely that the PAN will continue to shore up the PRI's position by playing its traditional role of loyal opposition. In contrast to the situation of six years earlier, the PAN's national convention in 1981 took a unified stand behind its candidate for the 1982 presidential elections, Pablo Emilio Madero. A nephew of Francisco Madero, he is a conservative politician with special appeal among the urban middle class. As a member of the business community, he led the CANACINTRA in 1969. He was a member of the Chamber of Deputies from 1979 to 1982. His leadership in the PAN's 1982 electoral resurgence was striking.

On the other hand, the PAN's remodeled profile has alienated a significant sector of traditional party supporters. These supporters, including respected leaders from earlier times, view with suspicion the thirst for power of the new group that controls the party. They have argued that the party's aspiration to represent a cross-section of Mexican society and its adherence to broad political principles associated with Christian democratic thinking have been abandoned. Relatedly, disenchanted PAN supporters complain about the open alliances established recently with business leaders and sectors of the conservative wing of the Catholic Church. An additional source of criticism has been the PAN's increasingly open identification with U.S. conservative groups, including the attendance of PAN representatives at gatherings of the Republican party; meetings with then U.S. Ambassador John Gavin; and the use of U.S. media based in the Southwest to denounce electoral fraud in northern Mexico. Finally, some attempts at forging a radical

PAN ideology and at legitimizing violence to attain electoral objectives are a major source of concern to the traditionalist and now politically displaced wing of the PAN.[35] A transformed PAN would neither want nor be able to maintain some significant long-standing if often tacit accommodation with the PRI. Indeed, PRI leaders have bitterly denounced the shifts within the PAN and have even contrasted the disloyal new breed with its predecessors.

We now turn to the former Communist party, whose candidate finished third in the 1982 presidential race. This party has also experienced internal divisions, and it has failed to establish itself as a stable unifying core for parties of the left.

Mexico's Unified Socialist Party (PSUM)

The Mexican Communist party (PCM) was the third largest electoral force in 1979, 1982, and (as part of the PSUM) 1985. Founded in 1919, ten years before the PRI began to evolve, it is the oldest political party in Mexico. It has survived internal strife and government repression. In 1978, after more than thirty years of being denied legal status, the Communist party applied for conditional registration under the new electoral law. It then received a permanent registration, and thus full legal status, following its success in the 1979 elections. The PCM participated in 1979 together with three other minor parties, the Mexican People's party, the Action Movement for Socialist Unity, and the Revolutionary Socialist party (a faction of the Popular Socialist party [PPS]). In the aftermath of the elections, it called upon all the parties of the left to form a united front in the 1982 presidential elections. Following extensive consultations with other leftist parties, the PCM merged with some of them to form a new party with its own identity, statutes, and objectives. But the Communist party failed to convince the PPS, the PST, and the PMT to sacrifice their individual organizations in favor of the new party. Some leaders charged the Communist party with being more interested in forming an electoral coalition for it own ends than with establishing a new, more moderate party with greater public appeal. Others complained that the Communist party has not devoted enough of its attention and resources to establishing links with mass-based working-class organizations, which remain affiliated with the PRI. (In reality, none of the small leftist parties can claim a large following among working-class organizations.)

The Communist party was formally dissolved on November 4, 1981, during a PCM party congress, and three days later, Mexico's Unified Socialist party was born. It nominated Arnoldo Martínez Verdugo, the former PCM secretary-general, as its presidential candidate for 1982.[36] Under his leadership, the Communist party had identified itself with the unorthodox, relatively moderate positions of the Italian Communist party of Enrico Berlinguer.[37] This moderate posture, together with the PCM's critical view of the Soviet Union's foreign policy and some aspects of its domestic system, could be aimed partly at bolstering the party's appeal.

During the 1985 electoral campaign, two events shook the PSUM. First, Martínez Verdugo was kidnapped by an extremist group, allegedly linked to the guerrillas led by Lucio Cabañas in the 1970s. The group complained that the former Communist party had never returned a ransom of 4 million pesos, which it had kept in custody in connection with the kidnapping of former Guerrero governor Rubén Figueroa. The group demanded 200 million pesos, to take account of inflation and of interest earned since 1974, before releasing Martínez Verdugo unharmed.[38] In addition to this embarrassing episode, one of the small splinter groups associated with the PSUM (and formerly with the PPS), led by Alejandro Gazcón Mercado, crossed party lines once again and ended up in the PMT. We now analyze the four leftist parties that have not agreed to join Mexico's Unified Socialist party. The left has simply not managed to form a stable electoral front, although by 1987 the PSUM led yet another attempt to build a unified socialist party (Mexican Socialist party, PMS).

Popular Socialist Party (PPS)

The PPS was formed in 1948 by Vicente Lombardo Toledano, the founder of the PRI's labor organization, when he became disaffected with some of the PRI's conservative tendencies. Although the PPS formally seeks the establishment of socialism in Mexico, it has gradually allied itself with the PRI, endorsing many of its candidates. The rationale for this strategy is that the PPS considers (U.S.) imperialism to be Mexico's worst enemy, and the PRI has ostensibly stood up to this challenge by pursuing whatever nationalistic and revolutionary policies have been possible, given political realities. Like the Communist and other parties of the left, the PPS supports greater state intervention in the economy and nationalization of mass transportation, minerals, and other economic areas.

The PPS is a party in electoral decline. In 1979, the majority (led by Gazcón Mercado) left the party to join the growing Communist party (before switching in 1985 to the PMT). Later in 1979, the leader of the faction that had spurned the Communists, choosing instead to perpetuate the PPS, became the first opposition member ever to gain a Senate seat. This illustrates how the regime and the PRI may tolerate and even reward "trustworthy" leftists who pose no significant challenge, especially when such arrangements undercut potentially more serious challenges. The PPS got fewer than 400,000 votes in 1979 (2.6 percent of the total) and received 425,000 votes in 1982 (1.9 percent of the total), continuing the trend leading gradually toward its probable political death.

Socialist Workers Party (PST)

The PST was founded in 1974 by some former leaders of the 1968 political movement who split away from the leadership of Heberto Castillo. The PST has received the support of the PRI and, some allege, of former President Echeverría. It seems interested in filling in the vacuum left by the declining electoral strength of the PPS. The PST could take a large share of the voters disenchanted with PPS policies and with its poor electoral showing. However, the PST failed to reach its goal in 1979. It lost the opportunity to capture the PPS's votes and finished poorly at the polls (2.1 percent). The same happened in 1982, when it received only 1.8 percent of the vote.

Interestingly, the PST publicly supported the corrupt oil union leadership when the latter was subject to severe criticism at the onset of de la Madrid's administration. As a result, the leaders of the oil workers passed a resolution during a general assembly encouraging union members to vote in 1985 for the candidates of the PST in those ballots assigned for proportional representation purposes.[39] This is said to have contributed to the increase of PST's votes to 2.5 percent of the total in 1985. Although the PST may be instrumental in weakening the position of more well-established parties on the left, like the PSUM, it does not seem to have a bright future of its own.

Mexican Workers Party (PMT)

Heberto Castillo has been a well-known professor at the school of engineering of the National University of Mexico. More important, he has been a well-known political leader for some time. Upon completing a jail sentence imposed for his part in the 1968 political movement, he convinced a group of university people and old opposition leaders, such as Demetrio Vallejo (who had led the 1958–1959 railroad workers' strikes), to form a new political party. The PMT claims today more than 25,000 regular members, primarily of working-class background and distributed mainly in the Federal District, Puebla, and Sinaloa. It did not participate in the 1979 and 1982 elections because it considered the recent electoral reform law to be anti-democratic. In particular, it opposed the government's control of the Federal Electoral Commission and the fact that there is no right to appeal decisions by that body. Before obtaining conditional registration in 1984, the PMT sought registration in 1981, but the commission denied it. Castillo, as we shall see later, led the way toward the opening of a public debate on Mexico's policies for oil expansion; Castillo has charged that for this reason the commission succumbed to presidential pressure not to grant his party legal status. Then the PMT entered negotiations with the Communist party, and for several months Castillo was considered the most viable presidential candidate of the emerging party of the left. By changing its mind at the last minute, the PMT lost an opportunity to measure its appeal among the electorate. The first opportunity in this regard came in the 1985 elections, when the PMT obtained 1.6 percent of the vote. The PMT supports nationalizations, price controls, indexing wages to price increases in order to protect the purchasing power of workers, and the use of oil resources for domestic consumption. It has agreed to join the latest attempt to build a unified socialist party.

Revolutionary Party of the Workers (PRT)

The PRT, the last party on the left, is inspired by Leon Trotsky's ideas and the Fourth International political movement. This means that the PRT is highly critical of the Soviet Union and of political parties that maintain close links with the Soviet Communist party. Prior to the establishment of the PRT in 1976, its founders for the most part were intellectuals who expressed their views in public universities. Lacking a mass constituency, the PRT remains an attractive option for a sector of the electorate that would not vote for the PSUM (the former Communist party) or for other parties on the left that are perceived as too compromised. The PRT claims to adhere to a more clear-cut and independent revolutionary orientation. After attaining conditional registration in 1981, it participated and obtained 1.8 percent of the vote in the presidential elections. The PRT thus secured permanent registration, even though its share of the vote for the Chamber of Deputies was only 1.3 percent and it did not get any representation in it. The reason the PRT obtained so many presidential votes was probably the personal appeal of Rosario Ibarra de Piedra, Mexico's first woman candidate for the country's highest office. Ms. Ibarra, who is not herself a member of this party, is a prestigious human rights leader and the mother of one of Mexico's young activists who "disappeared" due to political reasons. Ms. Ibarra has staged several protests, including some well-publicized hunger strikes, against police brutality and political repression.

In 1985, when the PRT again obtained only 1.3 percent of the vote for simple majority districts but was still assigned six seats in the Federal Congress, Ms. Ibarra became a member of Mexico's legislative body. It was argued in the Federal Electoral Commission that the PRT qualifies for these seats because it obtained a higher share of the vote in ballots for proportional representation.

We now conclude our analysis of political parties in Mexico by turning to two small nonleftist parties.

Democratic Mexican Party (PDM)

The PDM is an outgrowth of the fascist National Union Against Anarchy (Unión Nacional Sinarquista) founded in 1937. It struggled for many years, without success, for legal status. But it has endured nonetheless. It claims 86,000 members, most of them conservative Catholics (from rural areas) and small businessmen. It is particularly strong in San Luis Potosí, Guanajuato, Jalisco, and Querétaro. The PDM is critical of Mexico's mixed capitalist economy. It gives special attention to the rights of individuals and considers the family the center of society. To the right of the PAN on the political spectrum, the PDM is the most overtly conservative electoral option in Mexico. It got only about 2 percent of the vote in the elections for the Chamber of Deputies in 1979, 1982, and 1985.

Perhaps the most interesting feature of this party has been its ability to establish working alliances with other parties in certain regions. For example, a candidate supported by the PDM and the PAN was elected mayor of Guanajuato, the capital city of that leading mining state; and another candidate later became mayor of Comonfort in the same state. In the capital city of the state of San Luis Potosí, the PDM and a local political movement achieved a similar success. These are rare examples of formal coalition party politics in Mexico.

Authentic Party of the Mexican Revolution (PARM)

This rather obscure party was founded in 1952 by retired army generals alienated from the PRI. Like other parties, it soon began receiving public funds to conduct its activities on a regular basis. Like the PPS, it has supported most of the PRI's programs and candidates. Its ideology parallels the main principles of the PRI. The PARM received fewer than 300,000 votes in 1979 (1.8 percent of the national vote). In 1982, it failed to receive the minimum 1.5 percent of the national vote, thus losing its legal status until the government decided to give it another opportunity in 1984. It appeared to be following the PPS into oblivion when it gained surprising (though still very limited) success in the 1985 elections. It is the first opposition party other than the PAN to have obtained victories in simple majority districts since the implementation of the 1977 electoral reform.

CONCLUSIONS

Overall, political reforms have produced mixed results and left doubt as to how much true democratization the regime will allow in its major institutions and processes. For example, one question is whether Mexico is establishing a plural party system open to positions of the right and left, or whether it has only bolstered a *modified one-party system*, legitimizing it today with the presence of the PSUM, PST, PDM, and other emerging small parties, as it did yesterday with the PAN, PPS, and PARM. Analysis of electoral results in the 1980s suggests that the regime is not yet prepared to acknowledge and live with significant victories by opposition parties. Hope for continued reform has been kept alive by the recognition of opposition victories in regional elections, involving representation in state legislatures and even the administration of government in several state capitals. In addition, there seems to be a slow but gradual process toward a greater role of opposition parties in the national Chamber of Deputies. But the regime has favored small parties to prevent more well-established electoral forces from realizing their potential. Discussions about reforming the Senate to include opposition parties have never gone beyond the planning stage. And, as the elections of 1985 and 1986 showed, state governorships are still reserved exclusively for the regime's political party candidates.

Overall, the central issue is not so much whether the regime will be able to maintain control over elections at its own will; there is little the opposition can do regarding electoral fraud and repression. Rather, one is left to wonder how long the regime can resort to these methods before the public's interest and participation in elections wither. The reform has been instrumental to the regime by providing it with some breathing space in the current environment of popular discontent over economic problems; the regime may in fact find it easier to control the activities of an open than of a more repressed opposition.

Whether the wide political spectrum represented by the various parties will trigger a greater polarization of Mexican party politics is anyone's guess. There are confusing elements in the positions of many parties. And there are many objections to those parties, such as the former PCM, in which positions are more clearly defined. Furthermore, there are no clear indications that issue-oriented coalition politics will take hold in Mexico. Some alliances have been formed in the Chamber of Deputies, but mostly to oppose the PRI. Finally, an increase in public participation may depend on the political education the public receives from the political parties. If other parties succeed, the PRI may feel compelled to work more closely with its own supporters in order to expand their political education and participation.[40]

In addition to discussing the characteristics and the record of political parties and electoral participation, we have identified in this chapter the most important institutions and actors in the Mexican political system. We have reviewed the extraordinary concentration of power in the hands of the president and the competition for influence among key government agencies. Additionally, the background and the most significant features of organizations representing labor, the peasantry, and the business community, as well as some of their interactions with the government and the official party, have been analyzed. Such interactions have been a form of political participation of far greater importance than elections. With variable degrees of effectiveness, the actors here identified make demands upon the political system. In the following chapter we analyze how this variable political effectiveness, variable political freedoms, and policy changes have affected and been affected by political stability.

NOTES

1. For traditional voting patterns of Congress, see Pablo González Casanova, *Democracy in Mexico*, trans. Danielle Salti (London: Oxford University Press, 1970), p. 201.

2. See the interesting analysis of the role and powers of the Ministry of Programming and Budget by John J. Bailey, "Presidency, Bureaucracy, and Administrative Reform in Mexico: The Secretariat of Programming and Budget," *Inter-American Economic Affairs* 34, no. 1 (1980):27–59.

3. Jesús Lozano, "Se aplicó en ocho entidades el Plan DN-III: Arévalo Gardoqui," *Excélsior*, October 10, 1985.

4. His remarks are taken from an interview with Mexico City's weekly *Proceso*, September 22, 1980, pp. 6–8.

5. Reported in *Uno Más Uno*, December 10, 1980.

6. Marlise Simons, "US Said to Approve Jet Sale for Mexico's Military Buildup Plan," *Washington Post*, February 24, 1981; and Sadot Fabila, "Miembros de las fuerzas armadas acudieron a felicitar al presidente," *El Día*, January 3, 1980. See also the book edited by David Ronfeldt, *The Modern Mexican Military: A Reassessment,*

Monograph Series 16 (La Jolla, Calif.: Center for U.S.-Mexican Studies, University of California, San Diego, 1984), p. 3.

7. Ronfeldt, *Modern Mexican Military*, p. 98.

8. This argument is developed by Mario Ojeda and René Herrera, *La política de México hacia Centroamérica, 1979–1982* (Mexico City: El Colegio de México, 1983).

9. Phillipe Schmitter, "Still the Century of Corporatism?" in *The New Corporatism: Social-Political Structures in the Iberian World*, ed. Frederick Pike and Thomas Stritch (Notre Dame, Ind.: Notre Dame University Press, 1974), p. 86.

10. Jose Luis Reyna, et al., *Tres estudios sobre el movimiento obrero en México* (Mexico City: El Colegio de México, 1976); and Raúl Trejo, "El movimiento obrero: Situación y perspectivas," in *México, hoy*, ed. Pablo González Casanova and Enrique Florescano (Mexico City: Siglo XXI, 1979), pp. 121–151.

11. John J. Bailey, *Governing Mexico, 1976–1988: The Statecraft of Crisis Management* (London: Macmillan, forthcoming), Chapter 5.

12. See the "war of words" between the union and government authorities in the Mexico City press during the first two weeks of September 1984.

13. Héctor Adorno and Luis Segura, "De 33 detenidos la PGJDF consignó a nueve por los disturbios del desfile," *Excélsior*, May 3, 1985.

14. México, Secretaría de Programación y Presupuesto, "Acuerdo que establece normas que deberán observarse en la ejecución de obras públicas," published in *Diario Oficial*, January 30, 1984, pp. 8–11.

15. Aurora Berdejo, "No caigamos en alarmismos catastrofistas," *Excélsior*, January 9, 1986.

16. Interested readers are referred to Ian Roxborough, *Unions and Politics in Mexico: The Case of the Automobile Industry* (New York: Cambridge University Press, 1984).

17. Shlomo Eckstein et al., *Land Reform in Latin America: Bolivia, Chile, Mexico, Peru and Venezuela*, Staff Working Paper 275 (Washington, D.C.: World Bank, April 1978), pp. 16–21; and Gustavo Esteva, *La batalla en el México rural* (Mexico City: Siglo XXI, 1980), pp. 230–231.

18. Esteva, *La batalla en el México rural*, p. 230.

19. Salvador Cordero and Rafael Santín, *Los grupos industriales: Una nueva organización económica en México*. Cuadernos del Centro de Estudios Sociológicos 23 (Mexico City: El Colegio de México, 1977), Appendix. See "Coordinará fomento PROA actividades de las cervecerías Moctezuma y Cuauhtémoc," *Excélsior*, July 23, 1985.

20. An interesting study is by Angella M. Delli Sante, "The Private Sector, Business Organizations and International Influence: A Case Study of Mexico," in *Capitalism and the State in US-Latin American Relations*, ed. Richard R. Fagen (Stanford, Calif.: Stanford University Press, 1979), pp. 337–381.

21. Carlos Arriola, "Los grupos empresariales frente al estado," *Foro Internacional* 16, no. 4 (1976):449–495.

22. Soledad Loaeza, "La política del rumor: México, noviembre-diciembre 1976," *Foro Internacional* 17, no. 4 (1977):557–586.

23. The CCE published a paid advertisement in *Excélsior*, September 30, 1985, complaining about the regime. One complaint about the mayor of Mexico City is that he included in the expropriating decree over one thousand housing units that had not been affected by the quakes. As a result, a second decree was published to correct the initial error. "Rectifican 20% de las expropiaciones," *La Jornada*, October 22, 1985.

24. See COPARMEX's paid newspaper insertion, "Preservemos la libertad," *Excélsior*, November 9, 1985; and Minister Bartlett's response, "Incriminaciones falsas y vagas," *Excélsior*, November 14, 1985.

25. Alfredo Sandoval, "La modernización de México," speech delivered before the Forty-eighth National Assembly of COPARMEX, March 13, 1986.

26. John J. Bailey, *Governing Mexico*, Chapter 5.

27. There were twenty-nine states, two territories, and the Federal District. Subsequently, Baja California and Quintana Roo have become states, for a total of thirty-one.

28. Roberto Villarreal, "Ordena el presidente a Gobernación, cabal vigilancia al proceso electoral de julio," *Excélsior*, May 31, 1985.

29. This section draws substantially on our "Mexico: Challenges and Responses," *Current History* (January 1986):18–19. On the 1986 elections, see Delal Baer, *The 1986 Mexican Elections: The Case of Chihuahua* (Washington, D.C.: Georgetown University Center for Strategic and International Studies, The Latin American Election Studies Series, Report No. 1, September 1986).

30. John J. Bailey, "What Explains the Decline of the PRI and Will It Continue?" in *Mexico's Political Stability: The Next Five Years*, ed. Roderic A. Camp (Boulder, Colo: Westview Press, 1986), pp. 159–184.

31. This point is discussed in detail by John J. Bailey and Delal Baer, "Mexico's 1985 Midterm Elections: A Preliminary Assessment," *LASA Forum* 16, no. 3 (1985):4–10.

32. Carlos D. Salinas, "Tamaulipas: Mafias, caciques y cultura cívico-política," in *Electoral Patterns and Perspectives in Mexico*, ed. Arturo Alvarado, Monograph Series 21 (La Jolla, Calif.: Center for U.S.-Mexican Studies, University of California, San Diego, forthcoming).

33. Rafael Segovia, "Las elecciones federales de 1979," *Foro Internacional* 20, no. 3 (1980):397–410. We have drawn heavily from Segovia's work in our analysis of the 1979 elections. He is an expert on elections in Mexico.

34. Partido Acción Nacional, *A propósito de la reforma política* (Mexico City, 1977). For further reference, see Donald J. Mabry, *Mexico's Acción Nacional: A Catholic Alternative to Revolution* (Syracuse, N.Y.: Syracuse University Press, 1973).

35. Fernando Meraz, "Grave escisión interna enfrenta Acción Nacional," *Excélsior*, February 23, 1985; and Fernando Meraz, "Alto costo pagó por su expansión el blanquiazul," *Excélsior*, February 24, 1985.

36. The political views of Arnoldo Martínez Verdugo are presented in his *Crisis política y alternativa comunista* (Mexico City: Ediciones de Cultura Popular, 1979).

37. See Partido Comunista Mexicano, *Declaración de principios, programa de acción y estatutos del Partido Comunista Mexicano* (Mexico City, 1979).

38. Rogelio Hernández and Angel Soriano, "Exigen 200 millones al PSUM," *Excélsior*, July 3, 1985. It is interesting to read the exchange of views between the PSUM and Martínez Verdugo's captors in the Mexico City press, especially *La Jornada* and *Excélsior*.

39. "Del PST al pueblo de México," *Excélsior*, July 3, 1985.

40. For further analysis of the political reform, see Kevin Middlebrook, "Political Change in Mexico," in *Mexico–United States Relations*, ed. Susan Kaufman Purcell (New York: Academy of Political Science, 1981), pp. 55–66; Octavio Rodríguez Araujo, *La reforma política y los partidos en México* (Mexico City: Siglo XXI, 1979). Four books dealing broadly with Mexico's political institutions, actors, and processes, and therefore appropriate as suggested reading beyond this chapter, are Richard R. Fagen and

William S. Tuohy, *Politics and Privilege in a Mexican City* (Stanford, Calif.: Stanford University Press, 1972); Merilee S. Grindle, *Bureaucrats, Politicians, and the Peasantry in Mexico* (Berkeley: University of California Press, 1977); Bailey, *Governing Mexico;* Enrique Krauze, *Por una democracia sin adjetivos* (Mexico City: Joaquín Mortiz-Planeta, 1986).

4

The Politics of Stability

This second chapter on the political system shifts from a largely "micro" analysis of the system's actors, processes, and institutions to a basically "macro" analysis of the system as a whole. Its central concern is with regime stability. We have already discussed how extraordinary the stability appears in both cross-national and historical perspectives. But on what political terms has stability been achieved? Recent experiences of extended military rule in other major Latin American nations illustrate that political order may exact a substantial cost in terms of other political goals. Critics of the Mexican political system charge that it furnishes signal proof that long-term stability per se is no promoter of desirable politics, that it may in fact be an obstacle. This chapter analyzes the extent to which Mexico reconciles political stability with political freedom, political equality, and political change. In so doing, it considers some of the central paradoxes of a political system that has been variously characterized as free and repressive, inclusive and elitist, continually changing and remarkably unchanging, pluralist and authoritarian.

POLITICAL FREEDOM

Most prominent definitions of democracy focus on elections in which the citizenry selects its leaders. Mexico falls short of democracy on this count—but so do the overwhelming majority of nations.[1] Notwithstanding some stereotypical U.S. visions, however, Latin America is not a region of nondemocracies but one that has oscillated between nondemocracies and democracies. The restoration of electoral government in nations such as Argentina, Brazil, Ecuador, Peru, and Uruguay, alongside historically more novel electoral processes in several Central American nations, made for a sharp contrast between the 1980s and the military dominance of the 1970s. But without minimizing the differences between elected and nonelected governments, we should not accept an impression of considerable homo-geneity among the world's nondemocracies. Such an impression raises elections beyond their true importance both intrinsically and in promoting other freedoms. Elections do not in fact determine the extent of all other freedoms. Political systems without free elections vary enormously in how free they are.

Within the nondemocracies, the Mexican system is comparatively free, but we hedge with the term "comparatively free." One way to make the phrase meaningful is to identify salient patterns of freedom and limits to freedom, assisted by comparisons with other political systems. The purpose is neither to depreciate nor to legitimize the Mexican political system, but to gain a broader understanding of it.

Individual Expression and Organizational Action

As Chapter 8 will elaborate, there has been no viable organizational alternative to the regime, despite recent stirrings on the left and especially the right and despite some latitude for political freedoms. Among the reasons for this absence is the regime's intolerance of such alternatives. In fact, very different rules hold in Mexico for individual expression and organizational action. As Daniel Cosío Villegas has described it: "Complete personal freedom has existed" and "public freedom [has been] almost equally ample," but there has been a "failure of personal and public freedom to find an outlet in political action."[2] Some responsibility for this failure may lie with dissidents who do not take proper advantage of available opportunities, but most observers attribute the failure to repression by a regime that does not tolerate organized action that threatens its stability. Of course, no regime complacently tolerates such threats. A difference is what threatens them. Democratic regimes are not characteristically threatened to the core by independent critical organizations, and competition is open for government leadership positions. These regimes usually deny freedom of organizational action only to groups advocating regime overthrow. By contrast, the Mexican regime has not usually allowed strong independent organizations to challenge the basic development model even if they support maintenance (or expansion) of existing freedoms.

In this context, the Mexican regime's careful and recently reasserted restrictions on the party and electoral process can be understood. Free elections are inherently organizational or group processes, not simply vehicles for individual expression. Political parties are organizations that bring people together, and free voting itself represents an aggregation of individual expression. Thus, Mexican elections are steered outside the democratic process so that they do not determine who will rule.

Mexico's elections do serve certain purposes, but these do not include forming organized alternatives to regime control. Indeed, the purposes include organizing the population in continuing support of existing rule. In the best cases—the Cárdenas campaign is most frequently cited—candidates may learn about the citizenry. The citizenry has a chance to acquaint itself with its future leaders, who campaign as vigorously as if the results were completely in doubt. For example, de la Madrid reportedly made 1,800 speeches in the months prior to his inevitable electoral victory.[3] Strenuous efforts are also made in nonpresidential elections; in 1985, the PRI gubernatorial candidate in Sonora (whose victory *was* apparently in doubt) pledged to visit all 69 municipalities, including remote ones, to hear complaints and requests. But perhaps the campaign's main purpose is to promote stability through the illusion of popular sovereignty.

A similar analysis of limits on organizational activity could be made of the party system, and of the PRI in particular. Free parties generally try to aggregate and organize individual expression, bringing it to bear on the policy process. Mexico's party system does not fundamentally function on such a basis, although in the 1970s both the electoral and party processes were freer in Mexico than in most Latin American nations (where there were no elections whatsoever, or just plebiscites or elections without competition between parties, and where campaigns did not offer possibilities for free expression, let alone government change). But the region's renaissance of electoral and party activities in the 1980s made Mexico appear relatively unfree. Mexico's own political reforms, tarnished in the 1985 and 1986 elections, did not go nearly far enough to escape such invidious comparisons.

Thus, whatever the qualifications, freedom is still restricted in Mexico's electoral and party systems. The picture is very different, however, if the focus shifts to freedoms dependent less on organizations, more on individuals alone. The Mexican regime does not feel threatened by personal freedoms that many authoritarian regimes would not tolerate.

Religious freedom is an excellent example. It may seem a bit of an odd choice at first glance. After all, the revolutionary regime attacked the church, stripping it of much of its power. But therein lies the key factor. Churches are organizations and they bring individuals together. The regime would not tolerate the church *as a powerful political organization*, capable of influencing national policy and even challenging the regime. The modus vivendi meant that the church surrendered this political power in return for guarantees, legal and tacit, of its legitimacy as a religious organization. Today the church has the freedom to function as it sees fit, within this context. Grassroots activities by individual priests to organize the poor, as seen now in much of Latin America, or striking church calls to declare a moratorium on debt payments, or efforts by conservative elements within the church to ally the institution with antiregime forces on the right bear watching but have not to this point fundamentally undermined the modus vivendi.

Religious freedom for the individual is substantial. Mexicans have the right to worship as they wish, in whatever religion they choose, and they have the freedom not to worship at all. There are disquieting incidents, of course, and some would argue that the regime's pointed secularism in effect represses the church even as a religious organization, but by and large Mexico presents a contrast to the restrictions placed on religious freedom in some authoritarian countries. Nor is there any attempt, as sporadically occurs elsewhere in Latin America, to extol Catholicism as the official religion of the nation. Moreover, the Mexican regime supports religious freedom not only by its own lack of repression but also by strength. This strength helps protect citizens from the sort of persecution by fanatical or vigilante groups that has stalked Argentine Jewry, for example. And religious freedom in Mexico means more than the absence of active persecution. It means the opportunity to practice one's religion and to maintain vibrant religiously oriented institutions such as private schools.

Other individual freedoms exist; some flourish. Mexicans travel freely outside the republic, often more freely than their U.S. counterparts. Banned from visiting Cuba in the 1960s and 1970s, U.S. citizens bound for the island would most often make their way via Mexico. Nor does the Mexican government tell its citizens what jobs to take, just as it does not tell university students what careers to pursue. Allowing for exceptions, there are protections for property and for legal rights. Yet Mexico's "human rights" marks have not been exemplary. There has been increasing concern over missing persons, irregular detentions, forced confessions, and tortured political prisoners. As in the far more abusive Argentine case, especially in the late 1970s, it is often difficult to pinpoint the extent of government complicity in actions by hired thugs. The de la Madrid administration provided some information on the "disappeared," but the government's record seemed to compare unfavorably with, for example, that of the restored democracy in Argentina. Some human rights groups became very critical of Mexico. One alarming sign came when the 1985 earthquakes uncovered corpses that showed evidence of official torture.

A troubling issue arises even regarding the personal freedoms that do exist. Many are gratuitous freedoms for most Mexicans—what critics might call "bourgeois" freedoms, available only for those who can afford them. Party and electoral reforms may not mean much to most peasants. Few Mexicans will ever exercise their freedom to travel to Havana, New York, or Paris. Few will attend the university or send their children to private schools. Few will have a wide choice of jobs; the issue will often be work or no work. Few own much. Few will hire lawyers to take their grievances to court, where many legal provisions purposely protect privilege. Of course, similar questions could be raised about the extent of bourgeois freedoms in the United States, but there many more have the means to exercise those freedoms.

Furthermore, if the range of individual freedoms is expanded, Mexico does poorly. What Franklin Roosevelt spoke of as the "freedoms from" are not usually included in the U.S. concept of political freedom; the line between political freedom and socioeconomic freedom is thinner elsewhere, however, and the Mexican constitution gives testimony to the overlap. Yet so many Mexicans do not enjoy freedom from want, hunger, and disease. Without those freedoms, the more purely political ones may seem hollow. Critics can interpret Mexico's religious freedom in this light, arguing that the regime ceased its antagonism toward religion as the regime itself ceased being revolutionary; when it failed to deliver on its material promises, it once again encouraged the flow of "opium" to the people.

Up to this point we have divided political freedoms into more organizationally and more individually or personally oriented ones. Obviously, however, the distinction is not clear-cut. Freedom of speech, for example, has significant elements of both. Wide latitude for individual expression exists. A Mexican can stand on the proverbial street corner and say almost anything without government reprisal. He can say whatever he wants at the dinner table and to a friend on the bus or at a bar. Freedom of speech in Mexico becomes less certain as it becomes a less individual act, when more people are interactively involved. In the cases of freedom of assembly and freedom of the media, freedom of speech ceases to be a fundamentally individual act, yet it does not lie in as directly sensitive an area as electoral or political party freedom. Neither inherently raises an organizational alternative to the government.

There is ample freedom of assembly—up until such point as demonstrations are no longer ad hoc and instead develop a stronger organizational base. Demonstrations occur daily in Mexico. Not all are predominantly political in nature, and not all of the political demonstrations express dissent, but many do. Harassment comes in many forms, ranging from the organization of counterdemonstrations, to infiltration, to the hiring of thugs, to outright use of police or even the army. Restrictions on the freedom of assembly come from government, and they come from bullying by opposing groups. Freedom of assembly is neither fully respected nor dormant.

An interesting test of the freedom to assemble came in September 1980.[4] On the first of the month President López Portillo commented that constant demonstrations wreaked havoc with Mexico City's traffic and asked aloud what solutions might be found. Mexican presidents do not ask questions idly. The interior minister immediately "asked" Mexico City's mayor to talk with leaders of political organizations and registered parties, and on the fourth of the month an ambiguous but ominous communiqué was released by the city. It raised doubts about the legality of demonstrations outside the Plaza of the Republic, emphasizing that demonstrations caused "the disruption of normal life in Mexico City." Demonstrators should therefore restrict themselves to the plaza—but they should not feel deprived, because a sound system would be available and there would be access to officials in nearby government buildings! Many interpreted the government's statement as an attempt to restrict freedom of assembly. Not everyone accepted it. Some political parties expressed opposition, and demonstrations continued in the ensuing days, although police blocked some of them. Television channels dutifully interviewed irate drivers caught in traffic jams, eager to curb demonstrators.

Then, as quickly as the crisis had arisen, it subsided. Mexico City announced that no constitutional guarantees had been altered. The announcement tacitly ended what had been called "The Battle for the Streets." If the government had been trying a quiet, indirect way of restricting the freedom of assembly, the experiment had failed. Demonstrators in effect challenged the government to back down or enforce a clear policy through active repression. The government backed down. By not making its initial policy explicit, it could retreat without making its new policy explicit; it did not have to lose face by formally retracting any statement. It could have moved toward active repression but, apparently, only at the risk of considerable opposition, possibly violent opposition, and a loss of legitimacy.

Why then did the government act in the first place? One cannot overlook the truth in its stated premise: Demonstrations do aggravate the city's abominable traffic situation, and there were roughly 300 demonstrations in the previous year. But most demonstrations are not protests. They are symbolic political acts organized by the government or government-controlled institutions, and they are carried out in order to support policies or to greet a domestic or foreign dignitary. It lies well within the government's power to quarantine these demonstrations. Another possible explanation for the government action is that officials underestimated the opposition that would be engendered by their move. Yet another is that they planted the seeds for future action by drumming up widespread motorist resentment of demonstrators. But for the indefinite future, the right to free assembly had been reasserted.

Freedom of the Media

Like freedom of assembly, freedom of the media attracts our attention partly because it lies ambiguously between Mexico's ample individual freedoms and its restricted organizational freedoms. Moreover, freedom of the media is basic to a free society, certainly in the modern world. This section considers three principal issues: (1) general factors supporting or restricting media freedom; (2) variation in degrees of freedom; (3) substitutes for freer news coverage.[5]

1. *General factors supporting or restricting media freedom.* At first glance, Mexico would appear to have many of the requisites for media freedom. There are, for example, multifarious sources. Many newspapers enjoy a national circulation. Mexico City's residents can choose among *El Día, Excélsior, El Heraldo, La Jornada, Novedades, La Prensa, El Universal, Uno Más Uno,* and numerous minor newspapers. By contrast, the U.S. capital city and even New York City have but a few major dailies. Mexico also boasts an impressive number of news magazines, radio and television stations, and publishing houses. No government or official party vehicle is at all comparable to Radio Havana or the newspaper *Granma* in Cuba, although the government is *one* media owner. In fact, the great majority of all the media forms are privately owned. Beyond this, overt government censorship is exceptional, and freedom of the press is widely and constitutionally proclaimed.

On the other hand, significant sources of government influence exist. One lies in regulation of the resources necessary for media production. The government controls, distributes, and subsidizes all newsprint. PIPSA (Producer and Importer of Paper) is a virtual government monopoly, with private interests supplementing the government's controlling stock. Established in

1935, it purchases newsprint and sells it to periodicals wholesale. Almost all periodicals buy their newsprint from PIPSA, and to shop elsewhere, often abroad, means higher costs and less competitiveness. PIPSA can also provide excellent credit terms or it can be tough.

Another specific source of government control is advertising revenue. Mexican newspapers depend heavily on the government to buy space for announcements. Unprofessional and often corrupt advertising practices contribute to government influence and adversely affect independent news reporting still further. *Gacetillas* (publicity stories) can be bought and not labeled as advertisements. Insertions may be devoted to commemorative events, inaugurations, appointments, or government statements. Some of those working at Mexico's newspapers, often not satisfied with their salaries, have second jobs with firms sending in gacetillas. Similarly, they may collect *igualas*, monthly gratuities from business or government organizations involved in policy areas covered by them, to insure favorable reporting. Clearly, then, government interference is not the only obstacle to media freedom.

The patronage of private businesses could provide a buffer against government economic pressure, but it also carries its own strings in terms of not reporting certain kinds of news. Even where private ownership may be a hedge against government control, it does not necessarily imply free coverage of the news by competitive organizations. First, there is less competition than the plurality of media might imply. For example, while some newspapers are independents and some are cooperatives (owned by the employees), many belong to commercial chains, and a few big chains dominate. Much cross-ownership is found. Second, those who own the media, principally big businesses, rarely believe in an independent line. Their generally conservative interests are served pretty well by the development model. It would be easier to identify the bounds of freedom and repression if more of the private media identified themselves with the opposition or at least with the value of strict independence from the regime. The media would then attempt to act in conflict with the regime, and we would see how far they could go. In fact, however, the question may be less one of regime censorship, whether imposed ex post facto by the regime or a priori by media too frightened to criticize, than one of interest overlap. In fact, practices like those cited in the last paragraph often serve the interests of both government and media, while shortchanging the public.

Freedom requires individuals and organizations devoted to exercising it, a generalization that may be especially relevant in mixed authoritarian-free settings. Less opportunity exists in more authoritarian settings; less danger exists in freer settings. Of course, it is not easy for a strong professional ethos based on free expression and integrity to arise in the Mexican setting. For instance, as Mexican politics is group-oriented, so media cliques may be closed to news stories written by those from other cliques. Media cliquishness provides another illustration of the fact that restrictions on media freedom in Mexico do not all emanate from the government.

2. *Variation in degrees of freedom.* As media freedom in Mexico is not an all-or-nothing concept, so it is not a constant. We can identify certain

variables that determine when media freedom is stronger or weaker. One is the disposition of any particular administration. Echeverría, despite one jolting confrontation (analyzed below), clearly allowed greater freedom than did his predecessor. The media could take a more critical look at Mexico's general development model and its results. Government money actually supported cinematic efforts to depict poverty, corruption, and even political injustice. Of course, all this could be linked to Echeverría's own effort to alter the development model, but there was also greater latitude than before for criticism of ongoing government policies. Under López Portillo and especially de la Madrid, media freedom progressed still further. Reforms paralleled those made in the political party arena, and in fact, some direct links are found; as all parties have been allowed monthly television time to air their views, many presentations have been critical, vivid, and professionally prepared.

Freedom also varies according to the particular medium in question. A key factor is audience size. The government generally places more stringent limits on those media that reach more people; printed media are generally freer than "action" media. All this makes sense in terms of the greater limits placed on freedoms that involve greater organizational or interpersonal interaction. Cinema, for example, comes under a measure of regulation by the Interior Ministry.

But it is television that is increasingly the major medium and is especially important in urban areas. Audiences for the nightly news can reach about 20 million. Chiefly because of its large audience, television is subject to more licensing and regulations than are the print media. Nevertheless, we may focus on what private interests choose to do. In fact, private ownership runs television in ways that buttress the status quo.

Most of Mexican public television is educationally oriented, attracting limited audiences. When Echeverría bought an ailing private channel and made it into a public channel (thirteen), the powerful Monterrey Group of industrialists countered this perceived threat to the private sector by merging their channel eight with Mexico's major network system, thus forming Televisa. But private ownership (with government representation on Televisa's governing board) implies no fountain of dissent. In fact, compared to public television, Televisa has generally been a more ardent proponent of a conservative line within the stable development model. When, for example, public television took an anti-Somoza position in covering the 1970s insurgency in Nicaragua, Televisa tended more to emphasize the dangers of revolutionary Marxism. Probably the major point about television news coverage overall is that it very rarely covers events that are embarrassing to the government or criticizes government policies. Moreover, aside from restricted news reporting, television upholds the political system by transmitting the soap operas, comedies, and variety and other shows that often portray the social values of the privileged; such programs do not question the status quo.

Radio also mixes restricted news coverage with "safe" programming, conscious of government watchfulness. The government has the authority to regulate broadcasting to the "public interest." More directly, the government can require that radio stations allot considerable time for government programming, although the government exercises such authority less than it holds it in reserve. Yet there are pockets of dissent. University Radio, for example, speaks freely and even critically of the government, reflecting the general freedom exercised by the National University. Still, it is difficult to assess the actual limits on broadcast freedom; rarely are they boldly approached, let alone transgressed, by radio or television.

If the broadcast media give less critical coverage than daily newspapers, news magazines give more. The magazines range from very conservative, such as *Impacto*, to rather conservative, such as *Tiempo*, to more liberal, such as *Proceso*. Some, such as *Siempre*, have been open to divergent orientations. Mexico is not unusual in permitting weeklies to publish material that no daily would or could. Illustratively, Mexico's human rights abuses have received much more prominent mention in magazines than in newspapers. Additionally, the more critical newspapers and magazines usually have smaller audiences than their less critical counterparts (for example, *Uno Más Uno* versus *Novedades* and *Proceso* versus *Impacto*).

Two special kinds of journals present probably the most critical view of official Mexico. One, a popular one, is the comic book. Most comic books are nonpolitical, but a few have vigorously attacked government policies on an array of issues. Drawn in typical cartoon fashion, these magazines are scathingly satirical. The two most famous have been *Los Agachados* (literally the stooped ones) and *Los Supermachos* (super-machos). Eduardo del Río ("Rius") was their guiding light. With his freewheeling socialist bent, Rius did not go unmolested. But by the time he had to leave *Los Supermachos* the comic book claimed a circulation of roughly 200,000. Although *Los Supermachos* has not been the same since Rius's departure, Rius reactivated his challenge with *Los Agachados*, where he remained from 1968 to 1977; the new comic book achieved a peak circulation of roughly 150,000.[6] Like *Los Supermachos*, *Los Agachados* used Mexico's provincial towns for backdrops. There, the apparently simple and definitely beleaguered peasant asked the apparently simple questions that in fact cynically interpreted why he was beleaguered. U.S. imperialism was a favorite target, but the Vatican, private enterprise, *and* the Mexican government were also treated irreverently.

A second special kind of periodical is the scholarly journal. Several factors sustain its critical orientation. One is its relatively limited audience; another is its association with the university. The *Revista Mexicana de Sociología*, published at the National University, and *Foro Internacional*, published at El Colegio de México, are good examples.

Book publishing, with generally limited sales, also ranks closer to the freer than the more restricted end of the Mexican media spectrum. Surely self-censorship has existed, and interesting voids result. One, of special interest here, is that although many first-rate, incisive books by Mexicans are available on Mexican *history*, far fewer penetrating analyses are found on contemporary *politics*. Still, it is some indication of freedom that trans-lations of nearly all books on Mexican politics by foreign authors have been available, and many of these have been critical of Mexico's political system. Translations of more general works, from Karl Marx to Milton Friedman, have also been available. Additionally, if domestic "political science" has been relatively weak, prominent Mexican historians have dealt critically with contemporary affairs. Venerable figures such as Daniel Cosío Villegas and Jesús Silva Herzog, Sr., have repeatedly denounced restrictions on party, electoral, and press freedoms. Essayists, novelists, and poets have written sharply on political themes. Serious works of political criticism have been published by prominent private companies such as Siglo XXI and Nueva Imagen as well as by government-financed ones such as Fondo de Cultura Económica.

A recent trend has involved the publication of critical books that do reach relatively wide audiences. Among political gossip books, for example, is a lurid one by the assumed mistress of ex-president Díaz Ordaz. Also, a best-seller (*Lo negro del negro Durazo*) depicted corruption under López Portillo's Mexico City police chief. In general, however, the latitude for freedom has varied with the medium in question and has been greatest when audiences are small.

3. *Substitutes for freer news coverage.* What content is produced in the absence of wider freedom or independence? As book publishing cannot substitute for ongoing news coverage, and as little probably can be expected of the broadcast media, our attention focuses here mostly on the printed news media.

Readers find woefully little information on how and why political decisions are made. They will quickly see that the government raises wages, but not that the increases are inferior to the inflation rate. Nor will they find specifics on the decision-making process. They read the story of the PRI's congressional leader adjourning a legislative session, claiming that there was no quorum, and of opposition members yelling "antidemocratic," but they do not learn whether there really was a quorum. With rare but increasing exceptions, investigative reporting is not a major part of news coverage. Limited news reporting reflects the limited degree to which the ruled hold their rulers accountable. Mexico's government does not often forthrightly address citizen questions about why one policy is favored over another. After surprising the nation by firing those thought to be his most important and loyal cabinet ministers, President López Portillo "explained" his action as "for the national good." Lightly prodded for elaboration, he made it clear that he was the president in a presidential, not a parliamentary, system and therefore did not have to account for his decision. "At least tell me the latest rumors!" one columnist satirically pleaded. In practice, because officials rarely discuss intragovernment policy debates, even am-bitious reporters are handicapped by government secretiveness. A cycle develops in which Mexican newspapers become both perpetrators and victims of the lack of news.

Filling page after page without addressing the most significant news of the day becomes an art. Popular or "human interest" stories, indeed most nonpolitical stories, receive ample coverage. Entertainment, sports, fashion, medical news—there is no problem once one gets beyond section one, or basic news. The crux of the matter is what happens within section one. Publishers find many substitutes for critical coverage of Mexican politics. International news gets considerable space. The high ratio of international to domestic news in Mexico, higher than in the United States, may reflect Mexico's lesser parochialism or at least lesser self-sufficiency, but it is also true that greater international coverage helps limit domestic coverage.

Proclamations capture prominent space. These are grand statements, usually by government officials, that characteristically just repeat what is already well known. President López Portillo declares, "I will defend the Revolution," and newspapers have a headline piece. "I do not recommend a change" (in the six-year presidency), López Portillo declares; readers can only wonder who did. Some proclamations may be subtle or symbolic policy indications—the government's verdict on some matter under consideration. "Mexico Will Defend Its Independence" may suggest that Mexico is rejecting a U.S. proposal—but it also may be a cover for actual acceptance of a proposal. One might subscribe to what has been called a "mirror" approach to understanding Mexican government proclamations: Prepare yourself for the opposite. Most often, however, proclamations are mere banalities: If believed, they help legitimize the regime; if not, they at least fill space. Among those continually used as slogans during López Portillo's admin- istration were "To Justice by Liberty," "The Only Dogma in Our Constitution Is Liberty," "The Program of My Party Is My Program," "We Are All the Solution," "To Love Mexico and Understand the World." Such sloganeering diminished but persisted under de la Madrid.

Banalities are used as if there were a constant political campaign. And there is one of sorts, not against any specific opponent but against a feeling that the government has not satisfied its revolutionary promise. *Triunfalismo* (proclaiming triumphs) becomes especially intense in the last years of each *sexenio* (six-year presidential term). Mexicans see that a certain amount has been spent on expanding health facilities, for example, but they are rarely given a basis for evaluation. How does the amount compare to what the last administration spent? How does it compare to what other nations spend? What impact has it had? That such information does not flow from the government itself is one thing. That it is not provided by the media is another.

Mexican politics are rich in commemorations and these receive extensive media coverage. Heroes are extolled, holidays are celebrated. (In fact, the proliferation of holidays is an economic liability.) Coverage of commemorative events not only fills media space with empty news; it also serves symbolic purposes. When Mexican leaders pay homage to Zapata's peasant revolu- tionaries they reaffirm their allegiance to contemporary peasants and make it more difficult for dissidents to mobilize around Zapata's image. A few thoughtful columnists seize the opportunity to raise some doubts about the regime's faithfulness to Zapata's cause, but most simply publicize the government line.

Far removed from news trivialities and nonsense, readers can also find serious commentaries decrying the fundamental structure of the social-political-economic system. Unprepared observers may be startled at the profound, sweeping criticisms, often neo-Marxist criticisms, repeatedly leveled against the status quo. Of course, such critiques are more likely to be found in books and journals with small readerships, but they also appear in some newspapers. Why does a system sensitive to less profound criticism readily tolerate more profound criticism? The apparent paradox is rather easily unraveled. One type of criticism is dangerously policy-relevant; the other is not.

It might help to think of a distinction between "regime" and "state."[7] The state would be the broad "pact of domination" of the ruling classes, the very general guidelines within which privilege is assured. The regime would be the particular political and governmental configuration by which the pact is implemented. Much less variation exists among states (at similar levels of development) than among regimes in Latin America. Short of revolution, the Mexican state will not basically change. Columnists can elaborate the failures of Mexico's "dependent capitalist state" and the power of the high bourgeoisie and foreign interests. Government officials, far from clamping down on such broadly radical critiques, may even join in the moaning, skillfully portraying themselves battling the state. The high bourgeoisie and foreign interests are denounced in rhetoric, even as they are gratified in policy. Officials solemnly pledge to fight poverty and inequality, while they prudently attribute such evils largely to the nature of the state, immutable. Alas, little can be done to change the state. And so, profoundly sweeping commentaries are much more acceptable than specific, policy-relevant ones. Columnists can heatedly write what they choose, in general terms, about dependency, capitalism, and imperialism, but let them advocate specific tax or wage policies at odds with actual government decisions and press liberty gets a truer test. "Profound" criticism may even be *encouraged* insofar as it siphons off energy from policy-relevant specifics. So media freedom, like other freedoms discussed earlier, can in some respects be belittled as bourgeois freedom, freedom for expression that does not directly address—much less change—material policies.

In sum, Mexicans can follow the news media regularly and learn little about how policies are being made, what are the pros and cons, who supports each side, and what are the ultimate results. Instead, the news is covered ("covered" in the sense of hidden as much as in the sense of reported) with omissions, masks, mirrors, and metaphors. In nations with vibrant news media one may associate diverse headlines in different papers with free expression of multiple viewpoints. But in Mexico the fact that one newspaper features some stories and a second paper features others may reflect the lack of hard news coverage in both.

Case Studies in Media Dissent

Despite all the restraining factors on hard, especially critical, news reporting, there have been bold exceptions. After a brief look at two such exceptions, we focus on a particularly important and suggestive exception—the *Excélsior* case.

Kenneth Johnson has described how *¿Por Qué?* (literally, *Why?*), a leftist weekly journal, functioned from its inception in 1968 to its forced demise in 1974.[8] *¿Por Qué?* strongly attacked the status quo, even supporting guerrilla activities. Alleged government harassment included supply and price pressure from PIPSA, bullying potential advertisers out of doing business with *¿Por Qué?*, and imprisonment without trial of the journal's most prominent figure (who was implicated in guerrilla actions). Yet in 1972 *¿Por Qué?* still claimed a circulation of 100,000. One can emphasize either the harassment or the fact that such a radical publication as *¿Por Qué?* could function for as long as it did.

For a second example, occurring during a different presidential sexenio, consider the fate of *El ABC de Tijuana*. The newspaper began in January 1977, attracting dissidents from newspapers that would not publish their columns.[9] *ABC* quickly became a strong voice for the anti–status quo left. Critics charged that *ABC*, like *¿Por Qué?* for that matter, was highly sensationalistic. But also like *¿Por Qué?*, *ABC* was an independent political voice. Mediocre journalism did not make *ABC* unusual; independent journalism did. With the notable exceptions of a few journals, Mexico's provincial press does not report extensively or critically on such issues as the violent repression of peasants. It comes as no surprise, then, that the state government of Baja California repressed *ABC*.

Framing the issue was crucial. No official credence could be given to an image of a leftist, independent newspaper fighting a nonleftist, U.S.-oriented state government over substantive issues, certainly not over freedom of the press. So the government encouraged a labor strike at *ABC* and, under the cover of the strike, helped oust the paper's director. Using its "official left wing," the government brought in the PRI-affiliated peasant and worker unions to rally around labor's cause against *ABC's* management. Although the government identified this as a labor problem it belied its own posture by adding that newspapers should merely give the news, not judge it. The government received extensive support in the non-*ABC* media throughout the crisis. In the aftermath, the government offered only a withered olive branch, as *ABC's* director was invited to open a new but definitely transformed paper. The *ABC* one could find on the newsstands a few years later was quite different from its fiery predecessor, and its daily circulation would be only about 10 percent of the previous 35,000–50,000.

The events at *ABC* sensitize us to another important variable in patterns of freedom and repression. This is the factor of federalism. Chapter 3 established that ultimate authority lies with the national government, which can assert its will over any state government. But that does not mean that it always does. Ultimate authority cannot be invoked too often without diluting itself. The president makes a commitment to only so many issues, often leaving governors or other officials to bear the responsibilities of— and the resentment for—government repression. Freedom of the press as well as other freedoms varies according to the political situation in particular states.

Turning to the national scene, no single episode in recent years has attracted more attention to the issue of media freedom in Mexico than the *Excélsior* case in 1976.[10] Its significance stems from several factors. More than any other major newspaper of its time in Mexico, *Excélsior* exercised the freedom to dissent. Progressively oriented (since 1968), it criticized Mexico's domestic and foreign policies and continually called for increased political freedoms, broader distribution of the national wealth, greater worker participation in economic decision making, and more serious attacks on corruption. It also sold space to dissidents for their advertisements. *Excélsior* naturally angered many businesses, which proceeded to withdraw their advertising. Initially, however, the Echeverría government backed its rhetoric on press freedom with concrete actions and even picked up some of the advertising slack.

Excélsior provided a shining example not only of press freedom but of press quality. It counted among its columnists such well-known intellectuals as Daniel Cosío Villegas, Gastón García Cantú, Ricardo Garibay, Pablo Latapí, Vicente Leñero, and Rodolfo Stavenhagen. It earned a reputation for avoiding corrupt practices, for not selling headlines. In fact, *Excélsior* earned an international reputation. Its reports were used as evidence in U.S. congressional hearings on Latin America, and it established links with many of the world's finest newspapers. The London *Times* called *Excélsior* the most influential daily in Latin America. One prominent U.S. observer even called *Excélsior* "probably the last bastion of intellectual and press freedom in Mexico."[11] Thus it becomes especially important to take a careful look at just what the *Excélsior* case shows and does not show.

First question: *Why* did the government repress *Excélsior?* No single, definitive answer emerges, but probably the main factor was the perceived degree of dissent. Not just in frequency but in type and tenor of criticism, *Excélsior* went far beyond anything seen in other dailies. This was true of *Excélsior's* editorials, and it was truer of many of the articles written by its columnists, including some that came close to direct criticism of the president— a serious violation of the unwritten rulebook on political dissent in Mexico.[12]

More frequently, *Excélsior's* criticisms touched another sensitive nerve. They questioned the regime's progressiveness. The *Excélsior* case has this factor in common with the *¿Por Qué?* and *ABC* cases. Here, then, lies another clue to variable patterns of regime tolerance of dissent. The regime has been especially sensitive to criticism from the left because such criticism challenges the myths of its revolutionary legitimacy, of its commitments to political and economic equality. Criticism from the right may actually lend support to those myths and therefore even please the regime.[13] What better way to appear progressive than to be accused of pandering to peasants or workers or Cuba? Also, insofar as the right rather than the left is truly represented within the system, its criticisms have not usually suggested an independent alternative to the system. Granted, especially in the 1980s, political opposition is so much more strongly organized and potent on the right than on the left that the right constitutes the more visible and immediate challenge, but consider how much more preoccupied the regime might be if the more active threat came from the left.

Other motivations also emerge for the action against *Excélsior*. One widely circulated rumor was that Echeverría was trying to preserve his influence after his term expired and that a strong tool would be a loyal press. Additionally, Echeverría reportedly had an economic interest in an expanding editorial organization, a competitor of *Excélsior*. Others argue, however, that the economic motivation could have been only marginal and that Echeverría must have understood Mexican political history too well to suppose that he could be a strong power behind the throne. The best guess remains that the government moved against *Excélsior* mostly because of the paper's unusual independence.

Second question: *How* did the government act? Again, although no definitive answer emerges, strong likelihoods do. No open repression based on a straightforward statement of government dissatisfaction with *Excélsior's* dissent would be forthcoming. That would be uncharacteristically direct, and it would undermine the government's progressive image. Methods would be far more subtle—and insidious. Mexico's most progressive daily would have to be turned upside down for being too conservative.

Excélsior was depicted as an enemy of peasants and slum dwellers. On June 10, 1976, scores of landless Mexicans invaded land owned by *Excélsior* on the outskirts of Mexico City. *Excélsior* had purchased the land in 1959 precisely to insure itself a secure economic base, a base that could help sustain political independence. In 1976, *Excélsior* was seeking needed revenues by building a middle-class housing development on the land. Surely, the Mexican regime is not known for siding with peasants against the middle class. Standard procedure might be to expel the peasants or to seek some sort of accommodation. Instead, the squatter movement was led by a PRI candidate from the agrarian sector of the party, a sign of official backing. The government helped bring more peasants (in trucks, modern buses, and luxury cars), sheltered them, and staunchly rejected *Excélsior's* legal effort to expel them. Soon the squatters numbered more than a thousand. *Excélsior* had hoped that the initial invasion was a maneuver by a single governor or a mischievous trial balloon against dissent; perhaps Echeverría ultimately might repudiate it in the face of courageous *Excélsior* resistance. After all, the president had previously gotten along well with the paper's editor, Julio Scherer García. More important, the president had established a laudable record of permitting dissent, and many thought he would have to nurture it to pursue what were thought to be two of his fondest dreams—the Nobel Peace Prize and the UN secretary-generalship. But Echeverría publicly joined with the minister of agrarian reform in pressuring *Excélsior* to reach a compromise with the squatters. Involvement by the Agrarian Reform Ministry provided a nice touch, posing the problem as one of land reform rather than property rights and press freedom.

Simultaneously, the government orchestrated a strong media campaign. It withdrew its advertising from *Excélsior*, and it increased its financial support of competing dailies, in part by purchasing advertisements attacking *Excélsior*. Such attacks were not restricted to the printed press. In fact, the major media assault came through television's campaign against *Excélsior's* "lack of patriotism." Televisa's news program, "24 Hours," waged nightly warfare. *Excélsior* gamely tried to defend itself by reporting on the campaign against it. Its columnists even finally published a joint declaration on the need for a free press, especially in a society that lacked freedom in so many other institutions! Before that, however, the paper tried to mix independence with discretion. However reluctantly, editor Julio Scherer compromised principle by participating in the annual Liberty of the Press Day with colleagues he regarded as hypocritical enemies and with Echeverría himself. The day was filled with all-too-ironic declarations about how freedom of the press was respected.

In addition to its squatter, financial, and media offensives, the government also penetrated *Excélsior's* internal labor operations, another procedure reminiscent of the ABC case. *Excélsior* was a cooperative, owned by the workers; editor Scherer was not the paper's owner, but an employee. Although he was greatly admired by the editorial staff and columnists, he did not enjoy smooth relations with many of the rank-and-file workers. Many at *Excélsior* believed that the government exploited this opening to finance a dissident minority.

Early on the morning of July 8, 1976, came the coup, the culmination of the six-month anti-*Excélsior* campaign. Scherer and his supporters were strong-armed out; the printing presses were seized by the paper's minority (which cited Scherer's ineffective management of the squatter issue). The government insisted that the cooperative itself had legitimately changed its leadership. In any case, it was a conventional Mexican newspaper that came out the very next day. Its new directors congratulated themselves for restoring *Excélsior* to the mainstream of Mexican media. As happened at ABC, the periodical kept its name but lost its personality. Almost all the previous columnists resigned.[14]

The meaning of the *Excélsior* episode must be judged in light of not only the precipitating but also the ensuing events. While the international press (*Le Monde*, the *New York Times*, the *Washington Post*, and so forth) was predictably outraged, the Mexican press was predictably low-key, giving the coup only scant coverage. There were a few notable exceptions among magazines, such as *Siempre*. Some intellectuals expressed chagrin. Octavio Paz wrote of the triumph of "grey," the "color of conformity and passivity."[15] Reaction was also sharp in segments of the university community. On the other hand, author Carlos Fuentes offered a qualified defense of Echeverría. Echeverría himself predictably and bitterly denounced the prevalent foreign view as "anti-Mexican." Less predictable, at least for those who saw repression at *Excélsior* as clear evidence of the impossibility of press freedom in Mexico, was the nearly immediate stirring to reestablish an independent outlet for the ousted *Excélsior* team. Much to Echeverría's chagrin, the *Excélsior* episode was not over.

Scherer loyalists established a weekly magazine called *Proceso*, which Echeverría could not appear to repress without a legitimizing pretext. More important, Echeverría's presidential term would end within a month, and his further threats were backed by diminishing power. One Echeverría minister warned that a new independent journal could be considered unpatriotic, given Mexico's political-economic crisis. Echeverría himself strongly urged Scherer not to accept invitations to discuss the *Excélsior* case in the United States, as the United States was not truly interested in press freedom but only in attacking Mexico's anti-imperialist government. PIPSA made access to paper difficult, and *Proceso* had to buy what it needed at high black-market prices. Nonetheless, valor and freedom triumphed when *Proceso* appeared on November 6.

Outgoing President Echeverría continued to threaten *Proceso*, but incoming President López Portillo was now the key figure with whom to reckon. As PRI candidate, López Portillo had played the proper role of regime loyalist, agreeing that the crisis was internal to *Excélsior*. Yet he also gave Scherer a sympathetic ear and promised full press liberty starting December 1. As president, he allowed *Proceso* to flourish freely and critically (although it did not maintain its original quality). But however pleased they were with their success at *Proceso*, *Excélsior*'s dispossessed leaders realized they had come only halfway around. Weeklies simply do not have the impact of dailies. They wondered how the government would react to a new independent daily. Moreover, because there was no chance to get private-sector funding, the group was forced to seek government funds, despite the all-too-obvious risks of accompanying restrictions on press freedom.

López Portillo's response seemed to go beyond the Scherer group's imaginings. Why establish a new daily, the president asked, instead of simply returning to *Excélsior*? The president's possible motivation ranged from embarrassing and weakening Echeverría, to forestalling creation of a truly new and financially dependent daily, to upholding press freedom. With a mixture of hope and trepidation, Scherer's group accepted the president's offer and returned to *Excélsior*. Their hopes seemed confirmed when the Mexican press, perhaps signaling a new climate of tolerance, covered Scherer's acceptance of a prominent journalism award in New York City. But at this point the *Excélsior* saga took a sudden and bizarre turn. The *New York Times* broke the developing story of Scherer's return to *Excélsior*. Many Mexicans thought they smelled Yankee involvement, and Scherer's successor at *Excélsior* played his hand to the hilt by covering the *Times* piece on the front page. Scherer's plans to return to *Excélsior* soon fell apart.

In assessing the ramifications of the *Excélsior* case for Mexican press freedom, the negative side is clear. A uniquely independent, quality daily had been assaulted and transformed. On the other hand, a major newspaper had exercised considerable freedom for several years prior to the repression. The *Excélsior* case suggests the limits on dissent but also the latitude for it. It mocks the pious rhetoric of a free press but also indicates that such freedom can far exceed what is often found in some Latin American nations. The fate of Mexico's independent periodicals, subsequent to the *Excélsior* coup, also illustrates the mixed picture. Until 1982, *Proceso* labored in the *Excélsior* tradition, without significant government interference. Then, stung by criticism amid economic crisis and his own tarnished political image, López Portillo cut off government advertising revenue to *Proceso* and one other periodical, declaring that the government could permit dissent without having to subsidize it. Still, the López Portillo administration avoided any full-scale parallel to the 1976 repression of *Excélsior*. *Uno Más Uno*, a daily with many former *Excélsior* figures on its staff, has become one of the most important heirs to the *Excélsior* legacy. Moreover, one could point also to the vibrant dissent found in *El Heraldo*, *La Jornada*, and *Nexos*, and the heightened media (and other) freedoms that flourished under de la Madrid. The *Excélsior* case reminds us that repression lies within the regime's logic, but it does not prove that such repression is inevitable or constant. It also illustrates the regime's adeptness at acting in insidious fashion to accomplish ends that it would not openly declare.

POLITICAL EQUALITY

Rarely does a political system function equally freely, or equally effectively, for all its citizens. Yet Mexico appears unusual in the extent to which inequality characterizes the political system. We can speak meaningfully, if with qualification, of a free British political system, compared to an unfree Soviet system, whereas the contrasts within Mexico are so great as to constitute not qualifications but the essential characterization itself. "The" Mexican system is really (at least) two systems. Some Latin American political systems allow more freedom to their citizens and some allow less, but few, if any, allow more freedom to a sizable minority while allowing as little to the majority.

An analogy to Mexico's economic system is appropriate. Many nations are richer, many poorer, but few distribute wealth in the same unequal way as Mexico. Extremes of wealth and poverty usually coexist in countries in which only a very few enjoy the wealth while all but the few are impoverished. Although Mexico has the extremes, it also has a substantial middle class and lower middle class (including many workers). Rarely does such relatively widespread wealth coexist with abject poverty for perhaps one-fourth of the population (see Chapter 5). The political/economic parallel is of course no accident. Economic resources contribute to political resources and political resources contribute to economic resources.

The concern here is with inequality in political *power*. One definition of political power is the ability to get others to do what they would not otherwise do. A corollary is the ability to prevent others from doing what they would otherwise do, forcing "nondecisions" where decisions might have been injurious. Power and freedom do not always go together; one may be free to express himself, yet gain little power. In practice, however, great overlap exists, so that this section on power relates to the previous section on political freedom. The most common explanation for the correlation between freedom and power is that freedom brings power as groups have the opportunity to advocate, act, and influence. Accepting that, it is also true that power creates its own freedom, as power implies the means (influence, finance, expertise) to act (positive freedoms) and the ability to resist others' actions (defensive freedoms). Potential antagonists, including the regime itself, must pay a price to suppress the freedom of powerful groups.

The Less Powerful Sector

If we start by dividing the Mexican political system into two parts, one more powerful than the other, then most Mexicans find themselves in the less powerful part. The largest blocs within this subsystem are workers and peasants. Also included are the unemployed, grossly underemployed, squatters, marginals, and Indians; some individuals in these groups may also be workers or peasants. Our comparison of less and more powerful groups thus builds on the analysis in Chapter 3. There, we analyzed workers and peasants as political actors who have generally enjoyed little freedom or effectiveness in making demands on the state. Instead, these groups characteristically have had to accept the results afforded by a corporatist system, realizing that organized dissent carries strong risks of outright repression.

One of the great paradoxes of Mexican worker and peasant politics has been incorporation without power. The Mexican revolution brought many workers and peasants "into" a political system that could no longer simply ignore, exclude, or repress them. The PRI became the chief vehicle for incorporation, and that is one reason that the PRI—despite its limited role in policymaking—may be the most important political party in any nondemocratic Latin American nation. Yet (at least within the Western world) few if any systems that incorporate so many groups also give them so little freedom of action and so little material reward.

Two major qualifications are warranted. The first, elaborated in Chapter 3, is that a significant sector of organized workers, especially of skilled workers, has managed to bargain effectively with the state, reaping material benefits and thereby at least partly escaping the "less powerful" category. The other qualification is that even the less powerful are not necessarily powerless. To take one example from urban Mexico, consider the long-standing metro fare of roughly one peso, or just a fraction of 1 US cent prior to a 1986 hike to about 3 cents, whereas an unsubsidized price might be closer to 10 US cents. Explanations could center on the need to limit ground traffic or efficiently to deliver workers to their employers but could also involve calculations about the political costs of mass opposition to greatly increased fares. Turning to rural Mexico, the regime has generally regarded small plots (*minifundia*) and communal holdings (*ejidos*) as much less productive than large commercial farms. Yet it has been wary of the political costs inherent in repudiating the principle that every peasant is entitled to land. Finally, López Portillo and de la Madrid partially abandoned revolutionary rhetoric by disavowing *further* land distribution, thereby frankly elevating production based on economic rationality above distribution based on political concessions.

Even recent conservative policies have not implied the demise of peasant power. Instead, there have been continual examples of independent organizational initiatives by peasants. Compared to urban workers, peasants protest more frequently and strongly outside official organizations, which is one reason that they are more often repressed. Sometimes this repression is tempered by concessions; less often, tacit concessions may actually substitute for outright repression. Peasants who "invade" and squat on land, often defying legality in the name of revolutionary justice, may be ruthlessly evicted, even slaughtered—or they may be permitted to stay. Going still further, the regime has been known to provide both rural and urban squatters with money and tools, at the same time perhaps placating owners by paying compensation for their lost land. Urban squatters often pin their hopes on a similar sort of something-for-everyone solution. Some squatter movements even get away with brandishing radical ideology.

On the other hand, the illegality of squatting often provides a handy standby weapon for the government to wield against dissident organizations. Thus, in 1981, Mexico City police suddenly engulfed the Second of October Encampment, established in 1975 and named in commemoration of the dissident students slaughtered on October 2, 1968. As one leftist leader saw it: "The government didn't move against them because they were squatters. There are squatters all over the city. It acted because it cannot tolerate an independent organization that doesn't follow the political rules of the system."[16] Yet, it is also true that the government did tolerate the encampment from 1975 to 1981, mixing its tolerance with harassment and attempted co-optation.

Perhaps the most important political development in recent years has come in the aftermath of the 1985 Mexico City earthquakes. Some poor as well as middle-class Mexicans were critical of the de la Madrid administration's handling of the crisis (despite a comparative lack of corruption), including the president's disinclination to take the opportunity to galvanize the nation; others simply came to see their government, already overwhelmed by the economic crisis, not as a powerful shaper of events but as a largely impotent actor saddled with more than it could manage. Whether out of changed perceptions, disgust with the government, or sheer necessity, an increasing number of Mexicans bonded together spontaneously and voluntarily to form self-help groups such as tenants unions and construction teams and to avail themselves of assistance from religious and other nonprofit organizations. (See also the example of peasant *Coordinadoras* in Chapter 5.) Such groups may eventually breach the regime's guidelines against independent political organizations, but they may also add significantly to the degree of democracy found in Mexico.

Notwithstanding the exceptions and possible trends, were nearly all groups to enjoy only the limited power and freedom characteristic of the less privileged groups, the Mexican political system could properly be labeled authoritarian. There would be qualifications, of course, as there are for most inclusive system labels. But considerable concentration of power would reside in a regime relatively autonomous of society's rather powerless groups. Pluralism, the dispersion of power to various political actors, would be a basically irrelevant characterization for such a system.

The More Powerful Sector

The rules are different, however, for the middle class and business groups (including industrial, commercial, agricultural, insurance, manufacturing, and importing and exporting concerns). These groups have much more independent political power, much more freedom to chart their own policies, even in opposition to regime policy.

Within the state apparatus itself, middle-class employees have formed "bureaucratic enclaves that are relatively distinct from and independent of presidential authority."[17] Naturally, because the bureaucracy is part of the government, and because the president enjoys strong policymaking and appointive powers, there are important limits to bureaucratic independence. Nonetheless, other factors have encouraged some independence. These include the very size and intricacy of the bureaucracy as well as two factors discussed below: the prevalence of personal rather than systemwide loyalties and the growing role of technocrats reluctant to subordinate their special expertise to some political considerations.

An example involving structural autonomy from the state is the public university, which offers a good opportunity to analyze the degree of freedom and autonomous power possible in a middle-class institution. In fact, there is no more middle-class institution in Mexico than the public university.[18] Strong reasons exist to expect only limited freedom and autonomy. Dissent, usually from the left, is endemic at the university, and it has a potential organizational base there. The government invests substantial finances in the university, and the university is a leading center of national thought, as well as a socializing organization for most of the nation's budding political leaders. Furthermore, several authoritarian regimes elsewhere in Latin America have exerted considerable repressive control over university policy. And, indeed, the Mexican government does not tolerate organized political dissent that moves beyond the campus and challenges the regime. The most notorious incident occurred in 1968, when some 300 protesting students were killed by the government. This incident serves as a sobering reminder that the middle class is not exempt from brutal repression.

More generally, one finds co-optation, cooperation, and important overlap in both interests and personnel between the government and university worlds. Yet a pluralist or reconciliation model more than an authoritarian model characterizes Mexican government-university relations. The middle class, compared to the lower class, is usually given a wider area for dissent and even then punished less harshly for stepping outside this area. As Lorenzo Meyer has written: "When the opposition came from groups such as students, the intelligentsia, and the middle class in general, the response was much less violent and repressive."[19] In regard to ongoing political issues, the regime does not typically impose its will on the university, even when the regime itself is fairly united. Great autonomy is found in academic affairs such as curriculum. University leaders, like business leaders, are much less likely than peasant or labor leaders to be appointed by the government. The university itself basically decides how to distribute the block grants it receives from the government, and the size of these grants is determined much less by university compliance with government guidelines than by the size of the student body and by the lack of tuition; the economic crisis has allowed the government to initiate certain changes in admissions and tuition policy, but for decades government preferences have been thwarted. The tuition issue has epitomized the contrasting political power of privileged and unprivileged Mexico. Middle- and upper-middle-class students have received highly subsidized public higher education, while the government has dispensed scant resources to its woefully inadequate primary and secondary schools, especially in rural areas.

The relative autonomy of (middle- and upper-class) business groups has been more widely documented than the autonomy of any other group. Because the regime's economic policies have usually been basically favorable to business, it is often difficult to evaluate business power to oppose the regime. But conflict with the Echeverría administration provided a vivid example of business power. Of course, business frequently holds a veto power over government policy in nations where market economics dominate.[20] Mexican business may appear even more powerful because of the relative lack of power and autonomy of most other Mexican groups, including labor. Naturally, just as the less powerful groups are not powerless, so the more powerful ones are not omnipotent. Business-government relations were excellent during most of the López Portillo years, but business was dissatisfied with fiscal reforms, restrictive credit policy, high interest rates for borrowers, and increased government control over certain areas of the economy. Tensions obviously increased markedly with the 1982 government takeover of all domestic private banks, a startling assertion of the regime's political power to make public policy against business interests. As Chapter 3 suggested, tensions immediately diminished with de la Madrid's ascension but by no means gave way to an unambiguous picture of business power. In fact, much of the business establishment sorely felt its lack of power, and some observers have pointed to certain structural weaknesses in the political standing of the business community such as internal divisions; an ingrained public hostility possibly stemming from the revolution and perpetrated by much of the government and even the press; the lack of effective business-oriented means of political socialization, unless television fills the void; and the lack of ties even with the PAN, which, of course, still has little policy impact in any case.[21]

But whatever the limitations on business power, we would emphasize the greater power of business than of other groups just as we would emphasize the generally strong overlap between business and government interests. For all its complaints, the ability of business to pressure the regime is manifested in matters such as capital flight and the lack of domestic private investment. And de la Madrid's policies were directed largely at regaining business confidence, especially as most observers came to see the disaffection of business (not labor or the left as in the 1960s) as the major threat to political stability. In general, if business has not opposed the regime more often, this has been largely because it has usually achieved much of what it has wanted without substantial, active, open protest.

Basic comparisons between more privileged and less privileged groups lead us to the conclusion that there is a great disparity between constitutional provisions and the realities of political power. The Mexican government has more legal authority over business than it uses, and Mexican business has more political power than a reading of the constitution might suggest.[22] Mexico's masses, on the other hand, wield less power than the constitution would suggest.

Differences in the blends of repression, co-optation, partnership, and accommodation characterizing relations between the Mexican regime and various groups are essential to the ways the regime pursues political stability. Because of its development model, the regime has more in common with privileged than unprivileged groups. Only rarely, then, would privileged groups act to destabilize the regime. Partnership best characterizes the relationship between privileged groups and the regime, and when disagreement arises it is usually narrow enough to be bridged through accommodation. Regime repression is less frequently contemplated, and the costs would be high, given the power of these groups. The comparative powerlessness of mass groups, in contrast, makes the costs of repression and co-optation much lower. There is a vicious cycle. Mass groups lack power and therefore are vulnerable to regime policies—which make them less powerful. Furthermore, the costs of regime accommodation to independent mass movements would be high, given the grievances they could raise about the development model. If the regime is to get along peacefully with underprivileged mass groups, co-optation is a more suitable relationship than true partnership. As a very general rule, it costs the regime more to repress than to accommodate powerful groups and more to accommodate than to repress less powerful ones.

The stability of stable democratic regimes is generally based on greater equality. For example, the working class is freer in democracies than in Mexico. The democracies' policies are generally more favorable to it, and when disagreements do arise the working class can exercise independent political power. Blatant repression is unlikely, partly because interest conflict does not run that deep, partly because the costs would be high. Elsewhere, political stability may be compatible with great political inequality, but usually with more widespread repression than is found in Mexico. Co-optation is a partial substitute for repression of Mexico's less powerful groups, while partnership and accommodation are substitutes for repression of the more powerful groups.

The Mexican regime has pursued political stability through discriminating behavior patterns. One political subsystem operates for the freer and more powerful groups, and a second subsystem operates for the less fortunate groups. Mexico's political stability has not been incompatible with political inequality; rather, it has rested on pragmatically different relationships based on that inequality. This should not imply that Mexico has two political systems that exist independently of one another. For example, more powerful Mexico can often mobilize or otherwise use less powerful Mexico politically just as it does economically.[23] But such integration does not generally narrow the power gap between the two systems. Finally, to conclude that it is more appropriate to think of two political systems, rather than one, is not to overlook that more precision could come from a three-, four-, or eight-way discussion, sensitive to differences between, for example, well-organized and unorganized labor, the lower middle class and the upper middle class, and small and big business.

POLITICAL CHANGE

A crucial challenge for the Mexican political system has been the reconciliation of stability and change. Stability, after all, implies some continuity. Yet change is usually necessary to prevent continuity from deteriorating into stagnation, ineffectiveness, and, ultimately, instability. Many normative values also are frequently associated with political change. Some, like progressivism and representation of competing ideas, relate principally to *policy* change. Others, like personnel mobility and protection against extended tyranny, relate principally to *leadership* change. Obvious overlap exists between these two types of political change, but the distinction facilitates discussion of the Mexican case. Although leadership change proves to be more compelling and is therefore the object of greater attention here, we explore both types of change and their interrelationships.

Choosing the President

The great political event in Mexico is presidential selection. Mexico changes its top leader every six years without fail. Much is at stake, especially given the president's power, the extent of personnel change, and policy variation among administrations. Excitement is heightened by the way in which the selection process is publicized, like a great sporting or gambling event.

Few political events anywhere combine so much interest, even media coverage, with so much secrecy. The coverage is excessive, given the paucity of reliable information. Thus journalists and politicians alike repeatedly denounce *futurismo*, speculation about future political candidates, yet they themselves promote it. Already in 1979, newspaper headlines frequently quoted politicians explaining that it was too early to discuss what they were discussing, the 1982 elections. Similarly, futurismo was intense before the midpoint in de la Madrid's administration and became even more intense with a major cabinet shake-up in 1986. U.S. citizens may have become upset over their own system, in which more than a year passes with attention riveted on the presidential campaign; Mexico's gestation period is much longer. And it is more secret, less openly competitive. Futurismo diverts attention from present-day policy problems.

Futurism can be quite puzzling, as politicians play subtle games, sometimes through the media. Governor Rubén Figueroa of Guerrero suggested to the press in 1979 that Emilio Múgica Montoya would make a fine president. Any such "nomination" is "bad form," a blow to the nominee's chances, if he ever had any. When a journalist therefore asked Figueroa why he had spoken publicly, Figueroa responded cryptically that he had his reasons, that "politics is a scientific art that not everyone understands. If you understood it you wouldn't be a journalist but a governor, at least a senator. Well, the truth is that there are several messages, but I will not tell you them. You, the journalists, who are always bragging about your political expertise, should have sufficient talent to decipher them."[24] In sum, there is implicit disdain not only for the press but also for the public in the way that the nation's most important political event is handled. No single political event in Mexico provides more empty news.

Incumbent presidents are the key figures in appointing their successors, although it is uncertain how much they consult or even negotiate with their inner circles or with interest groups. Mexico's best-known scholar of sexenio politics sardonically dismissed claims of U.S. scholars to have discerned further rules.[25] The interior minister has been selected frequently, but by no means automatically. The closed nature of the selection process is reflected in words like *tapadismo* (the process of keeping the nominee under wraps or hidden, until formally "uncovered" to the public by the *gran dedo*, the great finger). The PRI's *tapado* always wins the general election. Certain parallels might be made with the way U.S. *vice*-presidential candidates are chosen by the presidential nominee. The gran dedo is the U.S. presidential candidate, choosing a vice-presidential tapado; he makes his decision in varying consultation with power brokers; factual secrecy is combined with wild excitement and speculation; public campaigning by U.S. vice-presidential candidates is considered bad form; the tapado will be the convention's vice-presidential choice, even though the convention could theoretically nominate a different running mate.

Echeverría spurred speculation about making Mexico's selection process less secretive. He discussed the process more openly than had any of his predecessors. Through a spokesman, he revealed in April 1975 the names of seven possible candidates, inviting an open evaluation of them. The press, he said, should investigate their personal fortunes and behavior. Others should comment on the candidate's qualifications. Some did. The right, for example, probably communicated its preference for Mario Moya Palencia or Hugo Cervantes del Río and its disapproval of Porfirio Muñoz Ledo, Gómez Villanueva, or Gálvez Betancourt. But such communications were nothing new, and most were still made privately. Representatives of private enterprise (as well as those of the United States, for that matter) repeatedly declared publicly that they would not interfere in any way whatsoever. And, if the Echeverría–López Portillo transition suggested some modification of the secrecy surrounding tapadismo, the López Portillo–de la Madrid transaction reversed the process. Typically cryptic preference signals from several groups hardly filled the information gap left by the tight silence of the front-running candidates right up until de la Madrid was selected. López Portillo issued no "short list" for public reaction. In fact, he "sprung" his decision early, perhaps to short-circuit any increasing interest in openness or any increasing group pressures, perhaps to begin sharing the burdens of economic crisis, perhaps to reassure business interests (thereby slowing capital flight), perhaps to detract attention from leftist attempts to form a coalition, perhaps to show personal decisiveness, perhaps partly to avoid appearing too predictable. Speculation is easy, definitive answers impossible. Ironically, whereas Echeverría had opened the process a little bit and then selected a dark horse, López Portillo kept the process tightly closed and then made a much more predictable choice.

The secretiveness of the selection process obviously limits our understanding of it. But that very secretiveness is suggestive. It shows, for example, that public opinion does not play a central role. Mexico's most important leadership change is not based on a public dialogue concerning either policy issues or even competing aspirants. No matter how obscure the details, at least one crucial result of the selection process is clear—its contribution to political stability. (Of course, the process is also a reflection of that stability.) Among the factors that we will consider are the certainty about the timing and wide range of leadership change, the ample opportunities available within the system, the periodic renewal of hope, the periodic policy adjustments, and the subordination of policy considerations.

Regular Transfers of Power

Continuing in office beyond one's legally prescribed term (*continuismo*) has been frequent in Latin American politics. Instability often results at these times, as incumbents face challenges from aspirants suffering the denial of legality or opportunity. Mexico, however, has overcome the problem. First, the revolution brought the principle of "free suffrage, no reelection."[26] There were attempts, in the early years, to defy the principle or to circumvent it—and leadership transitions were generally violent. Since 1935, however, when President Cárdenas turned back his predecessor Calles's attempt at maintaining power, continuismo has not been a major problem. If an ex-president holds political office, it is likely to be some relatively minor position, not a leadership post. Ex-presidents are neither generally seen in important places nor heard on important issues. The new president assumes a strong hand. Many have attributed the stability of the political system largely to the concentration of legitimate authority in the hands of its leadership.

If the principle of orderly and significant leadership change recently needed reaffirmation, López Portillo and then de la Madrid provided it. Many factors suggested some effort by Echeverría to perpetuate his own power—not actually to stay in office, of course, but to influence his successor. Of the seven possible candidates presented to the public, López Portillo was considered among the least likely. Perhaps as president, the relatively unknown López Portillo would therefore owe a special debt to Echeverría. Furthermore, López Portillo lacked his own strong personal following, a cadre of loyalists who could immediately dominate a new administration. Echeverría, by contrast, had been a energetic president, developing a personal following and trying to mold a long-range PRI program. In addition, he had economic holdings in the press and television and a claim to mass support based on progressive policies. Moreover, Echeverría was what his supporters might call a crusader, his detractors a fanatic; all would call him ambitious. Finally, he and his successor had been friends since childhood.

Yet López Portillo immediately established his independence, appointing many of his own associates and reversing some of his predecessor's policies. Echeverría consecutively became ambassador-at-large, representative to the United Nations Educational, Scientific and Cultural Organization (UNESCO), ambassador to Australia, and director of his own Institute of Third World Studies. Ex-presidents are suitable as ambassadors because ambassadors merely carry out presidential policy and because they are kept outside Mexico. By the time Echeverría returned home in 1979 he was greeted by headlines, perhaps purposeful, perhaps gratuitous or even vindictive, proclaiming his inability to influence the 1982 elections.[27]

De la Madrid did not confront a similar degree of speculation or challenge concerning his predecessor. Without underestimating how much Echeverría was discredited by 1976, we emphasize that López Portillo's position in 1982 was severely undermined by widespread revulsion over corruption and by the deepened economic crisis; also, perhaps unlike Echeverría, López Portillo realized he had no political future. De la Madrid did not give his predecessor even a symbolic government post; this was a complete and unambiguous break.

Sharing Opportunity

By restricting the time span of one administration, the political system leaves open the way for another. Sexennial (six-year) change involves the presidency, first and foremost, but it also involves widespread turnover. Most stable political systems combine change at the top with continuity below; Mexican officials come and go in groups, although individuals often reappear in new positions. A typical sexenio may draw on the previous one for roughly 20 percent of its important personnel and on the two before that for 15 percent more, therefore counting mostly on new faces.[28] For example, although de la Madrid's finance minister, Jesús Silva Herzog, had been López Portillo's finance minister, almost all of de la Madrid's other ministers had not served as ministers before. Nor is turnover restricted to six-year intervals. Few in López Portillo's cabinet at the beginning were in the same place at the end. In de la Madrid's administration a major change involved Silva Herzog himself, so powerful until his 1986 dismissal (discussed in the next chapter).

Lack of peaceful elite circulation contributed to violent power transfers in nineteenth-century Latin America, and certainly to the rebellion against Porfirio Díaz in Mexico. For all the parallels that may be drawn between the porfiriato and the present regime, this difference is crucial. A major contributing factor to political stability since 1929 has been political opportunity born of elite circulation. Aspirants to power need not change the system when they have reasonable chances for upward mobility within it. Another major difference is that there is no single power elite today as there was before the revolution. Instead, the political and economic elites are relatively distinctive. This gives the political system some autonomy to make the effective decisions that buttress its own stability, and it opens two relatively separate routes to advancement.[29]

The circulation of political elites provides opportunities not just for power but also for personal profit, as such opportunities are available to holders of Mexican political office. Naturally, corruption is a tricky matter to analyze. Governments do not publish data on the subject. There do seem to be unwritten rules on permissible corruption, however, in terms of both amounts and methods. Some administrations, such as Alemán's, earn reputations for excessive greed, others, such as Ruiz Cortines's, for unusual integrity. Corruption is also difficult to assess because no fine line distinguishes it from legitimate politics. Most corruption comes not from blatantly taking money out of public coffers but from peddling influence. Awarding public contracts to firms in which one has a personal interest is a typical method.

As we saw in Chapter 3, one factor contributing to corruption is that political actors need flexibility to see their demands gratified within an otherwise rigid bureaucracy. Another factor is the relatively small number of trained, professional civil servants, as opposed to political appointees. Yet another is the inadequate salary provided for many bureaucrats. Meanwhile, junior executives in many private firms enjoy salaries far greater than those of their government counterparts; to curb corruption among the latter could accelerate in some cases a brain drain from the public to the private sector. Of course, the expectation of corrupt income can then become a rationale for inadequate salaries. Besides, there is always sheer greed. Whatever the causes of corruption, the personalistic nature of Mexican politics promotes it, and once corruption pervades a system, it feeds on itself. In fact, while we focus here on government corruption, corruption pervades much of business, labor, media, and other realms.

Mexicans hold varied opinions about official corruption. Some will not begrudge one ex-president his houses in Acapulco, Cuernavaca, indeed "everywhere," because "at least he invests in Mexico," whereas another ex-president is berated for investing most of his profits outside Mexico. Some Mexicans excuse officials who steal if, at least, they also "do things" for the nation. Yet concern over corruption is rising. Police corruption, for example, is a source of great public displeasure. Vivid novels and exposés on this subject have become bestsellers.

It is against such a background that we can evaluate recent efforts to curb official corruption. López Portillo's declared attack on corruption was hardly the first to be publicized and to raise hopes. In fact, a few important officials were disciplined. But it is often unclear how much such ostensible attacks on corruption involve mere political jockeying. The arrest of Echeverría's last minister of agrarian reform was widely seen as a slap at the ex-president. (For another example, the right has often denounced bureaucratic corruption in order to discredit the public sector in general.) In any case, revelations about the unusual degree of corruption under and by López Portillo himself contributed to both public outrage and public cynicism. Partly because of that public reaction and how it appeared to increase the political costs of corruption, and partly because of personal conviction, de la Madrid then committed himself more resolutely than any predecessor to a program of "moral renovation." Many saw this as a real test case of whether corruption could be curbed.

At first, more hope than usual accompanied sober skepticism. The president invested his own prestige heavily on this issue and brought to office a reputation for integrity and comparatively few political debts to interest groups. Proclamations were issued concerning the public statement of salaries and punishment for nepotism and conflicts of interest. Enforcement offices were revamped. Mexico City's ex-police chief was extradited for trial in Mexico following eighteen months of imprisonment in the United States; his mansion was confiscated and opened as a museum, and the ex-head of PEMEX was imprisoned. Moreover, the assault was not limited to government workers; for example, de la Madrid pressured newspapers to take certain specific measures against the corruption that pervades their practices. Before long, however, the obstacles to change appeared. Immunity was tacitly granted to many. The attack on rampant corruption in the oil union was limited because the nation relies too heavily on oil production; political sensitivity also played a role in avoiding confrontations with the teachers union and the army. López Portillo and most of his allegedly guilty associates were not tried. De la Madrid found himself emphasizing the need to avoid a climate of terror or prosecution of anyone in the absence of full legal proof. Skeptics observed that investigations did not extend to officials in de la Madrid's administration. In addition to other factors, the economic crisis hampered the anticorruption drive by making it increasingly difficult for employers (like newspaper owners) to pay adequate wages or for government to run the political risks inherent in bold action.

Even if it proved technically feasible, diminishing Mexico's widespread corruption could actually undermine political stability. Many aspirants to political office now peacefully await their turn at corruption as well as power. Leaders who have taken care of themselves are more likely to leave office satisfied than to plot comebacks. And corruption decreases the chances of serious attempts at radical policy change insofar as political leaders have to work their way up by playing skillfully within the system as it is. If everyone is hostage, no one can rock the boat with impunity. In short, although the political costs of corruption in terms of public alienation and of delegitimation are great, the political costs of a relentless drive to curb corruption could be greater.

System Renewal and Policy Change

As leadership change promotes stability by offering opportunities to aspiring elites, it also promotes stability by providing hope for policy change to the nation as a whole. As one observer put it: "We Mexicans are given to live on hope, since we lack a good reality."[30] Sexennial change appears so dramatic that it offers new promise, partly by blaming present woes on the *last* leaders. Of course, continually frustrated hopes frequently turn to cynicism, but leadership change does promote system renewal.

Echeverría could disassociate himself from Díaz Ordaz's repression, even though he had been his right-hand man as interior minister. López Portillo was Echeverría's last finance secretary, but that did not stop him, as president, from disassociating himself from his former boss's economic policies. More important, Echeverría himself helped out, intentionally or not, by devaluing the peso before leaving office, thus saving the incoming president a politically onerous but necessary task. President-designate López Portillo lost no time making it clear that the consequences of devaluation were Echeverría's responsibility. He could subsequently justify conservative presidential policies as necessary to put the house back in order. The idea was that irresponsibility and inefficiency had left Mexico in a position in which major reform or even salary maintenance was impossible. Disassociation from his predecessor also let the new president wipe the slate clean and court key groups alienated by Echeverría. One of López Portillo's early actions was to meet, dine, and be photographed with the Monterrey Group in order to reassure the business community and, in turn, to secure its pledge to invest heavily during the ensuing years. The changeover itself seemed to revitalize a shaky Mexico. The peso began to recover, peasants in various parts of the country agreed to postpone disruptive actions, and industrial and agricultural producers, like foreign investors, were reassured and reassuring.[31] The new president would have his honeymoon period. Without the prospect of *institutionalized renewal*, the Mexican political system might have had more difficulty surviving the crises of Echeverría's tenure.

Another severe test of the ability of sexennial change to revitalize the system came with the 1982 López Portillo–de la Madrid transition amid renewed economic crisis. The fact that so many politically unpleasant responses (e.g., repeated devaluations and cuts in subsidies to consumers) to the economic crisis were made while López Portillo was still president would help de la Madrid to assume office in December 1982 without having to initiate those decisions. As López Portillo did with the economic crisis of 1976, de la Madrid could defend further unpleasant policies as necessary to combat an inherited crisis. Despite his position as head of the important Programming and Budget Ministry under López Portillo, President de la Madrid emerged as a new leader upon whom not only Mexicans but foreign investors and governments could place rejuvenated hopes. Even more than in 1976, a new president would emerge as a responsible alternative to a predecessor's perceived demagoguery.

But more than just hope or symbolism is involved. Renewal may encompass real policy changes. There is even a "pendulum" theory that sexennial politics involves swings between left and right, giving each side a chance. Outgoing presidents restrain themselves, or are restrained by others, from appointing like-minded successors, instead fulfilling an unwritten obligation to system renewal and stability.[32] The theory has some validity, but it has been exaggerated and appears to be decreasingly pertinent for recent sexenios. Policy variation has occurred from the left to the right only *within the establishment*, not over the entire political spectrum.[33] Nor has the pendulum swung each time from one extreme to the other even within establishment limits. Another pendulum theory postulates swings between activists and consolidators. After activists shake things up a bit, consolidators placate consequently alienated groups, insuring that political change will not endanger system stability.[34] Of course, this pendulum theory does not rule out incidents of ideological policy change.

Whatever its contours, policy change across administrations probably has less to do with a president's personal inclinations than with the system's needs. Labor Minister López Mateos had earned a reputation for liberalism and compromise, but President López Mateos, concerned over increased unrest, repressed labor. Minister Echeverría earned his reputation as a hard-liner tolerating little dissent, but President Echeverría, seeing the system's legitimacy in question after 1968, was relatively tolerant. Policy also changes within administrations because of similar factors. The Echeverría adminis-tration, by necessity at least as much as choice, pushed less actively for reform during the second half of its tenure than it had during the first. Thus, a new president's personal political background does not necessarily presage his policies, and even when outgoing presidents (e.g., Díaz Ordaz) try to choose like-minded successors (e.g., Echeverría), policies may change significantly. In this light, President de la Madrid's policies did not result from a simple pendulum swing away from, or from simple continuity with, his predecessor. For one thing, López Portillo did not leave office with the conservative pro-business credentials he had built in the first half of his tenure; instead, he zealously supported Nicaragua's Sandinistas, denounced the policies of the Salvadorean and U.S. governments, nationalized Mexico's private banks, and presided over a general economic collapse. In any case, a formidable pendulum swing might have seen de la Madrid emphasizing an attack on the deleterious social problems plaguing Mexico's masses. But de la Madrid's policies were dictated principally by a perceived need to reverse the economic decline and regain the confidence of domestic and foreign businesses. So much was this the case that de la Madrid could not even begin his sexenio, as most presidents like to do, by augmenting expenditures that finance popular initiatives; his lot was austerity.

Policy change across and within sexenios is limited by the system's subordination of policy to personnel politics. Leadership change is so extensive that many officeholders are inexperienced. It often takes some time before new administrations get under way. Additionally, incumbent "lame ducks" often lose some power in some areas during their last year in office, once everyone knows who the next president will be. Thus, analysts often see sexenios divided roughly into two consolidation years followed by but two key policy years and then two transition years.[35] On the other hand, an outgoing executive may feel free of interest-group pressures and take bold actions. In 1982, López Portillo devalued the peso, as Echeverría had done in his last year in office. In fact, it is frequently difficult to determine the point at which the president-elect may become more powerful than the incumbent, or how much is decided through consultation. For example, considerable speculation surrounded de la Madrid's role in the September 1982 bank nationalization decision, forcefully proclaimed by President López Portillo. To address the lame-duck issue, Mexico has recently cut the time period between the presidential election and the actual assumption of office, but incumbents are weakened long before the elections themselves are held.

Whatever the degree of power transfer prior to the official end of any presidential term, power surely passes from individual to individual, sooner or later. The point is that, on the whole, the political compromises on which the system rests simultaneously maximize the extent of personnel change and may limit the extent or impact of policy initiative and change.

Personnel and Policy Compromises

That personnel change is more extensive than policy change does not necessarily mean that it is more important to political stability; scholars have debated the relative importance of compromises based on shared opportunities and compromises based on issues. In fact, however, these are not mutually exclusive possibilities, and leadership change is designed to bring some policy change. Even so, the politics of leadership change demand that policy considerations be carefully circumscribed. *Personnel coalesce and advance mostly on nonpolicy criteria. Camarillas* are crucial. These are cliques built around central political figures, *not* policies. Members must pledge their first loyalty to the leader, not to whatever ideology they themselves may hold.

Loyalty provides organizational glue, and for good reason: Most political officeholders, even at lower levels, owe their jobs to someone. An individual's mobility depends on his camarilla. Here then is a critical link to the issue of elite circulation. One maintains loyalty to his camarilla and waits for it to get its chance. If the leader moves up, the group is likely to go with him. Camarillas clearly are based on hierarchy, on vertical relationships. An *Agachados* cartoon (October 29, 1975) depicts a puzzled peasant asking his impoverished friend why he personally congratulated López Portillo on his selection as PRI candidate, when the friend did not even know him. "Well, so he'd throw me a bone and in a year I'd stop being poor." Personal connections are important in politics almost anywhere; they are especially important in Mexico.[36]

Mobility is based on skillful bargaining and exchanging favors. It is not based on genuine and popular public policy records. Such appeals might in fact brand the politician as unreliable. The significance of personnel bargaining has even led to a reassessment of the traditional view that Mexican stability is based on strong institutions.[37] On the other hand, personnel mobility occurs within a well-developed set of structures and rules, and one does not get to the top in politics through uninstitutionalized routes. Suffice it to say here that Mexico's stability is based partly on institutions that facilitate the compromises, concerning policy and especially personnel, on which stability surely rests.

The Rise of the Technocrats

Too little attention in this book's first edition was given to a political change that, at least according to some observers, could itself alter some of the tenets of change just discussed. This is the growing influence of technocrats, or *técnicos*—those with specialized educational credentials that ostensibly equip them with skills for solving or managing problems on the basis of rationally efficient or apolitical criteria. The rise of the técnicos comes at the expense of traditionally trained *políticos*, or "politicians"— those whose experience is in electoral and partisan arenas and in bargaining and social intercourse. Both groups have increasingly been receiving advanced education, but the técnicos come even more disproportionately from Mexico's privileged classes and private universities, especially from graduate schools (predominantly in the United States). If the trademark field of study for the políticos has been law, for the técnicos it is economics (or a related administrative field).

Of course, the político to técnico shift is a matter of degree. Policymaking técnicos, for example, are necessarily politicians, but characteristics of political change that could be altered by the shift include the emphasis on long training in which one comes up through the political system, the distinctiveness of political and economic elites, and the centrality of cliques and of personal over programmatic politics. Overall we might see a movement away from some of the subtle and perhaps unique underpinnings of Mexican politics. Additionally, some observers are concerned about what they see as negative and dangerous consequences.[38] Among the concerns of these observers are that foreign models may be substituted for more suitably Mexican approaches; political mobility for the lower middle class may be restricted; técnicos may be less sensitive to mass needs and politics or at least may be less able to bargain with (manipulate?) groups such as labor and the peasantry; the role of the quintessentially political and once more influential PRI may continue to weaken; and the political system may lose much of its legitimacy as it loses much of its ability to rally electoral and popular support.

The de la Madrid administration represented an acceleration of a technocratic trend in evidence in previous sexenios. Fully 44 percent of the political elite under de la Madrid did graduate work abroad, and only one member of the cabinet had ever held elective office. Almost no one had either party or state or local political experience, whereas many had impressive backgrounds in finance and banking. The president himself had earned his master's degree in public administration at Harvard University and had then served in the Treasury Ministry and the Bank of Mexico before heading the Ministry of Programming and Budget. Like his two immediate predecessors, de la Madrid had never held elective office; in contrast, Díaz Ordaz and López Mateos had been senators, and Ruiz Cortines and Miguel Alemán had been governors.

The designation of de la Madrid evoked pained responses from labor and the PRI. For many, President de la Madrid has justified their fears. Although it can be argued that any Mexican president in the 1980s would have had to impose great austerity on the Mexican people, de la Madrid went far with "rationalization," chose to blame populist politics for many of Mexico's problems, and prescribed "scientific" solutions. Moreover, his tenure saw an increased penetration of técnicos beyond their established strongholds, such as the ones from which he himself emerged, into the PRI as well as elective offices. As we saw in Chapter 3, his concern over the PRI's slide did not preclude his weakening it and pushing its power more toward its centralized core, which was increasingly penetrated by técnicos, and away from the PRI's popular sectors (labor and the peasantry).[39] A perhaps more poignant manifestation of the president's approach to politics came in the aftermath of the 1985 earthquakes. As suggested earlier, many felt that de la Madrid was too reluctant to engage in the political mingling and symbolism necessary to rally a nation in distress.

But we should be careful not to exaggerate the impact of the move toward técnicos. If de la Madrid was a pragmatic manager, both Echeverría and López Portillo earned their reputations for demagoguery. Técnicos cannot be peremptorily dismissed as politically naive or unconcerned; on the other hand, a político can demonstrate a horrendous and tragic lack of political skills, as Díaz Ordaz did in 1968. Nor can técnicos be counted on for the positive impacts sometimes expected of them. López Portillo headed a strikingly corrupt administration; moreover, the técnicos have presided over a severe economic crisis. In fact, de la Madrid recognized at least some of the dangers of an excessive político-técnico imbalance and took some ameliorative steps. For example, bureaucrats were pressured to support the PRI actively. But such steps met with resistance. In sum, the technocratic surge has been significant in degree and probably in impact, but that impact remains difficult to identify precisely; we cannot know how government would act were it differently constituted.

PLURALISM AND AUTHORITARIANISM

The Mexican political system has been extraordinarily stable. There is no serious disagreement about that. But whether that stability has coexisted with democracy or with authoritarianism has been hotly debated. Less provocatively and more profitably put, the issue is really a matter of degree. Prior to the late 1960s, most major works emphasized the system's democratic inclinations. If Mexico was not yet democratic, it was evolving in that direction. Subsequent works, however, began to depict ostensibly democratic inclinations as but the trappings of a fundamentally authoritarian system. A different interpretation now seems appropriate. It rejects some important tenets of the authoritarian interpretation while affirming that it has come much closer to the mark than has the democratic interpretation.[40]

The Mexican political system is not democratic insofar as leadership change is not effected through a free, competitive process, and this, if we use but two categories, makes it authoritarian. But we have seen that great differences in political freedoms exist among nondemocracies. Variation is necessarily great in a category that encompasses most of the world's systems. Only Colombia, Costa Rica, and Venezuela, among the twenty republics of Latin America (excluding most of the Caribbean), might reasonably be said to have fit in the democratic more than in the authoritarian category for most of the 1970s, although the 1980s brought redemocratization to most of Latin America. All authoritarian systems place limits on pluralism, participation, and mobilization, but they differ significantly in the extent of these limits. Moreover, they differ significantly in terms of repressiveness, human rights and freedoms, political equality, political mobility, civilian-military balances—in short, on most important aspects of politics. Even in the electoral process, where the authoritarian label for Mexico has been much more apt, reforms have offered increased competition and choice.

Recognizing the breadth and consequent imprecision of the authoritarian category, scholars tied Mexico to the mode of authoritarianism found in most of Latin America's relatively developed nations. A key feature of this authoritarianism is the regime's ability to dictate its will regardless of, or even against, the will of once powerful political groups.[41] With that goes the political exclusion of many groups and the widespread and intense repression of their political freedoms.[42] Another feature is extended rule (usually military) with little or no provision for regular changes of political leadership.

Fortunately, however, the tendency to overidentify Mexico with such authoritarianism has waned.[43] The previously cited distinction between "state" and "regime" is helpful here. State "pacts of domination" favoring capitalist-dependent development and benefiting the upper bourgeoisie and industrial and urban interests—to the detriment of popular (especially rural) interests—may not be that different in Mexico, Chile, and Venezuela; nonetheless, the political regimes are fundamentally different. While those who see "who gets what" as the core of politics may emphasize fundamental similarities among states, those who also care about degrees of political freedom, human rights, participation, inclusiveness, civilian rule, regularized political change, and blatant repression may emphasize fundamental differences among regimes. The Mexican state has more in common with the Chilean and Venezuelan states than the Mexican regime has with their regimes.

Furthermore, the literature on authoritarian regimes, particularly on Mexico, has increasingly stressed the significant contradictions, tugs of conflicting goals and interests, and intrabureaucratic struggles within ruling coalitions. For the Mexican case, a "postauthoritarian" literature is now emerging that emphasizes these contradictions and shows how they link up with and affect societal groups, even though these groups cannot engage in an open democratic debate to determine policy. Documentation of these contradictions has been produced for educational, housing, family planning, and environmental policy.[44] Struggles between technocrats and politicians frequently figure into this picture.

Just as the breadth of the term "authoritarian" poses analytical problems, so does the restrictiveness of the term "democracy." Granted that Mexico is not democratic, one relevant question becomes the extent to which it is "pluralist."[45] Pluralist systems may or may not be democratic, but they require distribution of power and freedom of political action beyond central government officials. Pluralist policymaking and leadership selection depend largely on the demands and interests of various groups, on bargaining and conciliation among them.

Although no single, simple characterization of Mexican politics emerges, our analysis of political freedom, political equality, and political change suggests mixed and variable patterns of authoritarianism and pluralism. It also shows how the Mexican political system has struck its own balances, neither typically authoritarian nor pluralist, in reconciling stability with freedom, equality, and change. Thus, this chapter concludes by summarizing the relevance of authoritarianism and pluralism to these three political dimensions.

There is a complex, subtle, variable, and imperfectly defined degree of *political freedom* in Mexico. Imprecision stems not just from the difficulty of figuring out where the dividing line between freedom and repression lies. It stems also from actual variability. Two similar challenges may evoke two different responses. Some independent newspapers or squatter settlements or demonstrations may be repressed while equally independent ones may be tolerated. It is presumptuous to interpret specific cases of repression or tolerance as proof that either always occurs under certain given circumstances. All we can establish are probabilities and patterns. Thus we have considered variables such as individual expression versus organizational activity, the nature and source of criticisms, the size and composition of the participating groups, the specific issues involved, the posture of given national and state administrations, and the political-technical interface. The individual versus organizational dimension has received the greatest attention. Comparisons of freedoms with major (e.g., electoral), limited (e.g., religious), and intermediate (e.g., media) organizational bases show respectively limited, major, and intermediate ranges of freedom. To formulate the issue as a rational calculation: The regime permits freedom and dissent up to the point at which tolerance causes it less trouble than repression, and that point is different for different freedoms. Moreover, different officials see different dividing points. Of course, judgments are not always rational, let alone precise. Personalities and emotions make the picture less predictable.

Political freedom in Mexico clearly falls short of pluralism, let alone democracy, because of severe restrictions on organizational freedoms. But most personal freedoms are not simply tolerated; they fall logically within a system that is as "open" as it is "closed." Compared to most recent authoritarian systems in Latin America, Mexico allows more latitude even for organizationally oriented freedoms, but especially for individually oriented freedoms.

The Mexican regime obviously runs the risk that the considerable freedom and dissent it allows may undermine its stability. Thus, it responds in repressively authoritarian kind when it perceives itself threatened. That it does not feel threatened by many freedoms, however, means that it need not maintain ceaseless vigil or repression to maintain stability. It does not incur the costs of repression for the dissent that does not really pose an organizational alternative. Furthermore, Mexican freedoms have actually buttressed stability by enhancing the regime's image, legitimacy, and support base.

In terms of *political equality*, both freedom and power vary notably according to socioeconomic status. The personal freedoms cited above are exercised far more in privileged than in humble Mexico, whereas restrictions on independent organization apply far more to humble than to privileged Mexico. Pluralism better than authoritarianism characterizes the political subsystem for privileged Mexico. The regime may respond to and bargain with elite interest groups as much as it molds or controls them. Or it refrains from making policy that would offend powerful interests; that is, it makes "nondecisions." Examples include not imposing tougher taxes on business and not imposing tuition at the public universities. The regime is not an omnipotent or a unified center of power or policy initiative, and it does not select or control the leadership of privileged groups. Indeed, these groups are relatively autonomous of the government. In sum, plural centers of power exist.

Authoritarianism better characterizes the political subsystem for less privileged Mexico. The regime generally initiates policy, bringing affected groups into the policy process mostly for legitimizing support. Nondecisions in this subsystem usually concern issues on which potentially affected groups might like to see action but on which the regime prefers not to act; examples would include a much stronger government role in economic production and a radical reorganization of rural opportunities. Leaders of the less privileged groups are tied more to the regime, less to their constituencies. Of course, important qualifications could properly be made for both the pluralist and authoritarian subsystem characterizations, but far fewer than if either characterization were generalized to the system as a whole.

Surely, continual discrimination against the less privileged, especially as relative deprivation increases, poses a threat to political stability. Nonetheless, for decades that threat has not materialized. In fact, the discrimination, whatever else one thinks of it, may have promoted stability. Because the system assumes only a minimal burden for the less privileged, resources are left for the privileged, who are not constrained to share either their political power or economic well-being. And whatever the threat of popular revolution by less privileged groups, Latin American regimes more often fall to revolts inspired by privileged groups—often fearing the rise of those less privileged groups that, in Mexico, are kept in place. If Mexican business, for example, had less power within the system than it does, it might well oppose the system more strongly. Furthermore, by satisfying the demands of more privileged Mexico, the regime generally needs to incur the costs of repression only in dealing with less privileged Mexico, where, almost by definition, the costs are usually lower.

That *political change* is carefully and secretively controlled by a small elite mocks not only democratic but also pluralist criteria. Groups do not bargain openly over policies and candidates. Yet neither does political change follow patterns typical of authoritarian Latin America. It involves more contact with the populace, even if elections ratify more than they determine. More important, group interests and even demands are taken into account in changing both personnel and policy. Mexico's process is more regularized, yet more flexible. It is a civilian, not a military process, and it systematically allows for more personnel and even policy change. Turnover is not only greater but also smoother than it is in most authoritarian systems.[46]

Mexico has found its own solution for reconciling political change with political stability. Pluralist democracies generally meet this challenge through regular, competitive elections, based at least partly on public policy issues. Dictatorships generally have more difficulty with leadership changes. This applies not only to the Third World; communist systems too have notorious problems with orderly succession. Latin America has long suffered from continuismo and from instability, and many of the region's recent military governments have tried to forestall instability by proclaiming their intentions of ruling unchallenged for long terms. These intentions have been backed by force, often leaving few opportunities for peaceful policy change through leadership change.

In contrast, political change in Mexico has promoted political stability. Orderly rules have become institutionalized. There is little room for disruptive conflict over the timing of leadership change or for challenges by incumbents to the new leadership's policymaking authority. Regular and extensive turnover provides widespread opportunities for power and wealth, encouraging ambitious Mexicans to compete peacefully *within* the system. The system, in turn, can purge itself peacefully of the potentially destabilizing excesses born of leaders' unlimited tenure. Leadership change provides a fresh start, partly by supplying scapegoats for ongoing policy problems. It also provides real opportunities for policy adjustments based on the system's varying needs—relatively unburdened by accountability to the populace according to *its* perception of needs. Symbolic and psychological as well as policy renewal are thus provided within the system. Yet the potentially volatile politics of policy are subordinated to the carefully monitored politics of personnel. By restricting the role of policy choice, openness, and public accountability in leadership change, the system protects itself against victory from within by any proponent of radical policy changes in the system. The system has not, therefore, fallen under leadership that would promulgate policies considered populist, leftist, irrational, or irresponsible enough either to change the system fundamentally or to provoke a harshly authoritarian backlash takeover to prevent such change. Eschewing a truly pluralist process, the regime has also avoided the politics that sometimes help produce political regimes far more authoritarian than Mexico's.

So to call Mexico's political system authoritarian is accurate, but only in such a broad and vague way as to risk misleading characterizations. The same could be said of a pluralist identification. Extensive pluralist freedoms coexist with significant authoritarian restrictions in more sensitive areas. Pluralist dispersion of power in a subsystem for more privileged Mexico coexists with authoritarian concentration of regime power in a subsystem for less privileged Mexico. Pluralist compromises in effecting political leadership and policy change coexist with authoritarian denial of public influence and accountability. The Mexican political system is neither authoritarian nor pluralist—largely because it is some of both.

The very complexity of Mexico's hybrid authoritarian-pluralist political system, defying any single inclusive characterization, has a good deal to do with its extraordinary stability.[47] Stability is based on neither authoritarianism nor pluralism alone. Nor is it even fundamentally based on authoritarianism, allowing for mere pluralist trappings or marginal features, or on pluralism, allowing for authoritarian imperfections. It misses the mark to say that Mexico's political stability has been achieved *despite* significant political freedom and dissent or despite repression, despite the relative autonomy and power of privileged groups or despite political inequality, despite extensive leadership change or despite the limited scope of policy change. All these factors, and the complex interplay among them, have in some identifiable ways actually promoted stability.

NOTES

1. Two multi-volume works offer useful comparative insights into democracy, its definition, and the factors that favor its existence. Each of the two includes a

volume on Latin America that in turn includes a chapter on Mexico. See Guillermo O'Donnell, Philippe C. Schmitter, and Laurence Whitehead, eds., *Transitions from Authoritarian Rule* (Baltimore, Md.: Johns Hopkins University Press, 1986); and Larry Diamond, Juan Linz, and Seymour Martin Lipset, eds., *Democracy in Developing Countries* (Boulder, Colo.: Lynne Rienner Publishers, forthcoming).

2. Daniel Cosío Villegas, *American Extremes,* trans. Américo Paredes (Austin: University of Texas Press, 1964), p. 93.

3. Alan Riding, *Distant Neighbors: Portrait of the Mexicans* (New York: Knopf, 1985), p. 69.

4. Our account draws on Miguel Angel Granados Chapa, "La democracia en la calle," *Razones* (September-October 1980):10–12, and the editorial in the same issue.

5. For further sources and thoughts on the media and politics, see Daniel Levy, "The Political Consequences of Changing Socialization Patterns," in *Mexico's Political Stability: The Next Five Years,* ed. Roderic A. Camp (Boulder, Colo.: Westview Press, 1986), pp. 27–33. See also Roderic A. Camp, *Intellectuals and the State in Twentieth-Century Mexico* (Austin: University of Texas Press, 1985), pp. 177–207. For a comparative view see Marvin Alisky, *Latin American Media: Guidance and Censorship* (Ames: Iowa State University Press, 1981).

6. Charles Tatum, "Rius: Comic Book Writer as Social Critic and Political Gadfly," paper presented at the Sixth Conference of Mexican and U.S. Historians, Chicago, September 1981.

7. This is the distinction elaborated by Fernando Henrique Cardoso, "On the Characterization of Authoritarian Regimes in Latin America," in *The New Authoritarianism in Latin America,* ed. David Collier (Princeton, N.J.: Princeton University Press, 1979), pp. 33–57.

8. Kenneth F. Johnson, *Mexican Democracy: A Critical View,* rev. ed. (New York: Praeger Publishers, 1978), pp. 156–171. A recent study of press freedom has ranked Mexico in the top four (in both 1970 and 1975) among twenty Latin American republics. Kim Quaile Hill and Patricia A. Hurley, "Freedom of the Press in Latin America: A Thirty-Year Survey," *Latin American Research Review* 15, no. 2 (1980): 212–218.

9. Our account of the *ABC* episode is based mostly on Carlos Monsiváis, "El ABC de Tijuana," *Proceso,* no. 164, December 24, 1979.

10. It is difficult to be sure about all the details in a sensitive case involving conflicting claims and considerable maneuvering and secrecy, but our principal sources are good ones, supported by our numerous conversations with other involved parties. The principal sources are Armando Vargas, "Coup at Excélsior," *Columbia Journalism Review* 15, no. 3 (1967):45–48; Vicente Leñero, *Los periodistas* (Mexico City: Editorial Joaquín Mortiz, 1978); Alan Riding, "Mexico: Reinstating Editor Ousted by Former Regime," *New York Times,* May 14, 1977; other Riding articles in the *Times* and written correspondence with Riding, winter 1980; "Mexico: The Right to Edit a Paper," *Latin American Political Report* 10, no. 29 (1976):2229–2231. Our analysis focuses on the regime-*Excélsior* confrontation. As we mentioned, however, a private sector-*Excélsior* confrontation also occurred, starting before the regime itself attacked *Excélsior.* The role of U.S. subsidiaries in Mexico was especially noteworthy. For this aspect of the *Excélsior* case see Angela M. Delli Sante, "The Private Sector, Business Organizations, and International Influence: A Case Study of Mexico," in *Capitalism and the State in U.S.-Latin American Relations,* ed. Richard R. Fagen (Stanford, Calif.: Stanford University Press, 1979), pp. 370–377.

11. Johnson, *Mexican Democracy,* p. 54.

12. Other officials, like governors, are sometimes directly criticized. Moreover, presidents have been vilified immediately upon leaving office, and Echeverría and López Portillo became targets even prior to exiting. To his credit, President de la Madrid widened the latitude on permitted criticism of incumbents, although immunity remained the norm; thus, for example, labor generally criticized the government rather than de la Madrid himself for Mexico's austerity policies. Overall, however, the aura surrounding the presidency is not what it once was. And whatever the restrictions on criticisms through formal channels, de la Madrid was heckled in public by disillusioned citizens.

13. López Portillo, inevitably concerned with criticisms of his conservatism, reacted angrily when some journalists seized the 1979 midpoint in his administration as an opportunity to give midterm report cards. Although virtually all gave high marks on many counts, some hinted very strongly that his administration was rightist. "Unfair: I am not moving to the right," headlines featured the president's denial. "It offends my consciousness as a committed Mexican revolutionary to argue that I protect businessmen and therefore that I lean toward the right."

14. *Excélsior* subsequently recovered some of its independent standing.

15. Quoted in Leñero, *Los periodistas*, p. 232.

16. We draw the quote and details from Alan Riding, "Mexico, Crushing a Maverick," *New York Times*, March 19, 1981.

17. Rose J. Spalding, "State Power and Its Limits: Corporatism in Mexico," *Comparative Political Studies* 14, no. 2 (1981):149, 150–151. For further reading on bureaucrats, see the work of Merilee Grindle and Roderic Camp. For example, Grindle's "Power, Expertise and the 'Técnico': Suggestions from a Mexican Case Study," *Journal of Politics* 39, no. 2 (1977):399–426; and Camp's "The Middle-Level Technocrat in Mexico," *Journal of Developing Areas* 6, no. 4 (July 1972):571–582.

18. The summary of university, student, and middle-class power draws on Daniel Levy, *University and Government in Mexico: Autonomy in an Authoritarian System* (New York: Praeger Publishers, 1980), pp. 16–17, 43–63, 138–154. The summary refers to the public university; the private university's autonomy from the Mexican state is clearer. See Daniel Levy, *Higher Education and the State in Latin America: Private Challenges to Public Dominance* (Chicago: University of Chicago Press, 1986), pp. 114–170.

19. Lorenzo Meyer, "Historical Roots of the Authoritarian State in Mexico," in *Authoritarianism in Mexico*, ed. José Luis Reyna and Richard Weinert (Philadelphia, Pa.: Institute for the Study of Human Issues, 1977), p. 8.

20. See, for example, Charles E. Lindblom, *Politics and Markets* (New York: Basic Books, 1977), pp. 170–188. Specifically on Mexico, see, for example, Robert Shafer, *Mexican Business Organizations* (Syracuse, N.Y.: Syracuse University Press, 1973); and, especially, Dale Story, *Industry, the State, and Public Policy in Mexico* (Austin: University of Texas Press, 1986), pp. 79–105, including an analysis of the kinds of policy issues on which business is especially powerful.

21. Robert Shafer and Donald Mabry conclude that business is relatively weaker in Mexico than in the United States in political terms: see *Neighbors—Mexico and the United States: Wetbacks and Oil* (Chicago: Nelson-Hall, 1981).

22. Dale Story, "Entrepreneurs and the State in Mexico: Examining the Authoritarian Thesis," Technical Papers Series no. 30 (Austin: Institute of Latin American Studies, University of Texas, 1980), p. 2 and passim. Also see Susan Kaufman Purcell's account of how regime autonomy and business privilege sometimes blend, "Business-Government Relations in Mexico: The Case of the Sugar Industry," *Comparative Politics* 13, no. 2 (1981):211–232. On the other hand, for an analysis of how

the state developed relative autonomy from business, see Hamilton, *The Limits of State Autonomy: Post-Revolutionary Mexico* (Princeton, N.J.: Princeton University Press, 1982).

23. Larissa Lomnitz has shown how many of the urban poor or "marginals" (urban "hunters and gatherers"), by offering cheap and ready labor, may actually buttress the position of privileged Mexico. *Networks and Marginality: Life in a Mexican Shantytown* (New York: Academic Press, 1977), p. 208 and passim.

24. Quoted in Ignacio Ramírez, "No me lancé por amor," *Proceso*, no. 163, December 17, 1979.

25. Daniel Cosío Villegas, *La sucesión presidencial: Desenlace y perspectivas* (Mexico City: Cuadernos de Joaquín Mortiz, 1975), pp. 9–36.

26. The proscription of reelection is of interest primarily for political systems plagued by continuismo, but the idea of a single-term, six-year presidency has attracted considerable interest in the United States. Some presidents (e.g., Lyndon Johnson) have spoken in favor of it. Despite the dangers of diminished accountability, the hope is that the president could more often place the national interest above personal political interest. López Portillo himself was not bashful in recommending the Mexican model to others who might likewise look beyond petty politics to substantive policymaking and to history. "No recomiendo reformas," *Excélsior*, December 4, 1979. Yet Mexico may not serve as a good model of decisive, rational policymaking.

27. See Froylan M. López Narváez, "El retorno de Echeverría," *Proceso*, no. 163, December 17, 1979. Subsequently, Echeverría became more visible again, writing newspaper and magazine articles, and official spokesmen again reacted by saying that Echeverría had had his chance—and had not done too well with it.

28. Peter Smith, *The Labyrinths of Power: Political Recruitment in Twentieth Century Mexico* (Princeton, N.J.: Princeton University Press, 1979), p. 165. Roderic Camp has written extensively on political socialization, recruitment, and mobility in Mexico; see, for example, *Mexico's Leaders: Their Education and Recruitment* (Tucson: University of Arizona Press, 1980).

29. Smith, *Labyrinths of Power*, pp. 191–216. However much these routes to top positions have opened for men, they have not significantly opened for women. Women in high political office remain a decided rarity, notwithstanding the recent advances cited in Chapter 3.

30. Leopoldo Mendívil, "Lo malo es dejar de trabajar en el presente," *Impacto*, no. 1553 (1979):14.

31. The Echeverría–López Portillo renewal is usually discussed in terms of reassuring business, but the middle class, disturbed over inflation, urban deterioration, and Echeverría's brand of populism also needed reassurance.

32. The inability of outgoing presidents to influence their successors was captured twice over in a clever remark attributed to ex-president Díaz Ordaz, asked to give his opinion on outgoing President Echeverría: "He is more intelligent than I am; he knew how to choose his successor."

33. One account circulating before de la Madrid was nominated may be illustrative. It held that Díaz Ordaz solved the problem of public opposition but left a problem of political legitimacy, whereupon Echeverría solved the legitimacy problem but left an economic problem, whereupon López Portillo solved (sic) the economic problem but left a social problem; hence the next president would have to solve the social problem. The problem was that unlike the political crisis of 1968 or the economic crises of 1976 and the 1980s, the social crisis has been chronically characteristic of Mexican development. Also, measures to fight the 1980s economic crises aggravated the social crisis.

34. Susan Purcell and John F.H. Purcell, "State and Society in Mexico: Must a Stable Polity Be Institutionalized?" *World Politics* 32, no. 2 (1980):194–227. But it would be hard to classify any of the last three presidents as consolidators. Dale Story found quantitative evidence to dispute the ideological pendulum theory, despite qualitative evidence to sustain it: "Policy Cycles in Mexican Politics," *Latin American Research Review* 20, no. 3 (1985):139–161.

35. See, especially, John J. Bailey, *Governing Mexico, 1976–1988: The Statecraft of Crisis Management* (London: Macmillan, forthcoming). Most new leaders, given the personal more than policy base of allegiance and action, feel compelled to trumpet their own "new" policies. Thus personnel changes may stimulate policy *changes*, but they may also simply mean scuttling predecessors' policies and continually limiting the chances for effective, sustained policy, planning, and implementation. For two recent examples of these problems see Merilee Grindle, *Bureaucrats, Politicians and the Peasantry in Mexico* (Berkeley: University of California Press, 1977), pp. 166–175; and Miguel S. Wionczek, "On the Viability of a Policy for Science and Technology in Mexico," *Latin American Research Review* 16, no. 1 (1981):57–78. Note also de la Madrid's disassociation from his predecessor's SAM project, discussed in Chapter 5.

36. Smith, *Labyrinths of Power*, pp. 247–277, formulated twenty-two "rules of the game" for "making it" in Mexican politics, rules that emphasize personnel over policy concerns. Probably both the importance and obscurity of personnel politics are reflected in the special interest that the works of Camp and Smith have generated among Mexico's politicians and political observers. Furthermore, much of what we have said about personnel politics with regard to the presidency and national politics also applies to various other political arenas, from governorships to public university rectorships.

37. Purcell and Purcell, "State and Society," pp. 194–227.

38. See, for example, Roderic A. Camp, "The Political-Technocrat in Mexico and the Survival of the Political System," *Latin American Research Review* 20, no. 1 (1985):97–118; and Peter Smith, "Leadership and Change, Intellectuals and Technocrats," in Camp, *Mexico's Political Stability*, pp. 101–118.

39. For details, see John J. Bailey, "What Explains the Decline of the PRI and Will It Continue?" in Camp, *Mexico's Political Stability*, pp. 164–173. Steven Sanderson finds that de la Madrid's food program was run by técnicos from the Ministries of Finance and Programming and Budget whereas the Agrarian Reform Ministry and traditional agrarian political interests were bypassed. *The Transformation of Mexican Agriculture: International Structure and the Politics of Rural Change* (Princeton, N.J.: Princeton University Press, 1986), p. 283.

40. For a review essay on the major characterizations, see Lawrence E. Koslow and Stephen P. Murnane, "The Evolution of the Mexican Political System: A Paradigmatic Analysis," in *The Future of Mexico*, ed. Lawrence Koslow (Tempe: Arizona State University Press, 1979), pp. 47–98. Works that reject democratic evolutionary hypotheses while also emphasizing the limits on authoritarianism and regime power include John F.H. Purcell and Susan Kaufman Purcell, "El estado y la empresa privada," *Nueva Política* 1, no. 2 (1976):229–250; Spalding, "State Power"; Story, *Industry*; and Levy, *University and Government*. Also see Daniel Levy, "Comparing Authoritarian Regimes in Latin America: Insights from Higher Education Policy," *Comparative Politics* 14, no. 1 (1981):31–52. Reyna and Weinert's *Authoritarianism in Mexico* became perhaps the most prominently cited example of the authoritarian interpretation.

41. A major issue of scholarly debate has been the degree of presidential power in Mexico. Chapter 3 showed that presidential power is virtually unchallenged

within the government. Chapter 4 broadens the assessment by adding that presidential power can be no greater than government power, and therefore the president is not as nearly omnipotent as often portrayed; political and economic events during the de la Madrid administration appear to substantiate the point.

42. Our discussion, like most on Mexican authoritarianism, focuses mostly on repression by the government. Other forces, of various political persuasions, also restrict freedom in important instances. It may in fact be argued that political authority and stability are necessary, though insufficient, conditions for freedom.

43. See, for example, most of the references to Mexico in Collier's *New Authoritarianism*.

44. An analysis and sources will be found in a forthcoming book by Viviane Márquez.

45. Our definitional juxtaposition of authoritarianism and pluralism (or reconciliation) borrows from Levy, *University and Government*, pp. 8–13.

46. Smith, *Labyrinths of Power*, pp. 182–183.

47. Naturally we want to avoid automatically interpreting every feature found in a stable system as necessarily contributing to stability. For further books dealing broadly with the political system, see note 40; Roger D. Hansen, *The Politics of Mexican Development* (Baltimore, Md.: Johns Hopkins University Press, 1971); Johnson, *Mexican Democracy*; Susan Kaufman Purcell, *The Mexican Profit-Sharing Decision: Politics in an Authoritarian Regime* (Berkeley: University of California Press, 1975); Camp, *Mexico's Political Stability*; John J. Bailey, *Governing Mexico*.

5

Economic and Social Policy

Chapters 3 and especially 4 discussed the political stability that, at least until recently, has contributed to sustained economic growth. This chapter focuses on the other side of the relationship. The economic growth experienced during most of the last several decades has been highly instrumental in maintaining stability. It has promoted an alliance between the regime and key social groups favored by that process. It has benefited private business and the middle class mostly but has also touched sectors of the working classes. It has provided some opportunities for social mobility. In fact, stability has been maintained despite the limited numbers of people who have been able to take advantage of such opportunities. For example, Mexico has one of the world's most uneven profiles of income distribution. In that connection, this chapter also examines the social consequences of the growth model.

For decades Mexico achieved not only great economic growth but low inflation. The combination constituted something of a Latin American economic miracle, paralleling the longer-standing miracle of Mexico's political stability. But closer examination shows the economic record was mixed. As indicated, growth policies did not address the social problems of widespread poverty and terrible inequalities. Beyond this, economic growth was founded on certain bases that paradoxically contributed to severe economic crises in 1976 and especially in the 1980s. We try to analyze the economic successes in such a way as to help explain the social failures and to develop a context within which to understand the economic crises as well. At least in retrospect, then, we can see contemporary crises as rooted partly in past policies.

We turn first to the central features of the economic growth model from 1940 to 1970. Although Mexico began to consolidate its political stability in the decades prior to 1940, that year can be considered the starting point of Mexico's most spectacular period of sustained economic growth. There is wide agreement among experts on the Mexican economy that, throughout the ensuing three decades, the public sector was a major catalyst of economic activity.[1] In particular, the government provided basic infrastructure (e.g., roads and irrigation systems) and policy incentives (e.g., subsidies and protectionism) that have encouraged private investment and supported the growth process. Furthermore, several indicators presented

131

below (e.g., the public sector accounted until recently for about one-half of total capital formation) show a very important degree of public involvement in the economy. This situation is rather unusual for a capitalist economy, and it is worthwhile to analyze its development.

Mexico is one of many Latin American countries that adopted a strategy of import substitution industrialization (ISI) in the 1940s in order to pursue high rates of economic growth. Many of these countries previously had relied on exports of a few raw materials, using their export revenues to purchase all other products that they needed. The main objective of ISI has been gradually to replace imported products with goods produced locally. Entrepreneurs have been encouraged to concentrate their investments in order to fulfill that objective. The strategy worked well for many years, generating high rates of economic growth. Along with economic growth, however, several problems have emerged. These problems have concerned agricultural and industrial production, the disequilibria of public finances and of the external sector, and the distribution of new wealth in society. Such problems have not been properly dealt with and have therefore become important constraints on economic growth. The Echeverría and López Portillo administrations were faced with several of the problems associated with the pursuit of an ISI strategy; we analyze the manner in which their respective administrations attempted to handle those problems. In addition, we will focus on the economic policy of the de la Madrid administration, which represented a sharp break with those of his predecessors.

This chapter includes several tables with data on Mexico's economic performance from 1940 to 1985. We first use the tables in discussing the 1940 to 1970 period, and then, later in the chapter, we refer back to the same tables in discussing economic and social policy under Echeverría, López Portillo, and de la Madrid. One inescapable qualification is in order concerning the data. Acknowledging problems with the data's reliability, the Mexican government, in cooperation with several international organizations, has engaged in a continual effort to improve official records; we can claim only to try to analyze the best *available* data.

THE GROWTH MODEL, 1940-1970

The Mexican economy underwent a fundamental transformation in the period between 1940 and 1970, bringing about a number of no less dramatic changes in the nation's social structure. The average annual rate of growth for the whole period was more than 6 percent, which is comparable to that of only a handful of highly successful economies (e.g., postwar West Germany, Japan, Taiwan, and South Korea). In the process, Mexico turned into a semi-industrial country as people steadily migrated away from rural areas. Agriculture's contribution to total production diminished from 21 percent to 11 percent, while industry's contribution increased from 25 percent to 34 percent. Whereas two-thirds of the labor force was employed in agriculture in 1940, the figure dwindled to a little more than one-third by 1970.[2] Thus, many people moved to urban areas where they worked in industry and in the service sector. Mexico was an early industrializer in the Latin American context.

The engine of economic growth has been an industrialization strategy supported by various governmental policies and institutions. The creation of the Central Bank in 1925, the National Development Bank (NAFINSA) in 1934, and the nationalization of the railroads and the oil industry in the 1930s were all indications that political elites were committed to building a strong public sector that could play a crucial role in the economy. Government investment expanded the economy's infrastructure and productive capacity. The government also provided private investors with a series of incentives. Let us first analyze the objectives and targets of Mexican government investments.

Government Investments

The government has invested much of its resources to facilitate the movement of raw materials and goods throughout the country, thereby helping to integrate the national market. The building of roads, airports, railroads, and ports has improved transportation and communication (both important to the economy) between large and small towns. In addition, the government has invested heavily in agriculture and industry to promote the nation's productive capacity.

Gross fixed capital formation is a common measure of the national commitment to expand infrastructure and productive capacity. It tells us how much of the resources of the public and private sectors is invested to increase production facilities. In Mexico, capital formation increased steadily, representing only 8.2 percent of gross domestic product (GDP) in 1940 but 18.9 percent between 1965 and 1970. The latter compares well with ratios found in some of the most advanced industrial nations. Table 5.1 shows that the public sector has been very active in this respect, providing more than one-half of total capital formation during the initial years and an average of 40.5 percent during the 1940–1970 period overall. The public sector's share of capital formation fell from 56 to 42 percent during the Alemán administration (1946–1952). It then remained near the new level during most successive administrations. Therefore, this measure undercuts somewhat the view that, under President Alemán, public intervention in the economy was atypically low;[3] rather, Alemán reduced the public role to what would henceforth be the norm for decades.

Table 5.2 suggests certain tendencies regarding the functional distribution of public investment. Initially, a great proportion of resources was devoted to improving the communication and transportation systems; later, the level of these investments stabilized at about 20 percent of the total. This probably means that many of the facilities that had been built were not subsequently modernized. Problems have recently surfaced, revealing inadequate port, rail, and general transportation capacity. Furthermore, investments in agriculture were unusually high from 1947 to 1952 because

TABLE 5.1
Gross Fixed Capital Formation, 1941–1985 (in percentages)

Years	Average Share of Gross Domestic Product	Public Sector	Private Sector
1941–1946	8.2	55.5	44.5
1947–1952	13.7	42.1	57.9
1953–1958	17.2	31.6	68.4
1959–1964	16.4	38.9	61.1
1965–1970	18.9	34.3	65.7
1941–1970	14.9	40.5	59.5
1971–1976	20.5	37.5	62.5
1977–1982	23.1	44.5	55.5
1983	17.9	44.5	55.5
1984	18.9	39.5	60.5
1985	20.2	35.9	64.1

Sources: Banco de México, Producto interno bruto y gasto, 1970–1978 (Mexico City, 1979), pp. 43, 49; Nacional Financiera. Statistics on the Mexican Economy (Mexico City, 1977); and Banco de México, Informe anual 1985 (Mexico City, 1986), pp. 78, 79.

of the great efforts in irrigation. But then proportional investments in that sector were roughly halved for the duration of the period in question. This decreasing governmental effort has been one of several factors contributing to the agricultural output difficulties dealt with below.

Industry came to replace both communication/transportation and agriculture as the most favored recipient of public funds, taking 40 percent of investment resources from 1965 to 1970. This has reflected a special commitment to industrialization. The bulk of investments in industry has been aimed at securing the supply of various strategic products such as oil, electric power, and steel.

After years of relative neglect and stagnation, investments in the social sector (e.g., hospitals, schools) accounted for 25 percent of the total from 1959 to 1970. Finally, the low level of defense-related investments (referred to as "defense and administration" in Table 5.2), averaging only 2 percent between 1940 and 1970, supports our point that the external dimension of national security has not been a major concern to civilian leaders. Otherwise— as is the case in many Latin American nations—public investment for the military industry would have been much greater, putting additional pressure on the finances of the public sector.

Public Revenue Problems and
Incentives for the Private Sector

The public sector has been less and less able to finance its investments from its own resources. Starting in the early 1960s, it had to borrow

TABLE 5.2
Public Sector Investments by Economic Sector, 1941–1983

Year	Total (millions of current pesos)	Percentage of Total					
		Agriculture	Industry	Communications and Transport	Social	Defense and Administration	Unspecified[a]
1941–1946	4,309	15.7	10.2	51.6	12.9	1.8	7.8
1947–1952	14,090	22.0	18.9	40.2	13.3	0.2	5.4
1953–1958	29,673	13.0	30.2	36.3	14.3	3.0	3.2
1959–1964[b]	67,180	10.6	37.5	24.9	24.2	2.8	—
1965–1970	128,439	11.0	40.0	22.0	25.0	2.0	—
1941–1970	243,691	14.5	27.4	35.0	18.0	2.0	—
1971–1976	374,728	15.6	40.0	21.7	19.0	2.8	0.9
1977–1982	2,911,968	19.8 [c]	51.8	15.1	10.4	2.3	0.6
1983	1,365,427	19.1	48.3	21.1	7.8	2.8	0.9

aIn most cases this category refers to investments to expand tourist facilities.
bFigures were available for authorized rather than for actual investments during this period.
cBeginning in 1981, this figure includes investments for regional development programs.

Sources: For 1941 to 1964, Nacional Financiera, 50 años de la revolución mexicana en cifras (Mexico City, 1963), p. 133. For 1965 to 1976, Nacional Financiera, Statistics on the Mexican Economy (Mexico City, 1977), pp. 370–371. For 1977 to 1983, Banco de México, Informe anual (Mexico City, various issues).

increasingly from creditors (domestic and foreign), because its role in the economy expanded substantially while little was done to secure additional revenue.[4] To be sure, this has been a common problem in developing nations, and some efforts have been made in Mexico to increase the public sector's intake of available economic resources. For example, although the relation of public-sector income to gross domestic product remained stable (at about 10 to 12 percent) between 1940 and 1960, it increased significantly (to 19 percent) by 1970. However, such an increase was not enough to compensate for the growth of total public-sector expenditures, which rose at a faster pace. By 1970, the ratio of public-sector expenditures to gross domestic product had risen to 24 percent. And these trends have intensified since 1970.[5]

Why have officials done so little to prevent the deterioration of the public sector's financial position? For one thing (in addition to building a relatively adequate infrastructure), the government has showered private investors with policy incentives such as the provision of goods and services at substantially subsidized prices, a low level of taxation, and protection from foreign competitors. Such policies have involved high economic costs, borne by a relatively unremunerated public sector.

The government's generosity in providing these kinds of incentives very likely has reflected the general conception of Mexican society held by many politicians and their advisers. While they have encouraged the development of a strong public sector, a major objective has been *to support rather than to compete with private investors*. It is thus ironic that many private investors have been very critical of the government's role. Public enterprises are often accused of inefficiency and corruption, and the government is viewed as being responsible for the ills of the economy. More important, private investors fear that the government is becoming too involved in the economy at the expense of the private sector. The figures in Table 5.1 may lend some support to these fears, at least until de la Madrid's presidency. But the government has also gone a long way to facilitate capital accumulation in the private sector, and that sector's position has thus been strengthened.

That government policy has promoted the private sector is also seen in Mexico's taxation and subsidization policies. Mexico's low level of *taxation* can be explained by the fact that its tax system has sought to encourage investments more than to keep the government financially fit. Thus, in order to promote private investment, the government has sacrificed its financial health as well as resources that it could have used for income redistribution purposes. According to Robert Looney, the ratio of tax revenues to gross national product in Mexico at the end of the 1960s was 9.9 percent—one of the lowest in the world.[6] This ratio was due in part to problems with the tax collection system, but it was also a consequence of the purposes of that system. For example, contrary to the situation prevailing in most countries at a comparable level of development in 1976, Mexican wage earners and professionals together were contributing as much of total government tax revenues as were *all private enterpreneurs.* This shows the remarkable degree of official support for private capital.[7]

Subsidies constitute another way of encouraging private investment. There are no definite figures on the amount of subsidies granted by the government with the specific purpose of supporting private efforts at industrialization; instead, government reports group such subsidies with subsidies to consumers and with other items. According to experts, however, about one-half of total government subsidies are geared to promoting investments. The figures are impressive. The total value of said subsidies rose from 3.7 billion pesos in 1960, to 16 billion in 1970, to 428 billion in 1980.[8]

Given these figures, it is not surprising that the government has had to rely increasingly on credit in order to finance some of its own programs. Initially, domestic creditors were the main source of the public sector's borrowing. For example, the public internal debt rose from 7.2 billion pesos in 1960 to 53 billion in 1970.[9] However, in the 1970s the government began borrowing heavily abroad, driving up Mexico's foreign public debt. Of particular concern is the evolution of foreign public debt, expecially because a major indicator of the economic crises in 1976 and in the 1980s was the very high level of foreign indebtedness that the public sector had reached. Analysis of the external sector of the economy provides a broader framework within which to assess the characteristics and implications of this issue.

Public Revenue Problems
and the External Sector

Increased dependence on foreign funds is a corollary to the decreasing ability of the public sector to keep its finances balanced. Up to the mid-1950s, the government had financed its activities primarily through domestic credit and its own savings, but also by simply printing more money. Because many tensions arose from the resulting high inflation, the government resorted to foreign credit as a complementary means of financing its deficits. Thus, it could pursue a policy of domestic price stability for many years. Such a strategy, however, could be expected to show its own adverse effects in the long run. There is a limit to financing economic growth through foreign credit, just as there is a limit to excessive printing of money.

Resorting to foreign credit is not wrong in itself. If used wisely, borrowing abroad can play a positive role, assisting a country in its international transactions. In the Mexican case, foreign funds have aided the government in several critical areas. They have been instrumental in partially financing its investments and its imports of capital goods for public enterprises, and the government has used these funds to adjust Mexico's balance of payments.[10] In addition, foreign funds assisted the government in successfully pursuing exchange rate stability between 1954 and 1976. During that period, the value of the Mexican peso remained pegged to the U.S. dollar (at 12.50 pesos for US$1). Moreover, a policy of exchange rate stability was compatible for many years with a policy of domestic price

TABLE 5.3
Foreign Public and Private Debt: Structure, Service, and Relation to
Exports, 1946–1985 (in millions of dollars)

Year	Total	Public	Private	Exports	Service	DE Ratio
1946	485	485	—	395	na	na
1960	810	810	na	739	na	na
1970	6,091	4,262	1,829	2,933	720	.246
1976	25,893	19,600	6,293	7,371	2,548	.346
1977	29,338	22,912	6,426	8,404	3,837	.456
1978	33,416	26,264	7,152	11,925	6,287	.527
1979	39,084	29,757	9,327	16,131	10,180	.621
1980	48,781	33,813	14,968	24,819	7,681	.309
1981	73,218	52,961	20,257	30,810	9,543	.310
1982	80,463	58,874	21,589	28,919	9,982	.345
1983	83,772	62,556	21,126	28,282	8,416	.297
1984	95,900	69,338	26,562	32,902	11,715	.356
1985	97,903	72,080	25,823	30,178	9,917	.328

Note: na = not available; exports = total revenues from exports of goods and services registered in the current account of the balance of payments; DE ratio = debt service/ export ratio.

Sources: Banco de México, Informe anual (Mexico City, various issues); and México, Secretaría de Programación y Presupuesto, Información sobre las relaciones económicas de México con el exterior (Mexico City, 1979).

stability. The level of inflation from the mid-1950s to 1970 was remarkably low (an average annual rate below 5 percent), certainly by Latin American standards. The government could not have pursued these policies without relying on foreign credit to finance its deficits and deficits in the current account of the balance of payments. (The current account is a record of the international transactions of goods and services of any one country over a period of one year.)

Given the prevailing rules in the international economic system, however, heavy reliance on foreign funds has definite limits: Mexico was approaching those limits, that is, it was in danger of defaulting on its foreign debt payments. This danger was seen in the high level that its debt service ratio reached by 1970. The ratio of debt service (which is the sum of annual interest payments plus payments on the principal) to exports of goods and services is one of several indicators commonly used to assess the ability of a given nation to service its debt; the ratio provides a measure of its external financial solvency. Table 5.3 seems at first sight to indicate that, at least until 1970, the problems of increasing foreign debt and of servicing that debt were kept within manageable limits. When assessed from a broader perspective, however, the situation was more alarming. The Mexican ratio of 24.6 percent in 1970 was the highest ratio for all of Latin America and one of the highest in the world.[11] (Because hard data are lacking, these figures are only estimates of the total external debt and debt service.) Finally, the burden of servicing the Mexican government's foreign debt was accompanied by increasing private foreign debt. The latter rose from US$1.8 billion to US$6.3 billion between 1970 and 1976.

As a major concern of any country is to remain financially solvent, the question arises of what, if anything, could be done to solve the dilemma Mexico was facing. Mexico had to reduce its reliance on foreign credit to avoid eventual bankruptcy. But for many years it had relied heavily on borrowing abroad to finance public-sector imports and investments (which in turn promoted growth and employment) and to maintain a stable exchange rate, domestic price stability, and, ultimately, political stability. In theory, encouraging exports could have been a way out of this dilemma. Greater exports would have meant additional sources of foreign exchange, but the record shows that there was *a persistent deficit in the current account* from the 1950s to 1982. The fact that imports were consistently greater than exports thus had the opposite effect: It put additional pressure on the government to seek the foreign credit needed to stabilize the balance of payments.

Tables 5.4 and 5.5 provide a perspective on the current account and the composition and evolution of foreign trade. Actually, the export side of the current account has been characterized by a generally favorable performance. Thus, the value of total exports (in current dollars) rose from US$214 million in 1940 to about US$3 billion in 1970. Furthermore, although the share of agricultural exports fell somewhat between 1956 and 1970, the export shares of the extractive and manufacturing industries increased greatly during the same period. Hence, by 1970, manufactures accounted for 33 percent of total exports, reflecting Mexico's impressive industrialization. Services, tourism, and border transactions have always been pluses—bringing into the country more foreign exchange than the corresponding amount of Mexican expenditures abroad related to those activities.

Since 1970, *maquiladoras* have had a major impact on the external sector of the economy. Maquiladoras are U.S. firms operating on the Mexican side of the border (since 1965), assembling products for the U.S. market. The goods processed in Mexico return to the United States, with import duties imposed only on the value added in Mexico. The process benefits from cheap Mexican labor in exchange for provision of some jobs and payment of taxes to the Mexican government. Maquiladoras were intended to alleviate the problem of workers' migrating to the United States in search of jobs not found in Mexico. By providing over 200,000 jobs on the Mexican side of the border they have had this effect, but the number of jobs is still less than 1 percent of Mexico's work force.[12] The maquiladora program has become more significant in the 1980s because Mexico has desperately sought new sources of foreign capital to cope with foreign exchange and employment shortages. In fact, the success of the program has led to complaints by U.S. labor leaders that their own government encourages the loss of U.S. jobs

TABLE 5.4
Current Account, 1940–1985

	Amount of Transaction (millions of dollars)											
	1940	1950	1960	1965	1970	1976	1980	1981	1982	1983	1984	1985
Balance	22.6	58.7	-300.5	-314.4	-945.9	-3,068.0	-6,596.6	-12,544.0	-4,879.0	5,546.0	4,238.5	541.0
Exports of Goods and Services	213.9	826.7	1,371.8	1,989.1	2,933.1	7,371.7	24,819.5	30,810.0	28,919.0	28,282.0	32,902.3	30,178.6
Goods	94.4	493.4	738.7	1,113.9	1,281.3	3,315.8	15,307.5	19,420.0	21,230.0	21,399.0	24,196.0	21,866.4
Tourism	17.3	110.9	155.3	274.9	415.0	835.6	1,670.1	1,760.0	1,406.0	1,624.0	1,952.7	1,719.7
Border transactions	33.0	121.9	366.0	499.5	878.9	1,637.4	3,660.6	4,770.0	2,276.0	1,627.0	1,329.0	1,180.6
Maquiladoras	—	—	—	—	80.9	535.7	773.4	976.0	851.0	830.0	1,155.3	1,281.5
Other	69.2	100.5	111.8	100.8	277.0	1,046.6	3,407.9	3,884.0	3,156.0	2,802.0	4,269.1	4,130.5
Imports of Goods and Services	191.3	768.0	1,672.3	2,303.5	3,879.0	10,439.7	31,416.1	43,354.0	33,798.0	22,736.0	28,663.8	29,637.6
Goods	132.4	596.7	1,186.4	1,559.6	2,326.8	6,029.6	18,572.2	23,930.0	14,437.0	7,721.0	11,254.3	13,460.4
Tourism	8.0	9.3	40.5	119.1	191.4	423.1	1,010.8	1,571.0	788.0	441.0	648.6	668.0
Border transactions	20.0	76.5	221.0	295.2	563.3	1,192.7	3,056.4	4,584.0	2,417.0	1,457.0	1,520.0	1,594.4
Remittances	25.3	47.5	131.0	174.8	357.5	813.3	422.3	551.0	642.0	184.0	241.0	386.3
Interest on public debt[a]	—	11.2	30.4	62.2	229.2	1,266.0	3,957.6	5,476.0	8,400.0	7,346.0	9,700.0	6,857.0
Other	5.6	26.8	63.0	92.6	210.8	715.0	4,396.8	7,242.0	7,114.0	5,587.0	3,284.5	3,611.4

[a]These figures refer to *interest* payments on public debt only. They do not represent amounts comparable to those in Table 5.3, where figures refer to total debt service (interest payments plus amortization).

Sources: Nacional Financiera, *Statistics on the Mexican Economy* (Mexico City, 1977); México, Secretaría de Programación y Presupuesto, *Información sobre las relaciones económicas de México con el exterior* (Mexico City, 1979); Banco de México, *Informe anual* (Mexico City, various issues).

TABLE 5.5
Composition and Evolution of Foreign Trade, 1956–1985

| | Imports | | | | | | Exports | | | |
| | By Sector | | By Type of Goods | | | | By Economic Activity | | | |
Year	Public	Private	Consumer	Raw Materials	Capital	Other	Agricultural [a]	Extractive Industries	Manufacturing	Other
1956	na	na	16.6	36.6	46.8	—	54.2	31.8	7.4	6.6
1960	na	na	17.8	34.2	48.0	—	52.7	21.3	18.2	7.8
1966	17.2	82.8	17.9	35.9	46.2	—	52.7	16.9	20.4	10.0
1970	24.0	76.0	7.0	39.7	39.2	14.1	45.2	7.6	33.2	14.0
1976	35.7	64.3	5.8	43.3	41.1	9.8	34.8	20.7	27.4	17.1
1977	37.3	62.7	9.5	44.7	35.1	10.7	32.1	27.0	25.1	15.8
1978	37.6	62.4	7.3	49.0	33.6	10.1	26.1	34.6	23.8	15.5
1979	31.8	68.2	8.3	61.6	30.0	0.1	19.9	46.1	34.0	—
1980	36.6	63.4	13.1	59.2	27.5	0.2	10.1	67.8	22.0	0.1
1981	36.9	63.1	12.0	56.9	31.1	—	7.6	74.7	17.6	0.1
1982	37.4	62.6	—	—	—	—	5.8	78.2	15.9	0.1
1983	54.9	45.1	—	—	—	—	6.0	72.8	21.1	0.1
1984	42.5	57.5	7.5	69.6	22.9	—	6.0	70.8	23.1	0.1
1985	32.3	67.7	8.0	68.1	23.9	—	6.0	69.9	24.1	—

[a]Mexican government statistics usually include in this category fishing, livestock, and beekeeping.

Note: na = not available.

Sources: Same as for Table 5.4.

to Mexico. Japanese capital also has participated and benefited from low wages and Mexico's proximity to the U.S. market; what are in effect Japanese exports to the United States are disguised as Mexican exports.

Increased export revenues, however, have usually been overshadowed by the much faster growth in imports. The current value of imports rose from US$191 million to nearly US$4 billion dollars between 1940 and 1970. While Mexico began importing fewer consumer goods (which were being produced domestically), it increased its imports of raw materials and capital goods necessary to resupply local firms or to establish new industries. The public sector has been partly responsible for the higher deficit in current account, due to the combination of its greater imports of goods and higher interest payments on foreign public debt. Table 5.5 indicates that, by 1970, the public sector accounted for 24 percent of total imports. It also shows that foreign investors have been sending out of the country more foreign exchange than they have brought in (remittances).

Despite some obvious problems, the relatively good export performance of the economy during the 1960s, particularly in manufacturing exports, created the illusion in some circles that Mexico was attaining self-sustained economic growth. Other were more skeptical and pointed to the broader picture, putting special emphasis on the overall deterioration of the external sector. Such deterioration, it was argued, had been encouraged by government policies that fueled inefficiency on the part of both industrial and agricultural producers. Although industry had developed dramatically, it had done so partly at the expense of agriculture—which was entering a severe crisis. And the strategy of import substitution industrialization, which meant that industrial growth had been largely an inward-oriented effort, was also reaching its limits, as was true in some other large Latin American nations. Mexico's industry was highly protected, which kept it from developing its full export potential. Therefore, industry did not contribute sufficient foreign exchange resources in order to continue growing with an external sector in relative equilibrium. We have stated that there are some drawbacks associated with the implementation of an ISI strategy, and in addition to the emerging problems in the external sector just discussed, we must analyze the performance of industry and agriculture during the ISI years. Beginning in the 1970s, experts pointed out that unless the government took appropriate measures to make agricultural and industrial producers more efficient, constraints on economic growth were likely to become more severe.[13] The reality of the 1980s proved their prognosis. In what follows, some of the main economic features and problems of industry and agriculture, along with their political implications, are discussed.

Industrial Policy

During the initial stages of import substitution, protectionism is justified on the grounds that emerging local industries need time to make their products competitive with foreign goods. Protection can take several forms, such as imposing tariffs, limiting the amount of goods allowed into the country (quotas), and raising bureaucratic barriers such as Mexico's complex system of import licenses. Exchange rate policy can also be used for this purpose. At some point, however, it is expected that government incentives will gradually lead producers to cut down their production costs and prices in order to be more competitive and hence to increase their exports. But the Mexican government has long been spoiling domestic producers. Over-protection has been one aspect of governmental policy to encourage private investors to industrialize the country. It seems that once certain concessions are granted, the government finds it very difficult to remove them from those who have taken advantage of them. An example, discussed below, was the heated domestic debate that followed Mexico's first application to the General Agreement on Tariffs and Trade (GATT), an organization dedicated to ending protectionism. López Portillo, in 1980, changed his mind and decided not to join, following protests from sectors of the business community that resist giving up the benefits of protectionism.

In addition to the general problem of industry's export potential, there is the issue of domestic production of capital goods (i.e., production of machinery that is used for producing other goods). Table 5.5 shows that capital goods account for a substantial share of total imports. Ironically, a study by the World Bank (an institution typically wary of protectionism) claims that the low performance of the Mexican capital goods industry has been due, first and foremost, to the low level of protection granted to local producers. The study shows that private-sector importers pay very low tariffs and public enterprises pay no custom duties at all for this type of imports. As late as in 1975, more than 50 percent of total imports of capital goods were not subject to tariffs.[14] Thus, paradoxically, in a situation in which protection would have been justifiable, government action has been lacking. The study also contends that an inadequate exchange rate policy kept the Mexican peso overvalued for many years and that the lack of credit facilities through which Mexican producers could compete with the more favorable financing offered by foreign suppliers kept the pace of development of the capital goods industry very slow. In fact, in this respect Mexico lags far behind countries at a roughly comparable level of development, such as Argentina and Brazil.

Substituting imports of capital goods by encouraging domestic production is, according to some experts, one of very few remaining areas justifying protectionism. Other analysts contend, however, that the development of a domestic capital goods industry is a very costly and risky enterprise. The generally small size of the domestic market of developing countries and the need for complex technology constitute obstacles to sustained and sound progress. Instead, it is suggested that developing countries specialize in producing and exporting other types of manufactured goods. In particular, other policies, such as commercial and exchange rate policies, should aim to support the expansion of industries that make efforts to use labor-intensive technologies, thus using the "comparative advantage" of relatively cheap labor and also helping to reduce the unemployment problem that afflicts many developing nations.[15]

In short, several options existed for continued industrialization. The difficult choices included emphasizing a program to *develop the domestic capital goods industry*, primarily for import substitution purposes, but also for exporting. Alternatively, the government could have pursued an *export-led growth strategy*, cutting import restrictions to induce local industry to be more competitive. Hence, local industry would specialize over time in exporting certain products, and such activity would become the engine of economic growth.

There is no way to know a priori which policy is most appropriate. One policy might be more efficient in one country than it would be in another. Or a combination of policies would in some cases be both possible and desirable. As an example of the dilemma facing developing countries, Bela Balassa has presented evidence concerning the successful implementation of export-led growth strategies in Brazil, Taiwan, Korea, and a few other nations.[16] These newly industrializing countries have experienced very high rates of economic growth, expanded their exports substantially, stimulated investments in priority sectors, and achieved a great degree of sophistication in their industrial bases. But in some cases, such as the Brazilian, more open economies have become very vulnerable to external influences like high inflation and changing trade patterns, and little progress has been made in reducing social inequalities. It is ironic that the economic fortunes of these countries—which completed most successfully the process of import substitution—have come to depend once again on their export markets. They have come full circle without having achieved self-sustained growth or having diminished their socioeconomic inequalities, at least to the extent that was predicted. Taking into consideration the experience of such countries, Mexico eventually would have to work out a policy orientation for its future industrial development effort.

Agricultural Policy

A direct relationship has existed between public investment in irrigation and transportation and the general performance of the agricultural sector. While investment was high, from the World War II period until 1956, the average rate of growth was an impressive 7.6 percent. Lower investment was accompanied by growth that averaged only 3.8 percent during the following decade.[17] But government investment in irrigation and transportation systems does not tell us the whole story. Earlier, an important factor that accounted for high agricultural production was the accelerated pace of the agrarian reform program under the Cárdenas administration. Cárdenas provided new lands for cultivation, promoting favorable conditions to meet the growing foreign demand for Mexican agricultural products during World War II. And cheap food and raw materials were also made available to the urban population, permitting the development of the industrial and service sectors. Furthermore, the agricultural sector provided much of the labor force, savings, and foreign exchange that greatly benefited the industrialization process supported by the central government. Shlomo Eckstein and Reyes

Osorio made a rough calculation of the balance of resources taken away from agriculture and channeled to the rest of the economy between 1940 and 1961. They concluded that about US$250 million (1960 prices) was transferred to the rest of the economy by agriculture during those years of relative prosperity.[18]

In addition to both decreasing public investments in agriculture and the transfer of resources, government policy regarding access to good lands and to adequate inputs has favored large landowners for the most part. Their lands are generally the best in the country. These lands are located in northern Mexico and are provided with the best irrigation systems, fertilizers, and modern equipment.[19] These are the truly capitalistic enterprises that form the basis of Mexico's commercial agriculture. They are owned by individuals or by large companies linked to national and, increasingly, multinational firms engaged in the massive production and commercialization of food. A large share of this production is oriented to the U.S. market, which means that more foreign exchange resources have been available to facilitate imports of capital goods and raw materials to further industrialization. For many years, governmental support of these farmers was translated into a tacit political alliance that has been instrumental in maintaining political stability. This policy is consistent with the argument in Chapters 3 and 4 that the regime has been particularly supportive of privileged groups and only marginally of more disadvantaged groups. The alliance between government and large farmers has seldom been disturbed.

What have been the most important government policies toward the peasants? How has agricultural production been affected by these policies? From 1940 to 1970, peasants who owned lands, but who otherwise had very limited resources, were gradually forced to produce crops for which there was a secure but not very profitable market. They specialized in the production of maize, beans, and other basic foodstuffs, for which the government implemented price controls, and thus subsidized consumers in urban areas. Peasants have been often hurt by these urban-oriented policies. And peasant interests have been affected in other ways. Traditionally, the peasants have had to negotiate with several actors to obtain the resources necessary for production. We discussed in Chapter 3 peasant interaction with the Ministry of Agrarian Reform to obtain land; in addition, peasants have been forced to deal with local caciques who live off the political contacts that are necessary to get fertilizers, credit, and other resources. Furthermore, even when peasants have obtained these resources directly from governmental agencies, they have had to accept conditions in exchange for these inputs. That is, they have had to follow official production policies that, although designed by agricultural "experts," are not necessarily based on accurate knowledge of the environment. This often leads to failures and frustrations, the results of which obviously have adverse effects on peasant families more than on anyone else. Finally, peasants have had to deal with the market, which is largely beyond their control, for selling their products at given prices. They have been at the mercy of traders and a government monopoly (the National Staple Products Company, or CONASUPO)[20] wielding great resources to influence pricing and other decisions.

Thus, the peasants have been entrusted with the critical task of providing the basic foodstuffs central to the diet of the Mexican population, but they have not received enough governmental support. Their output began to decline sharply in the mid-1960s. Moreover, Mexican food production appeared to become oriented to exporting, and, as suggested in Chapter 1, national self-sufficiency in basic food products eroded. By 1970, Mexico, "the land of the green revolution," was no longer a net exporter of cereals. CONASUPO became second only to the state oil monopoly (PEMEX) as the major importer of foreign goods by the public sector. CONASUPO's food imports accounted for about 17 percent of public-sector imports in 1970.[21] This was an indication that agriculture, although for reasons other than those prevailing in industry, was also experiencing serious problems.

Mexico found itself in 1970 facing several structural problems in the external sector, industry, and agriculture that could constrain future growth. These problems are common to other countries that have followed the ISI strategy. Subsequent administrations would have to address these problems in order to maintain steady economic growth—and thus to maximize the prospects for continual political stability. Before we analyze their policies, however, we must more specifically discuss the other social problems that emerged during the years of ISI.

Social Outcomes of the Economic Model

At least two aspects of government policy have contributed to a very poor record in distributing the benefits of economic growth. One concerns the government's social expenditures aimed at providing the population with schooling, housing, health care, and other services. The other concerns official policies favoring industrialization; for example, low tariffs on capital goods imports have meant that many firms have preferred to use capital-intensive methods, which in turn have exacerbated the unemployment problem.

Government statistics at the aggregate level are likely to confuse the casual observer of the Mexican scene. Indeed, the government built many schools, hospitals, and other facilities during the ISI period, and Mexico's industrial plant achieved a relatively high degree of sophistication. However, only some sectors of the working classes have benefited from public services, and the social costs of industrialization have been high. Poverty still afflicts much of Mexican society. Those who argue that stability has been possible because of official control of the organizations of peasants and workers tell only half the story; strong unions have been able, in some cases, to negotiate agreements that have without any doubt raised the standard of living of their constituencies. But these legal provisions have seldom reached the *unorganized working classes*. A critical hypothesis is that political stability has resulted in part from the fact that much of the working class has not organized itself to protest the socioeconomic conditions in which it lives.

This should be kept in mind when looking at some of the indicators (presented below) of social development in Mexico.

In regard to *government social expenditures,* Mexico's are merely average (despite Mexico's enviable economic growth) when compared to those of other Latin American countries. Most of these expenditures have favored the population in urban areas, particularly near the nation's major industrial centers. Thus, the majority of the total population has been kept marginal. As a way of further illustrating this point, consider that the total public sector budget in 1979 was about US$55 billion, only 8.2 percent of which was spent on education, 10.4 percent on health and social security, and but 0.6 percent on housing.[22] On the positive side, these figures seem to have led to impressive achievements. The government provided schooling for more than 18 million and membership in public health institutions for 28 million. However, consistent with the data given at the beginning of this book, more than 4 million children annually still do not find a place in elementary schools, and 13 million will never reach the sixth grade. In the case of health, even if we assumed that the richest 20 percent of the population received private medical care, we would still be left with roughly 25 million who never receive modern medical care.[23] These figures lend support to our point regarding the limited number of working-class people who have benefited from state-sponsored social services.

Official policies in support of industrialization have also complicated various social problems. A case in point has been the encouragement given to industry to use capital-intensive technologies when Mexico has a huge labor surplus. Although accurate information about the extent of *unemployment* is very difficult to obtain, some aspects of the problem have been discussed in studies released by the Ministries of Labor and of Programming and Budget.[24] While Mexico's economy had been growing at rates of more than 6 percent (since the 1940s), and the population by an average annual rate of 3.5 percent, the Ministry of Labor found that the number of new jobs had increased by only 2.5 percent each year. The resulting rate of unemployment could be set at around 7 to 8 percent. But the major problem has been *underemployment:* People have either a part-time or seasonal job only or are paid less than the national minimum wage. Using such criteria, the underemployment level might have reached as high as 35 to 44 percent.[25] And, of course, the number of people unable to find jobs increased dramatically as Mexico plunged into severe economic crisis in the 1980s.

Another dimension of the problem is identified in the Ministry of Programming and Budget report. It shows that in 1950 about 32 percent of the population had jobs, but that proportion fell to 27 percent twenty years later. This means that from 1950 to 1970 proportionally fewer people were providing for the needs of the total population, one of the fastest-growing in the world. These figures also reflect the shifting age composition of the population, toward youth. In addition, the study notes that the ratio of employed women to total population increased from 4.5 percent to 5.5 percent during the same period, suggesting that both youths and women

TABLE 5.6
Income Distribution in Mexico, 1950–1977

| Income Group | Percentage of Income Earned | | | |
(deciles)	1950	1963	1969	1977
1–2 (lowest 20 percent)	4.7	3.5	4.0	3.3
3–5	12.7	11.5	11.0	13.4
6–8	23.7	25.4	21.0	28.2
9–10 (highest 20 percent)	58.9	59.6	64.0	55.1

Sources: For 1950 and 1963: United Nations Economic Commission for Latin America, La distribución del ingreso en América Latina (New York: United Nations, 1970); for 1969: World Bank, The Economy of Mexico: A Basic Report (Washington, D.C.: World Bank, June 1973); and for 1977: México, Secretaría de Programación y Presupuesto, Encuesta nacional de ingresos y gastos de las familias (Mexico City, 1979).

are exerting new pressures on the job market, in some ways further complicating the search for solutions to high rates of unemployment and underemployment.

Mexico's large pool of unemployed and underemployed people exerts downward pressure on *wages* and also affects *income distribution*. Information provided by the Central Bank and by the United Nations Economic Commission for Latin America shows a very erratic evolution of real minimum wages since 1960. An improvement in one year was followed almost systematically by a decrease the next year until the mid-1970s. A steady improvement over the period 1974 to 1976 was followed by four years of uninterrupted decline in real minimum wages (an accumulated 12 percent fall). And from 1982 to 1985, real wages fell further by a shocking accumulated index of 35 percent.[26] This means that wages were back at their level of two decades earlier.

From another perspective, organized workers in certain key industries have attained some fringe benefits over time that probably have affected relative factor prices. That is, the marginal cost of labor can exceed that of capital (machines), encouraging entrepreneurs to shift to capital-intensive technologies, thus aggravating the unemployment problem. For example, private employers in the manufacturing sector and the government both pay a 5 percent contribution toward improved housing facilities for their workers, about a 10 percent social security tax, a 1 percent educational tax, an 8 percent profit-sharing levy in some cases, and a bonus of a full month's salary at the end of the year. All such payments have made labor in manufacturing relatively expensive, and many entrepreneurs point to this fact in order to justify their adoption of capital-intensive technologies.

In regard to *income distribution,* Table 5.6 shows a steady deterioration between 1950 and 1969. By the latter year, 20 percent of the people garnered a mere 4 percent of national income. At the same time, the top 20 percent garnered 64 percent. Despite some improvement in the middle-income brackets during the Echeverría administration, the World Bank reported that Mexico still had *one of the worst profiles of income distribution of any nation on earth;*[27] the economic crisis of the 1980s has exacerbated the problem. The benefits of growth have indeed been maldistributed.

Social Policy and Private Initiative

There are, naturally, several explanations for Mexico's terrible failure in the social-welfare field. Many have focused on the regime's role, claiming that it has clearly favored stability over change and economic growth over distribution of wealth. Allegedly, while the state plays an overactive role in support of regressive industrialization policy, it generally provides far too little by way of resources and opportunities through the public sector. In fact, most recommendations for dealing with the social failure have centered on expanding the public sector.

But powerful political and economic factors have worked against such expansion. First, the regime has indeed placed a much higher priority on political stability and economic growth than on social change. Second, as we argue in this chapter, the regime has simply not been able or willing to extract from the economy the resources necessary to meet even its present expenditures. Third, the more powerful political groups, particularly business, generally have opposed such public-sector expansion as either economically unwise or at least not in their interests. This opposition, in turn, has meant that attempts at expansion, as under Echeverría and López Portillo, have jeopardized the regime's stability and growth priorities. These, then, are the major problems with implementing a major public-sector assault on Mexico's social problems—even if one assumes that the assault would "objectively" be the most appropriate policy to try. Conservatives, of course, argue that expanding the pubic sector, even if it were politically feasible, would be bad policy.

Despite all the obstacles, the public sector does sometimes expand significantly and sometimes its benefits do help alleviate social ills. It is also true, however, that powerful groups often manage to maintain their privileges even under such circumstances. For one thing, they may (through their resources, contacts, and knowledge) reap a disproportionate share of public-sector services. For another, they may shun the expanding public sector in order to buy special privileges in the private sector. Among the possible examples from many health and welfare fields, we look briefly at higher education.[28]

We have already seen (Chapter 1) that Mexico spends much more freely on higher education than on primary (or secondary) education and that (until recently) only a small minority enjoyed the privileges of higher education. Thus, the public sector of higher education has served mainly the elite. And when the public sector finally expanded greatly, offering opportunities not just to the elite but to the middle class as well, an interesting pattern developed: Much of the elite bypassed the public sector and established sanctuaries in private institutions. This shift, as in most of

Latin America, was largely a response to changes in the public sector. Elites reacted to the public sector's expanding social class base and to what they perceived as its terrible loss of prestige and quality, all amid recurring leftist political activism. Private-sector graduates generally receive more prestigious degrees than do their public sector counterparts, and they enjoy privileged positions in the job market. None of this alters the fact that Mexican higher education remains overwhelmingly public, maintaining its roughly 85 percent of total enrollments through the 1960s and into the 1980s. In fact, enrollments have grown as never before, from roughly 80,000 (1960) to well over 1 million by the mid-1980s. But as most groups first gaining access to higher education go to the (free) public sector, the fact that the private sector could hold at 15 percent means that it too has grown in unprecedented fashion and has done so by attracting social groups that once would have attended the public sector. Moreover, the private sector's 15 percent share is significant because Mexico's private sector is at least as private as any in Latin America (indeed, in the world) in terms of finance (virtually no government subsidy), governance (even more autonomy from the government than for public universities), and mission (both ideological and employment orientations toward private enterprise). Furthermore, the private sector is growing in relative importance. Not only does it far surpass the public sector in job placement for private enterprises, but significant inroads have appeared even in such traditional public university domains as recruitment to high positions in the public bureaucracy. Critics of the private sector fear rising private penetration of the state.

Thus, as in the economic sphere, the private-public balance raises important policy issues in the social sphere. Critics decry private higher education as elitist. With rare exceptions, only the wealthy can afford the tuition, and stiff entrance exams favor those, usually the wealthy, who have enjoyed better educational opportunities throughout their childhood. By attracting top students, the private sector represents a challenge to the quality of public facilities. Any political liberty to "choose" private institutions is seen as bourgeois liberty, for only those who can pay for it. Finally, private universities allegedly foster dependency by copying U.S. academic structures and policies and by encouraging many of their best students to pursue graduate work in the United States.

For others, the private sector represents voluntarism, competition, and superior services. It buttresses political liberty by providing choice, stability by satisfying powerful groups, economic growth by insisting on both academic quality and practical ties to private enterprise, and even national independence by training top Mexican talent that might otherwise choose study abroad over Mexico's public universities.

However one feels about the desirability of a strong private sector in a field like higher education, certain facts seem clear. The sector's strength does reflect, simultaneously, a substantial degree of socioeconomic inequality, political freedom, and openness to foreign influence, whether or not it contributes significantly to any of these. It tells us something about the flexibility of the Mexican political system, the ways in which goals such as depoliticization of social groups (such as students) and curbing of public expenditures can be partially achieved outside the public sector, thus lessening the government's felt need to repress the public sector to the degree found in many authoritarian nations. It also reminds us that there can be potent social as well as economic and political reactions to increases in the scope of the public sector. Privileged students can leave the public system just as privileged patients can bypass the public health system and just as private capital can flee an economy in which the public sector tries to expand its role. Unless the regime expands both its will and ability to impose changes in social policy, privileged groups will retain considerable leeway to shape the social policies not only within but also outside the public sector.

THE DEMISE OF THE ECONOMIC MIRACLE

Despite three decades of strong economic growth, Mexico entered the 1970s confronting severe economic as well as social problems. In structural terms, the ability of the public sector to play a positive role in the economy was being increasingly undercut by its financial problems. The Mexican regime—so often regarded as quite powerful—seemed unable to pursue certain fundamental options to gain the revenue necessary to meet its public-sector responsibilities. Its inability to tax business and wealth sufficiently was crucial. It also seemed unable to cut back on subsidies not just to industry but also to needy consumers. And because of the significance that a strong public sector has had in Mexican politics, selling public enterprises in order to balance the budget was not considered feasible. Thus, the question arises: Was the public economic posture weak mostly because the regime favored the private sector excessively? Or, perhaps even more important, did the regime really lack the political muscle to extract sufficient resources from society to maintain its powerful position? In addition to the public sector's financial health, other issues included the need to reinvigorate agriculture and industry. From the social perspective, unemployment, poverty, and exploitation of the poor remained salient features. These were the issues that Echeverría and López Portillo faced. Although these two administrations shared the objective of revitalizing the economic growth model, their policies were different in many respects. We turn to analyzing the evolution of the economy and of the social situation during the 1970s, a decade that witnessed the demise of the economic miracle. It became clear that significant steps should be taken to redefine the basic assumptions and major policies guiding the effort toward further industrialization and growth.

In 1970, a number of prestigious intellectuals and some of their friends in official positions published three volumes (*El perfil de México en 1980* [A Profile of Mexico in 1980]) on the desirable evolution of the Mexican socioeconomic and political systems for the new decade. The publication was significant both because it marked a partial rapprochement of some sectors of the intelligentsia with the political regime after the 1968 conflict and because some of the contributors would hold top positions in the Echeverría and López Portillo administrations. For example, David Ibarra became director-general of the National Development Bank during Echeverría's term and from 1977 headed the powerful Ministry of Finance. It is interesting to listen to what a man who would become one of the most influential economic policymakers of the 1970s had to say:

> The old revolutionary guard, in its time, just like the new generation of politicians in our time, congratulated itself on its own achievements. . . . And even some groups of dissidents have endorsed this [laudatory] assessment. . . . Only once in a while have problems surfaced that have called into question the capacity of the nation's institutions to adapt to socioeconomic changes.
>
> Unrest is still not generalized within the population, nor has it been so widespread as to force a fundamental and comprehensive reassessment of traditional approaches to economic and political policymaking. However, what would happen to the prospects for development should the major forces that have promoted such development during the last decades suddenly stall?
>
> It seems necessary, therefore, to begin defining new goals, that is, to elaborate clearly the objectives to be pursued and the tools and mechanisms needed to achieve them.[29]

A careful reading of the complete Ibarra essay and of the complete work indicates an awareness by intellectuals and by future holders of cabinet posts of some of the problems associated with the economic growth model during the previous decades. However, various authors express different views as to what caused the problems in the first place, and more important, which policies should be pursued to deal with such problems.

Naturally, different political actors hold different views as well. Thus, the left considers the labor unions' lack of autonomy from the regime a major determinant of the deteriorating standard of living of the working class. Labor leaders, for their part, put the blame on "unpatriotic entrepreneurs" who are not concerned with the well-being of all social sectors. The business community holds ineffective governmental policies responsible. By the same token, the various actors sometimes come forward with proposals to solve their grievances. In general, however, their input has been rather sporadic and has focused only on specific problems. That is, dissatisfied groups have rarely rallied behind a coherent set of policy proposals to deal with the social and structural shortcomings of the growth model. Thus, the government has had a free hand in initiating (or not initiating) actions to correct such problems. To some extent, this has been due to the lack of freedom for *organizational* alternatives, as discussed in Chapter 4. But it has also been due to the fact that until the 1970s and 1980s several key social groups generally did not feel threatened by the regime's social and economic policies. The evolution of the economy during the 1970s, however, was influenced to an important degree by President Luis Echeverría's loudly proclaimed commitment to effect a fundamental transformation of the traditional model of economic growth and by the adverse reaction of the business community to this proclamation.

The Economic Model Under Echeverría

In the early 1970s, under Echeverría, increasing public intervention in the economy was a major factor contributing to continued economic growth. The number of enterprises in which there was public participation, with shares ranging from very small to large, increased from 84 in 1970 to 845 in 1976, while the number of government employees doubled to more than 1 million.[30] This expansion of the public sector meant greater investments, imports of capital goods, expenditures for the growing bureaucracy, and so forth. All of the above were provided, *but not as a result of a substantial increase in government revenues following a major tax reform or changes in the amount and allocation of subsidies.*

It is true that some efforts were made to increase government revenues, but they fell short of compensating for soaring government expenditures. Thus, the ratio of public-sector income to gross domestic product increased from 18.9 percent to 27.4 percent between 1970 and 1976. At the same time, however, the ratio on the expenditure side rose from 23.7 percent to 33.9 percent.[31] To make up this gap, the Echeverría administration relied increasingly on a major tool used by its predecessors: *deficit financing.* Because of the lack of sufficient domestic sources of credit, the government borrowed abroad, and the level of foreign public debt skyrocketed from US\$4.2 billion in 1970 to US\$19.6 billion in 1976. The debt service/export ratio increased to the point that in 1976 one out of every three dollars collected from exports had to be used to service the debt (see Table 5.3).

During this period, the poor performance of the current account was no help to the rapidly deteriorating external sector. For example, despite a threefold increase in public investments in agriculture, output growth rates declined steadily and hit a record low of 1.2 percent in 1976. Imports of food in that year contributed significantly to an all-time record deficit in current account of more than US\$3 billion.[32] Imports of capital goods continued to account for a significant share of the deficit as well. At the same time, even though the government went out of its way to encourage exports, the rate of increase characteristic of the 1960s slowed. Furthermore, the manufacturing share of total exports actually declined from 33.2 percent in 1970 to 27.4 percent in 1976 (see Table 5.5). Echeverría founded the Mexican Institute for Foreign Trade, and he took entrepreneurs on his numerous trips the world over, with his government picking up the bill. However, many official policies that actually discouraged exports remained unchanged. Thus, for example, the government artificially maintained a fixed exchange rate for the Mexican peso, a policy that made Mexican goods more expensive in the international market than they would otherwise have been. Had the exchange rate been gradually adjusted to reflect the actual value of the peso, Mexican goods would have been more competitive, and exports could have been greater. Moreover, little if anything was done to reduce the excessive level of protectionism provided for domestic producers. The complex system of import licenses remained practically untouched, and producers of consumer goods did not feel pressured into becoming more competitive.

To make things even worse, several factors combined to produce rates of inflation of 20 to 25 percent, previously unknown in Mexico. First was an upsurge in aggregate demand, partly as a result of greater public involvement in the economy and partly due to gains in real minimum wages and income distribution. The profile of income distribution improved somewhat between 1969 and 1977, favoring mostly people in the middle-income brackets, who received 40 percent of the national income in 1977 (see Table 5.6). Because domestic production was insufficient to fulfill the demand for more agricultural and industrial products, some of these products had to be imported. As international inflation was widespread, the prices of many of these goods had risen, which also contributed to higher domestic inflation. However, some would argue that inflation would have been even greater had the government imposed import controls: Prices tend to rise when demand is growing and fewer goods are available.

Most important the government was losing the trust of key economic actors, a loss that is still felt in the economy. For one thing, the government engaged itself in ideologically charged confrontations with the business community, although in the end it did not even stand strongly by its public positions. Government attitudes toward foreign investors provide a good illustration. The government made considerable noise about its efforts to control direct foreign investment through a 1973 law.[33] According to this law, the majority interest (at least 51 percent) in all firms should be Mexican, and some industries (e.g., the automobile industry) are committed to produce locally an increasing share of components. In fact, direct foreign investment usually carries with it a number of positive as well as negative effects. On the plus side, it facilitates the flow of new technology, creates some jobs, and brings in foreign exchange. Even socialist countries have sought these benefits. At the same time, however, foreign firms have often created unwanted conflictive situations, especially in developing countries. Politically, they have sometimes interfered in domestic affairs, as in Chile in the early 1970s. And they have caused economic problems, as even a U.S. congressional study has shown. It points out that multinational corporations largely dominate the manufacturing sector in Mexico, as they do in Brazil, and that they control more than half the total assets of the 300 largest manufacturing firms in these countries. The study concludes that as a result of very high returns to capital, "resources are misallocated, and the distribution of income and wealth becomes more unequal. Moreover, innovation and growth are likely to be held below the rates attainable under more competitive conditions."[34]

But once it has been acknowledged that the international system exerts important influences over the economies of nations such as Mexico, we should also look at figures that suggest that the role of foreign capital has been more one of fitting into than of significantly shaping the domestic economic situation. In 1975, for example, foreign capital accounted for only

2.5 percent of total investment resources in the Mexican economy. U.S. firms accounted for about three-quarters of the cumulative US$4 billion of direct foreign investment up to that year. The proportion in 1985 was slightly smaller, about two-thirds of the US$14 billion total for that year.[35] In any event, despite the government's tough rhetoric and the 1973 law, direct foreign investment—which Echeverría blamed for many of Mexico's economic ills—actually increased during his tenure.

Another case in point concerns the domestic business community, which became terribly alienated from the regime. A pointed indicator of this situation was the level of gross fixed capital formation during these years. Despite the unprecedented level of public investments, total gross fixed capital formation fell by 2.7 percent in 1971 and again by 3.5 percent in 1976. That meant that private investors were withdrawing their capital from Mexico. The total amount withdrawn, sent primarily to U.S. banks, has been estimated at about US$4 billion.[36] Private investors feared they were being "crowded out" of Mexico's economy. They viewed excessive government spending as a major source of inflation and as a cause of the growing foreign debt. They also disliked wholeheartedly the social reform and foreign policy rhetoric of those years. So severe was their alienation that it has not been overcome even as the regime has moved away from leftist-oriented reforms.

It should be noted that the government had, and still has, its own list of grievances against the business community, some of them well founded. From the government's viewpoint, the crisis in agriculture, the insufficient production of industrial goods, and the capital flight from Mexico seemed unjustifiable. After all, the government had been providing various incentives for private investment—low taxes, huge subsidies, protectionist foreign exchange and commercial policies. Moreover, not all public expenditures were unproductive, despite private-sector claims. For example, 17 percent of the total public investments from 1970 to 1976 were devoted to the expansion of the oil industry alone. This helped end the need for oil imports and laid the basis for the greater production and exports of later years.[37] Thus, what the government expected, at a minimum, was that the business community would share the costs entailed in government policies to promote economic growth. Instead, the further deterioration of the economy during Echeverría's administration scared entrepreneurs so much that they ended up better organized than they had ever been. Recall the discussion (Chapter 3) of the 1970s rebellion, culminating with the establishment of the CCE, which became the major forum of private-sector organizations, the place where they form their common policy positions. Beyond all this, some have even argued that certain entrepreneurs control illegal paramilitary groups (primarily in Jalisco, Puebla, and Nuevo León) and that others are funding ultraconservative "independent" labor unions in those and other states in order to strengthen their position in the political system.

Thus, the regime has found itself confronting an intensified paradox, aptly summarized by Douglas Bennett and Kenneth Sharpe: "The national bourgeoisie, in many ways a creation of the state, acts now in ways that limit the power of the state."[38] Roger D. Hansen and E.V.K. Fitzgerald have also contended that the Mexican state's autonomy has been undermined to an important degree by the resistance of the private sector to cooperating in finding solutions to the problems associated with the pursuit of economic growth and by its growing capacity to exercise veto power over some of the government's economic policies.[39] Their analyses have been highly influenced by the pattern of events that resulted in the 1976 economic crisis. These analyses obviously square with the assertion in Chapters 3 and 4 that business exercises more autonomy from the regime than does any other political actor in Mexico.

In 1976, economic problems and the confrontation between the regime and the private sector reached a climax. By the end of the year President Echeverría, now a vanquished reformer, had little alternative but to comply with the rules of the international economic system that Mexico had repeatedly accepted in various formal conventions. These rules, for example, discourage excessive reliance on foreign credit to finance a large share of domestic investments and imports. Although debate rages about what precisely constitutes "too much reliance on foreign credit," the foreign public debt of nearly US$20 billion and the current account deficit of more than US$3 billion in 1976 were clearly too much. At the same time, the pace of the capital flight had accelerated, and so Echeverría announced during his last State of the Union address (September 1, 1976) his decision to devalue the Mexican peso. The following month Mexico put into effect some old agreements with the U.S. Federal Reserve and the U.S. Treasury Department, and it got a loan of US$600 million to support the peso. In addition, it signed a stabilization agreement with the International Monetary Fund (IMF), gaining access to as much as US$965 million from the fund's facilities. Mexico accepted in return a number of conditions to improve its economic situation, such as a US$3-billion-a-year ceiling on additional foreign public borrowing during the three years that the agreement was expected to last.[40] Certain major similarities would characterize the 1982 and subsequent economic crises and the bitter pills Mexico would have to swallow in order to gain foreign help in combating them.

Echeverría's term in office ended two months after the agreement with the IMF was signed. His successor, López Portillo, offered a different project to revitalize the economic model. In 1976, the economy had grown by only 2.1 percent, which meant a 1.1 percent decline in per-capita income, assuming a population growth rate of 3.2 percent. For one thing, a radical change in Mexico's long-standing oil policy was forthcoming. Mexico would become once again one of the world's leading oil producers and exporters. The expectations raised by this prospective change in oil policy probably explain how López Portillo could afford to remain largely silent during his campaign for the presidency. With oil, the new president-elect did not need to expound rhertorical promises to restore confidence in the Mexican government and economy. Furthermore, recent events had shown that any efforts to revitalize the economic model would have to be supported by a reassured business community.

The Economic Model Under López Portillo

Soon after López Portillo became president, he reaffirmed that Mexico was bound by the agreement with the IMF. He also expressed his determination to use oil as a means to improve the ailing economy. Expansion of the oil industry was expected to trigger the reestablishment of high growth rates, which occur with an external sector in equilibrium (thanks to foreign exchange resources provided by oil exports). The government could count on an additional source of revenue, so that it could lower the public deficit and reduce the need to borrow money abroad. These and other problems would be solved as PEMEX, the state's oil monopoly, increased its production of crude oil from 0.9 to 2.25 million barrels per day by 1982, half of it for export. It will be shown in Chapter 7 that such production and export targets were reached earlier (mid-1980) than originally planned. High economic growth rates were reestablished during 1978–1981, until Mexico fell into a new economic crisis toward the end of the López Portillo administration.

Other broad economic policy objectives were never fulfilled. In fact, as Mexico entered the 1980s, several of the structural and social indicators of the ills of the growth model that were the focus of attention during the 1976 crisis had deteriorated even further.[41] Moreover, the president alienated the business community with the expropriation of commercial banks in 1982.

Using traditional evaluative standards, one could compile a long list of problems with the economy of Mexico. Take, for example, some of the indicators used earlier in this chapter to present an overall view of the 1940 to 1970 period. During López Portillo's administration, similar trends prevailed in regard to *government finances*. Thus, although the ratio of public-sector income to gross domestic product reached 30 percent, the ratio in terms of expenditures increased to as much as 37 percent in 1980.[42] The ratio of public-sector deficit to gross domestic product, 7 percent in 1980, reached an all-time high of 18.5 percent in 1982. Subsidies continued to account for a large share of the public deficit, although some interesting changes in the tax system were introduced. While income taxes were reduced for lower income groups, a new value added tax (VAT) was effected with the objective of preventing tax evasion and improving the government's tax collection rate. VAT, however, has not had the positive effects on the general state of public finances that were sought.[43] The government also tried to add to its revenues through the sale of gold and silver coins and oil bonds.

The *current account* situation deteriorated even further under López Portillo (see Table 5.4). The deficit had been cut down from US$3 billion in 1976 to US$1.6 billion in 1977, but then it increased to the all-time record of US$12.5 billion in 1981, and it was still US$4.9 billion in 1982. The dramatic rise in oil's share of exports of goods is implied in Table 5.5.

In 1981, oil accounted for practically all of the 75 percent share of extractive industries in exports and for about 78 percent in 1982. At the same time, imports of capital goods, food, and the service of the foreign debt continued to account for most of the deficit. Were it not for huge revenues from increasing oil exports (US$14.6 billion in 1981 and US$16.5 billion in 1982), such a deficit in the current account could have become an insurmountable constraint on economic growth, a bad omen as an impending world oil glut would soon wreak havoc on Mexico's oil revenues.

The *foreign public debt* grew at an even faster pace than during the Echeverría administration. The figures below suggest that the change in traditional oil policy allowed López Portillo's government to continue relying on deficit financing, at least to some extent. In 1979, the debt amounted to more than US$29 billion (up from US$19 billion in 1976), and the debt service/export ratio was a staggering 62.1 percent. These figures mean, among other things, that two out of every three dollars received from export revenues had to be used to service the debt in that year. This fact, however, can be explained by the government's efforts to change the structure of payments on its debt. In 1978 and 1979, the government made advance payments on its short-term debt, which is due within one year and carries with it higher interest payments. Today, most of the debt is contracted on a longer-term basis and at lower interest rates. Thus, in 1980 the foreign public debt had increased to US$34 billion, but the debt service/export ratio of 30 percent was substantially lower than the ratio of 62 percent of the previous year (see Table 5.3). Strong signs of an imminent crisis appeared in 1981, when foreign public debt increased by a dramatic 50 percent in one single year—to US$52.9 billion. When López Portillo left office at the end of 1982, the foreign public debt stood at US$58.9 billion and the private sector's foreign debt at US$21.6 billion, for a total Mexican foreign debt of US$80.5 billion. The sheer increase in these numbers and Mexico's inability to pay back its creditors sent tremors throughout world financial markets.

In the *social* sphere, available figures add to the long list of records that the López Portillo administration unfortunately would come to hold. Table 5.2 shows that government social investments averaged only 10 percent during the period. Additionally, as already mentioned, real wages fell significantly. The working classes were particularly hard-hit by annual rates of inflation of 20 to 100 percent, not compensated for by corresponding wage increases.

Thus, ample evidence appeared for a bleak interpretation of the Mexican economy. Other indicators, however, suggested a reinvigoration from 1978 to 1981. One of the most significant improvements came in the area of employment: The number of jobs grew faster than the population due to the great increase in public works and in private-sector investments. Another positive feature was that income per capita, after decreasing again in 1977, rose in the three subsequent years. The economy grew by 6 percent in 1978, and by almost 8 percent from 1979 to 1981, compared to a rate of population growth of less than 3 percent.[44] Table 5.1 also indicates that the ratio of gross fixed capital formation to gross domestic product increased in real terms. In 1980, the ratio was 25.6 percent, the highest ever recorded, and it averaged 23.1 percent from 1977 to 1982. The public sector's share of the total (44 percent) was also unprecedented. Ironically, although public involvement in the economy was greater than ever, the attitude of the business community was a far cry from its confrontational tone of the mid-1970s. To be sure, disagreements remained, but the private sector seemed generally satisfied with the policies that restored high rates of economic growth. The cooperation of the business community, we have argued, is essential for securing political stability through steady economic growth. This cooperation was obviously shaken when López Portillo surprised everyone, in September 1982, by expropriating all domestic private banks; these banks, he charged, had encouraged a dangerous flight of capital from Mexico.

In the agricultural sector, a central goal of the López Portillo administration was to attain self-sufficiency in the production of basic foodstuffs. Although Mexico is a large agricultural producer, imports of products that are part of the basic diet of the population have been increasing at an alarming pace. For example, more than 10 million tons of maize, beans, wheat, and other basic foodstuffs, valued at US$1.5 billion, were imported in 1980 alone.[45] The administration implemented two main policies aimed at reducing food imports. First, the president announced in early 1980 the establishment of the Mexican Food System (SAM). A government study was completed, including detailed information pertaining to production of foodstuffs by region, as well as projections of output and consumption levels for the near future.[46] On this basis, SAM aimed to establish a formula for sharing risks between the government and the peasantry in order to reach certain production goals for maize, beans, and other products. The government committed itself to providing the peasant with fertilizers, seeds, and other inputs at very low prices; it promised to see that products would be bought at established prices; and it guaranteed a minimum income in the event that the crop is lost because of a natural disaster. The peasant, for his part, committed himself to devote his efforts, land, and labor to attaining official production goals. In this sense, a rather atypical relationship emerged between the state (as employer) and the peasant (as wage earner).

In addition to SAM, the highly controversial Agricultural Development Law was approved by Congress in 1981.[47] Before its passage, peasants were not allowed to lease their land, but Article 32 legalized what had been an unlawful and a very common practice. Thus, peasants would be allowed to integrate their lands with those of large landowners, ostensibly to increase productivity. In this manner, large agricultural enterprises are given a more secure environment to plan their long-term investments, which the government hopes will be helpful in reaching its own objectives. Large landowners were thus reassured that no more lands would be expropriated. In addition, they did not need to worry about coercively extending their territories at the expense of peasant lands. Now they could negotiate openly and directly with peasants to use their lands in exchange for a wage and an as-yet-indeterminate share in total profits. These enterprises, therefore, would control even if they would not own the land. And the peasant, as in the case of SAM and the state, would become a wage earner dependent on his employer. These new policies were of special significance at a time when the government decided to abandon one of the key commitments (land distribution) on which it has based its legitimacy. Of course, Chapter 4 noted that *policy change* has been an important feature of Mexican politics; that is, an administration may decide to emphasize once again its rhetorical commitment to fundamental land reform—although this certainly did not happen under de la Madrid. However, the regime undertook these risky new measures hoping that closer cooperation with the peasantry and large landowners would alleviate the crisis in the agricultural sector.

In industry, significant changes are also required, changes that are sometimes difficult both to understand and to implement. The situation is often complicated by the fact that many issues are debated in an environment characterized by a high degree of ideological prejudice. To illustrate this point, consider the debate that ensued over López Portillo's proposal to join GATT. GATT is an agreement signed in 1947, mainly by the industrialized nations. Its chief objective has been to "liberalize trade," that is, gradually to reduce all types of existing barriers to the free flow of goods across the borders of the negotiating parties. As of 1986, there were ninety-two member countries, which together accounted for 85 percent of the world's trade. Members that grant concessions to any nation are obliged to extend them to all members on a nondiscriminatory basis. There have been eight major multinational meetings, the more celebrated of which are known as the Kennedy and Tokyo rounds. In each session, the list of products exempted from trade restrictions has been expanded, although some escape clauses continue protecting certain domestic producers. It is assumed that greater trade leads to attainment of other goals, such as greater investment and employment, ultimately contributing to a better standard of living all around.

Analysts generally agree that GATT is very beneficial for the industrialized countries, but opinions vary about how appropriate it is for industrializing countries. For example, the bulk of exports of the latter countries are products that are still subject to protectionist policies in the industrialized nations (e.g., agricultural exports). Believing that the benefits of GATT would be mostly one-sided, several developing nations supported the establishment of the United Nations Conference on Trade and Development (UNCTAD) in 1964. To many, however, UNCTAD has over the years produced only good studies and resolutions, having little impact in the real world. Moreover, few deny that Mexico needs to take some measures to increase the competitiveness of its products, not only to increase its exports, but because of the positive domestic side effects of lower prices and better-quality products. It was against this background that representatives of the Ministry of Commerce of Mexico met with a team of GATT experts to discuss the prospective Mexican membership. After several months of negotiations, a broad agreement was reached opening the way for Mexico's formal application for membership. But because the government was aware that much was at stake in this crucial decision, it called upon business, professional, and other organizations to debate the issue.[48] Such calls for participation have generally been viewed, in studies of Mexican politics, as legitimizing covers for government policies that have already been decided.[49] Here, however, the issue was really still unresolved, the process vibrant indeed.

Proponents of GATT at the Ministry of Commerce soon found themselves isolated. Business organizations, however stereotypically identified with conservatism or imperialism, generally opposed the move, largely because they would have to bear most of the costs. In some quarters GATT proponents were simply accused of favoring U.S. interests, while its opponents were hailed for their firm stand in defense of "national interests." Professional organizations and some university professors pointed out that foreign actors have greater resources and experience and would therefore find it easy to push local producers out of the way. But was the only choice GATT and the end of protectionism with high costs versus the perpetuation of excessive protectionism? In fact, GATT is a multilateral negotiating forum in which developing countries like Mexico could find it very difficult to influence policy. Moreover, as most of Mexico's trade takes place with the United States, Mexico could opt instead to continue negotiating for trade concessions at the bilateral level. Mexico, some argue, has increased leverage, at least in times of international energy scarcity, because of its oil exports to the United States. It might be a better strategy to link an increase in exports to progress made in other areas of bilateral concern.[50] Still others point out that Mexico can take measures unilaterally to reduce excessive protectionism: The government could grant financial and other supports to smooth the transition toward a more open economy without having to overcommit itself by entering GATT or by abandoning the option of bilateral negotiations with the United States.[51] Thus, there are alternative courses of action to correct overprotection, one of the central policies associated with the traditional growth model; these alternatives were carefully evaluated by the de la Madrid administration, as membership in GATT subsequently became one of the critical issues confronting the administration.

In sum, a series of events during the 1970s contributed to the demise of the Mexican economic miracle. Echeverría's emphasis on the expansion of the public sector and the improvement of income distribution failed partly because he alienated the business community, partly because his programs were not funded with Mexico's own resources. When López Portillo took office in 1976, he faced a financial and a legitimacy crisis in his relations with powerful economic groups. However, as reports on the full extent of the nation's untapped oil and gas resources were confirmed, the national mood changed from caution to euphoria. As the slogans would have it; Mexico should prepare itself "to manage abundant resources and wealth," because "a new, proud, and wealthier Mexico was at last going to rise in the world of nations."

The Mexican regime realized too late that it was unlikely to solve, with oil revenues alone, a set of complex problems whose solution required the vigorous and systematic pursuit of several new and imaginative policies. That is, rather than following a moderate course funding some key programs with oil revenues as these became available, the López Portillo administration (and the business sector) fell victim to the false perceptions and expectations characteristic of countries that suddenly acquire abundant wealth. In fact, the experience of other oil-exporting developing nations provided warning signs.[52] But the Mexican government elaborated a grand design to change the economy and society in fundamental ways over too short a span of time. In addition to oil, the government expanded significantly the steel and petrochemical industries, it engaged itself in an expensive program to modernize ports and the national railway network, and it funded the expensive Mexican Food System, among others. Many business firms were as ambitious as the government and expanded their operations beyond advisable levels. When President López Portillo turned power over to his successor, Mexico was immersed in its most severe economic crisis in fifty years, and many feared for the fate of the political system itself.

Relying on cheap and abundant foreign credit or increasing oil exports was not an option President de la Madrid could count on because conditions in international capital and oil markets had turned unfavorable. The president had to devise new policies to confront Mexico's economic situation in 1982, including a negative rate of growth—the first in decades—and 100 percent inflation. The peso exchange rate in relation to the U.S. dollar had fallen from 26 to 45 in February 1982 and then to 70 in September and 150 when de la Madrid took office in December. Finally, the task of restoring business confidence in the economy was a complex one, and the regime's traditional bases of support (organized labor and the peasantry) were jeopardized as strict economic and social austerity program were prepared.

ECONOMIC POLICY UNDER DE LA MADRID

Miguel de la Madrid assumed office realizing that he had scarce public resources at hand and that, in contrast with his predecessors, the prospects for any significant increase of these resources were poor. A central dilemma of his presidency can be summarized as follows: De la Madrid was committed to honor Mexico's international payment obligations at the same time that he had to allocate resources for resuming economic growth; and he knew he had to invest whatever resources were left to encourage the restructuring of Mexico's inefficient economy in the long run. If these seemed to be formidable tasks in themselves, capital flight, collapsing oil prices, and the 1985 earthquakes dashed any hopes that Mexico would show substantial progress on the social and economic fronts during de la Madrid's presidency. Only optimists expected even modest short-term results. We analyze de la Madrid's policies in detail because they represent major changes in the economic sphere and because these changes have substantial social and political ramifications.

Many of de la Madrid's policies involved high immediate costs but represented perhaps the only feasible way to set Mexico's economy on the right course. To be successful, however, the government had to command significant support in Mexican society, and this proved an elusive goal. Debate raged as to whether the credibility problem that afflicted President de la Madrid was a result of his lack of leadership skills and statesmanship or simply of limited opportunities for a chief executive who inherited a government plagued by poor administration and widespread corruption over the previous twelve years.

Government Initiatives

The objective here is not to exonerate Miguel de la Madrid's government, but rather to point out that many of its policies suffered because they were not given a fair test in the first place. For example, de la Madrid went far to encourage the growth of non-oil exports, and he sold public enterprises back to private owners in order to enhance the external sector of the economy and public finances. He did so at high political risk, and yet the cool response of wealthy Mexican entrepreneurs proved to be a persistent problem.

The original austerity program implemented during 1983 exceeded the expectations of the International Monetary Fund and international bankers (with whom Mexico had signed an economic stabilization agreement in November 1982). Political observers were amazed at the ability of Mexico's political system to avoid the disruptive effects usually associated with putting in practice a stabilization program of such magnitude. (In military-ruled Brazil and Chile civilian dissatisfaction with similar programs often erupted into significant demonstrations.) If it is at all feasible to express in one single quantitative indicator the extent of economic adjustment efforts in Mexico in 1983, consider the reduction of the public sector's deficit in relation to gross domestic product. That deficit fell from 18.5 percent in 1982 to 8.7 percent in 1983. Praise for the efforts of Mexico's financial authorities was found in leading international economic journals at that time. Inflation was brought down from over 100 to 80 percent, and the current account surplus of US$5.5 billion was the first registered in three decades (Table 5.4). Meanwhile, *negative* economic trends also suggested how profound Mexico's austerity effort was. Economic growth, which abruptly halted in 1982—a negative 0.5 percent compared to the average 8 percent growth of 1978 to 1981—declined markedly in 1983 (5.3 percent). Overall investments contracted by more than 20 percent, and despite modest increases in two subsequent years, the level of investments in the economy in 1985 was only at the same level of the mid-1970s (Table 5.1). We have noted already the devastating effects of this adjustment program for Mexico's working and middle classes (e.g., falling real wages, low government investments for social services, and increasing unemployment).

In 1984, when the outlook seemed more promising, it was difficult for the government to resist the temptation to stimulate economic growth. Inflationary pressures had been receding, public finances experienced a slight surplus early in the year, negotiations to reschedule foreign debt service payments had succeeded, and many private firms had been able to put their finances in order without laying off most of their employees. By the end of the year the economy had grown once again by a respectable 3.5 percent, inflation was down to 59 percent, and the current account surplus was US$4.2 billion. Moreover, non-oil exports, led by manufactured products, rose by an outstanding 18 percent, fueling hopes that investments to restructure Mexico's inefficient industry were already showing results. There was a dark side to this story, however. The annual rate of inflation and the public sector deficit (7.6 percent of gross domestic product), while showing some progress over the previous year, were substantially above the targets Mexico set with the IMF in November 1982. Were it not for the economic calamities that hit Mexico in 1985, perhaps investors could have overlooked the government's decision to spend more in order to encourage the growth effort. But indicators went from bad to worse in 1985, and the government's economic management increasingly faltered.

Negative Reactions

When the first signs of fiscal indiscipline manifested themselves, Miguel de la Madrid's government became suspect in the eyes of the business community. Businessmen often stress their disappointment with the Echeverría and López Portillo administrations, when the government usually failed to meet the targets of economic performance it had set for itself or when continued assurances that the peso enjoyed a stable position were routinely followed by devaluations. This legacy of distrust meant that any show of laxity in government economic behavior was bound to hurt prospects for restoring the business community's trust in the government's capacity for economic leadership. From such a perspective, it did not matter whether the inability of the government to keep the public deficit and inflation low (to give but two examples) was due to factors beyond government control. The fall of oil prices during 1985 represented a loss of over US$2 billion to the public treasury, and the resources required to fund the task of reconstruction in the aftermath of the 1985 earthquakes reached about US$4 billion (according to a United Nations study). Yet the government did not receive understanding from business leaders, who instead pointed to the increase of the 1985 public sector deficit to 9.9 percent of gross domestic product and to inflation's rise to 64 percent. Not only were these outcomes seen as major setbacks, but when the government, also in 1985, took bold measures to reduce its expenditures, the business community was simply not impressed. In 1985, the federal budget was cut on three occasions, 22,000 bureaucrats were laid off, and an additional 80,000 positions that were vacated in 1983 and 1984 would not be refilled. It is noteworthy that over 100 high-paid federal government jobs disappeared, including 15 undersecretaries and 50 positions at the rank of assistant undersecretary.[53]

To be sure, other grievances of the business community may explain its reluctance to operate in Mexico in a more committed fashion. One such grievance refers to the growth of the so-called "social sector" of the economy discussed in Chapter 3. Unions are gaining control of an increasing number of productive firms that enjoy large government subsidies, which leads to further competition with the business sector for credit resources. Moreover, credit is scarce and very expensive because the government's monetary policy aims at reducing inflation by funding the public deficit with domestic savings instead of printing more money. In addition, by maintaining interest rates at high levels (i.e., above inflation) the government has attracted savings into the national banking system and thus has combated capital flight in some measure. However, annual inflation rates of above 60 and even 100 percent have pushed interest rates over 100 percent to allow for a profit margin for both savers and the banks that provide the money. The cost of credit thus has become prohibitive.

The diminished availability of credit hurts investment and employment opportunities. Ironically, larger investors have met their resource needs by bringing back into Mexico funds previously deposited in U.S. banks. In 1985, about US$1 billion flowed back to Mexico as some sort of "reverse" capital flight; a similar amount flowed back during 1986.[54] To put these figures in perspective, a conservative estimate of capital flight from 1975 to 1986 amounted to US$36 billion. The problem is that only a limited number of businesses have their savings abroad in positions from which they can draw funds once credit becomes scarce within Mexico.

Furthermore, analysts and leaders of business organizations complained that changes in government policies were often slow to materialize and were sometimes misdirected. For example, it was not until the midpoint of the de la Madrid administration that the government significantly reduced the bureaucratic redtape limiting foreign trade and investment flows. Approval in 1985 for an IBM project to produce computers and sophisticated software in Mexico, on condition that IBM maintain full control and ownership of its operations, came only after a great deal of hesitation. In the end, IBM agreed to invest US$91 million over a five-year period, to export 92 percent of its output, and to sell the remainder in the domestic market at no more than 15 percent above comparable international prices.[55] (Business criticized the government's delay in making up its mind, particularly given the low investment amount involved.) Moreover, in December the government went so far as to authorize foreign firms to establish new plants, relocate old ones, and/or increase their controlling share beyond the 49 percent ceiling permitted by the 1973 Law on Foreign Investment.[56] Thus, the government relaxed tough regulations on foreign investors at a time when these investors were least likely to commit further resources because of negative factors in the Mexican economy. It could be argued as well that providing major concessions under such conditions was an ill-advised negotiating strategy if Mexico had hoped to gain something in return.

In the view of many business leaders, cutting the public deficit across the board rather than selectively illustrates misdirected government policy. Such indiscriminate cuts sometimes hurt the financial stability of entities that have been performing well and providing valuable services. It would be better to strengthen such entities and in certain cases help to cure ailing ones.[57] Meanwhile, reduced government expenditures resulted in the lowest levels of public investments in years. Table 5.1 shows that the share of public investments in total gross fixed capital formation shrank to about 36 percent in 1985. Although under different circumstances many business groups would have welcomed this trend, protests this time were expressed by those businesses that depend on government investment projects.

During times of austerity it is obviously quite difficult to satisfy all sectors of society. Thus, it is not surprising that those government decisions that have been praised by business have often drawn stern criticism from labor leaders and the left. For example, the government made great efforts to channel foreign exchange so that private investors could purchase inputs abroad as well as meet their foreign debt obligations. Data presented above suggest that there was an increase in the business share of total imports both in 1984 and 1985. In addition, the government established a mechanism known as the Foreign Exchange Protection Trust Fund (FICORCA), which allowed private firms to purchase U.S. dollars at a price below the free market exchange rate in order to meet interest and other foreign debt payment obligations. Labor and the left charged that the government in effect subsidized the financial indiscipline and the excesses of business during the years of high growth.

The sale of public enterprises also elicited mixed responses from Mexican society. At one extreme, Gastón García Cantú, a venerable leftist historian and political commentator, accused the government of selling out to foreign interests and of weakening the state. White-collar employees at Mexicana Airlines, however, welcomed press reports of the imminent sale of their firm because they had bitterly complained when the government took it over to save it from bankruptcy. By contrast, blue-collar workers of state-owned enterprises that closed their doors, like Monterrey's *Fundidora* steel mill, feared for their future. In any event, when negotiations to put together yet another emergency financial rescue package for Mexico (1986) seemed to approach a dead end, the government stepped up efforts at selling and in some cases closing down public enterprises. The bureaucracy and workers have been hit hard by the economic crisis, and they have in the process lost the protection and the long-term security once represented by government jobs.

Of course, the government could go only so far in closing down its agencies to reduce expenditures. The mere suggestion that CONASUPO might disappear was met with such widespread opposition that the government immediately provided assurances that it would continue selling products for the basic diet of the working classes at subsidized prices. The role and certain operations of CONASUPO were reduced at the same time that the government went on to negotiate the survival of that state firm with the IMF. In general, however, the views of organized labor were not very influential, and its role was limited largely to defusing growing worker frustration. An editorial in a Mexico City weekly expressed this succinctly in its reference to the CTM's long-time boss: "A Fidel Velázquez ya no le hacen caso" (They no longer take Fidel Velázquez seriously).[58] Successive calls by the CTM and other organizations to halt payments to international creditors and to increase wages above inflation fell on deaf ears. Furthermore, government-labor relations under de la Madrid were strained over attempts to curb union corruption—especially among the oil union leaders (see Chapter 3).

It is interesting to note that although blue-collar workers, bureaucrats, and the middle classes often did not find effective ways of influencing policies that hurt their interests, sectors of the peasant population succeeded in strengthening their organizations in some respects. López Portillo's SAM program has been assessed positively by numerous authors. Not only did the agricultural sector grow by 6.7 percent in 1980–1981, before experiencing a 0.4 percent decline in 1982, but SAM perhaps signaled a shift in government policy aimed at strengthening the mass legitimacy of the political system.[59] The SAM, however, was one of the victims of de la Madrid's efforts to disassociate himself completely from his predecessor. A new agrarian reform law was enacted at the end of 1983 whose basic purpose was to decentralize certain decisions away from Mexico City and from the president's hands. For example, state governors were empowered to allocate lands to *ejidatarios* (owners of communal lands) and to decide on new land petitions put forward by peasant organizations; and the Ministry of Agrarian Reform would decide on whether to protect agricultural holdings from attempts to expropriate and redistribute lands.[60] The objective was to demobilize the peasantry and thus reduce the hundreds of protest marches from rural areas to Mexico City that take place every year.

But with the centers of decisionmaking transferred to individual states, the peasantry was able to strengthen its local and regional organizations. This was facilitated by the inability of official agencies like the CNC to provide leadership, and thus independent organizations gradually filled the political vacuum. The most significant institutional expression of this trend is the surge of the Coordinadoras.[61] These are networks of regional organizations that maintain their own autonomy and design their own objectives, programs, and policymaking mechanisms (usually decisions are made by consensus). The Coordinadoras are dedicated to struggle for lands used for livestock and cattle-raising, which they want to put to work for agricultural produce.[62] They also seek direct access to credit outside the present framework, which involves the unfair enrichment of several intermediaries, and they seek to commercialize their own products and raise official prices to improve profit margins. The outlook of the Coordinadoras, according to an analyst involved in their work for years, seems particularly bright because the government needs the peasants for several critical reasons. One is to increase agricultural production at home so that import needs are reduced and some output can be exported. Another is to prevent revolt; the PRI also needs the peasant vote to help it defeat the growing opposition it has faced in urban areas. Finally, the government and the army need peasant support to fight the bloody war against illegal drugs.[63]

Further Efforts at Reform

With the assistance of a favorable climate, the agricutural sector grew by an average 2.7 percent from 1983 to 1985. The record of the industrial sector, however, fluctuated pretty much along the lines of the overall economy. An abrupt decline in 1983 was followed by moderate growth rates in 1984 and 1985 (an average 4 percent) and then by a contraction when the economy entered into a recessionary phase in 1986. The oil industry was particularly affected as a result of shrinking foreign sales and the collapse of oil prices. Mexican oil was selling for an average US$25 per barrel in January but only about US$10 by midyear. Thus, manufacturing became once again the focus of attention and of expectations to pull the rest of the economy through its difficulties.

The problems afflicting the industrial sector included the low levels of operating capacity and of new investments, given prevailing economic uncertainties and the scarcity of domestic credit. Government efforts to increase productivity and to encourage industry toward foreign markets did not fulfill expectations. For example, the government followed an aggressive foreign exchange policy, keeping the peso undervalued to make Mexican products more attractive; and it provided fiscal and commercial incentives to facilitate exports. Most of all, de la Madrid signed a memorandum of understanding with the U.S. government (April 1985) affecting bilateral trade relations. Mexico committed itself to reduce gradually alleged subsidies for its exports, and the United States agreed not to impose compensating duties unless Mexican products are subjected to the "injury test" following a complaint by domestic economic agents.[64] In 1985 President de la Madrid also sent a negotiating team to Geneva seeking membership in GATT, and in July 1986, Mexico became the ninety-first member nation of that trade organization.[65]

This time the presidential directive regarding GATT was so definitive and conclusive that hardly any opportunity arose for the sort of public debate aired in 1979. The new policy question revolved only around the extent to which adhering to GATT rules would actually encourage the growth of exports.[66] National economies do not become more productive and competitive primarily as a result of an executive decree or abstract rules included in an international treaty. Mexico had to take a hard look into its recent export growth experience, which was by no means very encouraging. Export revenues increased substantially from US$3.3 billion in 1976 to US$21.2 billion in 1982, but of the latter figure three-quarters were composed of oil exports. By contrast, non-oil exports grew much more modestly from US$4.7 billion in 1980 to US$7.1 billion in 1985. This means that the success at diversifying the profile of Mexican exports in terms of their geographical destination, where oil exports to Japan and Europe played a key role, was not matched by comparable success in diversifying the commodity structure of exports (see pertinent data in tables presented in Chapter 7). Therefore, oil's shares in total exports remained uncomfortably high.[67] On the import side, 65 percent of all 1985 products were no longer subject to licences; instead, tariffs were imposed, ranging from 10 to 50 percent of the product's value. It remained to be seen whether these trade liberalization measures would help reduce inflation, enhance the quality of domestic products, and more generally encourage greater Mexican industrial competitiveness.

When the Mexican government signed a new agreement with the IMF in July 1986, there were expectations that the stage was set for some economic recovery. Under the agreement Mexico would receive up to US$12 billion in financial assistance through the end of 1987.[68] The World Bank, the Inter-American Development Bank, and the governments and banks of key industrial nations would also be important contributors to this unprecedented financial package. The agreement was inspired by the so-called Baker Plan, which was proposed by the U.S. secretary of the treasury, James Baker, during a joint IMF–World Bank meeting in Korea (1985). At that conference, Baker stressed the need to approach the debt issue by providing sufficient funds to allow debtor nations to resume growth on a long-term basis. Furthermore, an innovative feature of the Mexico-IMF agreement established that the flow of new money lent to Mexico could change according to the evolution of oil prices. That is, higher prices and therefore growing export revenues would result in a lower amount of money made available to Mexico, and vice versa. This constituted a truly revolutionary concept that would have been unthinkable just a few years ago. U.S. critics asked how their government could endorse such a measure while neglecting assistance to its own hard-pressed domestic oil industry and bankrupt farmers.

In addition, the IMF, in an unusual show of flexibility, accepted at face value Mexico's contention that the ratio of public sector deficit to gross domestic product be calculated exclusive of government payments on its own internal debt. The latter had grown tremendously as a result of high interest rates affected in turn by domestic inflation and other fiscal and monetary policy considerations discussed above. At the time of the agreement, payments on the domestic debt represented 10 of the total deficit ratio (to GDP) of 13 percentage points; excluding the former, the public deficit ratio was only 3 percent, and Mexico committed itself to bring that figure down to zero. Thus, what in early 1986 appeared to be a situation that could well lead Mexico into default, turned into one of relief.

The process that led to the IMF agreement was complex. Disagreements within de la Madrid's cabinet had been sharpened by the economic downturn that preceded the accord. The dust had hardly settled in the aftermath of the 1985 earthquakes when the much-feared outbreak of an oil price war put the Mexican government's economic plans for 1986 in shambles. Projections of a 45 percent inflation rate, a surplus in the foreign trade account of US$8 billion, a public deficit ratio of 4.9 percent, and economic growth ranging from −1 to +1 percent appeared ridiculously optimistic almost as soon as they had been published.[69] Business leaders were dismayed at the lack of governmental ability to include in their projections worst-case scenarios—especially because these are the scenarios that have materialized in recent years. Further, the president delivered dramatic speeches in 1986, stressing that "the dead can no longer meet their commitments and the bankrupt cannot be expected to strike deals."[70] Speculation regarding an imminent Mexican default was fueled by the three-hour visit to Mexico City made by the chairman of the U.S. Federal Reserve, Paul Volcker, in June. A week later the outspoken and internationally (as well as domestically) respected minister of finance, Jesús Silva Herzog, resigned abruptly.[71]

Intracabinet disagreement with Silva Herzog's handling of the debt negotiations had been leaked to the national press. The "opposition" was headed by minister of programming and budget Carlos Salinas, which led to speculation that (as happened in 1981 when several ministers got rid of key presidential contender Jorge Díaz Serrano) the departure of Silva Herzog enhanced the prospects for other presidential hopefuls. But those who disagreed with Silva Herzog included some of his own associates, such as the head of the Central Bank and the president's chief of economic advisers (respected economist Leopoldo Solís).[72] A consensus gradually emerged within the economic cabinet, led by the newly appointed minister of finance, Gustavo Petricioli. Upon his return from negotiations in Washington, Petricioli summarized Mexico's views as follows: "Any solution to the debt problem must allow for moderate economic growth in 1987 and 1988 and should take into account the brutal effects of falling oil prices on public finances and on the balance of payments." It was to his credit that the IMF approved his plan. In time difficult negotiations were completed with foreign banks and governments willing to finance yet another expensive rescue package for Mexico.[73]

CONCLUSIONS

Since the 1970s, Mexico has faced profound difficulties in trying to achieve economic growth rates commensurate with prior rates, expectations, and the expanding population. Throughout this period, however, sound economic management has been a major political problem, and there has been a problem of credibility and of mutual distrust in government-business relations in Mexico. Without underestimating this political dimension of the problem, however, it should be stressed that it has been particularly trying for many affected actors to adjust to the new economic realities—to turn from an economy where the public sector's leading role and the substitution of imported goods with local products constituted the engine of growth to one led by a business sector pressured to orient itself toward world markets. This transition turned out to be especially difficult because of the false expectations and the distortions introduced by the expansion of the oil industry from the mid-1970s to the early 1980s. Then, natural disaster and collapsing oil prices contributed to economic crisis. In 1987, as in 1982, total financial disaster was averted, but Mexico continued to grapple with the very formidable economic problems and challenges that have been identified in this book.

In subsequent chapters we will explore the relationship between the oil industry and the economy, as well as the broader debate regarding the kind of development strategy that various actors prescribe for Mexico's future. First, however, realizing that Mexico's domestic political and economic systems do not exist in a vacuum, we turn our attention to Mexico's position in the international system.[74]

NOTES

1. Raymond Vernon, *The Dilemma of Mexico's Development: The Roles of the Private and Public Sectors* (Cambridge, Mass.: Harvard University Press, 1963); Roger D. Hansen, *The Politics of Mexican Development* (Baltimore, Md.: Johns Hopkins University Press, 1971); Leopoldo Solís, *La realidad económica mexicana: Retrovisión y perspectivas*, 10th ed. (Mexico City: Siglo XXI, 1980).

2. Nacional Financiera, *Statistics on the Mexican Economy* (Mexico City, 1977), pp. 5, 13–15.

3. Sanford A. Mosk conducted a study showing that the Alemán administration went out of its way to support young and ambitious entrepreneurs, many of whom became leading figures in the industrialization effort. While President Alemán's sympathy for the business community is no secret, it is also true that the public sector remained an important economic actor during his tenure. See Mosk's *Industrial Revolution in Mexico* (Berkeley: University of California Press, 1954). For a pathbreaking work assessing Mexican government policy through its expenditures, see James W. Wilkie, *The Mexican Revolution: Federal Expenditures and Social Change Since 1910* (Berkeley: University of California Press, 1967).

4. E.V.K. Fitzgerald's comprehensive study on this topic arrives at conclusions similar to the analysis that follows. However, his data and ours are not strictly comparable because they are arranged differently in terms of time-series. See Fitzgerald's *Patterns of Public Sector Income and Expenditures in Mexico* (Austin: University of Texas, Institute of Latin American Studies, 1978).

5. Roberto Anguiano E., *Las finanzas del sector público en México* (Mexico City: UNAM, 1968); Banco de México, *Informe anual*, various issues.

6. Robert E. Looney, *Mexico's Economy: A Policy Analysis with Forecasts to 1990* (Boulder, Colo.: Westview Press, 1978), p. 49. Fitzgerald reported an even lower ratio of taxes to gross domestic product during the 1960s and a 9.1 percent ratio for 1975 (*Patterns*, p. 8).

7. See the analysis by Mexican tax expert Luis Bravo, "La política impositiva," in *Opciones de política económica en México: Después de la devaluación*, ed. Gerardo Bueno (Mexico City: Tecnós, 1977), pp. 161–198.

8. An unusual discussion of this subject can be found in President López Portillo's fourth annual State of the Union Address. México, Secretaría de Programación y Presupuesto, *Cuarto informe de gobierno* (Mexico City, September 1980), pp. 25–26.

9. Fitzgerald, *Patterns*, p. 16.

10. A thorough analysis of the debt-related issues is presented by Rosario Green, *El endeudamiento público de México, 1940–1973* (Mexico City: El Colegio de

México, 1976); see also her article "Endeudamiento externo y debilidad estatal," *Foro Internacional* 20, no. 1 (1979):73–117.

11. Inter-American Development Bank, *Economic and Social Progress in Latin America* (Washington, D.C.: IDB, 1980), p. 101; World Bank, *World Development Report* (Washington, D.C.: World Bank, 1980), pp. 134–135.

12. Peter Vander Spek, "Mexico's Booming Border Zone: A Magnet for Labour-Intensive American Plants," *Inter-American Economic Affairs*, 29, no. 1 (1975):33–48.

13. L. Antonio Aspra, "Import Substitution in Mexico: Past and Present," *World Development* 5, nos. 1/2 (1977):111–124; René Villarreal, "The Policy of Import-Substituting Industrialization, 1929–1975," in *Authoritarianism in Mexico*, ed. José Luis Reyna and Richard Weinert (Philadelphia, Pa.: Institute for the Study of Human Issues, 1977), pp. 67–108.

14. World Bank, *Mexico, Manufacturing Sector: Situation, Prospects and Policies* (Washington, D.C.: World Bank, March 1979), p. 56. For a more general discussion about the role of the public sector in encouraging domestic production of capital goods in developing countries, see the study by the World Bank, *The Capital Goods Sector in LDCs: A Case Study for State Intervention?* Staff Working Paper 343 (Washington, D.C.: World Bank, July 1979).

15. Villarreal, "Policy." Another study that questions the wisdom of a capital goods import substitution policy in developing nations is by the World Bank, *Fostering the Capital Goods Sector in LDCs: A Survey of Evidence and Requirements*, Staff Working Paper 376 (Washington, D.C.: World Bank, March 1980).

16. Bela Balassa, *The Newly Industrializing Countries in the World Economy* (New York: Pergamon Press, 1981).

17. Solís, *La realidad económica mexicana*, p. 111.

18. Shlomo Eckstein and Reyes Osorio, "Desarrollo polarizado de la agricultura mexicana," in *La sociedad mexicana: Presente y futuro*, ed. Miguel Wionczek (Mexico City: Fondo de Cultura Económica, 1973), pp. 30–31.

19. Vania Almeida and Kristen de Appendini, *Agricultura capitalista y agricultura campesina en México*, 2d ed. (Mexico City: El Colegio de México, 1977).

20. CONASUPO is a state monopoly supplying poor people with some basic products, primarily food, at substantially subsidized prices.

21. México, Secretaría de Programación y Presupuesto, *Informe sobre las relaciones económicas de México con el exterior* (Mexico City, 1979), p. 62.

22. Inter-American Development Bank, *Economic and Social Progress*, p. 309.

23. México, Secretaría de Programación y Presupuesto, *La población de México, su ocupación y sus niveles de bienestar* (Mexico City, 1979). In its first evaluation of the Global Development Plan, the government acknowledged that 18 million people do not receive any modern medical care. See México, Secretaría de Programación y Presupuesto, *Plan global de desarrollo: Primer informe de avance, 1980–1982* (Mexico City, 1981), p. 18.

24. México, Secretaría del Trabajo y Previsión Social, *Proyecto. Plan nacional de empleo, 1980–1982* (Mexico City, November 1979); and Secretaría de Programación y Presupuesto, *La población* (1979).

25. Saúl Trejo Reyes, "La política laboral," in Bueno, *Opciones*, p. 150. Regarding women in the work force, it is worth noting that a few have recently ascended to very prominent positions; Mexico has only recently had its first female governor and its first female minister.

26. Banco de México, *Informe anual*, various issues; United Nations Economic Commission for Latin America, *México. Notas para el estudio económico de América Latina* (Washington, D.C.: United Nations, 1979).

27. World Bank, *World Development Report*, 1980, pp. 156–157.

28. The analysis draws on Daniel Levy, *Higher Education and the State in Latin America: Private Challenges to Public Dominance* (Chicago: University of Chicago Press, 1986), pp. 114–170. On social-welfare policy, see, for example, Rose Spalding, "Welfare Policymaking: Theoretical Implications of a Mexican Case Study," *Comparative Politics* 12, no. 4 (1980):419–438.

29. David Ibarra, "Mercados, desarrollo y política económica: Perspectivas de la economía mexicana," in *El perfil de México en 1980*, by the editors of Siglo XXI (Mexico City: Siglo XXI, 1970), Vol. 1, pp. 186–187.

30. México, Secretaría de Programación y Presupuesto, *Segundo informe de gobierno, anexo I* (Mexico City, September 1978), pp. 295–300.

31. Banco de México, *Informe anual*, various issues.

32. México, Secretaría de Programación y Presupuesto, *Informe*, p. 58.

33. México, Secretaría de Patrimonio Nacional, *Law to Promote Mexican Investment and to Regulate Foreign Investment* (Mexico City, 1973).

34. John M. Connor and Willard Mueller, *Market Power and Profitability of Multinational Corporations in Brazil and Mexico* (Washington, D.C.: Government Printing Office, Report to the Subcommittee on Foreign Economic Policy of the Committee on Foreign Relations, U.S. Senate, April 1977), pp. 5–12.

35. Mauricio de María, "Política y resultados en materia de inversiones extranjeras," *Comercio Exterior* (special issue, July 1976):32; Banco de México, *Informe anual*, various issues; and Mexico, Secretaría de Programación y Presupuesto, *Segundo informe de gobierno: Anexo sector comercio y fomento industrial* (Mexico City, 1984), p. 214.

36. Banco de México, *The Mexican Economy in 1977* (Mexico City, 1978).

37. Nacional Financiera, *Statistics*, p. 370.

38. Douglas Bennett and Kenneth Sharpe, "El estado como banquero y empresario: El carácter de última instancia de la intervención económica del estado mexicano, 1917–1970," *Foro Internacional* 20, no. 1 (1979):72.

39. Roger D. Hansen, "The Evolution of U.S.-Mexican Relations: A Socio-Political Perspective," in *United States Relations with Mexico: Context and Content*, ed. Richard D. Erb and Stanley R. Ross (Washington, D.C.: American Enterprise Institute, 1981), pp. 39–48; E.V.K. Fitzgerald, "The State and Capital Accumulation in Mexico," *Journal of Latin American Studies* 10, no. 2 (1978):263–282.

40. Lawrence Whitehead, "La política económica del sexenio de Echeverría: ¿Qué salió mal y por qué?" *Foro Internacional* 20, no. 3 (1980):484–513; and Sidney Weintraub, "Case Study of Economic Stabilization: Mexico," in *Economic Stabilization in Developing Countries*, ed. William R. Cline and Sidney Weintraub (Washington, D.C.: Brookings Institution, 1981), pp. 271–296.

41. For an analysis of the relationship between oil policy and broader economic policy objectives, and the implications for Mexico's domestic and foreign policies, see Gabriel Székely, "The 1976 Oil Export Decision: Effects of the Oil Boom on Mexico's Political Economy," Ph.D. dissertation, George Washington University, 1983.

42. Banco de México, *Informe anual*, various issues.

43. It is difficult to assess the impact of the elimination of income taxes for the poorest groups, because inflation has been so high, because many people do not receive the minimum wage, and because of the introduction of indirect taxes (VAT) that are paid by everyone.

44. Chapter 1, fn. 7; Banco de México, *Informe anual*, various issues.

45. Ibid., 1980, p. 84. All tons are metric.

46. Oficina de Asesores del C. Presidente de la República, "Sistema Alimentario Mexicano" (Mexico City, 1980), unpublished draft. This study includes twenty projects, of which only fourteen are available to the public.

47. México, Secretaría de Gobernación, "Ley de fomento agropecuario," in *Diario Oficial* (Mexico City, January 2, 1981), pp. 9–25.

48. For the debate, see "Opiniones sobre el ingreso de México al GATT," *Comercio Exterior* 30, no. 2 (special issue, February 1980); and "México ante el GATT," *El Economista Mexicano* (special issue, January-February 1980). For a good analysis see Dale Story, "Trade Politics in the Third World: A Case Study of the Mexican GATT Decision," *International Organization* 36 (Autumn 1982):767–794.

49. Susan Kaufman Purcell, *The Mexican Profit-Sharing Decision: Politics in an Authoritarian Regime* (Berkeley: University of California Press, 1975).

50. The linkage of oil to negotiations on other bilateral issues was expounded, notably, by former foreign minister Jorge Castañeda, "En búsqueda de una posición frente a Estados Unidos," *Foro Internacional* 19, no. 2 (1978):292–302; in the United States, see the supporting statement of former undersecretary of state for economic affairs Myer Rashish at New York's Center for Inter-American Relations, "North-American Economic Relations," September 22, 1981.

51. See the position paper of the National Association of Economists of Mexico, *Excélsior*, May 26, 1979.

52. Alan Gelb, *Capital-Importing Oil Exporters: Adjustment Issues and Policy Choices*, Staff Working Paper 475 (Washington, D.C.: World Bank, 1981).

53. Aurora Berdejo, "Congelación de sueldos a funcionarios: Salinas de Gortari," *Excélsior*, July 25, 1985; and Gilberto d'Estrabau, "Reorganizar la administración no causará desocupación masiva," *Excélsior*, July 26, 1984.

54. Estimates provided by Banco de México.

55. The Ministry of Commerce and Industrial Development approved the IBM and other investment projects worth US$350 million on July 23, 1985, as reported in "Computación, farmacéutico y turismo, son algunos: SECOFIN," *Excélsior*, July 24, 1985.

56. See the December 6, 1985 issue of the *Diario Oficial*, published in Mexico City; also, Edith Jiménez, "Júbilo en la IP por la modificación a la ley de inversiones extranjeras," *Excélsior*, December 7, 1985.

57. Rogelio Ramírez, "Presupuesto y política fiscal," paper presented at the conference Government and Private Sector in Contemporary Mexico, organized by the Center for U.S.-Mexican Studies of the University of California, San Diego, April 16–18, 1986.

58. *Proceso*, July 21, 1986.

59. Jonathan Fox, "The Political Dynamics of Reform: The Case of the Mexican Food System, 1980–1982," Ph.D. dissertation, M.I.T., 1986. See also Cassio Luiselli, *The Route to Food Self-Sufficiency in Mexico: Interactions with the U.S. Food System*, Monograph series 17 (La Jolla, Calif.: Center for U.S.-Mexican Studies, University of Calif., San Diego, 1985).

60. Comisión de Reforma Agraria, Cámara de Diputados, "Proyecto de decreto que reforma, que adiciona y que deroga diversas disposiciones de la Ley Federal de Reforma Agraria" (Mexico City, December 29, 1983).

61. Gustavo Gordillo, "El futuro de la participación política en el campo mexicano," paper presented at the weekly seminar at the Center for U.S.-Mexican Studies of the University of California, San Diego, May 26, 1986.

62. Mechthild Rutsch, *La ganadería capitalista en México* (Mexico City: Editorial Línea, 1984).

63. Gordillo, "Futuro."

64. "Entendimiento entre Estados Unidos y México sobre subsidios e impuestos compensatorios," *Diario Oficial* (Mexico City, May 15, 1985).

65. The following are key documents to understanding the process of negotiations between Mexico and GATT: "Instrucciones presidenciales," *Comercio Exterior* 35, no. 12 (1985):1195–1196; in the same issue, Tomás Peñaloza, "La adhesión de México al GATT," pp. 1160–1167. Also, the "Memorandum sobre el régimen de comercio exterior de México," *Comercio Exterior* 36, no. 2 (1986):189–202; and Patricia Muñoz, "México firma hoy con el GATT," *El Financiero*, July 15, 1986.

66. Claudia Schatan, "The Political Economy of Import Liberalization in Mexico," in *Government and Private Sector in Contemporary Mexico*, ed. Sylvia Maxfield and Ricardo Anzaldúa (La Jolla, Calif.: Center for U.S.-Mexican Studies, University of California, San Diego, 1987).

67. Gabriel Székely, *Mexico's Economic Relations with Industrialized Powers: Oil and Trade Diversification* (1987), mimeo.

68. Peter Kilborn, "Mexico Reported Near Agreement for New Loans Up to $12 billion," *New York Times*, July 22, 1986; Art Pine, "Mexico-IMF Pact Is Seen Easing Cash Crunch, Altering Economy," *Wall Street Journal*, July 23, 1986.

69. Miguel de la Madrid Hurtado, "La política económica para 1986," *Comercio Exterior* 35, no. 12 (1985):1179–1188.

70. "Ajuste de la deuda externa a la capacidad real de pago: MMH," *La Jornada*, February 22, 1986; "Pagaremos si podemos crecer," *El Financiero*, June 3, 1986.

71. Aurora Berdejo and Jesús Rangel, "Petricioli, titular de hacienda por renuncia de Silva Herzog," *Excélsior*, June 18, 1986.

72. See "El informe público 1985 del Banco de México, maquillado," *Proceso*, May 5, 1986, pp. 8–9; and "Cambio inmediato de políticas, aconsejan los economistas al presidente," *Proceso*, June 2, 1986.

73. Jesús Rangel, "Habrá resultados en 30 días," *Excélsior*, July 1, 1986; Aurora Berdejo and José M. Nava, "Confirmó ayer por vía telefónica," *Excélsior*, July 10, 1986.

74. For further reading, see Clark Reynolds, *The Mexican Economy: Twentieth Century Structure and Growth* (New Haven, Conn.: Yale University Press, 1970); Jorge Domínguez, ed., *Mexico's Political Economy: Challenges at Home and Abroad* (Beverly Hills, Calif.: Sage Publications, 1982); Donald Wyman, ed., *Mexico's Economic Crisis: Challenges and Opportunities*, Monograph Series 12 (La Jolla, Calif.: Center for U.S.-Mexican Studies, University of California, San Diego, 1983); Pablo González Casanova and Héctor Aguilar, eds., *México ante la crisis*, 2 vols. (Mexico City: Siglo XXI, 1985).

Photo Section

View of El Angel (The Angel) monument and modern areas of Mexico City. (Photo courtesy of Bud Lewis)

Mexico City's famous Plaza de las Tres Culturas (Plaza of the Three Cultures) at Tlatelolco. (Photo courtesy of Bud Lewis)

View of Mexico City at night. (Photo courtesy of Bud Lewis)

Sunday entertainment, reflecting Mexico's heterogeneity, at Chapultepec, Mexico City's largest park.

The western city of Morelia. The building is adorned with one of the regime's ubiquitous political slogans ("We Are All The Solution").

Rural scene near Cuautla, close to Mexico City.

Outdoor cantina in the southern state of Chiapas. (Photo courtesy of Lynne C. Rienner)

Peasant house in southern Mexico. (Photo courtesy of James P. Brochin)

Agricultural activity in the central state of Hidalgo. (Photo courtesy of James P. Brochin)

Mayan ruins in southern Mexico. (Photo courtesy of James P. Brochin)

6

Foreign Policy:
In the Giant's Shadow

Poor Mexico: So far from God and so close to the United States.
—attributed to Porfirio Díaz

The first element of Mexican foreign policy is . . . its relations with the United States. . . . This is, I repeat, an irrefutable reality, not a political option. It cannot be denied by past problems or historical experiences; it is simply a fact of life.
—Jorge Castañeda, June 1980[1]

Our two quotations, from two distinct eras, suggest a profound continuity in Mexican foreign policy—the centrality of the United States. Surely, as discussed in Chapter 1, Mexico is increasingly important to the United States. But Mexico is one among many important nations for U.S. foreign policy, whereas the United States is probably more important than all other nations combined for Mexican foreign policy. When, for example, a U.S. ambassador apologized for bothering Mexico's foreign minister with a trivial matter, the minister reassuringly dismissed the apology, explaining that 85 percent of his time was devoted to relations with the United States.[2] A different indicator, to be explored shortly, is that Mexico has relied on the United States for roughly two-thirds of its import and export trade.

Mexico has made significant efforts, especially since 1970, to become more assertive, to build a foreign policy less covered by the giant's shadow. Although some success has been achieved, the shadow remains large indeed. This chapter first summarizes the evolution of Mexico–United States ties. It then analyzes the increased breadth and assertiveness of contemporary Mexican foreign policy beyond the United States, recognizing that Mexico–United States relations are affected by this change. Finally, the chapter returns to major, specific issues in contemporary Mexico–United States relations and highlights Mexico's deepened dependency on its neighbor in times of economic crisis.

183

EVOLUTION OF MEXICO-UNITED STATES RELATIONS

Annexation

Products of very different colonial heritages, Mexico and the United States had little contact until the nineteenth century. Before long, however, contact was intense and conflictual.

When Mexico achieved independence it was not yet clear that it would be much the weaker neighbor, but within two decades the United States had established its superior strength. Although still relatively equal to the United States in land size, Mexico had fallen far behind in population.[3] Crucially, the United States had avoided the brutal cycle of economic crisis and political instability that had characterized Mexico. Thus, when the two nations went to war in 1846, the United States proved itself far stronger than Mexico.

The issue was Texas. After Mexico complained that the first U.S. ambassador meddled in Mexico's domestic politics, the United States appointed a successor who meddled even more, actively plotting against Mexico's interests in Texas. U.S. settlers had been immigrating into Texas. Fearing revolutionary consequences, Mexico limited the legal flow in 1830. This should be remembered, in one of history's ironies, as the year that Mexico slammed the border shut on the United States—or attempted to do so. The measure proved impossible to enforce, just as contemporary U.S. laws fail to keep Mexicans out, and the first wave of "illegal aliens" crossed the border. In 1836, Texans declared their independence from Mexico and soon defeated General Santa Anna's Mexican troops. Although President Andrew Jackson happily recognized Texan independence in 1837, the United States initially rejected Texan requests for annexation and statehood. Abolitionists opposed the addition of another slave state, and there was some concern that Mexico not be provoked any further. But pressures built, and President Polk was a powerful proponent of U.S. expansion.

In 1845, the United States annexed Texas, and a lopsided war ensued. From Mexico's point of view the war's cause was clear: U.S. aggression. Not only did the United States annex Texas, but it claimed boundaries for Texas that Mexico simply could not accept. The United States resorted to more complex rationalizations, ones that could not unite U.S. opinion. Polk did get his war resolution through the Senate with only two dissensions— the same number that would defy President Lyndon Johnson's Gulf of Tonkin resolution for military action in Vietnam more than a century later. As with the Vietnam War, however, considerable dissent quickly developed. Some leaders in the South feared that the United States was going too far against Mexico, while many northeasterners decried "Mr. Polk's War"; the Massachusetts legislature condemned the U.S. role. Prominent dissenters ranged from literary figures such as Henry David Thoreau and Ralph Waldo Emerson to political figures such as young Abraham Lincoln. Unlike the Vietnam War, however, the war with Mexico represented the ascent of the

United States as an active—or overactive—international power and ended in striking military success. Indeed the war itself was short. General Winfield Scott captured the key port of Veracruz and marched on to take Mexico City. Mexico's most treasured war memory lies in the heroism of six young cadets who jumped to their death rather than surrender themselves at Chapultepec Castle. Today prominent monuments to the *Niños Héroes* are found throughout Mexico, from the castle itself, to a subway station, to streets in many major cities, to significant attention in public school textbooks.

However militarily undramatic the war was, the settlement reached with the Treaty of Guadalupe Hidalgo was dramatic—and unjust. Mexico lost about one-half of its territory, including all or parts of what are now Arizona, California, Colorado, Nevada, New Mexico, and Utah. As a post-script, the United States swallowed still more Mexican territory with the Gadsden Purchase of 1853, when Mexico—desperately in need of money— sold off a chunk of its land. That chunk would eventually include copper mines and create an unnatural border, actually splitting cities in half. Moreover, the war obviously hurt Mexican efforts to build unity, stability, and prosperity in the new nation.

It would be difficult to understand contemporary Mexican attitudes toward the United States without reference to the enormous land grab of the mid-nineteenth century. This does not mean that most Mexicans feel an active anger about the war or advocate "taking back the land." Rather, sentiment remains like a dormant volcano in the historical consciousness. There is a sense of resentment based on the unhappy role Mexico played in U.S. expansionism. The war may not be an explicit political issue, but it is a vital historical referent and symbol. Consequent "wounded nationalism" perhaps serves today as a useful foreign policy bargaining chip: Mexican policymakers can tell their U.S. counterparts that, restrained by sensitive public opinion, they must negotiate tenaciously.

From Accommodation to Revolutionary Conflict to Accommodation

As Mexico next came to suffer at the hands of a different foreigner, France, relations improved with the United States. President Abraham Lincoln continued to recognize the regime of President Benito Juárez throughout the period of French intervention. Outstanding claims between Mexico and the United States were settled in 1868. Mexico–United States relations deepened when the porfiriato replaced the reform and created just the sort of domestic environment that pleased U.S. economic interests. Unaffection-ately dubbed "father of foreigners and stepfather of Mexicans," Porfirio Díaz extended further the already attractive invitations to foreign investors. He eased requirements for acquiring land in border regions and on use of subsoil resources and generally encouraged increased foreign economic activity in Mexico. Most important, Díaz secured the political stability that foreign investors demanded. Mexico's doors opened not just for its northern neighbor but for West Europeans as well; nonetheless, the United States took greatest advantage of the opportunities and established its predominance among foreigners in Mexico's economy. There was even increased foreign penetration of the priesthood, to the dismay of many Mexican clergy.

As the Mexican Revolution replaced political stability and friendliness to foreign investment with instability and nationalism, Mexico–United States relations predictably worsened. And, unfortunately for Mexico, the United States was in an imposing muscle-flexing period. Its easy 1898 victory in the Spanish-American War and its construction of the Panama Canal reflected the emergence of the United States as a true world power, including a heightened preeminence in the New World. If subsequent events are viewed within this political-economic context—Mexico torn by revolutionary instability, the United States prepared to impose its will—then the machinations of individual political actors may count for little. Still, individual behavior not only helped shape events but left scarring symbols in Mexico's memory. U.S. Ambassador Henry Lane Wilson, for example, is perhaps a stereotypic villain. In complicity with Mexico's counterrevolutionary leaders, he is widely believed to have participated in the sinister assassination of President Madero, the elected and conspicuously nonrevolutionary democrat. The ambassador hoped to return Mexico to his own conception of peace, progress, and prosperity.

President Woodrow Wilson, by contrast, emerged as perhaps the higher-minded villain. Whereas the preceding president, William Howard Taft (1909–1913), had clearly based his actions on U.S. self-interest, without trying to "improve" Mexico's own system, Wilson was a human rights activist, a zealous democrat, albeit a paternalistic one. This is not to say that he would subordinate U.S. material interests to moral concerns, but that he identified them with a type of political regime that Mexico did not have. Whatever justifications he saw, Wilson was an interventionist, to the point of using military force and the threat of further military force. He managed to antagonize not only those he opposed but also those he favored. He helped to topple the Huerta government (which the United States itself had helped install) by denying diplomatic recognition, cutting off Huerta's European arms supply, authorizing arms sales to Huerta's opponents, and seizing on a limited provocation for the capture of Veracruz (by now a favorite U.S. pressure point).

Differences of opinion exist over the extent to which the United States shaped Mexican domestic politics in the early revolutionary years. Suffice it to say that the United States did not create all the strife but did intervene forcefully to influence the outcome. At various points, the United States supported Madero, Huerta, and Villa, before settling on Carranza as the most likely figure to win the military battle, establish stability, and deal with U.S. economic interests in an acceptable manner.[4] As with Indian disunity and Cortés's conquest, or nineteenth-century disunity and the U.S. and then French actions, so again in the early years of the revolution, Mexican independence was undermined by domestic disunity and instability as well as by blatant foreign intervention.

Angered over U.S. intervention on behalf of Carranza, Villa undertook vengeful raids across the border. U.S. general John Pershing unsuccessfully pursued him through northern Mexico, thus inadvertently contributing to Villa's immortalization. Even today, Villa remains the hero of numerous popular ballads. Although tensions mounted still further, additional Mexico–United States hostilities were ultimately averted. Mexican politics stabilized somewhat, and Wilson and Pershing were soon preoccupied overseas with World War I. Nonetheless, bilateral bitterness lingered. Mexico did not support the United States and its allies in the world war. It did, however, reject the tantalizing Zimmerman note in which Germany opportunistically solicited Mexican support in exchange for a promise that a victorious Germany would return to Mexico the lands previously taken by the United States.

The main source of conflict now became compensation for U.S. properties nationalized as a result of Mexico's revolution. As general and then president, Carranza proved to be more of a nationalist than the United States had hoped. Diplomatic recognition of Carranza's successor (Obregón) was delayed three years, until Mexico in 1923 signed the Bucareli Agreements, promising not to apply certain legislation retroactively. Only a mini-era of good feeling would follow the Bucareli Agreements. By 1925, Mexico's new president, Plutarco Elías Calles, had toughened national policies on oil and land; one provision declared that disputes would be handled by Mexican adjudication, not U.S. adjudication. Both oil and land proved to be tough issues, major problems for Mexico–United States relations.[5] The new U.S. ambassador undiplomatically proclaimed Mexico on trial. Additionally, Calles unleashed a brutal attack on Mexico's church, provoking many conservative Catholics, both in Mexico and in the United States, to solicit U.S. intervention.[6]

The crisis abated, partly through the efforts of the new U.S. ambassador, Dwight Morrow, a Yankee Wall Streeter who demonstrated respect for Mexican political independence and enthusiasm for Mexican culture. Deeper roots for Morrow's success lay in Mexico's inclination to temper further reforms. When Lázaro Cárdenas assumed the presidency in 1934, Mexico's economy, save agriculture, was possibly more controlled by foreign interests, certainly by U.S. interests, than in 1910, after the porfiriato's noted coziness with foreigners.[7] Mexico's most renowned revolutionary president then began to alter the ownership balance, nationalizing the railroads and—most important—petroleum (see Chapter 7). At that point another deep root for improved Mexico–United States relations developed. Despite the challenge to U.S. business interests, a historical pattern was broken: Mexico–United States relations did not sharply deteriorate as Mexico asserted its independence. Franklin Roosevelt's Good Neighbor Policy set a new tone of acceptance, prevailing over considerable domestic pressure for retaliation. The change was symbolized by the friendly ambassadorship of Josephus Daniels, himself formerly the secretary of the navy that had occupied Veracruz; his assistant had been F.D.R. As with the Mexican revolution and World War I, so with Mexican nationalization and World War II: A "soft" U.S. policy toward Mexico was motivated largely by widening U.S. foreign policy concerns.

With World War II came increased Mexico–United States cooperation. Mexico declared war on the Axis powers in 1942 and made a strong contribution to the war effort. Mexican soldiers did not participate significantly in active combat, but they did add to the manpower reserve. Most important, the Mexican economy accelerated its production of raw materials, and Mexico and the United States entered into the *bracero* program that brought Mexican workers to the labor-drained United States; in fact, these two contributions would further integrate the Mexican economy into the U.S. economy, thus shaping future Mexican foreign policy.

As we reach the era in which Mexico's regime institutionalizes and stabilizes itself, no longer subject to repeated fundamental policy reorientations, we shift from a chronologically to conceptually oriented account. Grand historical disputes over territory, property rights, debts, diplomatic recognition, and active intervention gave way to lesser problems, mostly economic, over water rights, fishing, tariffs, migrant workers, and drugs. In time, some of these disputes would become very intense, but during the 1940s, 1950s, and 1960s, Mexico–United States relations were comparatively smooth. If the Cárdenas-Roosevelt era represented a transitional stage away from continually tense conflict, the new equilibrium would generally hold for the ensuing three decades. Mexico's domestic development clearly favored a stable industrialization that encouraged secure, profitable U.S. investment. The Mexican Revolution, by all serious accounts, was over. Naturally, the United States was eager to foster this sort of (nonrevolutionary) relationship. In 1947, President Truman paid the first U.S. presidential visit to Mexico City since the revolution, and President Eisenhower met with Mexico's president on several occasions. John Kennedy's trip to Mexico evoked an enthusiastic response by millions to his Alliance for Progress concerns, his youth and glamor, his religious affiliation (as the United States's first Catholic president), and the promise of a better future through bilateral cooperation. Johnson's early, friendly contacts were soon overshadowed by his preoccupation with the Vietnam War and by both his and President Díaz Ordaz's domestic troubles, and the Nixon and Ford administrations paid only intermittent attention to improving Mexico–United States relations. Oil, the Central American crisis, and Mexico's own economic crisis made Mexico a major concern for presidents Carter and Reagan alike.

REACHING BEYOND THE UNITED STATES

Mexican foreign policy is not determined wholly by Mexico–United States relations. The tug between the efforts to achieve greater independent breadth and the constraints encountered therein forms one of the themes of Mexican foreign policy. For decades, "universalism" and "leftism" have suggested a respectable degree of independence. These concepts will be defined and then examined in Mexico-Cuba relations. Additionally, since 1970, Mexican foreign policy has entered an era of greater assertiveness. The respective efforts and constraints involved in this change will be examined in terms of Mexican policy toward the Americas in general and Central America in particular. Finally, the Iranian crisis of 1979 will be reviewed as an example of Mexico's independent orientation in foreign affairs *beyond* the Americas.

Universalism, Leftism, and Cuba

A foreign policy obedient to U.S. leadership would befriend U.S. allies and reject U.S. foes. Mexico has generally repudiated such criteria in favor of more universal diplomatic ties. The universalistic approach is poignantly proclaimed in the Estrada Doctrine, issued in 1930: Mexico grants diplomatic recognition to any government. Mexico does not judge others as the United States continually judged Mexico or still judges others. Instead, Mexico champions a host of platitudinous principles, widely popular at least in rhetoric: national sovereignty and self-determination, equality among nations, nonintervention, peaceful settlement of disputes. Thus, it opposed veto power for Security Council members at the United Nations, favoring greater weight for the General Assembly, in which all members have equal representation. At least until recently, Mexico was one of the nations to honor most the Latin American tradition of providing asylum for political refugees. "Friend of all" is the way official Mexican propaganda sometimes likes to characterize it, although noted exceptions have qualified that approach to the point where Mexico has sometimes disavowed not only friendship but even diplomatic recognition. In fact, the breadth and vagueness of such platitudinous principles leave great flexibility for Mexico's president. He can justify almost any foreign policy with consecrated principle. Universalism provided a sure rationale for ignoring the U.S.-led boycott of the 1980 Moscow Olympics in the aftermath of the Soviet invasion of Afghanistan, but had Mexico wished to boycott, it could have claimed to be defending Afghanistan's national sovereignty. Universalism has been one major component of Mexican foreign policy, but it is not automatically applied.

Mexico is a participant and supporter of international organizations, including the Organization of American States (OAS), Inter-American Development Bank, and Association for Latin American Integration (formerly the Latin American Free Trade Association), and beyond the Americas, the United Nations, International Monetary Fund, and World Bank. But Mexico tries to balance participation with independence. It is wary of U.S. domination in the inter-American organizations. It has joined neither the Organization of Petroleum Exporting Countries (OPEC), nor the movement of nonaligned nations. It did however, enter the 1980s by assuming a seat on the UN's Security Council for the first time since 1946. Mexico is striving to increase its participation in international fora when such participation would not jeopardize its independence. And, as we have seen, in 1986 Mexico joined GATT.

Beyond its universalistic, rather than pro-U.S., posture, Mexico sometimes seems to relish the "leftism" of its foreign policy. By "leftism," we mean Mexico's sympathy for leftist movements outside Mexico. Why, paradoxically, does a regime that is conservative at home propagandize a leftist foreign policy? One reason is genuine conviction, genuine support for nationalist or popular movements. To dismiss this factor is to indulge in over-cynicism and to impute too much surreptitious calculation to every decision. Another reason is to maintain, and trumpet, some independence from the United States. Another, however, is to divert attention from unprogressive domestic policies.[8] A populist foreign policy, "easy leftism," comes at relatively little cost to Mexico's rulers; a populist domestic policy would involve far greater sacrifices. After the 1968 demonstrations against Mexico's lack of democracy, the two biggest Mexico City demonstrations in the 1960s and 1970s were against the Vietnam War and the 1973 coup in Chile, demonstrations that not only cost the government nothing, but even provided it opportunities for popular rhetoric. Another example: President López Portillo pointedly refused to attend the 1977 Washington, D.C., signing of the Panama Canal treaty, protesting that it did not go far enough for national sovereignty and that the event was marred by the presence of certain South American military dictators. A cartoon in the satirical comic book *Los Agachados* (March 17, 1976) captured the domestic policy-foreign policy paradox: A Mexican leader pontificates that Mexico will resume diplomatic relations with Spain (then under Franco) only after the dictatorship is overthrown and democracy established, to which the Spanish general replies: "In Mexico." In fact, the Spanish political system did shortly become more democratic than Mexico's.

Relations with Cuba offer a revealing case of the domestic politics component of Mexico's foreign policy. Mexico was the only Latin American nation that did not break diplomatic or commercial relations with communist Cuba, despite strong U.S. and OAS pressure. It has opposed the U.S. embargo against Cuba (although it did not criticize the United States in the 1962 missile crisis) and helped persuade the OAS to lift its sanctions against Cuba in 1975. One motivation has been to defend Cuba's national sovereignty in the face of (U.S.) intervention. At the same time, Mexico has asserted its independence of the United States and gained a degree of revolutionary legitimacy. President López Mateos used recognition of Cuba and criticism of the 1961 U.S.-backed Bay of Pigs invasion to support his claim to be "within the constitution, of the extreme left." President Echeverría repeatedly tried to reap revolutionary credibility via the Cuban connection. President López Portillo, usually conservative at home, strengthened the Cuban connection in the second half of his administration. For example, his visit to Cuba gave Castro a tremendous boost at precisely the moment that he suffered what many considered the international humiliation of seeing thousands of disenchanted Cubans grab a sudden opportunity to flee their island. Indeed, Mexico has been helping to reintegrate Cuba into Latin American organizations, although de la Madrid was more circumspect than his two predecessors in dealing with Cuba.

The Mexican government's domestic exploitation of Cuba's revolution goes beyond seizing leftist legitimacy. It has even included skillful manipulation of the Mexican left.[9] By not joining in U.S pressures against Cuba, the Mexican government denied its left an exclusive claim to favorable Mexican public opinion on Cuba. Moreover, the government carefully monitored its left. It did not oppose the strong anti-Cuba campaign launched by Mexico's church, press, and conservatives in general. In fact, in the early 1960s, facing economic troubles, the government was looking for support from the foreign and domestic business community. It is also plausible that the government welcomed the prospect of winning part of the new U.S. sugar market opened by the U.S. embargo on Cuba. In any case, when leftist pro-Cuba demonstrations seemed to pose the danger of formidable domestic mobilization, the government clamped down. It was made clear that the Cuban revolution was relevant to Mexican domestic policy only insofar as the regime could shore up its own revolutionary credentials through a leftist foreign policy. In return for its friendly foreign policy, the Mexican government expects Cuba to stay out of Mexican domestic politics.[10]

Increasing Assertiveness

Mexico's universalism and leftism have represented a degree of foreign policy independence. Yet Mexico's foreign policy until 1970 has also been described as essentially defensive and limited in geographical scope.[11] Mexico's international relationships were generally more ceremonial than important, even in inter-American affairs. The point should not be overstated. Mexico has asserted its independence in foreign policy in ways that many Latin American nations have not. For example, it has played a prominent role in negotiations concerning disarmament and the law of the sea.

Whatever the balance between defensiveness and assertiveness prior to 1970, assertiveness then increased markedly, for which there are several explanations. One concerns the decline of bipolar international dominance, especially the diminished U.S. ability to have its way in international affairs. The Mexican government itself has spoken hopefully of the "activism of middle-range powers." Certainly, Mexico could not pretend to undo its strong ties to the United States, but it has tried to break the fatalistic acceptance of the idea that nothing important could be done about it; Mexico has tried to increase its *degree* of independence. Additionally, some believed that fundamental problems with Mexico's development model required not just domestic but foreign policy change. Disenchantment with Mexico–United States economic relations was deepened by new U.S. protectionist trade policies. Finally, inheriting a crisis of political legitimacy, the Echeverría administration could enhance its popular image by emphasizing its independence of the United States.[12]

Foreign policy leftism, that mixture of true independence and guile, became more pronounced. Mexico sought leadership in the Third World. In 1975 alone, Mexico established diplomatic relations with thirty-three developing nations. It also pushed the Charter of Economic Rights and Duties of States, championing Third World positions, although in reality the developed world's objections to widespread redistribution seemed to leave Mexico with only a symbolic diplomatic success. Similarly, Echeverría's attempt to broaden diplomatic and trade relations with communist nations yielded only mixed results, although Mexico has markedly strengthened ties with Western Europe and Japan. If most presidents since the 1940s have traveled widely to demonstrate their independence of the United States, Echeverría outdid them all. He was dubbed the "around the world in eighty days president." Wherever he went, Echeverría damned superpower politics, multinational corporations, and indiscriminate foreign investment. He accepted, perhaps even pridefully, the wrath of U.S. elites.

Mexico under Echeverría provided many examples of using foreign policy as a showcase for leftist expression, but also instances of truly asserting, successfully or not, a more active, independent foreign policy. Within Latin America, Echeverría improved relations with Cuba. More dramatic was his almost ostentatious support of Chile's Marxist president, Salvador Allende. Echeverría did not simply stand by the traditional Mexican position of nonintervention, serving notice that Mexico would once again criticize U.S. moves to topple a Latin American experiment in socialism. He repeatedly proclaimed Mexico's enthusiasm for Chile's experiment, much to the chagrin of Mexico's right but with the approval of much of Mexican public opinion and, predictably, of the officially organized political groups. He and Allende exchanged solidarity visits. Allende praised Echeverría's progressivism in standing up to Uncle Sam. And when Allende was toppled, Mexico did not restrict its criticism to U.S. interventionism but extended it forcefully to Chile's ensuing military regime, labeling it a pariah and breaking diplomatic relations (which were not restored under López Portillo or de la Madrid). Mexico welcomed a tremendous influx of Chilean refugees. Here was an important case of moving beyond universalism to a more assertive posture of identifying with friends and actively opposing enemies. Previously, Mexico's opposition to Franco's Spain, a special case involving the mother country and the political regime hated by the many prominent Spanish refugees who had settled in Mexico, was an unusual example of such active negativism (including nonrecognition) in Mexican foreign policy.

Beyond Latin America as well, Echeverría's bid for Third World leadership often involved both leftism and independence of the United States. One notorious failure was Echeverría's ignominious support, which set Mexico apart from most of Latin America's major nations, for a 1975 UN resolution equating Zionism with racism. Mexico soon tried to disavow the vote, but not before provoking a strong outcry and a tourist boycott. Even economic expediency could not have explained Echeverría's blunder, for Mexico is one nation invulnerable to the Arab oil weapon.[13] The episode contributed to an image of Echeverría's impulsiveness, symbolic leftism, and ultimate ineffectiveness.

Overall, Mexico had moved further away from defensive, U.S.-oriented foreign policy toward greater activism in favor of friends and even challenges to foes. Paradoxically, however, Mexico's initial period of jarring assertiveness may have led to "much more dependence on the exterior,"[14] perhaps illustrating the limits to independence, or at least to overzealous expressions off it. Presidents López Portillo's and de la Madrid's challenges included sustaining Mexico's increased assertiveness while restoring confidence in the underlying pragmatism of Mexican foreign policy. Activism associated with any one leader, however bold, might have appeared transient, even irresponsible. Sustained activism might be seen as fundamental to Mexican foreign policy, institutionalized, and highly responsible. Parallels emerge with domestic policy and the desire to depart from the pre-1970 development model in a pragmatic way that would effectively sustain, even revitalize, other aspects of the model.

Throughout most of López Portillo's administration, success was achieved in restoring credibility. In this the president was helped by his foreign minister, Jorge Castañeda. More important help was provided by oil, the economic resource with which to back national resolve. Indeed, in retrospect, the 1978–1981 period illustrates how assertive Mexico can appear when economic and other conditions make it stronger and the United States weaker than is usually the case.

López Portillo enthusiastically symbolized Mexico's foreign policy assertiveness in direct meetings between heads of state. After López Portillo had become President Carter's first official foreign visitor, Carter returned the visit—and his host wrote a new chapter on standing up to Uncle Sam. The Mexican president immediately delivered a symbolic statement at the airport by making Carter walk over to greet him. It was to be at best a calculatedly cool visit. Some will remember February 14, 1979, as a Valentine's Day massacre. Cruel jokes circulated contrasting Carter's presence to the proximate ones by truly welcome superstars like Brigitte Bardot and Sophia Loren, not to mention the pope and, for a fairer comparison, the president of France. A low point came when Carter's undiplomatic attempt at a humorous comment about Moctezuma's revenge met with stony silence. López Portillo's visible pride earned him high marks—and provided some revolutionary legitimacy with which to blunt criticism of conservative domestic policies.

The Mexican government shrewdly affected surprise over the negative U.S. reaction to Mexican treatment of a beleaguered President Carter. After all, Mexico had simply spoken frankly, as a confident equal, not a scrappy troublemaker. Carter, Mexico argued, had been reasonable, not weak. To his credit, Carter spoke some in Spanish, an appreciated gesture. To the Mexicans, the fact that his statements acknowledging Mexico's rightful interests should cause a stir in the United States only reflected U.S. "media hype" and the persistence of colonial "gringo" mentalities.

These years of Mexico's comparative strength in the bilateral relationship soon appeared to mark an exception rather than a secular change, however. At least as a matter of degree, López Portillo's "businesslike," pragmatic approaches yielded to behavior even his own foreign minister would later indirectly characterize as indiscreet.[15] U.S. self-assurance soared with Reagan's presidency and the nation's strong economic recovery. Most of all, oil prices fell substantially, and Mexico lapsed into economic crisis. However much his own ideology or leadership style may have led de la Madrid to curb foreign policies that antagonized the United States, a major determinant was Mexico's dependency. Massive assistance was required from private and public U.S. sources at both the onset and midterm of the de la Madrid administration.

At the same time, the Reagan administration was inconsistent and internally divided over how much Mexican independence it would abide, over how much it wanted to exploit Mexico's dependency. On the one hand, aid packages were extended, and Mexico's domestic recovery programs (and even its regional peacemaking efforts) were periodically praised. Additionally, the administration at least partly distanced itself from the diatribe launched from Senator Jesse Helms's Senate subcommittee.[16] The 1986 Reagan–de la Madrid meeting highlighted the administration's friendly and soothing tendencies. On the other hand, right-wing ideologues and hard-liners from the Republican party, the CIA, the National Security Council, and federal drug agencies continually portrayed Mexican policies as deeply threatening to U.S. interests. These right-wingers blamed Mexico's domestic problems on corrupt policies and a lack of U.S.-style market economics and characterized Mexico's foreign policy as either naively or opportunistically anti-American and pro-leftist. In short, the hard-liners favored heavy U.S. pressure on the Mexican regime, including contacts with the PAN and disgruntled business interests, to force fundamental policy changes or even to change the political system. Such an approach not only provoked sharp responses from Mexicans including the president but rejected a fundamental tenet that had for decades guided State Department thinking and most U.S. policy: that bilateral differences have been tolerable, if naturally irritating, given the enormous benefits of having a stable, legitimate government and trading partner across the border. In our view and probably the view of the overwhelming majority of scholars of Mexican politics and Mexico–United States relations, this sort of rejection would mark a tragic shift in U.S. policy. It appears unlikely, but shifts are usually matters of degree, and threats of shifts can themselves be influential.

Even far short of a major hard-line shift, Mexico has had reason to conclude that its powerful neighbor still treats it as a junior partner, not a nation with an independent foreign policy meriting first-class recognition. For example, despite the elevation of Mexico within U.S. foreign policy concerns, the choices of recent U.S. ambassadors to Mexico have been seen as slights. President Carter selected Patrick Lucey, ex-governor of Wisconsin, hardly a diplomat steeped in knowledge of Mexico (although sympathetic to immigration). Lucey spoke no Spanish. When he subsequently resigned to return to domestic U.S. politics, Carter left the position vacant for an unusually long time. He finally appointed Julián Nava, the first Mexican-American to serve in the post, who was regarded as hostile by many of Mexico's foreign policymakers. President Reagan then appointed John Gavin. Like the president an ex-actor, Gavin was known in Mexico mostly as the rich, erudite gentleman in a prominent Bacardi rum commercial. The appointment was greeted by many Mexicans with dismay and ridicule. But others pointed out that Gavin's mother was Mexican and that Gavin, fluent in Spanish, held a degree in Latin American studies and had some experience with the OAS. He could be seen as more professionally prepared than Lucey, more sympathetic than Nava. Still, the new ambassador had been primarily an actor and really had no record on Mexico, except perhaps for one speech in which he advocated, of all things not likely to win Mexican confidence, a North American common market. The appointment was especially disturbing after rumors had circulated that former Senator Jacob Javits would be selected. With his extraordinary experience and prestige in foreign affairs, Javits might have been a symbol of U.S. acceptance of Mexico's claims to increased foreign policy significance. Mexican dissatisfaction with Gavin intensified in 1982, when the ambassador rather undiplomatically, if indirectly, raised questions about Mexican political stability and also suggested that Mexico join GATT. In fact, right up until his 1986 resignation, Gavin's propensity for outspokenness, unorthodox behavior, and criticism continually stirred such dissatisfaction. Not surprisingly then, the appointment of Charles Pilliod as Gavin's successor was greeted with some relief in Mexico. A former businessman, Pilliod moved swiftly to rebuild cordial diplomatic relations.

Overall, Mexico's quest to assert itself has followed a relatively successful course but an erratic one that includes setbacks and continual reminders of the constraints accompanying dependence on Mexico's imposing neighbor.[17] The assertiveness has probably been most notable in Mexico's relations with Central America and the Caribbean.

Relations with Central America and the Caribbean

No region outside the United States has recently been more important to Mexican foreign policy than Central America and the Caribbean. Geography obviously accounts for that. Mexican policy toward the region has expressed many of the key tenets of Mexican foreign policy in general. One has been the principle of nonintervention. Mexico opposed the U.S. ventures into Guatemala in 1954, Cuba in 1961, the Dominican Republic in 1965, and Grenada in 1983, all to thwart leftist forces. Mexico saw each U.S. action as a blow to the sovereignty of small nations. Furthermore, in the late 1970s and 1980s, it has made clear that it strongly opposes U.S. military intervention in Nicaragua or El Salvador. It also opposed Guatemalan moves to assert its territorial claims over tiny Belize, formerly controlled by Great Britain and independent only since 1981. Mexico itself had territorial claims in Belize, to the point that hostilities with Guatemala seemed possible in the mid-1970s, but Mexico then renounced its claims as inconsistent with nonintervention and self-determination.

Nonintervention has been relaxed to allow for growing assertiveness. In fact, the last few years of the López Portillo administration marked an unprecedented upsurge in Mexican assertiveness. Mexico gave strong public support to the Sandinista insurgency against Somoza's government in Nicaragua. The Estrada Doctrine notwithstanding, Mexico broke diplomatic relations with the besieged dictatorship. It also supported the insurgent left in El Salvador, although it pushed more for a political accommodation when the guerrilla's 1981 offensive failed to topple the regime. With France, Mexico publicly urged recognition of the guerrillas as a "representative political force" with which the government should negotiate. The initiative was rejected not just by El Salvador and the United States, but also by most of Latin America's powerful nations. In a switch, Mexico was criticized for violating principles of nonintervention. More conventionally, in 1981–1982 Mexico offered itself as a "communicator" to help reach wide-ranging compromises between the United States and each of its regional adversaries: the Salvadorean guerrillas, the Nicaraguan government, and even Cuba. When Reagan suggested a "get tough" policy on Cuban interference in El Salvador, López Portillo responded indirectly but clearly by praising Cuba, even calling it the country "most dear" to Mexico's heart. Mexico urged greater restraint by all parties, including a "truce of silence" to reduce tensions. In return for leftist moderation, especially in terms of not exporting revolution, the United States was urged to renounce the use, support, or threat of force. The Reagan administration responded with interest in elements of Mexico's proposals but also with resentment against what it perceived as Mexico's indiscreet diplomacy and excessive tolerance for leftist political forces, and it soon became clear that the United States had implicitly rejected the Mexican initiative.

A good illustration of Mexico's increased assertiveness came in an April 1981 meeting between López Portillo and the president of Venezuela. The two leaders extended their oil program from nine to eleven nations. But the meeting's main purpose was to demonstrate determination to check foreign influence in the region. While Venezuela pointed its finger principally at Cuba, Mexico pointed its finger principally at the United States. López Portillo denounced "paternalistic" pretexts for foreign intervention based on the alleged prior intervention of others (Cuba and the Soviet Union) as an "insult to intelligence." Instability, he reminded everyone, is rooted not in communist infiltration but in social injustice. He joined the Venezuelan president in calling for aid to Nicaragua's revolutionary regime, just a week after the United States had cut off its economic aid because of alleged Nicaraguan support of the insurgent left in El Salvador. Similarly, later in 1981, Mexico pledged to aid leftist Grenada, despite U.S. antipathy to that island's "Cuban tendencies." In both the Caribbean and Central America, Mexico's specific policies have clearly had the common purpose of asserting influence. "Our voices in unison," López Portillo declared, "are raised loud and strong in our region."

But more recent Mexican policies on Central America also show a retreat from the peak period of assertiveness and distancing from U.S. policy.[18] President de la Madrid restricted aid to Nicaragua and improved relations with both El Salvador and Guatemala, at times infuriating the Sandinistas and the leftist rebels in the latter two nations. Mexico reoriented its leadership, perceived by many as overly favorable to the Sandinistas, to stress accommodation among the parties in conflict. In 1984 Mexico hosted monthly meetings between Nicaragua and the United States. But the main initiative was Contadora, a peace process in which Mexico joined with Panama, Venezuela, and Colombia to press for a regional settlement. Contadora sought a reduction in arms, tensions, and external interference. Although Mexico was the Contadora partner most sympathetic to Nicaragua, Contadora advocated positions that departed seriously from both U.S. and Nicaraguan policies. Among the common explanations for the foreign policy reorientation under de la Madrid were differing presidential viewpoints and styles, changed circumstances within Central America itself, and Mexico's worsened economic situation (which made Mexico more dependent on the United States).

Clearly, however, the reorientation was a matter of degree and did not represent a return to the pre-1970s status quo in Mexican foreign policy. How then do we explain Mexico's active and independent (from the United States) Central American policy? Those in the U.S. government and elsewhere who perceive merely naivete and leftist propensities fail to perceive well. In fact, Mexican policy is based fundamentally on a concern for Mexico's own stability, although other factors relate to that. Just as the United States wants a stable Mexico, Mexico wants a stable Central America on its border. Mexico's dominant view of the threats to regional stability differs from a significant U.S. view. Mexico emphasizes that attempts to resist change in Central America are doomed to fail and would lead to protracted instability. Mexico does not see the prime threat as communist military subversion but fears that U.S. perceptions along those lines can convert regional conflicts into East-West and military confrontations.[19]

Of course, Mexican policy is "leftist" compared to U.S. policy, and one finds in Mexico much sympathy for what are considered progressive forces. But considerable evidence suggests that pragmatic politics, not ideology, guides Mexican actions; this evidence on Central America is consistent with our general notions about leftism in Mexican foreign policy. First, Mexico has not befriended merely the left. Oil aid, for example, has gone to Cuba and Nicaragua but also to nations such as Honduras and Guatemala and Caribbean democracies like Jamaica. Additionally, Mexico's strong endorsement of Nicaragua's Sandinistas did not come until it was clear that the Sandinistas would triumph. Support for the Salvadorean guerrillas was diminished once the government showed electoral strength and the guerrillas showed military weakness; rebel leader Guillermo Ungo complained that he was being restrained from saying things in Mexico that he had once freely expressed there. Moreover, Mexico never supported the guerrillas in Guatemala, where they were comparatively weak. Mexico even showed considerable restraint in tolerating the Guatemalan army incursions into Mexico (mentioned in Chapter 3) and, subsequently, to the delight of the government and dismay of the guerrillas of Guatemala, moved refugee camps from the nations' border to further inside Mexico.

A second aspect of Mexico's pragmatic preoccupation with stability is that it seeks to moderate leftism in the region. It believes that supporting moderate change helps to avoid irresponsible and threatening extremism. Notably, Mexico has contested Cuba for leadership in Central America and the Caribbean, which it did not actively do in the 1960s. Furthermore, Mexico could claim a restraining influence on Nicaragua, and the latter has probably resented the strings that Mexico has attached to its aid. (Mexico's own economic crisis certainly also played a part in reducing aid.) And a third aspect to consider is that Mexico, by lending support for some leftist movements outside Mexico, has brought itself protection against leftist advances within Mexico. As in the Cuban case, this is so in part because the Mexican left is denied exclusive claim to popular issues and in part because leftist movements outside Mexico at least tacitly agree not to undermine the comparatively supportive Mexican government.

One could argue that Mexico has seen fit to become more active in Central American affairs precisely to achieve goals once assured with less active diplomacy. Chief among these is guaranteeing that foreign issues strengthen or at least do not weaken domestic legitimacy and stability. The Central American conflicts inevitably push many problems onto Mexico, and Mexico believes that it is better to assume an active role than passively to brace for the consequences of those problems. One relevant threat is that actual armed combat could spread to the Mexican border; even the threat has been used to modernize Mexico's military. So far changes in the military have not undermined civilian political control, but the military has assumed an increased role in some issues related to national security. A more potent impact has already been felt from the influx of hundreds of thousands of refugees fleeing the strife of their own countries. Mostly Salvadoreans and Guatemalans, they differ considerably from the refugees Mexico traditionally welcomed with pride (for example from the Spanish Civil War in the 1930s). The numbers are far greater and less regulated by the Mexican government, and the refugees now are mostly poor and needy. They compete with Mexico's own poor for scarce resources. Government help to the refugees runs the risk of alienating Mexicans who feel bypassed, yet government inaction provokes criticism from international humanitarian agencies. Additionally, mistreatment of vulnerable Central American migrants within Mexico opens Mexico to unflattering analogies regarding the mistreatment of Mexican migrants in the United States. Despite the expressed preferences of some international agencies, for example, Mexico has claimed that the Central Americans in its midst have fled their nations for economic reasons and therefore are not eligible for political asylum; the parallel with U.S. policy on refugees from El Salvador and Guatemala is striking.

A final threat to Mexican internal stability concerns polarization. Foreign policy issues have not usually divided Mexico too dangerously. But, in keeping with its generally increased vocalness, the right has become increasingly visible in this foreign policy area. It has served notice that it no longer sees foreign policy as marginal to its interests or as the province of an establishment that inclines left of center on such issues. Elements of business and the media are staunchly anticommunist, opposed to assuming much burden for the Central American refugees and fearful of alienating the United States. On the left, some grassroots clergy activity with the poor, including refugees, should be considered alongside predictable criticism of the government from the academic community. Even the government itself has been divided, although Foreign Relations has remained in charge on overall orientations. Some ministries such as Finance have expressed reservations about the economic costs of helping refugees, and Interior puts a premium on what it sees as internal security threats.

Clearly, issues as complex as the Central American conflicts do not automatically point the Mexican government to any easy or consensual policies. And several variable factors stimulate policy changes, as we have seen. Nonetheless, these changes fall mostly within a general framework, one with significant features distinct from key features guiding U.S. policy. Normally, the U.S. government has reconciled itself to Mexican independence on such issues, but (in keeping with our comments above on some elements within and others associated with the Reagan administration) Mexico has been subject to pressure to assume more pro-U.S. stances (despite the fact that Mexico's positions generally have had more legitimacy in the Americas and beyond, including much of the Western alliance). It is difficult to determine how much short-term "success" these pressures produce, when applied amid conditions of exacerbated economic dependency. Two things do seem clear, however. One is that the pressures have not pulled Mexico outside its basic framework, for that framework is based on now established Mexican views of regional events and appropriate responses to them. The other is that short-term gains could come at the expense of more important damage to Mexico–United States relations. If our analysis in this chapter and throughout this book is correct, and were accepted, then even U.S. conservatives would acknowledge that their interests are well served by a regime that has pursued the development model that Mexico's has, insured stability on the southern border of the United States, and shown considerable adeptness at constructing a foreign policy suitable to its own domestic needs.

Relations with South America

Relations with South America have generally illustrated Mexico's limited presence beyond the giant's shadow (as trade figures will show below), but here again we see some escape. In fact, for decades Mexico's relative diplomatic isolation from South America derived in part from Mexico's independence from the United States. Mexico was more a maverick than a leader in inter-American affairs.

Mexico has purposely limited its role in inter-American organizations— largely because it recognized U.S. dominance within them. For example, Mexico has favored the UN over the OAS. The United States is much less powerful in the UN; illustratively, U.S. efforts to isolate Cuba were backed in the OAS but not in the world body. Also, Mexico has consistently opposed U.S. attempts, especially forceful in the early 1960s, to create an inter-American military force.[20] Indeed, at a 1954 Caracas conference, Mexico proposed an amendment barring action against fellow OAS members to a U.S. proposition on international communism; the amendment was soundly defeated. When Mexico voted against the 1962 OAS resolution to expel Cuba, it found itself together with Cuba in a group of two. OAS nations were more likely to look to Argentina or Brazil for leadership. Mexico may have been respected for its independence, but that very independence often set it apart. Even Mexico's role in the world's North-South relations, where it championed redistribution toward the South, ironically made Mexico a leader more to some African and Asian than South American nations.

Recently, Mexican–South American relations have become closer. Although it was not a leader, Mexico sided with almost all of Latin America in supporting Argentina in its 1982 South Atlantic war with Great Britain. More telling examples have followed changes within South America itself. Redemocratization helped as Mexico had sometimes harshly criticized the dictatorships of the 1970s. Even preceding redemocratization, several nations had moved closer to some of Mexico's once maverick positions. Restored diplomatic relations with Cuba offer a good example. But perhaps the most visible cooperation came on two shared concerns. One was the debt. In 1984 (during an optimistic break in its own economic crisis), Mexico joined with others to help Argentina handle its debt problem. The other concern was Central America. In addition to the San José plan with Venezuela and Contadora activity with Venezuela, Colombia and Panama, Mexico interacted with the Contadora support group of Argentina, Brazil, Peru, and Uruguay. Moreover, Mexico was closer than the United States to the Central American policies favored by most South American nations.

Relations with Canada

If Mexico's relations with South America have been decreasingly limited, a look northward, beyond the United States to Canada, underscores the general lack of diversification in Mexico's foreign relations. (See Chapter 7 on oil's impact on relations with Western Europe and Japan.) Were political desire more powerful than economic reality, Mexico would probably achieve more balance in its involvement with its two northern neighbors. Mexico and Canada share some foreign policy objectives and a search for independence in the giant's shadow. These are the only two nations bordering the world's richest nation. Parallel difficulties mark certain aspects of Canada–United States and Mexico–United States relations. There is concern over fishing rights, cross-border pollution, cultural penetration, and, especially, economic penetration, even control. Both Mexico and Canada have feared U.S. inclinations toward some sort of North American common market. Both already receive heavy U.S. investment, and although Mexico is the United States's third major trading partner, Canada is the major partner;

whereas Mexico was the second foreign nation President Reagan visited, Canada was the first. Many Canadian workers depend on U.S. business, and tourism is a major industry. The United States has become concerned with Canada's stability (threatened by regionalism), and it has disapproved when Canada seemed friendly toward Cuba or permissive toward leftist movements in Central America; Canada, for its part, has feared U.S. intervention in that region. On all these points substantial overlap of interests exists between Canada and Mexico. Perhaps poignantly, the 1981 North-South meeting in Mexico was cohosted by the chief executives of Mexico and Canada, both critical of what they saw as Reagan's unhelpful posture toward the South.

The hard reality for both U.S. neighbors, however, is that they must deal with the giant between them as a giant. Although Canada shares many development characteristics with the United States, it does not afford Mexico an important counterweight to U.S. power. There have been steps to increase Mexico-Canada trade and diplomacy, but these are infinitesimal compared to the relationship of each with the United States. Canada absorbs roughly 2.5 percent of Mexico's exports and provides 3 percent of its imports.[21] For all their common interests, Mexico and Canada cannot jointly minimize their dependency on the United States. As a Canadian diplomat was quoted: "The Canada-U.S. relationship often is described as that of a mouse sleeping with an elephant. If Mexico climbs into the same bed, it merely means that two mice will be sleeping with the elephant."[22]

Mexican Policy Outside
the Americas: The Iranian Case

Mexico's relations with nations beyond the Americas, despite their increasing prominence, are still rather marginal in Mexican foreign policy. It is nonetheless worth noting that Mexico does pursue an *independent* line in those relations. The Iranian crisis of 1979 provides a vivid example. Mexico pointedly rejected what the United States saw as Mexico's proper role. Instead, Mexico saw its own broad foreign interests in conflict with U.S. interests and made no apologies for asserting an independent position. We analyze this episode not in terms of its complex details, but in terms of the conflicting viewpoints held by many in the United States and Mexico respectively. Not all these viewpoints were held with equal strength, and certainly not all were equally based on facts; some may have been frivolous, others grossly inaccurate. We are interested here in perceptions.

In November 1979, militant Iranian students took over the U.S. embassy in Tehran. For the return of the more than fifty hostages, their principal demand was the return to Iran of the (ex-) shah. The shah was temporarily in the United States for medical treatment that he claimed he could not get in Mexico, where he had been living. The United States refused to extradite the shah and expected him to return to Mexico. Very much to the United States's chagrin, Mexico refused to have him back.

Seen from the U.S. side, Mexico's refusal to readmit the shah was a blatant betrayal, not just of the shah himself, but of the United States.

Mexico is the United States's friend and neighbor. It boasts a proud tradition of extending asylum to political exiles, regardless of ideological stripe. The shah had lived in Mexico from June 10 to October 22, and nearly everyone expected him to return after receiving U.S. medical attention. Mexico's foreign minister confirmed the expected return just weeks before the shocking reversal. The official U.S. version did not go beyond this. But the White House left the clear impression that it supported angry statements by Senator Lloyd Bentsen of Texas accusing Mexico of selfishness and cowardice; Mexico had let the United States down when the United States was most vulnerable. Adding insult to serious injury, Mexico subsequently criticized U.S. economic sanctions against Iran as "aggressive and precipitous."

Why then, according to the United States, did Mexico refuse the shah? Not provoking Iranians into sabotaging Mexican interests around the world was most significant. In this the United States saw capitulation to a terrorism that threatens all civilized nations—however ironic that view appeared in the aftermath of U.S. arms sales to Iran just a few years later. Moreover, Mexico was also out to prove its independence of the United States, to look progressive in foreign policy, and to placate its own left, especially by declaring gratuitously that the shah himself bore considerable responsibility for the militants' actions. Whatever the motivation, the suddenness of Mexico's announcement, allegedly without prior notification to a neighbor now to be plunged into still deeper trouble, was seen as a horrible blow. Some in the United States would believe that López Portillo's own admonition, only recently thrust at the United States over a different issue, seemed to fit: "Between permanent rather than casual neighbors surprise moves and sudden deceit and abuse are poisonous fruits that sooner or later will have an adverse effect."

Seen from the Mexican side, national interest was the key factor. Mexico's foreign policy must be independent. It must be based on Mexican, not U.S. interests. There is more to Mexico's place in the world than its relations with the United States. The United States, arrogant yet hurting, still thought of Mexican foreign policy as but an extension of Mexico–United States relations. Such a vision was, at best, outdated. Hostile U.S. reactions simply reflected the frustrations of a shrinking imperial giant, one that had fully realized neither that it no longer had the power always to have its way nor that its still considerable might did not give it right. Just as the United States would not accept Mexico's revolutionary assertion of sovereignty decades ago, so it still resisted it. The "Colossus of the North" would not accept that Mexican foreign policy must reflect Mexican interests. Images of U.S. imperialism could only be aggravated by the prominent involvement in the case of David Rockefeller and Henry Kissinger, symbols par excellence of U.S. international influence.

Why, López Portillo asked aloud, should Mexico become embroiled in "a conflict that is not ours"? He vehemently denied that there were any Mexican "commitments." He specifically blasted U.S. news reports that (1) he had assured the shah in writing and in person that the shah could return and that (2) the White House knew of and counted on this. He acknowledged only that he had visited the shah before the shah went to the United States and that he had told the shah that he was welcome to come back while his visa was good (six months from issuance). U.S. charges were dismissed as part of a vicious anti-Mexico campaign. Therefore, Mexico's reaction was predictably animated, to say the least. Mexican newspapers cranked out combative articles under colorful titles: "Here Come the Gringos!" "Gratuitous Hostility," "No One Manipulates Us," "The U.S.: Unleashing Passions." The Mexican Congress quickly jumped into line. The leader of the Chamber of Deputies pointed out that if Senator Bentsen (head of the U.S. delegation to the United States–Mexico intercongressional committee) was a friend, Mexico hardly needed enemies. Labor provided revolutionary legitimacy. Its official leader, Fidel Velázquez, said of Bentsen: "This gentleman does not know that this is a sovereign country that rejects pressures of any kind." A more leftist labor leader denounced Bentsen as a mere voice of "imperialist exploiters" who feel that Latin Americans "should be on their knees."[23]

To understand this clash more fully it would be necessary to analyze the viewpoints of different groups within the United States and Mexico. Still, the general lines of a government-versus-government confrontation, each supported relatively broadly by its society, are clear. Although misunderstandings played a part, basically conflicting interests were at stake. Mexico's perceived interests obviously undermined the United States's perceived interests. And Mexico asserted itself forcefully.

The Iranian crisis was only a passing issue in Mexico–United States relations, but it reflected ongoing differences. Mexico feels that it must and will pursue its own broad foreign policy objectives—whether the United States approves them or not. Yet, inescapably, most of Mexico's major foreign policy issues remain fundamentally bilateral ones with the United States. Ultimately, this is where independence meets its most critical test.

PRINCIPAL BILATERAL ISSUES

The Asymmetry of Economic Interdependency

Specific bilateral issues must be seen against the background of the vital U.S. role in the Mexican economy. Political assertiveness is one thing, economic sovereignty another. Nationhood is one thing, independence another. Economically, Mexico is profoundly dependent on the United States— despite U.S. dependency on Mexico. As with cultural interdependency, Mexico–United States economic interdependency is asymmetrical. (Asymmetry does not necessarily imply economically favorable outcomes for the predominant partner; note, for example, how Mexico's economic crisis has negatively affected U.S. jobs, exports, and trade deficits and has necessitated public and private loans to avert the U.S. banking catastrophe that could result from a Mexican inability to repay earlier loans—and to avert the sort of political unrest that could threaten U.S. interests.)

Whereas Mexico now ranks behind only Canada and Japan as a leading trading partner for the United States, U.S. trade is spread widely across many nations. But Mexico relies overwhelmingly on the United States as its principal trading partner. Figures for 1980 (just prior to Mexico's volatile economic crisis) show Mexico taking in only 5.4 percent of total U.S. exports and sending off what would amount to 3.7 percent of total U.S. imports. By contrast, Mexico sent 61.8 percent of its exports to the United States and took in 62.3 percent of its imports from there. And even these figures represent a recent decline in Mexico–United States trade asymmetry; that is, Mexico had previously accounted for even less of U.S. trade, and the U.S. had accounted for even more of Mexican trade. Moreover, Mexico exported less to the United States (US$12.5 billion) than it imported from the United States (US$15.1 billion). From 1982 to 1985, the volume of Mexico's total trade diminished because more foreign exchange was used to service the debt and less was available for imports. In fact, Mexico registered during those four years a surplus in trade accounts, the first such surplus in over three decades; in 1983, Mexico exported goods worth US$12.3 billion to the United States (57 percent of Mexico's total exports); and US$4.9 billion (63 percent) of Mexico's imports in that year originated in the United States.[24]

Oil has helped to redress basic trade asymmetries, but it also has led to increased Mexican demands for U.S. goods. Perhaps more important than changes in Mexico–United States imbalances is that the volume of trade—this basically asymmetrical trade—has increased enormously. The volume dwarfs Mexican trade with other countries, including the rest of Latin America. Mexico sends roughly 2 percent of its exports to Central America and the Caribbean and only 4 percent to the rest of Latin America. Furthermore, universalism and leftism notwithstanding, the entire communist world accounts for only about 1 percent of Mexico's exports and imports.[25]

U.S. investment in Mexico is also increasing, again deepening an asymmetrical economic relationship. The United States accounts for two-thirds of the roughly US$14 billion in accumulated (up to 1985) direct foreign investment received by Mexico, while Mexican investment is but a small part of foreign investment in the United States.[26] The United States invests more in Mexico than in all but a few nations anywhere. Moreover, U.S. capital is concentrated in critical areas, including many of the fastest growing and most profitable. Whereas foreigners historically invested in mining, increased investment in the last few decades has focused on services (including tourism) and especially on industrial manufacturing (automobiles, chemicals, pharmaceuticals, cosmetics, processed foods, and drinks). Trying to relieve the underdevelopment syndrome of exporting agricultural for manufactured goods, Mexico has developed some new exports in recent decades. Agriculture (sugar, coffee, beef, tomatoes) is still important to Mexico, although extraordinary problems came to the fore in the late 1970s (see Chapters 1 and 5), and oil has become preeminent.

Certainly Mexico has tried to diminish its economic dependency on the United States, e.g., by broadening trade with other areas, including South America, Europe, and Japan. But powerful factors, even beyond the obvious geographical ones, maintain the U.S. role. The Mexican private sector is in many ways tied to U.S. economic interests, and binational organizations promote favorable policies. The Mexican middle class demands U.S. exports. U.S. lobbies, governmental and private, press for close economic ties. Nor has official Mexican policy clearly opposed foreign economic penetration, despite unease about the huge U.S. share. On the one hand, the regime has usually upheld protectionist policies, defending domestic producers; on the other hand, it has encouraged foreign investment and trade and maintained the low wages, political stability, and general economic industrialization model that foreign economic interests want. Whatever the ideological preferences of Mexican policymakers, a terrible constraint is simply the recent failure of the domestic economy. Herein, for example, looms the threat of the "food for crude" crisis alluded to in Chapter 1. If Mexican agriculture cannot feed Mexico, then Mexico is forced to rely on the United States.

Whether or not most Mexicans have supported the bilateral economic status quo, the point is that the interests of many powerful groups, indeed the central domestic development policies themselves, have basically encouraged it. Basic encouragement, however, hardly means full or conflict-free acceptance. From the U.S. side, some isolated protestations about imperialism and dependency excepted, the common perception is that U.S. economic activity in Mexico is a result of natural and beneficial economic forces. Again, however, this attitude hardly precludes heated debates over specific policies.

Each of the following specific issues is too complex for detailed analysis and evaluation here. Certainly, we make no pretense at offering solutions. Instead, we again concentrate on contrasting Mexican and U.S. perceptions of the key factors. Again, we neither endorse any of these perceptions nor assert that all have factual validity, much less equal moral validity. While we emphasize government perceptions, we acknowledge intragovernmental disagreements and dissent by some nongovernmental actors. Thus, bilateral cooperation and conflict involve more than intergovernmental agreement or disagreement.

Trade: Tariffs and Quotas

The issue of trade is obviously central to economic policy and therefore was largely treated in the last chapter. Of particular relevance here are the discussions of the recent GATT decisions, border economics, and, especially, the role of trade in Mexico's economic growth model. Rather than reformulating those discussions here, this brief section focuses on conflicting Mexican and U.S. perceptions of proper tariff and quota policies.

Mexico–United States disputes over tariffs and quotas are so repetitive that they become fairly predictable as different products capture the headlines.

Mexico's fundamental viewpoint is usually clear. Mexico wants to sell its products competitively in the United States. Does not international capitalism mean that laws of free trade and comparative advantage should hold? If Mexico can produce shoes, textiles, and agricultural products cheaply because its labor costs are low, U.S. consumers should buy from Mexican rather than more expensive U.S. producers. Only with such revenue can Mexico afford to buy the more sophisticated, capital-intensive goods that the United States is better suited to produce. Only with such sales can Mexico employ its population. To deny Mexico its market for labor-intensive goods is to increase Mexican unemployment and force job-seekers across the border. To deny Mexico its rightful market is to contribute to the astronomical foreign debt, block Mexican progress, and encourage disorder. If the United States wants good relations with Mexico, it must offer Mexico a fair chance. In fact, Mexico has gone beyond this and asked for a "special relationship" in which its goods would be given privileged treatment in the United States. That would be seen as a genuine and important measure to bolster Mexican economic development and political stability. Yet the United States has generally insisted that it cannot give special treatment to Mexico without undercutting its relationships with other countries. Instead, Mexican products have been either slapped with tariffs that destroy their competitive edge in the U.S. market or denied access altogether by restrictive quotas or tough sanitary requirements. In fact, a major bilateral conflict has involved the U.S. practice of "graduating" advanced developing nations into a category wherein they lose favorable trade treatment. In 1980 and 1984, many Mexican products were removed from duty-free status.[27]

Why has U.S. policy not been more accommodating? A major factor is that powerful U.S. domestic interests conflict with Mexico's desires. Labor fears a loss of jobs if consumers reject U.S. products for less expensive foreign ones. Small businesses in particular see trouble for their own precarious situation. Besides, the United States asks, how open has Mexico been to foreign competition? Mexico obviously has mustered greater policy agreement for free exporting of its own products than for free importing of foreign products. It has declared its right to select specific trade policies that serve Mexico's interests rather than to adhere doctrinally to free-trade principles. Rightly or wrongly, some in the United States believe that Mexico has unduly thwarted free competition by subsidizing some of its own exports, by claiming extensive sea and fishing rights off Mexico, by unilaterally terminating a fishing agreement with the United States, by its zeal for "revolutionary" nationalizations, and (in the 1970s) by its toughened restrictions on foreign investment and technology transfers. A culminating point came in 1980 when Mexico declined to enter GATT. But by 1985 and 1986 U.S. complaints had to be modified. Whatever the role of U.S. pressure, the de la Madrid administration perceived a need to move further toward market solutions to economic crisis. These solutions included reversing the earlier anti-GATT decision and signing the first Mexico–United States trade agreement in nearly a half century (see previous chapter).

Recent accords do not, however, signal the end of the basic bilateral differences cited above. Nor should we minimize the differences within each nation over how much to accommodate to the position of one's trading neighbor. For example, Mexico's decision to join GATT received support from COPARMEX, northern exporting businesses, and the PAN while engendering opposition from CANACINTRA, relatively small industries, unions, scholars, and leftist parties. U.S. opinion also is significantly divided on key trade issues. Naturally, consumers want inexpensive products. What emerges is a classic domestic political struggle between smaller, organized groups and larger, unorganized groups. U.S. pluralist democracy generally makes the organized groups stronger than numbers alone would suggest. And because domestic U.S. politics obviously affects foreign policy, it is hard to overstate the importance to Mexico of understanding the complex U.S. maze. In 1976, to take an example of conflict over quotas, the U.S. government came under tremendous pressure from shoe producers demanding a limit on the import of shoes. Congress supported the call. So did the International Trade Commission and the Treasury Department, but the Department of Commerce opposed the move, fearing trade retaliation by Mexico and other affected nations. The State Department and National Security Council also opposed the quotas, not wishing to jeopardize good relations or to cause unrest abroad.[28] Mexico obviously wanted to export its shoes as freely as possible.

A good example of bilateral tariff disputes concerns winter vegetables. Florida growers and truckers complain that Mexico has captured much of the U.S. consumer market. Mexicans allegedly "dump" tomatoes and squash, peppers, cucumbers, and eggplant cheaply on the U.S. market in order to drive producers out of business. The producers therefore pressured the Treasury Department to impose tariffs. Otherwise, U.S. interests would not be able to compete with Mexico's cheap labor, government production subsidies, and laxer laws against insecticides. Mexico, in turn, argued that tariffs would be unfair, drive up prices to U.S. consumers, drive up U.S. inflation, put Mexicans out of work and onto the road northward, and adversely affect bilateral relations. What a terrible irony: Mexicans are forced north where they help produce food in the United States that Mexico is forced to import. How could the United States put the clamps on one of Mexico's few major exports while Mexico consumes so much from the United States? In fact, although these basic differences over trading fairness are critical, the conflict is not a clearcut, bilateral one. Some U.S. producers are hurt by the imports, but the impact is different in Florida and California, for example. Many U.S. distributors control, profit from, and therefore encourage the Mexican imports. And "Mexican" production often really is tied to large international corporations; it is awkward to complain that Mexican pineapples compete unfairly with U.S. pineapples when Del Monte is a key actor on both sides of the border.[29]

Drugs

Mexicans have argued that U.S. tariffs on legitimate goods like vegetables push Mexican farmers into a more lucrative agricultural activity—
the cultivation of drugs. Although ranking depends on variable estimates,
the year in question, and the type of drug, Mexico now stands near or at
the top of exporters to the United States. Mexico's importance as an exporter
of drugs accelerated when World War II interrupted heroin supplies from
the Middle and Far East. A second wave was inaugurated in the 1970s by
Turkey's crackdown on poppy growing, the attack on the "French connection," and the communist takeover in Vietnam. Mexico came to supply
the United States with perhaps 10 million pounds (45,000 kg) per year of
marijuana, or 70 percent of U.S. consumption, plus 70–80 percent of U.S.
heroin and some cocaine. Drugs have been grown in poor states such as
Guerrero and Oaxaca and in richer ones such as Sinaloa. Sinaloa's drug
income may exceed its income from legitimate agriculture, even though
Sinaloa has more irrigated land than any other state in Mexico.[30]

Leaving aside U.S. drug users, who not unlike consumers of other
agricultural products might like to see their goods flow across the border
even more freely, *the United States tends to blame the drug traffic on Mexico.*
Mexico (1) fails to encourage legitimate agricultural alternatives; (2) tacitly
encourages the drug enterprise, which brings jobs and fabulous income into
Mexico, some into the hands of corrupt government officials; (3) has run
inadequate, corrupt antidrug campaigns; (4) lacks the will to confront local
bosses or guerrillas on their home turf; and (5) fails to cooperate adequately
with the United States, exacerbating tensions by mistreating U.S. citizens
imprisoned on drug charges. Even when the United States acknowledges
that the drug traffic has its perpetrators in both nations, it sometimes implies
that only one government has resolved to confront the problem.

The Mexican side of the story is quite different. *Prime or equal
responsibility is placed on the United States.* One must look at the *demand*
side of the equation; without U.S. demand Mexicans would not grow the
supply. Millions of U.S. consumers are in fact all too eager to pay billions
of dollars for their habits and illicit pleasures. Moreover, U.S. drug pushers
benefit from the trade. In other words, "corruption" is as much a U.S. as
a Mexican affliction; interestingly, this view of a corrupt U.S. society
demanding drugs was endorsed by Ambassador Gavin. Furthermore, drugs
are often traded for guns, which are easily available in several Southwest
U.S. states.

Bilateral relations have oscillated between periods of higher and lower
tension. A contentious point was hit in 1969 when President Nixon embarked
on the sort of unilateral action dictated by the hard-line U.S. view of the
drug problem. Under Operation Intercept careful border searches were
launched. The operation angered Mexicans and hurt them economically, for
it significantly slowed tourism and frontier trade. Within days, Operation
Cooperation followed as a less offensive substitute. By the mid-1970s, the
bilateral Operation Condor was under way, bringing Mexico's military and

judicial forces into action. Mexican manpower combined with U.S. money and reconnaissance technology. Mexico–United States cooperation had indeed materialized. In 1976, an unprecedented prisoner exchange symbolized this new cooperation.

By the early 1980s, Mexico's estimated share of the U.S. market had dwindled to about a third for heroin and to only a few percent for marijuana. But by 1986 Mexico reportedly reassumed its position as the primary producer and source of heroin and marijuana and surged into second place (behind Colombia) as a conduit for cocaine. The U.S. Drug Enforcement Administration and the U.S. Customs Service launched damning attacks on allegedly corrupt, inept, and cowardly Mexican officials; they even pointed the finger at specific officeholders. These charges echoed ones made in 1985 after a U.S. drug agent was murdered in Mexico. Mexico responded by reemphasizing the international and economic roots of the problem, which was aggravated as the economic crisis steered many growers from legal to illegal crops. Mexico also pointed to its own substantial enforcement efforts and sacrifices and rejected what it saw as brazen U.S. attempts to simplify a thorny issue into an attack that would further weaken Mexico's ability to resist U.S.-imposed solutions to its economic woes. At their 1986 meeting (marred by the beating of another U.S. drug enforcement official by Mexican police) de la Madrid and Reagan recommitted their governments to cooperation, with Operation Alliance. The new program would involve more personnel, funds, and some measures previously unacceptable to Mexico; however, Mexico pointedly defended its sovereignty by rejecting a U.S. proposal to allow U.S. planes to pursue suspects across the border.

What has been at the heart of the bilateral drug controversy, therefore, is not fundamental misunderstanding but conflicting interests. In each country, some groups want to help solve the problem whereas others do not. According to one view, only when the Mexican government came to see its own interests threatened did greater cooperation emerge.[31] But even if we were to assume that both governments were fully committed to fighting the drug problem, no societywide Mexico–United States consensus would emerge as long as many people rely on drugs to provide their jobs, illicit incomes, pleasures, or escapes.

Tourism

Tourism is usually one of the least conflictual issues associated with Mexico's international economic relations. It shows instead the strong mutual interests between Mexico and the United States. During the 1970s, the number of U.S. citizens visiting Mexico increased from slightly more than 2 million annually to nearly 3.5 million annually and up to roughly 3.8 million by 1984.[32] Moreover, tourism is a reciprocal Mexico–United States industry. There is a good deal of advertising in Mexico for U.S. attractions such as Disney World, Las Vegas, and New York City. Roughly 2.5 million Mexicans visited the United States in 1979.

As in all major Mexico–United States economic relations, however, a strong degree of asymmetry exists. Whereas 13 percent of U.S. foreign travel reaches Mexico, 95 percent of Mexican foreign travel reaches the United States. Whereas Mexicans are one foreign group among many visiting the United States, U.S. citizens make up the vast majority of tourists in Mexico (although the percentage fell from 93 percent in the early 1970s to roughly 80 percent in 1984), and the vast majority of Mexico's roughly US$2 billion annual tourist income. Tourism ranks second only to oil, at least among Mexico's legal and measurable income sources.

Various Mexican regions have grown primarily because of tourism. Acapulco, a small town before World War I, has become one of the world's best-known vacation spots. Puerto Vallarta, Mazatlán, and Cancún are other favorite coastal resorts. Mexico's attractiveness for tourists is easy to understand. Hotels, food, entertainment, and handicrafts are inexpensive by U.S. vacation standards. Most of all, Mexican proximity to the United States makes for low-cost round-trip transportation, especially from populous areas such as southern California and Texas. If the following sounds like a tourist promotion, it also indicates how Mexico can sustain a profitable industry. Mexico is blessed with beautiful, extensive, and warm beaches. Tourists can choose from modern entertainment and fine tourist accommodations, "quaint" folklore, or archeological treasures. A visit to Mexico City offers not only the sights of a huge metropolis, but short side-trips to a great number of tourist attractions: pyramids, hot springs, Taxco ("the silver city"), Cuernavaca (the "city of eternal spring"), Querétaro (a charming colonial city), and Puebla (a historic metropolis with Spanish influence). Acapulco and Veracruz are fewer than eight hours by car or two by plane from the capital.

Although foreign interests own much of the tourist industry, Mexican businesses also profit. And tourism creates jobs. According to Mexico's Ministry of Tourism, tourism brought 220,000 new jobs to Mexico from 1977 to 1979. So the Mexican government treats the industry carefully, building necessary infrastructure and maintaining strong tourist bureaus to prevent mistreatment of tourists. It advertises avidly and skillfully, catering especially well to what U.S. tourists want to hear.[33]

Many problems surface, however. Tourists are walking symbols of the development gap between Mexico and the United States. Such symbols are especially resented when they play the "ugly American" role of patronizing local society. Even short of this, many tourists naturally do not acquit themselves well in Mexican eyes. For instance, "the majority of the tourists are more interested in admiring the countryside and the famous monuments than in feeling a live culture. They react only to their own expectations. . . . They do not visit a country but the image of a country."[34] In fairness, one can respond that not every tourist need be an anthropologist. Yet, unlike most of their South American counterparts, Mexicans see so many U.S. tourists that they may well tire of them. Despite some conventional assumptions, tourism does not necessarily lead to greater understanding among peoples.

Many Mexicans, especially on the left, see their country catering too much to tourist desires. Their government often moves quickly, and brutally if necessary, to suppress local disturbances that could frighten away tourists. Development projects are often chosen to make Mexico attractive to foreigners rather than to Mexico's masses. The Tourism Ministry, for example, is known to push against ejido ownership because small communal landholdings are harder to seize and turn into tourist sites. Coastal regions are being "denationalized," many charge. Foreign investment and control are found in much of the tourist industry. Finally, Mexico cannot assert itself with the United States too much on other issues because it must fear repercussions in its vital tourist industry. According to this negative view, the Mexican government zealously pursues its tourist policies because they fit so well into the regime's development model—rewarding those the regime caters to, regardless of the consequences for others.

Events in the mid-1980s illustrated Mexico's vulnerability and heightened Mexico–United States conflict. For example, in 1985 U.S. officials, angered over an alleged lack of cooperation in the drug murder case cited above, imposed tedious car-by-car searches on the border. To make U.S. citizens wait for hours to reenter their country is to cripple border tourism and commerce. More generally, U.S. government statements about corruption and potential instability in Mexico are also hurtful deterrents.

Vulnerability to economic as well as political pressures has also been manifested. Ironically, Mexico's good fortune with oil presented problems by boosting inflation. If prices soar, Mexico loses some competitive advantage over other tourist spots, and privileged Mexicans are themselves attracted to vacation outside their country. Yet renewed economic stagnation in the 1980s brought massive peso devaluations, which made prices once again very attractive for U.S. tourists. Whatever the future, Mexico's tourism has usually benefited not only from the country's geographical and natural beauty, but from Mexico's economic weakness compared to its northern neighbor and from a development model that has preserved political stability.

Migration

If tourism is the principal factor motivating U.S. citizens to cross the border, the principal factor for Mexicans is work. Mexico's leading exports to the United States are not foodstuffs or drugs, but oil and people. "Green-card" holders work legally in the United States; debate focuses on the millions who cross the border without legal U.S. documentation.

So thorny is this bilateral problem that the Mexican and U.S. governments cannot agree even on what to call the migrants. Mexico regards the label "illegal alien" as pejorative, perhaps implying that the migrants are not quite human. Mexico refers instead to "undocumented workers." The United States generally regards this label as too benign: Most Mexican migrants are in violation of U.S. law, and not all are workers. We refer here simply to "migrants," a label that addresses neither the legality nor the desirability of the influx.

The migration problem is very difficult yet serious, and no easy answers emerge. At least each side should better understand the other's dominant positions.

First, Mexico argues, *the United States rather hysterically exaggerates the problem.* William Colby, former director of the Central Intelligence Agency, hyperbolically called the migrants, not the Soviet or Chinese communists, the greatest menace to U.S. security. Others talk of a "silent invasion." Estimates of the total number of migrants in question range from 3 to even 12 million; Mexicans tend to accept the lower figure, allowing that well over half are Mexicans. Furthermore, many are in the United States only temporarily or seasonally.

Second, Mexico argues, *migration is a natural or even inevitable phenomenon* where wealth and poverty are in close proximity. There are more jobs in the United States. More important, these jobs offer perhaps three or four or even seven times as much salary for comparable work.[35] Just as Switzerland attracts Italians, Venezuela attracts neighboring South Americans, and Mexico itself attracts Central Americans, the United States attracts Mexicans. Contemporary migration in Western Europe seems to offer a parallel better than even historical Mexico–United States immigration to contemporary Mexico–United States immigration. Beyond legal guest-worker programs, many emigrate from nearby less developed nations to work in Europe's more developed nations. Migrants today seek work in capital-intensive societies in which the demand is less for labor than for cheap labor, in societies with elaborate and costly social services that would have to be made available to native workers or to legally admitted immigrants. It takes two to migrate. That is, there must be demand on the receiving end. Someone in the United States wants the migrants, just as someone wants the drugs. Mexico feels that the United States overemphasizes the factors that "push" people out of Mexico, ignoring the factors in the United States that "pull" in people. U.S. quotas, for migrants as well as for agricultural goods, block free trade. Yet laws forbidding migration are like laws against prostitution, gambling, or alcohol: They are hard to enforce because they run counter to strong impulses and incentives.

A corollary of the principle that migration is a natural phenomenon is that the United States reaps many benefits. The point is especially pertinent for employers and consumers but also relevant to U.S. taxpayers generally. Whereas most migrants pay U.S. taxes, they often do not claim the full benefit of U.S. welfare, health, education, or food stamps because of their short stays and particularly their fear of exposure. Indeed, U.S.-based empirical studies have tended to document overall positive benefits to the U.S. economy.[36]

Another corollary is that if Mexicans must suffer all the natural disadvantages of proximity to a colossus, at least they should also be allowed the natural benefits. They note that many U.S. citizens enjoy more luxurious lives in Mexico than they possibly could in the United States. *Los Agachados* (March 9, 1976) has satirized U.S. concern about Mexican migrants by affecting reverse hysteria: The gringos are out to do what they did to Texas— move in, cause trouble, and annex! "Unfortunately, YES, the news is correct: More gringos live in Mexico than Mexicans in the U.S. . . . The only

Mexicans that you still see on the *Reforma* [one of Mexico City's major streets] are the traffic cops."

A third Mexican argument is that *U.S. policy crassly manipulates the flow.* The United States could relax barriers to the entry of Mexican goods, thereby promoting employment opportunities in Mexico. It could raise the *legal* quota for immigration and grant more seasonal work permits. Instead, the United States has historically pursued narrowly self-serving policies. Until the late 1920s it allowed unrestricted immigration to fill its need for cheap labor. The Great Depression brought Operation Deportation, to remove competition for scarce jobs. World War II then brought the bracero program to attract needed workers for a shorthanded nation at war. Although Mexicans were legally admitted to harvest crops until 1964, the United States predictably cut back the program almost immediately after the war, in 1947. In 1954, Operation Wetback entrusted to a military general the task of deporting more than 1 million Mexicans, "excess" workers. No wonder this has been called the flower-petal policy: "I need you, I need you not, I need you. . . ." In the 1960s and 1970s, quotas on Western Hemisphere nations, including Mexico, became more rather than less restrictive. Mexicans then saw U.S. unemployment problems provoke Operation Jobs, a 1982 roundup and forced departure of thousands of Mexican migrants, just when Mexico found itself mired in its own economic crisis and when Mexico once again felt victimized by tariff policy. Mexico then decried an unfairness in U.S. officials' strident attacks on increased migration in the mid-1980s when Mexico's economic crisis deepened alongside a reinvigorated U.S. economy.

Fourth, Mexico argues, *U.S. attitudes about migrants lead to violations of human rights.* The violations include unlawful arrests, forced confessions, beatings, and emotional abuse. Several incidents at the border itself have embarrassed the beleaguered and understaffed U.S. Immigration and Naturalization Service. The whole migration issue presents a difficult moral issue. A *Los Angeles Times* poll (reported July 15, 1979) indicates that perhaps 90 percent of the population of Mexico City believe that Mexicans working illegally in the United States are being abused. In 1974, Mexico successfully urged the UN to approve a resolution that nations should accord foreign workers, regardless of their legal status, the same human rights as citizens. No nation voted against the resolution, but the United States, aware of the finger-pointing, was one of four abstaining.

While not challenging all the tenets of the other's position, the two nations have tended to see different dimensions and to emphasize different factors. First, the United States argues that *the migration problem is serious, intensifying, and fundamentally rooted in Mexico itself.* Whether because of irresponsible population growth coupled with ineffectual economic policies, or because of general problems of underdevelopment, Mexico produces an excess work force. The worsening of Mexico's economic crisis in the 1980s offered a ready example, as the peso was repeatedly devalued, and employment opportunities were grim in Mexico. Apprehensions of migrants by U.S. authorities soared. They reached roughly 1.8 million by 1986, a 50 percent increase in just a single year, a doubling over 1976 and a quadrupling over 1971, and officials estimated that those caught are outnumbered from two to ten to one by those not caught. In fact, officials complained about the "greatest surge in history" across the U.S. border.

Moreover, the United States is concerned over qualitative changes in the migration, arguing that more new migrants are coming and more are bringing their families and staying permanently, having given up on Mexico. Such changes have allegedly placed vastly increased burdens on schools, hospitals, and law enforcement agencies in many U.S. states. And not just U.S. but Mexican studies have shown that today's migrants are more urban and educated than their predecessors, facts that arguably cause increased job competition with native U.S. workers.

Second, the United States argues, *Mexico benefits from a problem dumped on its prosperous neighbor.* The welfare burden on the U.S. government represents a relief for the Mexican government. Thus a crucial "safety valve" allows Mexico to export its social burdens. Moreover, Mexican migrants send home huge sums, with estimates running as high as US$3 billion a year, more than Mexico's tourist income;[37] this remittance is seen as money taken out of the U.S. economy. The Mexican political system also benefits because of the safety-valve effect. Mexico need not address fundamental problems in population, agriculture, employment, and so forth as long as it can release many of those it cannot satisfy. Another reason the Mexican regime may not want to stem emigration is that Mexicans migrate not just to the United States but, within Mexico, to the more populated areas. Mexicans migrating to the United States no longer come predominantly from rural areas, and if fewer migrants went to the United States more would remain in already overcrowded Mexican cities. Could Mexico address such burdens?

A third argument made in the United States is that *Mexico proposes no viable alternative* but instead merely complains about U.S. policy, calls for further study, and hopes that oil and industrialization will eventually create more jobs in Mexico. This argument follows from the first two, which hold that Mexico has the responsibility but not the incentive to tackle the problem. Indeed, López Portillo acknowledged that Mexico could not provide sufficient employment for all its workers during this century.[38] Although migrants may represent a loss of useful human capital, a brain drain, the loss would pale before the benefits Mexico presently reaps from its policy of benign neglect.[39]

Despite virtual consensus in the United States that Mexico benefits from the migration, in fact no U.S. consensus exists on what adverse consequences the United States suffers. Strong opposition to Mexican migration comes from labor unions. The AFL-CIO has opposed plans to legitimize or increase the flow of migrants, legal or illegal. Thus a fourth argument heard in the United States is that *U.S. unemployment is aggravated,* especially among the poor, in the agricultural, service, and manufacturing sectors where many Mexicans find work. If Mexicans cannot be prevented from coming, then many U.S. opponents advocate stiff penalties to discourage potential employers from hiring them.[40] Labor maintains that the migrants are robbing U.S. citizens of jobs and increasingly usurping better jobs; no longer are migrants confined to jobs unwanted by domestic workers. Moreover, foreign workers indirectly deflate the wages of domestic workers by expanding the available labor pool. They have been used, historically, to prevent or weaken unionization. Such effects are felt today mostly where low-income domestic labor is involved. Along with some Chicano leaders, representing U.S. citizens of Mexican descent, Black leaders have been wary of the Mexican influx (just as they were wary of the 1980 Cuban influx). Some have argued that talk of the United States's ability to absorb immigrants is based on the history of an era, a bygone era, in which the United States was an expanding society seeking more laborers.

Although U.S. public opinion probably tends to agree with labor that Mexican migrants basically constitute a problem, U.S. scholarly opinion tends to be more sympathetic to Mexico's arguments. And many U.S. conservatives see the migrants in positive economic terms. The United States itself may increasingly experience labor shortages because of its stagnant population growth and aging work force. More specifically, big agriculture and many small businesses are delighted with the large and *cheap* pool of eager laborers, either satisfied with the wages offered or afraid to complain. In fact, some conservatives advocate diminishing international constraints on the free flow of capital and labor. Cheap Mexican labor allows U.S. business to produce goods (such as fruits, vegetables, wine, and clothes) that are priced more competitively on the international market and more inexpensively for domestic consumers. Remove cheap Mexican labor and many U.S. businesses would close, raise prices to uncompetitive levels, or relocate outside the United States in places where cheap labor *is* available. Besides, the United States gets an instant work force, one it does not have to train expensively through its public-school system. Furthermore, some detect a paradox: If the U.S. pressures Mexico to slow migration, it must be prepared for domestic Mexican policies that put job creation ahead of capital-intensive growth—that is, for policies alien to the Mexican growth model that has basically worked for U.S. private business.

U.S. domestic political forces have tended to line up something like this: On the antimigration side, labor and the Treasury Department have hoped to keep Congress inclined toward their position. On the other side, the Department of Agriculture has responded to agricultural interest groups in the Southwest, and the Departments of State and Justice have added that harsh proposals to "seal the border" would hurt relations with Mexico.[41] In fact, U.S. authority on migration policy has been fragmented among the Departments of Labor, Education, Health and Human Services, Justice, and State, the Immigration Service and frontier patrol, Congress, and interest groups ranging from unions and businesses to Chicanos and police. It is more difficult for the United States than for Mexico to form one coherent official position.[42]

U.S. opinion is also fragmented on whether migrants should be counted in the census. To do so is to grant them legitimacy and to reward localities (with government funds based on population) for attracting them. Not to do so is to deprive localities of revenues that they desperately need to support services used by migrants and to have "taxation without representation" insofar as migrants do pay taxes. It is ironic that some who claim that migrants do not really drain welfare resources also claim that their localities need more such resources because migrants do use them. Similarly, great debate continues, especially in border states, over whether children without legal residency status should be allowed in the public-school system. Those in favor argue that the children are innocent victims of circumstances and that to deny them access to education is unconstitutional and unjust and sows the seeds of civil disorder. Opponents maintain that U.S. taxpayers should not have to finance the education of persons here illegally and that to do so can only encourage more to come. But opponents lost an important 1982 court case concerning migrant children living in Texas.

We have focused more on the conflicting viewpoints on both sides of the border than on the hard facts in the case. This is because our main purpose is to understand how the parties themselves see things, because there are only so many unambiguous, provable facts, and because limited space precludes the attempt to deal with empirical details. Suffice it to reiterate these probabilities: that most Mexicans come to the United States either to find employment or higher salaried employment than they can find at home; that most do return home, although many come back periodically; that most take jobs unwanted by U.S. citizens; that they may adversely affect unskilled labor's interests; that they lower costs for U.S. employers and probably consumers; that they send important revenue back to Mexico; that they give some relief from Mexico's terrible employment problem; and that many are treated abusively in the United States.[43]

At least until recently, the debate has only rarely gotten beyond the level of unproductive charges and countercharges, and when it has, it has become painfully clear that no neat solution exists. It is not even granted by all that a solution should be found, for while some suffer, others benefit from the migration. The Mexican government makes little pretense at having the answer, arguing nonetheless that more enlightened U.S. policy could ameliorate the situation. Both the Carter and Reagan administrations advocated policies to legitimize the status of those in the United States while cracking down on continued migration. One Reagan plan would have put many Mexicans living in the United States on a ten-year track toward legalization but would have made it more difficult and dangerous for employers to hire migrants. A major sticking point concerned the possibility of an identification card. Without it, the government would find it difficult to compel employer compliance. With it could come a bureaucratic nightmare and perceived threats to human rights. Reagan also proposed doubling the size of the guest-worker program for a two-year experimental period, but at other times proposed harsh policies involving emergency power.

In fact, the Reagan administration was as ambivalent about migration as about several other Mexico–United States issues. On the one hand, free-market inclinations and appreciation that the "safety valve" helps preserve Mexican political stability argued against restrictive initiatives. On the other, a tendency to vocalize displeasure with Mexico's political economy, coupled with fears about the adverse impacts of immigrants in the United States led the Immigration Service, for example, to advocate heavy employer fines and several measures to make it harder for Mexico's working migrants to legalize their status (e.g., through marriage). The administration also sent ominous signals to Mexico about its readiness to tighten borders by restricting the flow of tourists. Overall, the administration supported some reform but left the initiative to Congress.

The major congressional initiative was the Simpson-Mazzoli-Rodino legislation. Like the presidential plans mentioned above, it centered on legalizing the status of migrants who had already been in the country for several years ("amnesty") while cracking down on new migration though employer sanctions and bolstered law enforcement. Such legislation appeared consistent with public opinion polls showing widespread support for im-migration restrictions and passed the Senate several times and the House in 1984, but the chambers could not agree on a package until late 1986. Predictably the 1986 legislation included the following: amnesty for those living in the United States continuously since January 1982; penalties for employers hiring workers without legal documentation; considerable am-biguity about many provisions; quick executive approval from President Reagan; denunciation from large employers, unions, and ethnic groups, which had together helped block previous legislative attempts; and denun-ciation by Mexico for the measure's unilateral effort to legislate a solution to a market problem without getting to the deep causes (such as trade) while increasing the potential for human rights abuses.

Unfortunately, measures that might seem more adequate to address the roots of the problem usually seem impossible to implement. Mexico could change its development model so as to create more and better employment. The United States could lend massive assistance to Mexico's development efforts, especially in labor-intensive agriculture. But such mea-sures would run counter to the general development approaches pursued by Mexico and the United States. Similarly, the United States has not seriously considered legalizing an unimpeded flow, regulated only by U.S. economic demands, nor a drastic opening for U.S. importation of Mexican goods. (Some Mexicans have expressed interest in a bilateral agreement to allow a large guest-worker program, with appropriate safeguards, although others fear that such a program would mostly help U.S. employers and promote the migration of semiskilled and skilled workers needed by Mexico.) Short of an unimaginable narrowing of the Mexico-United States development gap, the United States will continue to "pull" Mexicans across the border. Even if Mexico drastically cut its unemployment, for example, Mexicans would still be attracted northward by higher wages. The only other road that might weaken the "pull" further would be a severe U.S. recession or a radical program of border and employment vigilance and probably repression, beyond anything yet seriously contemplated.

The improbability of the root solutions makes it imperative to consider limited alternatives, even though these too engender little easy agreement. Whatever help better understanding of the specific causes and consequences of Mexican migration to the United States may provide, officials would still face an entanglement of conflicting cross-national economic, social, individual, moral, and political interests. In a sense, migrants, employers, and indirectly, consumers—more than the two governments—have been making migration policy.

CONCLUSIONS

Surprising as it may seem from reading the news, contemporary Mexico–United States relations are comparatively good.[44] Of course, very important points qualify this positive view, such as increased tensions since 1970 and including those of the mid-1980s. But one has only to compare the last fifty years to the hundred preceding them to appreciate the improvement. No longer is there warfare, or the threat of it. No longer do U.S. warships blatantly bully Mexican politicians by seizing Veracruz. No longer is diplomatic recognition problematic. A sense of history puts contemporary problems into perspective.

The key explanation for good contemporary relations is that both sides have benefited. Mexican development has been tied to imports of U.S. goods, capital, and technology and to U.S. imports of Mexican products and workers. In return, the United States sees in Mexico an unusually close, secure, and profitable land for investment, a large market for U.S. exports, a needed supplier of energy and even workers—and a stable, noncommunist southern neighbor. Domestic politics and foreign policy are vitally intertwined, and for roughly fifty years Mexican domestic politics have served U.S. interests well.

A quick historical overview supports the proposition that bilateral relations have been harmonious when Mexico's domestic politics have promoted political stability, economic growth, and investment opportunities, more than when they have prompted instability or popular reform. One example would be the good relations during the porfiriato. Conversely, relations were bellicose during the 1840s when Mexico's internal problems made it especially vulnerable to U.S. aggression. Relations were also strained during the early decades of the revolution, when U.S. economic interests were threatened. Thus, the end of U.S. gunboat diplomacy is really as much a reflection as a cause of improved relations. The United States can penetrate the Mexican economy without recourse to the most blatant forms of political intervention. On balance, contemporary Mexican policies have promoted good relations with the United States, despite the important strains since 1970. Mexico's universalism has rarely been sustained by diminishing economic relations with the United States, and leftist foreign policy has not produced leftist or radical domestic policies, which could be far more dangerous to U.S. economic interests.

Nonetheless, Mexico's foreign policy is strikingly independent for a nation that is so much weaker than its superpower neighbor. Mexico is no Finland, bound to support the foreign policy of the superpower on its border. Mexico's positions on foreign policy often clash with those of the United States, and Mexico is a tough negotiator with the superpower on bilateral issues. In short, Mexican foreign policy is no mere appendage of U.S. policy. The United States generally accepts this because of the strength of the Mexican position, its own increased dependency on Mexico, and the perceived importance of Mexican stability. If Mexico's independent foreign policy provides some cover for conservative domestic policy, it is also true that successful domestic policy—in terms of stability and growth—has allowed Mexico to strike an independent foreign policy. By the same token, Mexico's economic crisis, and the desperate need for U.S. support, has undermined Mexican independence. Surely, U.S. policy toward Mexico is influenced by Mexican foreign policy, but it is probably influenced more by Mexican domestic policy.

Good relations do not depend on Mexico's serving U.S. interests alone. Significant Mexican interests are also being served. This chapter has repeatedly shown that bilateral problems are rooted in conflicting interests, not just misunderstandings; similarly, the fundamentally harmonious aspects of Mexico–United States relations are rooted in overlapping interests. "Poor Mexico" is still poor partly because it is so close to the United States, but significant benefits also stem from that proximity. There can be legitimate debate over whether such proximity is, on balance, good for Mexico, but less doubt concerning whether it serves Mexico's dominant political economy. Of course, to write of "Mexico" is to oversimplify. Some Mexicans benefit, others suffer. A key factor is that *powerful* groups in both nations have tended to benefit and therefore to promote the present bilateral pattern. Those (particularly in Mexico) who have not had much influence over foreign policy may well be suffering from that pattern, just as they may suffer from the domestic policy with which the foreign policy is consistent.

In sum, if Mexican foreign policy is too "dependent," the causes lie not only in foreign influence but in Mexico's development model and in Mexico's geography. Given its domestic development model and its geographic position in the giant's shadow, contemporary Mexico has forged a remarkably independent foreign policy.

NOTES

1. The "Poor Mexico" phrase is generally attributed to Díaz, but it may have been coined by someone else. We hope that readers already familiar with Mexico will forgive yet another citation of this quotation; we use it here in juxtaposition to the quotation of Castañeda, Mexico's foreign minister in 1980 (at the forty-second annual Council on Foreign Relations meeting, June 6, 1980).

2. Robert McBride, "U.S.-Mexican Relations," *Princeton Alumni Weekly*, March 13, 1978, reporting on a 1969 incident.

3. Karl M. Schmitt, *Mexico and the United States 1821–1973: Conflict and Coexistence* (New York: John Wiley, 1974), pp. 44–50. Also on Mexico's potential strength see Daniel Cosío Villegas, *American Extremes*, trans. Américo Paredes (Austin: University of Texas Press, 1964), p. 35; and Jesús Silva Herzog, *Trayectoria ideológica de la revolución mexicana* (Mexico City: S.E.P., 1973), p. 188. For a recent and brief overview of the history of Mexico–U.S. relations (to the present), see Josefina Zoraida Vázquez and Lorenzo Meyer, *The United States and Mexico* (Chicago: University of Chicago Press, 1985).

4. On Wilson's changing preferences, see Schmitt, *Mexico and the United States,* pp. 126–149.

5. On the centrality of revolutionary nationalism in Mexico–United States conflicts, see Lorenzo Meyer, *Mexico and the United States in the Oil Controversy 1917–1942* (Austin: University of Texas Press, 1977).

6. There is a traditional anti-U.S. strain in the Mexican Catholic Church. This orientation stems from a rejection of U.S. Protestantism, liberalism, individualism, and materialism. Changes occurred in the twentieth century, however; a foreign policy factor was the Catholic Church's kinship to the anticommunist crusade led by the United States.

7. Wayne A. Cornelius, "Nation-Building, Participation, and Distribution: The Politics of Social Reform Under Cárdenas," in *Crisis, Choice and Change: Historical Studies of Political Development*, ed. Gabriel Almond, Scott Flanagan, and Robert J. Mundt (Boston: Little, Brown and Co., 1973), p. 399.

8. These three reasons are not mutually exclusive, and given foreign policies may be based on mixed motivations. For example, the regime may support a leftist cause partly to express genuine sympathy, partly to oppose U.S. intervention, and partly to strengthen its support among many intellectuals, bureaucrats, and other nationalists. Such policies may even make it easier for some intellectuals to accept public office. None of this means that the domestically most conservative presidents pursue the most leftist foreign policies. Díaz Ordaz, for example, was not as leftist in foreign policy as his predecessor (López Mateos) or his successor (Echeverría), and de la Madrid was generally seen as more conservative than his two predecessors in both domestic and foreign policy.

9. The best account of Mexico's Cuban policy, an account sensitive to nuance', is Olga Pellicer de Brody's *México y la revolución cubana* (Mexico City: El Colegio de México, 1972). Our summary draws especially on pp. 22–29, 95–103.

10. Wolf Grabendorff, "Mexico's Foreign Policy—Indeed a Foreign Policy?" *Journal of Interamerican Studies and World Affairs* 20, no. 1 (1978):87–88. There is also an interesting interplay between domestic policy and foreign policy with the Soviet Union. Mexico shores up its leftist and independent credentials while the Soviet Union praises the regime's independence, even if that means undercutting Mexico's Communist party. On the eve of the 1976 elections, for example, the Soviet ambassador publicly brought Echeverría the "friendly greetings" of the Soviet Communist party.

11. For a brief overview of the defensive component of Mexican foreign policy, see Rosario Green's "México: La política exterior del nuevo régimen," *Foro Internacional* 18, no. 1 (1977):1–9. Notwithstanding the tensions, a number of significant agreements were concluded between Mexico and the United States on air quality, air transport, water rights, flood and other natural disaster control, wildlife, sanitation, and extradition procedures. Compared to such issues as trade and migration, these are the "easy" issues.

12. For a basic account of these motivations, see Olga Pellicer de Brody, "Cambios recientes en la política exterior mexicana," *Foro Internacional* 13, no. 2 (1972):139–154.

13. Soon, however, relations with Israel returned to normalcy and cordiality, involving cultural and technological interchanges as well as Israel's need for oil.

14. Mario Ojeda, "México ante los Estados Unidos en la coyuntura actual," *Foro Internacional* 18, no. 1 (1977):33.

15. Some see a retreat to a lack of assertiveness even as early as the López Portillo administration; see, for example, Olga Pellicer de Brody, "Veinte años de política exterior mexicana: 1960–1980," *Foro Internacional* 21, no. 2 (1980):152–159. If one also sees López Mateos's activism curtailed by Díaz Ordaz, then we get some image of a pendulum swing in foreign affairs, paralleling swings in domestic politics. But it is with de la Madrid that a retreat from Echeverría's sort of assertiveness is more definitively found.

16. Helms and witnesses before his subcommittee blasted Mexico on issues of drugs, migration, corruption, and so forth. Responding to echoes of such charges within the Reagan administration, juxtaposed to more conciliatory statements from the same administration, the *New York Times* (editorial, May 17, 1986) justifiably wondered if the administration was playing "good cop, bad cop," intimidating and then soothing Mexico. For a strong argument that intensified U.S. scrutiny and criticism of Mexico are counterproductive to U.S. ends, see Jorge G. Castañeda, "Mexico at the Brink," *Foreign Affairs* 64 (Winter 1985–1986):287–303.

17. See, for example, the overview by Lorenzo Meyer: "México–Estados Unidos: Lo esencial de una relación," in *México–Estados Unidos, 1984*, ed. Manual García y Griego and Gustavo Vega (Mexico City: El Colegio de México, 1985), pp. 15–30.

18. The ensuing paragraphs draw on Daniel Levy, "The Implications of Central American Conflicts for Mexican Politics," in *Mexico's Political Stability: The Next Five Years*, ed. Roderic A. Camp (Boulder, Colo.: Westview Press, 1986), pp. 235–264, and on sources cited therein. See also Mario Ojeda, ed., *Las relaciones de México con los países de América Central* (Mexico City: El Colegio de México, 1985).

19. The U.S. government did not want its position stereotyped as opposite Mexico's. President Carter called for political solutions based on what he regarded as reformist, centrist compromises. President Reagan's defenders made similar claims, whereas critics dismissed that president's talk of peaceful solutions as window dressing. One of Reagan's plans for regional economic development, the Caribbean Basin Initiative to help small nations in the area, received a mixed Mexican reaction. Mexico generally praised the search for political solutions through economic assistance but regarded the plan as piecemeal and too tied to armaments policy.

20. Mario Ojeda, *Alcances y límites de la política exterior de México* (Mexico City: El Colegio de México, 1976), pp. 58–61. One astonishing indicator of Mexico's independence from the United States is that it received only 0.2 percent of U.S. military assistance to Latin America from 1950 to 1967.

21. Mexico, Secretaría de Programación y Presupuesto, *Tercer informe de gobierno: Anexo Sector Comercio y Fomento Industrial* (Mexico City, 1985).

22. See *U.S. News and World Report*, March 9, 1981.

23. Statement of the secretary of the Sindicato de Obreros Libres (Free Workers Union), quoted in "La política," *Ocho Columnas* (Guadalajara), December 19, 1979. Interestingly, Mexico's conservatives remained relatively quiet during the crisis, but many did rebuke Mexico's foreign minister for allegedly misleading everyone just shortly before the decision to readmit the shah. Responsibility for such inconsistencies logically falls on the president, but conservatives did not violate the unwritten code

against public criticism of the chief executive. (U.S. aerial bombardment of Libya in 1986 brought a mild protest from Mexico, denouncing military reprisal but also terrorism.)

24. On Mexico's number three ranking, see U.S. House of Representatives, *U.S.–Mexico Relations: An Update,* Hearings before the Subcommittee on Inter-American Relations of the Committee on Foreign Affairs, June 10, 1981 (Washington, D.C., June 1981). On the 1980 figures, see U.S. Council of Economic Advisors, *Economic Report of the President* (Washington, D.C.: January 1981), p. 350; Departamento de Planeación, "Intercambio comercial México-Estados Unidos," *Comercio Exterior* 31, no. 4 (1981):469; José López Portillo, *Quinto informe de gobierno* (Mexico City: Secretaría de Programación y Presupuesto, September 1981). On the 1983 figures, see Secretaría, *Tercer informe.*

25. See Secretaría, *Tercer informe.*

26. Also, Mexico relies on the United States for most of its credit. The latter provides about 80 percent of all private bank loans to Mexico. (See Chapter 5.)

27. See Guy F. Erb and Cathryn Thorup, *U.S.–Mexican Relations: The Issues Ahead,* Development paper 35 (Washington, D.C.: Overseas Development Council, 1984), p. 15. For a good presentation of Mexican views on how U.S. policy thwarts free trade, see part II of García y Griego and Vega, eds., *México–Estados Unidos.*

28. Tomás Peñaloza, "La formulación de la política exterior en los Estados Unidos de América y su impacto sobre México," *Foro Internacional* 18, no. 1 (1977):26. Ultimately, President Ford decided against imposing quotas.

29. Steven E. Sanderson, *The Transformation of Mexican Agriculture: International Structure and the Politics of Rural Change* (Princeton, N.J.: Princeton University Press, 1986), pp. 64–116, and passim. Indeed, recent scholarship has emphasized the impacts of transnational corporations on Mexico. See Gary Gereffi, *The Pharmaceutical Industry and Dependency in the Third World* (Princeton, N.J.: Princeton University Press, 1983); Douglas C. Bennett and Kenneth E. Sharpe, *Transnational Corporations Versus the State: The Political Economy of the Mexican Auto Industry* (Princeton, N.J.: Princeton University Press, 1985).

30. We use the word *drug* loosely (not in a medical sense) to include marijuana. Among the sources we consulted are the U.S. State Department's Bureau of Public Affairs, *Gist* (December 1978); and "Mexico: The Connection," *Latin American Political Reports,* March 17, 1978, pp. 85–86. We draw on the social science/detective work of Richard Craig; see his two articles in the *Journal of Interamerican Studies and World Affairs,* "La Campaña Permanente: Mexico's Antidrug Campaign," 20, no. 2 (1978):107–132; and "Operation Condor," 22, no. 3 (1980):345–364.

31. Craig, "Operation Condor," pp. 359–361. Craig argued that Operation Condor was spurred by Mexico's realization that the drug issue had become an international embarrassment, that drug use was growing among middle- and upper-class young people, and that tremendous drug revenues threatened to create excessive power outside the central government. Further evidence for such perceptions of threat appeared in subsequent years. See also Samuel del Villar, "La narcotización de la cultura en Estados Unidos y su impacto en México," pp. 63–88, and James Van Wert, "El control de los narcóticos en México: Una década de institucionalización y un asunto diplomático," pp. 89–104, both in *México–Estados Unidos, 1985,* ed. Gabriel Székely (Mexico City: El Colegio de México, 1986).

32. Our data on tourism come from Departamento de Planeación, "Intercambio," p. 479; Instituto Nacional de Estadística Geografía e Informática, *Estadísticas históricas de México,* Vol. 2 (Mexico City, 1985), pp. 703, 709; and Joseph B. Treaster, "One Thing More for Mexico to Rebuild: Tourism," *New York Times,* October 8, 1985. The US$2.2 billion figure is for 1984.

33. Tourists may find a handsome bilingual publication, *A Giant Awakens* (Mexico City: Ministry of Tourism, 1979), in their hotel rooms.

34. Jacques Bugnicourt, "La otra cara del turismo: Sus efectos culturales," *Comercio Exterior* 28, no. 5 (1978):593.

35. Wayne Cornelius, "La migración ilegal mexicana a los Estados Unidos: Conclusiones de investigaciones recientes, implicaciones políticas y prioridades de investigación," *Foro Internacional* 18, no. 3 (1978):402; Kenneth Johnson, *Mexican Democracy: A Critical View* (New York: Praeger Publishers, 1978), p. 198. Most studies of the migration problem have been based on field research in the United States. A pioneering attempt to gather data and insights from within Mexico itself is headed by Jorge A. Bustamante, "Nuevos hallazgos," *Uno Más Uno*, December 10, 1979; and "El estudio de la zona fronteriza México–Estados Unidos," *Foro Internacional* 19, no. 3 (1979):471–516.

36. See, for example, Thomas Muller and Thomas J. Espenshade, *The Fourth Wave: California's Newest Immigrants* (Washington, D.C.: The Urban Institute Press, 1985). Silvia Pedraza-Bailey contrasts the treatment of Mexicans with that of Cubans (who are more favorably received) in the United States in *Political and Economic Migrants in America: Cubans and Mexicans* (Austin: University of Texas Press, 1985).

37. "Los ilegales mexicanos," *Comercio Exterior* 28, no. 7 (1978):804. But Alba concludes that estimates vary greatly on the amount of money sent to Mexico and that probably the sums are sufficient to help many families with consumption but insufficient to help Mexico much with saving or investment. See Francisco Alba, "El patrón migratorio entre México y Estados Unidos: Su relación con el mercado laboral y el flujo de remesas," in García y Griego and Vega, eds., *México–Estados Unidos*, pp. 212–215. In the same volume, a broad case is made that tougher U.S. border restrictions would have less impact on Mexico than most Mexicans fear: Manuel García y Griego and Francisco Giner de los Ríos, "¿Es vulnerable la economía mexicana a la aplicación de políticas migratorias estadounidenses?" pp. 221–272.

38. U.S. House of Representatives, Committee on Science and Technology, *U.S.–Mexico Relations and Potentials Regarding Energy, Immigration, Scientific Cooperation and Technology Transfer* (Washington, D.C.: Government Printing Office, 1979), p. 18.

39. See Barry W. Poulson, "The Brain Drain from Mexico to the United States," in *U.S.–Mexico Economic Relations*, ed. Barry W. Poulson and Noel Osborn (Boulder, Colo.: Westview Press, 1979), pp. 245–260.

40. Such, for example, was the strongly voiced opinion of Carter's secretary of labor, F. Ray Marshall, "Economic Factors Influencing the International Migration of Workers," in *Views Across the Border: The United States and Mexico*, ed. Richard W. Weatherhead and Stanley R. Ross (Albuquerque: University of New Mexico Press, 1978), pp. 178–179.

41. Peñaloza, "La formulación," pp. 26–27.

42. Within their respective domestic political contexts, the Mexican president has a freer hand than his U.S. counterpart in making foreign policy. Less division exists, at least less public and intragovernmental division, than in the United States; similar points could be made about certain other bilateral issues. Mexican foreign policy consensus should not be exaggerated, however. For example, some Mexicans favor a new guest-worker program, while others strongly oppose it. One way to approach the plurality of views in both nations is through "linkage," considering bilateral issues integrally instead of separately. The United States has generally been more wary of linkage than Mexico has. On linkage, see Richard E. Feinberg, "Bureaucratic Organization and U.S. Policy Toward Mexico," in *Mexico–United States*

Relations, ed. Susan Kaufman Purcell (New York: Academy of Political Science, 1981), pp. 32–42; Erb and Thorup, *U.S.-Mexican Relations,* pp. 3–33. An alternative is to conclude that not all bilateral problems are solvable by government (government may even aggravate some problems) and to encourage conflict resolution through private and incremental procedures.

43. Additional sources on migration include the entire issue of *Foro Internacional* 18, no. 3 (1978); Antonio Ríos-Bustamente, ed., *Mexican Immigrant Workers in the U.S.* (Los Angeles: UCLA, 1981); Wayne Cornelius, Leo R. Chávez, and Jorge Castro, "Mexican Immigrants and Southern California: A Summary of Current Knowledge," Working Paper no. 36 (La Jolla, Calif.: Center for U.S.-Mexican Studies, University of California at San Diego, March 1982). Some policy suggestions are offered in Jorge A. Bustamente, "Migración indocumentada," *Foro Internacional* 19, no. 2 (1978):317–325.

44. Schmitt, *Mexico and the United States* (p. 193), described the 1945–1970 period as more "harmonious and carefree" than any previous period in Mexico-U.S. history, with the possible exception of the porfiriato. Among the recent works that provide overviews of contemporary Mexican foreign policy, especially concerning the United States, see Richard D. Erb and Stanley R. Ross, eds., *United States Relations with Mexico: Context and Content* (Washington, D.C.: American Enterprise Institute, 1981); George W. Grayson, *The United States and Mexico: Patterns of Influence* (New York: Praeger Publishers, 1984); Purcell, *Mexico–United States Relations;* Carlos Vásquez and Manuel García y Griego, eds., *Mexican–U.S. Relations: Conflict or Convergence?* (Los Angeles: UCLA, 1983); Mario Ojeda, *México: El surgimiento de una política exterior activa* (Mexico City: Secretaría de Educación Pública, 1986). The annual publication by El Colegio de México, *México–Estados Unidos,* is a formidable contribution, and the same institution's *Foro Internacional* remains the journal that deals most fully with Mexican foreign policy. A good official journal published by the Mexican government is *Revista Mexicana de Política Exterior.*

7

Oil Policy: A Case Study of Mexican Development

In 1973, Mexico produced fewer than 1 million barrels per day of crude oil and gas equivalent, a production insufficient to meet its own demand. By late 1981, output had increased fourfold. *Oil had become Mexico's principal export.* Estimates of potential Mexican oil and gas production and exports for the 1980s found in various studies conducted by U.S. government agencies proved hopelessly conservative. Mexico's proven hydrocarbon reserves rose from 5.4 billion to more than 72 billion barrels of crude oil and gas equivalent during the 1973–1981 period.[1]

During the 1980s, however, Mexico's energy development fell prey to the volatility characterizing so much of the nation's economics and politics. Dramatic expansion and optimism were countered by sharp declines and pessimism. Crude oil output peaked in late 1982 at about 3 million barrels per day (mbd), before stabilizing at 2.75 mbd, of which 1.5 mbd, or 55 percent, was being exported. Then, in 1986, oil production fell drastically to 2.3 mbd as PEMEX (Mexico's state oil company) proved unable to export more than 1.2 mbd. Excess production capacity in the world market triggered a price war among producers. Gas production experienced a similar upsurge and decline. From 1980 to 1984, gas output reached more than 4 billion cubic feet per day (bcfd), which is equivalent to an additional 800,000 barrels of oil per day. Because only 2.7 bcfd of total gas production were being consumed domestically and only 0.3 bcfd were being exported to the United States, gas flaring (gas burned into the atmosphere) amounted to close to 1.0 bcfd. Mexico's gas output declined, and Mexico no longer exported gas to the United States.

Notwithstanding such disheartening reversals, Mexico is today among the world's top four nations in terms of three crucial factors: crude oil reserves, production, and exports. A very large gap still separates Mexico from the largest oil powers; in terms of production, for example, the Soviet Union, the United States, and Saudi Arabia each produces more than twice what Mexico produces. Nevertheless, everyone who follows the news knows that Mexico is itself now a leading oil producer. Less well known is that

225

Mexico was a leading oil producer in the early 1920s. At that time the Middle East and Venezuelan oil fields had not been developed, and Mexico accounted for one-fourth of the world's oil production. As a result of Mexico's oil revival, many politicians, private entrepreneurs, and scholars in oil-importing and oil-exporting nations have developed a special and sudden interest in Mexico. Some have expressed concern over the disruptive effects of rapid oil development on domestic political and socioeconomic relations. Others have speculated about the potential effects of increased Mexican oil production and exports on world oil supply and price levels. For many years, rising oil prices, and the continual fear of another Arab oil embargo, put additional pressure on already tense world economic and political relations. Thus, Mexico's decisions regarding its oil production and exports have been linked to other nations' economic, political, and even military interests.

The focus of this chapter, however, is more restricted than the possibilities for research offered by this topic might suggest. After briefly reviewing the significance of oil in historical perspective, we analyze the various reactions of key domestic actors to Mexico's official oil policy as set forth in 1976. Thus, this chapter offers the reader an opportunity to apply some of the concepts about Mexican politics developed in earlier chapters. Oil became, after all, the most important new factor affecting Mexican politics and the development model. We argued that in 1976 the economy was a shambles, the political environment tense. The new oil export policy helped to restore confidence in the development model—at least until 1982. We conclude this chapter by discussing some of the links between the new oil policy and Mexico's economic and foreign relations.

HISTORICAL BACKGROUND

The history of Mexican oil can be divided into five phases.[2] Each has witnessed important changes in regard to *resource ownership* and *the primary goal or destination of production.*

The first phase extended from precolonial times to 1884. During that period, the state owned the resource, but no commercial production took place. Oil was known to the Mayas and Aztecs, who used the term *chapopote* to refer to the large oil seepages found primarily in southern regions, but their use of this natural resource was only marginal. So it would also be under the Spanish crown. Yet Spanish law, which influenced independent Mexico, provided for public ownership of underground natural resources.

The second phase began when a new law allowed the government to grant property titles to foreign companies, a telling illustration of Porfirio Díaz's tendency to encourage foreign entrepreneurs' participation in Mexico's first major drive for industrialization.[3] Exploratory efforts started in 1886 in southern Mexico. By 1901, commercial production of oil began. Ironically, the first shipment of oil exports left Mexico in 1911, just when Porfirio Díaz himself boarded the *Ipiranga* on his way to exile in France. Mexican society had exploded in revolution.

The third phase opened with the provision in Article 27 of the new 1917 Constitution, establishing that underground natural resources were considered once again the exclusive property of the Mexican state. Understandably, this law set the stage for an eventual confrontation between the government and the foreign companies operating on the basis of the 1884 law. Their differing positions over resource ownership rights gradually evolved into a conflict that did not end until the 1940s. Interestingly, revolution and turmoil had not stymied oil development. In fact, output picked up, and by 1921, Mexico accounted for 25 percent of the world's total production. Mexico was the world's single largest oil exporter! During this period, most production coming from Mexico's famous golden belt (*faja de oro*) was exported to the United States, which was slowly increasing its use of oil and gas to fulfill its growing energy needs.

Our analysis in Chapter 2 of the effects of Mexico's revolutionary assertion of its economic sovereignty on Mexico–United States relations deliberately left details of the oil controversy for our discussion here. Washington withheld diplomatic recognition of the revolutionary regime for some time, in part because of the 1917 Constitution's provisions regarding private property and social policy issues, which were perceived by the United States as too radical in their material effects on U.S. interests. Normalization of diplomatic relations followed Obregón's ascendency to power in 1920, but only after the signing of the Bucareli Agreements (1923) on oil and other matters.[4] In particular, the government of Mexico committed itself not to implement retroactively the provisions of Article 27. The U.S. government accepted, for its part, that the companies' property titles be referred to from then on simply as "concessions." Because concessions are usually granted for a limited time only, the U.S. position left open the possibility of an eventual end to the presence of foreign oil firms on Mexican soil.

Bilateral relations became strained once again following the decree of a new Petroleum Law in 1925 by President Plutarco Elías Calles. The decree demanded that companies register their titles with local authorities, and it limited concessions to a maximum of fifty years. The companies, already disturbed by the Bucareli Agreements, found these provisions unacceptable and lobbied heavily against them in the United States. In an attempt to strengthen their domestic base of support, some went so far as to advocate the use of military force to settle once and for all the list of outstanding issues with Mexico. In 1927, Calles dramatized the situation by ordering General Lázaro Cárdenas, then commander-in-chief of the oil provinces, to set the fields afire if the United States conducted any kind of military action against Mexico. But several events combined to prevent that scenario from unfolding. For one thing, Calles did not push the companies to comply immediately with the law; more important, the new U.S. ambassador, Dwight Morrow, played a conciliatory role that led to an eventual revision of the law, to the satisfaction of some oil firms. In any event, the uncertainty generated by the controversy over resource ownership was among several factors that caused the major oil companies to concentrate their efforts in other lands. Large oil fields were found in Venezuela in the 1920s and in the Middle East in the 1930s; production costs were lower in these areas than in Mexico. Cost was a crucial consideration because oil was competing with cheap and abundant coal, the major source of energy in the industrial world.[5] Thus, the center of world oil production shifted from Mexico and the United States to the Persian Gulf and Venezuela. Note that in the 1920s—quite unlike the 1980s—Mexico was a leading producer of a resource that was *not* the world's principal energy source.

The fourth phase in Mexico's oil history began in 1938 with the nationalization of the oil industry by President Cárdenas. Mexico was no longer a major oil exporter, partly as a result of the declining production that accompanied the prolonged struggle between the foreign companies and the government. At the same time, domestic demand for hydrocarbons increased steadily as Mexico engaged in a new drive for industrialization after 1938. The decision to nationalize the industry followed the challenge to Mexico's judicial authorities by foreign oil firms. The courts had ruled in favor of union demands to improve workers' living standards. Unions were particularly strong because President Cárdenas had supported the establishment of the Confederation of Mexican Workers in 1936. This is a good example of how the political dynamic that followed the revolution affected oil development. The state could rely on a strong and well-organized actor (labor) to face the challenge of the foreign companies. After long and hard bargaining, the companies refused to comply with the recommendations of the courts. President Cárdenas believed that this questioning of the legitimacy and the authority of the regime was intolerable, and he proceeded accordingly. In his own words:

> It is clear that the problem presented to the national executive power by the disobedience of the Supreme Court's verdict is not simply a problem of implementing the verdict, but a situation that must be resolved at once. . . . It is the nation's sovereignty itself that could be exposed to maneuvering by foreign capital, which has forgotten its previous commitment to respect national laws, and is now seeking to avoid fulfillment of its duties as dictated by the country's authorities.
>
> It is a clear-cut case, and it leaves the government no choice other than to apply the current Law of Expropriation.[6]

Although talk again of imminent U.S. military intervention in Mexico circulated, overall U.S. foreign policy objectives at the time rendered such an event highly unlikely (see Chapter 2). Roosevelt's Good Neighbor Policy was intended to keep the nations of the Western Hemisphere together when the outbreak of world conflict was most feared. Partly for this reason, the U.S. government opted instead for pressuring Cárdenas to compensate the firms as they requested. It was only the amount of compensation, then, that was at issue, because the Mexican government had already expressed its intention of following the constitution, which included compensation rights for those affected by this kind of government action. But the companies wanted to go much further and to teach rebellious Mexico a lesson, hoping that in the future other host countries would refrain from effecting nationalizations—especially after Bolivia's attempts to nationalize its oil industry in 1937. They pressured the U.S. government to cut down imports of Mexican silver, Mexico's main source of foreign exchange. In fact, a complete boycott of Mexican oil products and of other exports ensued. But because a growing share of Mexican oil was diverted to the Axis powers, U.S. government policy soon shifted. This time, the U.S. government put pressure on the companies to come to an agreement with Mexico, on the grounds of national security. It was thought that Mexican oil production could be increased on short notice should an emergency require it. In that sense, it was critical to maintain good relations with Mexico. A final settlement came in 1942, when a bilateral governmental team worked out an agreement whose terms were accepted by the U.S. companies. Total compensation amounted to only a fraction of the $400 million once demanded by U.S. Secretary of State Cordell Hull.[7]

Today, a constitutional ban prohibits the involvement of foreign firms in most aspects of the oil industry, primarily due to their intolerable behavior in the past. However, the government has not hesitated to ask for foreign assistance when the country's capacity to fulfill certain needs (e.g., domestic consumption needs) has been in jeopardy. That is, economic independence is a recurrent theme in Mexican politics, but it can be compromised in order to attain a different or even a higher priority, such as economic growth. Thus, for example, President Miguel Alemán allowed PEMEX to sign several contracts, in 1949 and 1951, with U.S. firms to conduct exploration works in the Gulf of Mexico. The companies, if successful, would be paid partly with a share of 15 to 18 percent of the value of production. Although these contracts were honored until their respective expiration dates twenty years later, Article 27 of the constitution was amended in 1958 with the specific purpose of preventing any similar kind of contracts in the future.[8]

Since the 1938 nationalization, a top priority of governmental policy has been to supply sufficient oil and gas, which together have accounted for about 90 percent of total domestic energy needs during the rapid industrialization since the 1940s. Because domestic consumption was rising rapidly while hydrocarbon reserves had increased more modestly, from 1.2 billion barrels in 1938 to 5.2 billion in 1964, the search for oil and gas went on during the 1960s. President Díaz Ordaz supported greater exploration efforts in the Gulf of Mexico. In 1967, according to the *Wall Street Journal*, PEMEX officials estimated total reserves from that area at about 10 billion barrels of crude oil and gas equivalent.[9] Those estimates were not then confirmed, but it did not take many years before press speculation regarding potential huge deposits of oil and gas in Mexico started anew.

On March 18, 1973, during the annual commemoration of the oil nationalization, the director general of PEMEX referred publicly for the first time to the oil and gas findings. A few months later, President Luis Echeverría himself spoke about the "oil discoveries" in southern Mexico, during his State of the Union address.[10] In some quarters, these declarations were not taken seriously at first. After all, Mexico had stopped exporting crude oil in 1969, and the country had been a net importer of oil in recent years. Nonetheless, others became increasingly interested in what was going on in Mexico's oil and financial circles. The issue was discussed by President Echeverría and President Gerald Ford during their meeting in October 1974.[11] In the eyes of the U.S. president, the issue probably looked uncomplicated. Mexican authorities began to talk publicly about the new oil fields before the energy crisis of late 1973 and early 1974. That was an indication that Mexico had an independent interest in selling oil. Now that the United States could be subjected to an Arab oil embargo, and now that oil prices were rising quickly, friendly Mexico would presumably find it even more appealing to increase its oil output and exports. And the United States, for geographical reasons, is in purely economic terms the natural market for Mexican oil exports. But things looked more complex to President Echeverría. He was aware that some domestic resistance would arise to any sharp break from the oil-for-domestic-consumption-only policy of the last decades. In addition, his self-image as a "leader of the Third World" could be damaged if the effectiveness of an Arab oil embargo were undercut by Mexican oil exports to the United States.

Despite these considerations, and even though Echeverría did not dramatically depart from traditional oil policy, his policies helped lay the foundations so that a new administration could pursue a fundamentally new oil policy if it wished. One critical rationale, as discussed in Chapter 5, was quite unintentionally provided by the state of economic disarray when Echeverría left power. López Portillo made a strong case that the constraints on growth imposed by the disequilibria in the external sector of the economy (e.g., lack of foreign exchange and the growing foreign debt service) could be overcome much sooner with greatly expanded oil production than without it. Yet figures show that there is a greater degree of continuity in oil policy among administrations than is usually assumed. The oil sector accounted for 17 percent of total public investment during Echeverría's tenure, and PEMEX received several foreign loans, totaling about $4 billion, to fund its expansion. The results were satisfactory by most standards. Output rose from 0.8 mbd of oil and gas equivalent in 1970 to 1.3 mbd in 1976. More than half of total output in 1976 came from the new fields. Similarly, the nominal production capacity of the national network of refineries increased by 55 percent. During the period, Mexico's status changed from that of a net oil importer to that of a net oil exporter. The 1975 figure of nearly 100,000 barrels per day (which was soon to be surpassed) was the highest crude oil export level since 1928.[12] In short, when López Portillo came to power he did not have to start from scratch to implement a new oil policy. Rather, the efforts of the previous administration made it easier for him to move swiftly in that direction. The 1973–1976 period may be considered a transitional stage between the fourth and fifth phases in the history of Mexican oil policy.

The fifth phase, the present phase, started in late 1976. Resource ownership was no longer an issue, as the decisive 1938 nationalization was initiated and implemented in the fourth phase. But domestic production was once again more than sufficient to satisfy national energy needs, and for the first time in decades, Mexico would begin exporting oil and gas in substantial amounts. López Portillo in fact went much further than his predecessor in expanding the oil industry. PEMEX is a giant enterprise. Its budget in 1980, at the height of its expansion, amounted to US$15 billion (about one-quarter of the total budget of the public sector), and it ranked thirty-fourth on *Fortune*'s list of the 500 largest enterprises in the world.[13]

Three weeks after the inauguration of the new government, PEMEX director general Díaz Serrano announced that the figure for proven reserves had been increased from 6.3 billion to 11.1 billion barrels of oil and gas equivalent. PEMEX invited a prestigious U.S. firm, De Golyer and Mc-Naughton, to certify the authenticity of these figures. But why are reserve figures important in any case? At a minimum, reserve figures indicate the capacity of any country to export oil for some period of time. In Mexico, at current rates of production and consumption, 11 billion barrels would be expected to last twenty-three years. Because experts agree that a well-balanced reserve-to-production ratio should be equivalent to at least fifteen years, it was safe and justifiable that Mexico engage in an oil export program. How long beyond twenty-three years Mexico could remain an exporter would depend on the success of its exploration in adding to current reserves. A closely related factor was that PEMEX needed to secure foreign loans to finance its ambitious development program. There could hardly have been anything more valued than oil to convince foreign banks and international financial institutions that, despite the general economic chaos prevailing in Mexico, lending money to PEMEX was still a wise financial policy. Further, it was expected that oil might help to put the economy back in good shape and thus improve the prospects for continued political stability. Mexico could put its finances in order with the assistance of oil export revenues. It turned out that when the specifics of PEMEX's expansion plans were publicly known, not only bankers but also many industrialists, and even some governments, became very enthusiastic. Many hoped to do business with PEMEX or simply saw Mexico as a more secure source of oil imports than OPEC countries.

PEMEX's budget for 1977–1982 was estimated at US$40 billion, with investments alone accounting for about one-third of the total. By 1982, Mexico's crude oil output was expected to have increased to 2.25 mbd; output of natural gas was expected to be some 4 bcfd. Originally, it was planned that half of total crude oil output would be available for export, but no mention was made of gas exports. Other major goals included doubling the nominal refining capacity to 1.7 mbd, as well as a threefold increase of production capacity of basic petrochemicals to 18 million tons per year by 1982. How did PEMEX's expansion plans evolve, and how were they implemented? And how did domestic political actors react to the new oil policy?

THE DOMESTIC DEBATE
OVER CONTEMPORARY OIL POLICY

It took several months before the first dissenting voice was raised. Moreover, for some time it seemed as if there were only two participants in the debate. One of them, predictably, was the PEMEX director general. He represented and defended the government's position. Less predictably, the other participant was Heberto Castillo, a university professor and founder of the small Mexican Workers party. He has the distinction of having initiated the debate that eventually drew the attention of intellectuals and other actors previously inactive in this respect. Castillo advocated a return to the old oil policy on grounds that hydrocarbons are a nonrenewable natural resource, a natural resource on which Mexico depends heavily to satisfy its own energy needs. He further argued that because alternative energy sources had not yet been fully developed, and the technology required would be largely beyond Mexico's control, it would make sense to stretch the lifetime of hydrocarbon reserves as long as possible. He also contended that the main value of hydrocarbons is not as a fuel but as a raw material for production of other goods, like plastics and fertilizers. Fertilizers presumably would help to increase output of food that would help feed Mexico's needy, ensure national economic independence, and improve the peasants' lot.[14]

Castillo made a strong case, but he had little chance of success. The government perceived oil as the best means to overcome quickly the economic crisis. And Castillo did not command enough political resources to press his view. Still, his criticisms became the focus of the debate because, for some months, he systematically embarrassed the government by presenting evidence of the incoherence and inconsistency of the information presented by PEMEX in support of its development program. For example, Díaz Serrano went before Congress in October 1977 to explain a new project—PEMEX wanted to invest an additional US$1 billion to build a gas pipeline (*gasoducto*) that would reduce gas flaring. (As oil is extracted, gas also emerges; and because Mexico has not found adequate outlets for the gas, it must destroy it.) The gas surplus, Díaz Serrano argued, could be sent to the United States through the gasoducto, with exports reaching more than 2 bcfd by 1982. But many of PEMEX's statistics, such as the official record of how much gas was being flared, were inconsistent. Furthermore, the financial calculations to justify the gas project were not totally accurate.[15] Thus, Castillo found in the gasoducto affair an additional focus for his criticism of government policy. He appealed to nationalist feelings, warning that Mexico would become more linked than ever to U.S. national security. Mexico could even become a target of Soviet missiles during a superpower confrontation. He suggested that Mexico instead use the surplus gas domestically or liquefy it and send it overseas, despite greater financial costs.[16]

The Castillo-PEMEX controversy did not directly influence actual policy. In fact, PEMEX's plan fell through temporarily because the U.S. government did not approve the gas export contract signed by PEMEX and six U.S. gas firms in the summer of 1977. The pricing system for natural gas in the U.S. was being hotly debated in Congress, and the terms of the gas deal with PEMEX (US$2.60 per 1,000 cubic feet of gas) went beyond what was acceptable to the U.S. Congress at the time.[17] An embarrassed Mexican government ended up conducting a program to substitute gas for oil as a fuel in many of the nation's industries. And when an agreement was reached two years later to export 300 million cubic feet per day of gas to the United States, it was of a far more modest nature than was originally planned. Nonetheless, the Castillo-PEMEX controversy is interesting as an indication of the changing political environment in Mexico. In 1968, Castillo had been put in jail for criticizing the government during the university confrontation with the regime. Ten years later, granting that the nature of the challenge was different, he could express his opinion through a largely independent magazine and even elicit a civil public response from government officials.

A return to an oil policy without exports remains highly unlikely. If the government decided to eliminate oil exports, public finances would deteriorate dramatically, and the country's capacity to import would be severely restricted. There is no reason to believe that the government would make a decision that would most certainly aggravate Mexico's ongoing foreign exchange shortage. At the risk of oversimplifying, one can identify two main positions regarding the preferred course of Mexican oil development. One can be termed the *moderate oil development program*, the other the *all-out production and export program*. In what follows, the central arguments in support of each position will be discussed. Actors publicly advocating one or the other of these positions will be identified. A note of caution, however, is that these alternative policies have not been presented with the degree of coherence that is implied here. Nor are the actors on one side or the other necessarily working together to further their views. Mexican politics simply does not characteristically lend itself to such coherent public debate, unrestricted participation in policymaking, mobilization, or organizationally based coalition building. In addition, given the collapse of oil prices in 1986 and the continued glut in the world oil market, it appeared improbable that Mexico would have an option to increase substantially its oil output and exports. At the same time, however, we have learned that dramatic changes in such a market occur unexpectedly. A revolution, a regional war, or other events could restrict the availability of oil and drive prices up at any time. Therefore, looking carefully at the oil policy debate that developed during the López Portillo administration constitutes a useful analytical exercise partly because conditions encouraging a higher oil output and exports could present themselves once again in the future.

The Moderate Oil Development Program

López Portillo's decision to develop oil resources rapidly took many by surprise. Furthermore, it was soon realized that the issue was no longer whether to return to the old oil policy without exports, but rather how much and at what pace oil and gas would be produced and exported. Those who feared that excessive reliance on oil would exacerbate rather than solve Mexico's socioeconomic and political tensions gradually rallied in support of the *original* oil development program discussed earlier. They presented several arguments in support of their efforts to establish a fixed ceiling to oil and gas production and exports.

From the point of view of *resources*, the moderates argue that PEMEX should be careful not to rush, in its quest to fulfill its production targets, to a point that could risk depletion of resources. At the same time, the country should be allowed sufficient time to invest in developing alternative energy sources. Initial investments have in fact been made in nuclear and geothermal energy projects, with the hope that Mexico will gradually reduce its excessive dependence on hydrocarbons. But this process requires time, and only hydrocarbons can guarantee that time by insuring that Mexico will not have to face energy shortages at the turn of the century.

A concern with the varied effects of oil development on the *rest of the economy* is also central to the moderate position. Oil might be indispensable in coping with some of Mexico's short-term economic problems, but it is not a substitute for implementing necessary reforms in the tax system, income distribution, and other areas. Beyond this, a new strategy for increased agricultural production and industrialization must be developed, in which oil is but one of many factors to be considered. In addition, there should be enough time available to work out solutions to insufficient storage facilities and transportation systems (bottlenecks) and to control inflation. Finally, oil development should be expected to have positive side effects on the economy only if domestic entrepreneurs are granted sufficient time to produce locally many goods that otherwise would have to be imported. In short, moderates were right in that they saw fundamental problems in the development model that rapid oil expansion would only temporarily cover, not solve. In fact, covering over may have diminished the chances for realistic long-run policy.

To a greater or to a lesser extent, several actors identified themselves with the moderate position. Within the government itself, as we saw in Chapter 3, different ministries hold different ideological and policy orientations. The minister of national resources and industrial development under López Portillo was the strongest advocate of a moderate oil development program. He is, by law, the chairman of PEMEX's Board of Directors; but in fact PEMEX's director general has exercised much greater power, as he has been a closer associate of the president. Nevertheless, under the leadership of José Andrés de Oteyza, the Ministry of National Resources provided two important documents: the National Industrial Development Plan and the National Energy Plan.[18] Although these plans were superseded by those elaborated after 1982 by de la Madrid's administration, they are noteworthy in two respects. One is that some of their critical provisions were included in the newer development and energy plans. In addition, in their original version these plans provided, for some time, a rallying point for all those groups and individuals who disagreed with PEMEX's policy of rapidly expanding oil production and exports.

The Industrial Development Plan proposed annual rates of economic growth of up to 10 percent, starting in 1979 and continuing through 1990. Industry was expected to grow at an annual average rate of 12 percent, petrochemicals and capital goods at 20 percent. The plan discussed the instruments and incentives the public sector would have to provide to private investors. It was designed to decentralize Mexican industry geographically by encouraging it to move outside Mexico City. For example, for those investing outside Mexico City, it granted substantially subsidized prices for oil, gas, and petrochemical products (up to 30 percent below already low domestic prices). A more specific link ties the Industrial Plan and oil policy. The plan was based on the assumptions that crude oil output would have stabilized at 2.25 mbd at the end of 1980 and that any subsequent rise in output would only compensate for the growth of domestic demand. Revenues from exports of 1.1 mbd of crude oil would be instrumental to achieving the objectives of the plan. Gas exports were not considered at all, probably because the negotiations with the United States were at a standstill. As has been shown, the production and export targets of the *original* oil development program (which were included in the Industrial Plan) have been revised substantially. PEMEX's crude oil production of 2.25 mbd was reached two years ahead of schedule, gas was exported as early as January 1980, and the *new ceiling for oil production alone*—which implies a higher output of oil plus gas associated with oil—was increased to 2.75 mbd.

By giving great publicity to the government's commitment to a certain oil output ceiling, Oteyza may have earned some added leverage with the president regarding decisions to change that ceiling. An indication of this situation is that Oteyza got the president's approval for his National Energy Plan in November 1980. On the other hand, the president's approval probably reflected his own receptivity to the plan's major trends, for no ministry pushes the president against his will.

In presenting the National Energy Plan, Oteyza stressed that "any expansion in energy production should be a function of the nation's global development needs only. It should not be a function of the volumes of reserves *per se*, nor of greater demand by foreign economies."[19] Specifically, departing from the oil production ceiling of 2.75 mbd set earlier by López Portillo, the plan established an export ceiling of 1.5 mbd of crude oil and 300 million cubic feet per day of gas (the level of gas exports to the United States in 1980). In addition to this new attempt to freeze oil and gas production and export levels, the plan established that oil exports be diversified. That is, no more than 50 percent of Mexican oil should end up in the same country, and no country should come to depend on Mexico to fulfill more than 20 percent of its oil import needs. What was the meaning of these export rules? From 1974 to 1979, before those rules existed, more than four-fifths of Mexican oil exports had gone to the United States. By 1981, that proportion had fallen sharply, to about 50 percent. Thus, Mexico fulfilled its goal, at least temporarily, of not sending too much of its oil to the United States.[20] But fears of excessive U.S. reliance on Mexican oil, and thus of potential U.S. meddling, were naturally heightened by the 1982 economic crisis and Mexico's agreement to sell the United States increased quantities, at preferential cost. The continued economic crisis, so interwined with a deepening world crisis for oil producers, undermined Mexico's attempts at diversification and heightened vulnerability to U.S. pressure.

The minister of national resources under López Portillo had some allies within the administration, as well as some influential sympathizers elsewhere. In official circles, for example, economic policymaking authorities consistently expressed their concern with the effects of oil development on rising inflation. Further, as we argued in Chapter 5, the National Development Bank has a special interest in promoting the development of a domestic capital goods industry that, in time, could supply a share of the needs of PEMEX and other industries. And the Ministry of Finance and the Central Bank would like to exert greater influence on decisions regarding where and how oil revenues should be invested.

The governors of oil-producing states, particularly of Chiapas and Tabasco in the south, can also be counted among those who would rather support a moderate oil development program. Not only do state governments see a very small share of the oil money, but, at the same time, they have to deal with rising tensions, such as those resulting from expropriated peasant lands and delays in paying compensation. They also have to deal with pollution in lakes, the ocean, and farms. In fact, there are reports, many published in Mexico's generally cautious press, of protests by peasants and fishermen affected by PEMEX's activities. In addition, complaints in oil-producing states are growing because inflationary rates are even higher there than in Mexico City, urban areas are overcrowded, crime is on the rise, and so forth.[21] In other words, some of the threats to stability discussed in Chapter 1 are manifested particularly in the oil-producing states.

Although they are mostly of secondary importance due to the distribution of political power in Mexico, other potential proponents of the moderate policy include some private investors who need time to reap the full benefits of increasing aggregate demand; opposition political parties concerned with rising government corruption and waste of public funds; and university professors concerned with the hazardous environmental, social, and political effects already brought about by PEMEX expansion.

How far can PEMEX go? Some major actors have expressed support for development of the oil industry at a pace much faster than has been the case so far. They would like to see PEMEX producing and exporting higher levels of oil on the basis of its huge reserves. But their position was severely weakened with the first signs of shrinking world demand for oil in the summer of 1981. The continued glut in the world market in ensuing years led several nations to lower their oil output, but even then producers could not prevent the fall of oil prices, from the peak of nearly US$40 per barrel in 1981 to about US$10 in 1986. This situation made it quite unattractive for any nation to invest in the expansion of its oil industry. Nonetheless, conditions in the world oil market are changing constantly and unpredictably. Some political actors have continued to hope that Mexico would develop its oil industry much more rapidly.

The All-Out Production and Export Program

With the benefit of hindsight, the arguments that were put forward in support of a more ambitious development of the oil industry seem astonishing. To be fair, these arguments were presented when radically different expectations about and conditions in the international oil market prevailed.

It was argued at the time that Mexico was confronted with a unique opportunity brought about by a combination of fortuitous conditions. The world's demand for oil was high and on the rise. Furthermore, Mexico already had great hydrocarbon reserves, which could increase even further, as only one-tenth of its potential oil-bearing territory had been explored. And oil prices had increased more than tenfold, from about US$3 (since Mexico discovered the southern fields before 1973) to US$40 a barrel in some cases. Additionally, Mexico has long lacked sufficient capital to solve its unemployment and other critical social problems. With added capital from oil revenues, the opportunities for enhanced economic growth would multiply, with expanded benefits for all social sectors. The Mexican economy need not be distorted by the great infusion of oil funds. In contrast to most OPEC nations, Mexico has a sophisticated industrial base, human resources, and managerial skills in both its private and public sectors. It also has a broad natural resource base that includes resources other than oil (e.g., silver, steel, copper, uranium). Moreover, oil revenues can finance projects to develop the alternative energy sources on which the country will have to rely at some point in the future in any event. In a broader sense, oil can be an agent of modernization in terms of fueling greater interaction with the industrial countries, particularly in the areas of trade and technology. In sum, the proponents of the all-out position have argued that not many countries have been blessed with such an opportunity as that offered to Mexico by its wealth in a resource in such high international demand. Mexico would be well advised to reap the full benefits of such an opportunity. Of course, Mexico's economic troubles since 1982—attributed by many to rapid oil development—have dramatically weakened this position.

Among those officials who identified themselves publicly with this position, the former PEMEX director general, Jorge Díaz Serrano, stands out. Although he resigned in 1981 following an intragovernmental controversy over the pricing of oil exports, and was subsequently jailed for his alleged involvement in corrupt practices, the following discussion is still relevant as an illustration of support from influential figures for the more radical oil development position. Díaz Serrano's political and managerial talents stunned many in Mexico and abroad. He led PEMEX to a position of great power. Recognizing the central policymaking role of the president, Díaz Serrano's first success was to convince his friend and then presidential "candidate," López Portillo, to commit himself to a new oil policy. Recognizing the important role of the United States in Mexico's political economy, Díaz Serrano also tried to convince U.S. oil and financial circles that Mexico's oil findings were notable indeed and that they should support PEMEX's expansion plans. Under attack by some of his opponents, he turned his attention back home and added to his list of achievements. For example, despite domestic opposition from many groups and the initial failure of the gas export deal with the United States, he carried on with the gasoducto project. Construction of the gasoducto was completed in late 1979.[22]

More relevant for our purposes is that as soon as it became clear that PEMEX would, in 1980, reach its 1982 production target, the debate within the government focused on what limits to establish on increasing oil and gas production capacity. Here lies the importance of the concept of an *oil production ceiling* discussed earlier. Díaz Serrano had repeatedly emphasized that such a ceiling might be subject to change. For example, he told former French president Giscard d'Estaing during a visit to Mexico City that it was conceivable that Mexico might be producing 4 mbd of crude oil in 1982.[23] That was not official policy, but Mexico's proven reserves had increased, justifying greater production (at least on technical grounds alone). In any event, Díaz Serrano succeeded in raising the official oil production ceiling from the original 2.25 mbd to 2.75 mbd.

There is another important factor to be considered. Mexico's port facilities were expanded to accommodate oil supertankers and greatly increase export capabilities. The mastermind of this project was Rodolfo Moctezuma Cid, who had been one of López Portillo's chief economic advisers and his first minister of finance. Following an unusual public dispute over official economic policy with Carlos Tello (López Portillo's first minister of programming and budget), López Portillo fired both Moctezuma and Tello in 1977. But he eventually went on to appoint Moctezuma to succeed Díaz Serrano as director general of PEMEX, thus working closely with Moctezuma to implement Mexico's all-important oil policies. Previously, however, the president had appointed Moctezuma to head a major commission, the Special Development Projects. The central task of this commission was to build four major industrial ports on the Gulf of Mexico and the Pacific. Many firms would set up their facilities near these ports in order to cut transportation costs. It is hoped this will also help to alleviate the already overburdened national railway network; that is, the ports are expected to help solve one of the major development bottlenecks (lack of adequate outlets for transportation and trade) discussed in Chapter 5. But more important, these ports, together with the ports of Pajaritos and Dos Bocas built by PEMEX, established a total oil export capacity of close to 4 mbd by 1985.[24] It may well be that Mexico's new, impressive sea-based oil-exporting capacity will remain idle, especially in the face of unfavorable world oil market conditions. However, insufficient facilities will not stand in the way of a future government decision to increase oil exports substantially, under favorable international conditions.

One of the most obvious proponents of the all-out policy is PEMEX's labor union itself. With about 125,000 members, it is the strongest of the national industrial unions discussed in Chapter 3. The salaries and fringe benefits enjoyed by most oil workers are such that there have been abundant reports regarding corrupt union leaders who sell jobs for several thousand pesos. The more PEMEX expands, the greater the number of positions available for sale. And enhanced economic power is usually accompanied by more political power. Another, more disturbing source of corruption is encouraged by concessions given the union by PEMEX's management. Because Mexico did not have the technology needed to conduct oil-well perforations offshore, it had to rely on U.S. firms such as Brown and Root. PEMEX has given the contracts to two Mexican firms, Gulf's Offshore Perforations and Proyectos Marinos, which in turn have subcontracted Brown and Root and others. Previously, however, PEMEX had to negotiate with the union that enjoys exclusive rights over perforation works. It has been reported that an agreement was reached whereby the union keeps control over 40 percent of contracts given to third parties for these perforation works. Much money is involved in that operation, inviting even further corruption.[25] This is why the 1984 government decree that banned all subcontracting of third parties is so important in curbing corruption (see Chapter 3).

All those private firms that are able to keep pace with the increase in aggregate demand caused largely by PEMEX's expansion are potential backers of this position. And, as we argued in Chapter 4, business is Mexico's most powerful political actor, other than the government itself. The all-out position may also have the backing of a much less significant but partially reemerging political actor: the military. The military is in charge of security and protection of all oil installations. Its public assertiveness, which already increased during the stage of the moderate oil development program, would be further increased. The military may hope to parlay its legitimacy, based on its role as guardian of Mexico's economic lifeline, into expanded political power.

Here we outline two conclusions to be drawn from this section. First, a more open political system in Mexico flourishes today, but by and large, key strategic decisions are still a result of intraelite discussions only marginally influenced by most societal actors and public opinion. The heads of PEMEX and of the Ministry of National Resources tried at some point to rally the support of other key (rather than marginal) actors in order to influence the future course of Mexico's oil policy. Second, the particular case of oil policy shows that, contrary to much rhetoric in Mexico and to misperceptions in the United States, the strength of vaguely defined concepts such as "nationalism" in influencing public policy have been exaggerated. For example, despite the opposition from the left to the gasoducto project and despite Mexican "strident nationalism," the gas export deal with the United States went ahead, and foreign firms are assisting PEMEX in its expansion plans. Under López Portillo, most oil policy decisions originated in the government's evaluation of the broader economic policy objectives to be attained with the assistance of oil. López Portillo's task was facilitated by the steady expansion of world demand for oil that permitted Mexico to realize its full crude oil export potential (1.5 mbd). By 1981 and 1982, however, severe economic setbacks indicated that oil was not fulfilling the promise many had expected. At the same time, conditions in the international oil market deteriorated for producing nations that had invested huge amounts of money in expanding their oil industries. Some have been more successful than others in adjusting to the new market realities.

OIL POLICY IN CRISIS

The analysis of the Mexican economy since 1976 (Chapter 5) shows that despite the successful achievement of oil production and export targets in both the government's original and revised plans, many of the problems associated with the underlying development model remained largely unsolved even before the economic crisis deepened in the 1980s. During the López Portillo administration, a key strategic objective was to reduce the unusually high level of inflation that prevailed during the Echeverría years before actively pursuing high rates of economic growth. López Portillo wanted to avoid repetition of a painful episode in recent Mexican history. Following the economic boom brought about by huge agricultural exports to the United States during World War II, Mexico experienced a decade of economic growth combined with high rates of inflation. This led eventually to a devaluation of the peso in 1954. The regime then opted for relying on foreign funds to help maintain price stability at home and to support the value of the Mexican peso. That policy worked well for about twenty years, followed in the 1970s by a short period of no growth, combined with high inflation.

The late 1970s saw the return of high economic growth rates combined with high inflation. The Mexican economy grew by an annual average of 8 percent from 1978 to 1981, while inflation ranged from 20 to 30 percent. In addition, the record shows a continuing deficit in public finances, a deficit in the current account of the balance of payments (US$12.5 billion in 1981, in spite of oil export revenues that amounted to more than US$14.6 billion), an ever-increasing foreign public debt (US$53 billion in 1981, up from US$19 billion in 1976), declining exports of manufactures, increasing imports of foodstuffs, and so forth. Moreover, the government needed more revenues to fund the ongoing expansion of port facilities, railroads, capital goods, and petrochemical plants—all necessary to the oil and other industries— and to support its new agricultural production programs. In short, all this meant that the government needed extra revenues to finance its various projects and to revitalize the development model. And given traditional trends characteristic of Mexican economic policy, changes in tax and subsidy policies were expected to have only a marginal effect in supplying total governmental revenue needs.

It followed for many that greater oil exports were the needed and most likely source of additional government revenues. But whatever the

TABLE 7.1
Oil and Mexico's Foreign Trade and Foreign Debt Service, 1980–1985
(in billions of U.S. dollars)

	1980	1981	1982	1983	1984	1985
Total Exports	15.3	19.4	21.2	21.4	24.2	21.9
Oil (crude and products)	10.4	14.6	16.5	16.0	16.6	14.8
Non-oil	4.7	4.8	4.8	6.3	7.5	7.1
Agriculture	1.5	1.9	1.2	1.2	1.5	1.3
Minerals	0.5	0.7	0.5	0.5	0.5	0.5
Manufactures	2.7	2.7	3.0	4.6	5.4	5.2
Total Imports	18.6	23.9	14.4	7.7	11.2	13.4
Trade Balance[a]	-3.2	-4.5	6.8	13.7	12.9	8.4
Foreign Debt Service Payments	7.7	9.5	9.9	8.4	11.7	9.9

[a]Figures for exports and imports have been rounded off, which affects the balance reported in the table.

Sources: Banco de México, *Informe anual,* various issues; Inter-American Development Bank, *Economic and Social Progress in Latin America. External Debt: Crisis and Adjustment* (Washington, D.C.: IDB, 1985), Table 62 in the appendix.

general merits of that approach, Mexican authorities soon realized that they could no longer resort to increasing oil exports to address their country's financial needs. For one thing, the domestic economic crisis and the unwillingness of foreign bankers to continue lending money to Mexico restrained the availability of government funds to further expand oil output. More importantly, oil consumption in the industrial countries fell by an extraordinary 20 percent from 1980 to 1983.[26] Although a detailed analysis of this issue falls beyond the scope of this book, it should be stressed that economic recession, energy conservation programs, and the development of alternative fuels in the industrial countries account for their success in cutting down oil consumption and imports. Further, although in 1984 industrial countries resumed their economic growth, their consumption and imports of oil increased only moderately. Thus, as Table 7.1 shows, revenues from Mexican oil exports stabilized at about US$16 billion from 1982 to 1984—before oil prices fell in 1985 and plummeted in 1986.

In fact, certain points merit elaboration in assessing the data presented in Table 7.1. In spite of falling world demand for oil, Mexico maintained an oil export average of 1.5 mbd from 1982 to 1984. A key to Mexico's success was the coincidental increase of output of heavy crude oil (*Maya*), at a time when the major oil refining companies in the world were hardpressed by growing competition and demanded more heavy crude to secure an acceptable profit margin. In contrast to light crude oil, such as Mexico's

Itsmo, the price of heavy crudes has never been subject to negotiations within the framework of OPEC. As a result, producers have been able to set prices in response to market conditions. Mexico's prices for Maya heavy oil have generally been quite attractive to consuming nations. Maya represented 32 percent of Mexico's total oil output in 1980, but over 60 percent by 1984. In addition, Mexico's decision in 1980 to diversify its oil export markets provided it with a greater degree of flexibility in finding new customers. As Table 7.2 shows, a number of industrial nations purchased a growing share of Mexico's oil exports.

Mexico also experienced a fall in oil export revenues of close to US$2 billion in 1985 (compared to the previous year). Although price levels were already slipping in 1985, the real problem was that Mexico failed to respond effectively to market signals. Many oil producers had been selling oil in the spot market and at discounted prices early in that year to keep their share of the world market. Thus, it was not surprising that several customers approached PEMEX asking for oil price reductions in order to continue buying Mexican oil. What was surprising was that their request was rejected, on the grounds that "Mexico was not prepared to break ranks with OPEC producers," who still maintained official prices. As a result, Mexican oil exports, which had averaged only 1.3 mbd in April and May, fell precipitously in June to less than 800,000 barrels a day. Quite a high cost was involved in allowing Mexico's oil export pricing policies to become the subject of political rivalries. Francisco Labastida, the energy minister at the time, had convinced President de la Madrid of the virtues of maintaining solidarity with OPEC.[27] Labastida was in the minority within the government's Committee for Oil Exports (COCEP), which decides on oil export volume and prices, but he had the ear of the president, and prices were not adjusted in time to prevent a dramatic fall of foreign oil sales.

The COCEP includes representatives from several government agencies that deal with economic policy issues. It was established by de la Madrid to forestall a repetition of the 1981 summer events, when domestic politics got in the way of oil export pricing decisions and Mexico lost huge revenues as a result. This governmental body worked well until the 1985 events unfolded. More important, the evolution of the international oil market in 1986 made it painfully clear that Mexico was caught off guard by a hostile market dominated by the largest oil-consuming and oil-importing countries. In particular, PEMEX lacks sufficient experienced personnel to fight aggressively in international trading centers to preserve Mexico's share of the world oil market. Investments for training managers in this area seemed unnecessary for many years because world oil demand expanded steadily and, when it fell, industrial countries had economic and political reasons to purchase more oil from Mexico. During that period, Mexico could afford to express its solidarity with OPEC at the same time that it did not hesitate to offer attractive prices to expand its oil exports worldwide. When the reversal in the world oil market situation was completed and prices hit bottom in mid-1986, however, Mexico was unable to respond effectively.

TABLE 7.2
Mexico-OECD[a] Oil Trade, 1975–1985 (thousand barrels per day)

Year	Total Mexican Exports of Oil	OECD, total	United States	Canada	Japan	OECD, Europe	France	Great Britain	Spain
1975	94.2	94.2	94.2	—	—	—	—	—	—
1976	94.4	94.4	73.3	—	—	21.1	—	—	—
1977	202.0	178.0	176.8	—	—	1.2	—	—	1.2
1978	365.0	343.0	324.9	2.4	0.9	14.8	—	—	13.6
1979	532.8	492.0	448.8	—	—	43.2	—	—	42.9
1980	827.7	736.5	562.5	4.2	35.2	134.6	42.1	—	92.5
1981	1,098.0	915.7	546.7	46.1	76.5	246.4	71.7	18.3	151.5
1982	1,492.1	1,276.3	729.3	47.9	112.7	386.4	84.8	83.7	169.9
1983	1,534.8	1,347.4	823.2	39.7	120.1	364.4	82.6	85.4	161.8
1984	1,525.6	1,363.1	750.9	43.2	159.1	409.9	91.5	100.8	168.5
1985	1,438.2	1,280.1	744.0	34.6	145.0	356.3	85.5	72.6	158.2

[a]The Organization for Economic Cooperation and Development (OECD) comprises all the industrialized countries with a market economy. It is based in Paris, France.

Sources: Petróleos Mexicanos, Anuario estadístico, 1982 (Mexico City, 1983), p. 117; Gerencia de Análisis y Evaluación del Mercado Internacional; OECD, Annual Oil and Gas Statistics, 1976 and 1977 (Paris: OECD, 1977, 1978).

Crude oil exports averaged only 1.2 mbd during 1986, thereby further aggravating Mexico's financial problems.

At another level of analysis, whereas Table 7.2 shows that the policy to diversify oil export markets worked remarkably well from 1980 to 1985, Table 7.1 demonstrates Mexico's failure to diversify the commodity structure of its exports.[28] For example, Mexico's exports of manufactures in 1984 and 1985, about US$5 billion each year, are not commensurate with an economy of Mexico's size. These figures compare poorly with Brazil's and Korea's manufacturing exports of close to US$20 billion in each of those years.[29] Such a performance is explained by a series of economic problems that successive Mexican administrations have been unable to resolve (Chapter 5). The crisis of oil export revenues has exposed this more important economic problem and the need to solve it.

Finally, for many Mexicans it has been painful to realize that a substantial share of the revenues generated by oil exports has been used every year to service the country's huge foreign debt. Some have argued that the much-feared "denationalization" of the oil industry, in the sense that oil is being exported simply to pay Mexico's dues to foreign creditors, has materialized. What is even worse, the oil price collapse in 1986 suggested that oil export revenues could no longer foot the bill for Mexico's most essential imports, let alone for servicing Mexico's foreign debt. Mexico's revenues from oil exports in 1986 totaled US$6 billion, less than one-half the total revenues of the previous year.

OIL AND FOREIGN POLICY

We close this chapter with an analysis of how oil has affected foreign relations, particularly how it has reinforced trends, analyzed in Chapter 6, toward a diversification—however constrained—of Mexico's foreign policy away from its traditional focus on the United States. The United States has been and will continue to be the largest consumer of Mexican hydrocarbons, a factor reinforcing the U.S. orientation of Mexico's foreign policy. But oil may nevertheless provide an economic base to help sustain the often-proclaimed goals of national independence, universalism, and diversification that had frequently seemed more rhetorical and unsubstantiated than real. Mexican foreign policy toward nations beyond Latin America has become important. Mexico's relations with oil-importing and oil-exporting nations will be analyzed, as well as Mexico's recent attempts to play a mediating role in the disputes that have characterized relations between these two blocs of nations.

Mexico and the Oil-Importing Nations

Some significant tensions with the United States have arisen over Mexico's oil development program. The initial failure of the gas export deal discussed earlier and the 3-million-barrel oil spill in the Gulf of Mexico—the accident at the Ixtoc oil well in 1979 was the worst of its kind in history—are the clearest examples. Nonetheless, in general, the United States is pleased with its imports of Mexican oil. Beginning in May 1982, Mexico became the leading foreign source, supplying over 20 percent of total U.S. oil import needs. And gas flowed from Mexico to the United States from early 1980 until shipments were suspended in late 1984. (Disagreements over prices and Mexico's declining gas output account for that suspension.) We have said that some have gone as far as to propose the establishment of a *North American common market* that would include Canada, the United States, and Mexico.[30] But because the coordination of energy, monetary, and other policies among countries of unequal power, resources, and aims is perceived as a potential threat to the national sovereignty of the weaker parties involved, Canada and Mexico have so far rejected the proposal.

Others have advocated developing a *special bilateral Mexico–United States relationship* on the grounds that stability in Mexico is essential to U.S. national security interests and that the United States should be prepared to pay the costs that such a situation entails.[31] Thus, for example, the United States could grant significant concessions in the immigration and trade areas in exchange for Mexico's commitment to increase oil exports to the United States. Henry Kissinger and David Rockefeller have been among the most enthusiastic supporters of such a bilateral relationship.

In contrast with the central assumption implicit in the two proposals outlined above, a third view advises against allowing Mexican oil to be used as a pretext to intensify bilateral relations. According to this view, a greater degree of interaction between the United States and Mexico might further complicate the relationship rather than increase cooperation. Instead, the United States should concentrate its efforts on bringing Mexico into *multilateral fora* (as it did to help Mexico join GATT), where existing bilateral tensions could be more easily defused and hence become more manageable.[32] Any of these three options could become official U.S. policy in the future, but the United States has not yet developed an overall energy policy, let alone a particular energy policy toward Mexico. In any event, suffice it to say that oil remains one of many factors that together make up a complex but generally friendly relationship between Mexico and the United States. On the other hand, as recent U.S. presidents have learned from their Mexican counterparts, Mexico has asserted its independence from the United States on oil and related energy issues.

Oil has played a decisive role in the diversification of Mexico's economic and political relations with other industrial oil-importing nations—especially with West European nations and Japan. These countries depend heavily on oil imports to satisfy their energy needs; hence they seek secure supplies. Because Mexico has a long record of political stability and is more reliable than OPEC—especially OPEC's radical Arab members—Mexico is generally perceived as a more secure source. Thus, some have even been willing to pay more for oil from Mexico than they would for oil coming from OPEC countries located nearer their borders. In addition, Mexico has been able to strike a series of bilateral deals including greater investments, loans, and technological assistance from these countries in exchange for long-term Mexican oil export contracts. For example, Spain has allowed PEMEX to take a majority interest in a refinery, Petronor, to process Mexican oil and compete in the European market. Japan, which is playing an increasingly crucial role in the Mexican economy, is assisting Mexico with the most advanced technology available to expand port facilities and the national railroad network.[33] Before Mexico's financial crisis led the government to shelve most plans for developing the nuclear energy industry, Canada, France, and Sweden competed for a contract to sell Mexico the particular kind of nuclear energy production technology they know. Finally, all these industrial nations encouraged a greater flow of private capital to Mexico, and banks from these nations have underwritten many of Mexico's loan operations in the international financial market. Mexico has indeed awakened new interest and respect abroad. Following the controversy over Mexico's oil export prices in the summer of 1981, relations with these countries—especially with France—were temporarily strained. Contracts for oil purchases were terminated in some cases. Subsequently, PEMEX's relations with its customers worked out smoothly, until some disagreements arose once again in 1985 and 1986 over Mexico's oil export prices.

We argued in the preceding chapter that oil has also been instrumental in Mexico's policy toward Central America and the Caribbean. PEMEX has won several contracts to conduct oil exploration works in Cuba, Panama, and Nicaragua. More important, Mexico and Venezuela signed the San José Agreement, whereby they provided oil to some dozen nations in the area on preferential terms. The two major oil exporters in the Western Hemisphere agreed to supply up to 80,000 barrels per day each of crude oil. According to the initial agreement that was signed in August 1980, the beneficiaries have to pay only 70 percent of the market price, and the rest becomes a credit to be paid according to either of two formulas. One is a credit for five years at an annual interest rate of 4 percent. However, if these financial resources are invested in priority economic development projects or in developing alternative energy sources, the terms of the credit change to twenty years at an annual interest rate of only 2 percent.[34] This agreement has been renewed during six subsequent years, although the specific credit terms have changed somewhat due to Mexico's and Venezuela's own financial constraints. In addition, in the mid-1980s Venezuela suspended all shipments to Nicaragua and Mexico reduced them substantially on grounds that the Nicaraguan government was not honoring its payment obligations. Although there has been speculation that Mexico's decision followed U.S. government pressures, it seems plausible that Mexico's own needs led to that course of action. In any case, what others have seen as Mexico's and Venezuela's generosity can be attributed to the fact that both nations are concerned with the ongoing political turmoil in the region. Masters of political co-optation at home, the Mexicans agreed with the Venezuelans to try this formula in regional relations. It is hoped that lower oil prices will ease, if only to a certain degree, the economic and political tensions afflicting Central America and the Caribbean. As at home, political co-optation involves clear costs to the Mexican government, but, as at home, the costs seem well worth assuming.

Mexico and the Oil-Exporting Nations

While Mexico's crude oil output rose from 0.5 mbd in 1973 to a peak 3 mbd in late 1982, world crude oil production since the latter date has held near the 1973 level, about 56 mbd.[35] This means that Mexico's share of total world crude oil production has risen from less than 1 percent to over 5 percent during the period. Because a substantial share of this output has been exported, in some cases displacing competitors, Mexico's relations with other producing countries have come under stress.

To be sure, it is very difficult to assess the actual effect of greater Mexican oil production and exports on world oil prices. To date, Mexico has avoided direct confrontation with OPEC's price hawks by staying out of that organization. And it was only in the early 1980s that higher Mexican oil production and exports combined with surplus conditions in the world market. Nonetheless, as the relative weight of Mexico in the world oil market increases, it would not be surprising if Mexico has to face new pressures from parties that may feel injured in the process. From this perspective, it is in Mexico's interest to evaluate thoroughly the advantages as well as the costs resulting from future decisions to increase its oil production and exports. Some would argue that Mexico should become a member of OPEC, or at least coordinate its production policies with OPEC in order to avoid affecting real oil prices negatively. However, we argued earlier that a policy of solidarity with OPEC would not be attractive; maintaining solidarity at all costs would hurt Mexico's objective of preserving its share of the world oil market. OPEC states are generally much more experienced than Mexico because the latter resumed oil exports only in the mid-1970s. This is why questions have been raised in regard to Mexican officials who have publicly expressed their support for closing ranks with OPEC even though key members of that organization have failed to honor formal agreements on oil output and export price levels.[36]

These are difficult issues to which Mexico must give special consideration. Oil has inevitably introduced new variables into the foreign policymaking process, but some have expressed the hope that Mexico will resist getting caught up in the intricacies of oil diplomacy. Domestically, for example, the Ministry of Foreign Relations has to protect against potential challengers (such as PEMEX) to its authority, who might want to make some decisions affecting relations with other nations independently, and the dreams of many who either have viewed or will view oil as a means to increase Mexico's political influence abroad.[37] Beyond its borders, Mexico will be dealing with oil-importing and oil-exporting nations with different interests and objectives. Partly to avoid a clear-cut identification with the demands of one single bloc of these nations, Mexico has been seeking to play the role of broker or mediator.

Mexico as Mediator

When market conditions are favorable for oil producers, Mexico has shown its readiness to tie its oil policy to its progressive foreign policy rhetoric and to back that rhetoric with resources. Consider President López Portillo's proposal before the United Nations General Assembly on September 27, 1979. The president argued that energy resources should be managed in a way that helps to fulfill the needs of all nations, avoiding the chaos that has recently characterized world economic relations and that has the potential to spill over into political-military conflicts. He proposed a *world energy plan*[38] with participation of all nations, although the details of such a plan and the means to implement it were never clear. Mexico is not the first nation that has declared its intention to help resolve the disputes that result from the fact that only a few nations are well endowed with a resource that is of strategic importance for the economies of the world. Henry Kissinger led an effort to bring all parties to the negotiating table. The United States convened a meeting of all major industrial nations in Washington in February 1974. In Kissinger's mind, the meeting should have been followed by another session with participation by all other oil-importing nations. After reaching a common position, a world conference including OPEC oil producers would be called. However, the project fell through at its first phase because the industrial nations themselves could reach no common position.[39]

In 1975, French president Giscard d'Estaing tried to use the prestige enjoyed by his country among some developing nations by convening the North-South Dialogue in Paris. The agenda linked oil to discussion of a complex set of issues such as aid, foreign debt, and trade and monetary relations. Once again, the effort fell apart after two years of frustrating negotiations.[40]

In a more recent effort to revive the exchange of views between North and South, former West German chancellor Willy Brandt was appointed to head a commission composed of world-renowned figures, which produced a report calling for the reestablishment of the North-South Dialogue.[41] At that point, the heads of state of Austria and Mexico entered the picture. Austria is a neutral country par excellence, both in the European context and along the axis of East-West relations. And Mexico is a developing country that enjoys international prestige, is an important oil producer, and is *not* a member of OPEC. Following a preparatory meeting in Vienna in March 1981, it was agreed to invite several nations from all continents to a summit meeting in Cancún, Mexico. The Soviet Union declined to attend, but the heads of state or government of twenty-two other nations met at Cancún on October 22 and 23, 1981. The meeting was supposed to be chaired by the presidents of Mexico and Austria, but the latter fell ill, and Canada's prime minister, Pierre Trudeau, took his place. The meeting was very informal: There was no agenda, and no actual negotiations took place. Its main objective was to strengthen support for the idea of a *global round of negotiations* dealing with various aspects of the world's deteriorating economic and energy situation. In this respect, the gathering could be termed a success, as all the participants agreed to conduct such negotiations in the near future within an institutional framework provided by the United Nations. Otherwise, as expected, the meeting did not produce any tangible outcome. Why, then, did Mexico spend so much time and effort to organize the summit?

Mexico's prestige was no doubt enhanced as a result of the Cancún Summit. In particular, Cancún highlighted Mexico's aspirations to universalism and national independence—two major goals of Mexico's foreign policy. And by being at the forefront of the efforts that made Cancún possible, Mexico reasserted the trend toward diversifying the focus of its foreign relations away from the United States. It was as if Mexico wanted "to jump away from the giant's shadow" and show the world that it had its own initiatives and could press its own views to help solve international problems. All this is, of course, highly symbolic—as was Cancún.

Another factor probably explaining Mexico's role in Cancún is that, at the time, oil-exporting nations were feeling increasingly pressed to respond to the plight of oil-importing developing countries. The latter experienced phenomenal difficulties adjusting to the international economic situation. In particular, some nations came close to declaring themselves bankrupt because they could not cope with the rising prices of strategic imports, especially oil imports. Conducting a *global round of negotiations* that would take into consideration the needs of all parties is perceived by many nations as the only means available to try to stabilize the world economy. A common view holds that a very strong and direct link exists between adequate oil supplies and the economic (and political) health of every country. However, as oil prices fell, oil-importing developing countries would no longer blame their fellow oil-exporting developing nations for contributing to their economic ills through high oil prices. The developing world focused its attention on meeting payment obligations associated with servicing its huge foreign debt. Rather than agreeing to global negotiations, the approach of governments and bankers in the industrial countries has followed a case-by-case basis. As far as Mexico is concerned, although de la Madrid was generally sympathetic toward Latin American debtors who wanted to take a unified and tougher stand in dealing with their creditors, his government's role within the Cartagena Group of Latin American debtor nations was one of moderation.

CONCLUSIONS

In this chapter, we have analyzed some aspects of the role oil has played in Mexico's history, economy, and foreign policy.[42] For one thing, oil is a very important symbol of national independence. It is also a good example of the key role of the public sector in the economy. The government has provided oil abundantly and at low prices for industry and other consumers, contributing to economic growth. More recently, oil became the primary source of funds for those projects that are supposed to propel Mexico into a new era of industrialization. These revenues are also instrumental for the government's programs to increase agricultural production. However, the economic reforms discussed in Chapter 5 must be implemented if oil is to make its best possible contribution to Mexico's economy. Oil alone will not solve Mexico's economic problems, as became painfully evident in the 1980s.

Oil has provided still another illustration of a common feature of Mexican politics: the centralization of power at the top. Decisions on this issue of national interest have been made by only a privileged few, without significant participation by the public. None of the societal actors analyzed in Chapters 3 and 4 is known to have influenced oil policy, although there has been freedom to express dissent. That is, political power to influence such an important policy has been lacking, while political liberty to oppose that policy has been maintained. Two important qualifications should be added, however. The first is that Mexico's oil policy has generally pleased most of the business community, and the second is that very little group- or class-based dissent has found an *organizational* expression. Thus, the regime has not been seriously challenged by the individual expressions of dissent that have indeed been allowed.

We have tried to present as clearly as possible the little that is known about the ongoing debate among those who do affect oil policy. Significant differences exist concerning the role that oil should play in current attempts to revitalize the growth model. Some political forces, such as the business community, opposition parties, and intellectuals, have elaborated their own views about oil and, more generally, about other matters affecting the future course of Mexico's development. Analysis of their views on that future course is the focus of the concluding chapter of this book.

NOTES

1. Contrary to common practice in the international oil industry, PEMEX includes crude oil *and* gas in its proven reserve figures. In fact, only about 70 percent of total reserves are crude oil; gas, liquids, and condensates account for the rest.

2. For a comprehensive reading of various aspects of this history, see Lorenzo Meyer, *Mexico and the United States in the Oil Controversy, 1917–1942* (Austin: University of Texas Press, 1977); México, Secretaría de Relaciones Exteriores, *La expropriación petrolera* (Mexico City, 1974); Jorge Basurto, *El conflicto internacional en torno al petróleo de México* (Mexico City: Siglo XXI, 1976).

3. The 1884 law was actually passed during the administration of President Manuel González, but he was only a proxy acting, for all practical purposes, on behalf of the dictator from 1880 to 1884.

4. Cole Blasier, *The Hovering Giant: U.S. Responses to Revolutionary Change in Latin America* (Pittsburgh, Pa.: University of Pittsburgh Press, 1976), p. 118.

5. Oil became the leading energy source in the United States only in 1950, and in Japan and Western Europe in the 1960s. Oil companies kept prices down for many years in order to gradually displace coal. OPEC was born in 1960, partly as a reaction of host governments who were interested in higher prices so that they

could collect higher taxes and revenues from the companies operating in their territory. See Anthony Sampson, *The Seven Sisters* (New York: Viking Press, 1975); and Michael Tanzer, *The Political Economy of International Oil and the Underdeveloped Countries* (Boston: Beacon Press, 1969).

6. Universidad Nacional Autónoma de Mexico, *General Lázaro Cárdenas: Voz viva de México* (Mexico City, 1978), p. 7.

7. By contrast, British firms persuaded their government to break diplomatic relations with Mexico. These relations were reestablished following a compensation agreement in the early 1940s.

8. See Lorenzo Meyer, "La resistencia al capital privado extranjero: El caso del petróleo, 1938–1950," in Bernardo Sepúlveda et al., *Las empresas transnacionales en México* (Mexico City: El Colegio de México, 1974), pp. 107–156. President Miguel Alemán wrote a disclaimer following public release of copies of the contracts by the U.S. National Archives in 1974. See his *La verdad sobre el petróleo en México* (Mexico City: Editorial Grijalbo, 1977).

9. James C. Tanner, "Model Monopoly: National Oil Organization So Successful It Worries Industry," *Wall Street Journal*, January 26, 1967.

10. The complete story regarding *when* PEMEX found out about the full extent of the oil and gas fields, and *why* such information was withheld from the public for some years, has yet to be written. It seems that an internal governmental debate developed around the very issue of disclosing the new reserve figures, although details are still largely unknown. It is also quite likely that the U.S. government learned of the information early and became very interested, although speculation on Washington's pressures on Mexico City to increase oil exports seems exaggerated. Some useful clues are provided in the following documents: PEMEX, *Informe del Director General, 1973* (Mexico City: PEMEX, 1973); México, Secretaría de la Presidencia, "Tercer informe de gobierno," *El gobierno mexicano*, (Mexico City, September 1973); *Platt's Oilgram News Service*, September 13, 1974; and articles in the *New York Times*, October 20–22, 1974.

11. *U.S. Department of State Bulletin*, November 18, 1974.

12. PEMEX, *Anuario estadístico, 1978* (Mexico City: PEMEX, 1979), p. 30; and Gustavo Ortega, *La industria petrolera mexicana, sus antecedentes y su estado actual* (Mexico City: Secretaría de la Economía Nacional, 1936), p. 34.

13. "Aspectos del Presupuesto de 1981," *Comercio Exterior* 31, no. 1 (1981):14–19; and "The Largest Industrial Companies in the World," *Fortune*, August 10, 1981. Venezuela's PETROVEN and Brazil's PETROBRAS are the only two Latin American firms that are larger than PEMEX.

14. Castillo's arguments are similar to those made in the early 1960s by Juan Pablo Pérez Alfonso, Venezuela's minister of mines. Pérez Alfonso was a central figure in the efforts to establish OPEC in 1960. See Franklin Tugwell, *The Politics of Oil in Venezuela* (Stanford, Calif.: Stanford University Press, 1975).

15. For the PEMEX program and the gas project, see Instituto Mexicano del Petróleo, *Comparecencia del Sr. Ing. Jorge Díaz Serrano, Director General de PEMEX, ante el H. Congreso de la Unión* (Mexico City, 1977). See the data for gas flaring in annual speeches of the PEMEX director general (which he reads before the president); they are not consistent with much higher gas-flaring figures reported in PEMEX's own annual report, *Memoria de labores*.

16. See Heberto Castillo's frequent articles in the weekly *Proceso* and his best presentation, *Necesario plan de energéticos* (Mexico City: Servicios y Representaciones de Ingeniería, 1978).

17. For a discussion of the reasons that the gas export deal did not materialize but instead became entangled in U.S. bureaucratic politics, see Richard Fagen and

Henry R. Nau, "Mexican Gas: The Northern Connection," in *Capitalism and the State in U.S.–Latin American Relations*, ed. Richard Fagen (Stanford, Calif.: Stanford University Press, 1979), pp. 382–424.

18. Secretaría de Patrimonio y Fomento Industrial, *Plan nacional de desarrollo industrial, 1979–1982* (Mexico City, 1979); and *Programa de energía. Metas a 1990 y proyecciones al año 2000* (Mexico City, 1981).

19. "Programa de energía," *Energéticos* 4, no. 11 (1980):1–3.

20. PEMEX, *Memoria de labores, 1980* (Mexico City: PEMEX, 1981); and U.S. Department of Energy, *Monthly Energy Review*, various issues in 1980 and 1981.

21. An interesting study of the initial social effects of the oil boom in the south is by Leopoldo Allub and M. A. Michael, "Petróleo y cambio social en el sureste de México," *Foro Internacional* 18, no. 4 (1978):691–709. See also reports in the *Washington Post*, June 10, 1979, and January 20, 1981. The best and most comprehensive study in this area has been edited by Alejandro Toledo: *Petróleo y ecodesarrollo en el sureste de México* (Mexico City: Centro de Ecodesarrollo, 1982).

22. Guillermo Zetina, "Ningún extranjero perfora pozos: Díaz Serrano," *Excélsior*, September 21, 1979.

23. "Guessing Game Continues over Mexico's Oil Reserves," *Latin American Economic Report*, March 16, 1979.

24. Sources in both Mexico and the United States confirm the extent of this superproject. For technical details of the port development program, see Proyectos Especiales de Desarrollo, *"Programa de puertos industriales"* (Mexico City, November–December 1979), unpublished draft. The estimate of total oil export capacity for 1985 is found in U.S. General Accounting Office, *Prospects for a Stronger U.S.-Mexico Energy Relationship* (Washington, D.C.: GAO, May 1, 1980), p. 46. In May 1986, Japan and Mexico reached an agreement whereby Japan will invest up to US$4 billion to help Mexico complete several steel mill projects. Part of this money will be used to put nearby port facilities into operation. See "Invertirán empresarios japoneses 4,000 millones de dólares en Las Truchas," *Excélsior*, May 15, 1986.

25. Francisco Ortiz, "A cambio de contratos, el STPRM cede su exclusividad en la perforación de pozos," *Proceso*, October 24, 1977; and Francisco Salinas, "Acepta el STPRM, como excepción," *Excélsior*, November 30, 1977. More recently, new allegations surfaced about funds illegally pocketed by oil union leaders. See Rafael Medina, "Nunca ha formado parte del patrimonio del STPRM el 2% por concepto de obras en PEMEX: Barragán," *Excélsior*, February 5, 1984.

26. International Monetary Fund, *World Economic Outlook* Washington, D.C.: IMF, April 1984), p. 128.

27. For an analysis of this episode, see Gabriel Székely, "México y el petróleo: Crónica de amargas lecciones, 1981–1985," *La Jornada*, September 1, 1985.

28. This is one of the most important aspects of the relationship between oil development and Mexico's overall development strategies in the 1980s. A systematic study of these issues is presented in Gabriel Székely, *Mexico's Economic Relations with Industrial Powers: Oil and Trade Diversification* (1987, mimeo).

29. United Nations, *International Trade Yearbook* (New York: United Nations, 1984 and 1985).

30. For the particular case of energy, see Kenneth E. Hill, *North American Energy: A Proposal for a Common Market Between Canada, Mexico and the US* (New York: Blyth Eastman Dillon and Co., 1979).

31. The best study about the various scenarios under which such a special relationship could materialize, although the author is not enthusiastic about the option, is Henry R. Nau, "U.S.–Mexican Oil and Gas Relations," in *United States*

Relations With Mexico: Context and Content, ed. Richard D. Erb and Stanley R. Ross (Washington, D.C.: American Enterprise Institute, 1981), pp. 195–211.

32. Raymond Vernon has analyzed this position and its implications in "Trade and Investment in Mexican–US Relations," in *United States–Mexico Relations: Economic and Social Aspects*, ed. Clark Reynolds and Carlos Tello (Stanford, Calif.: Stanford University Press, 1983), pp. 167–180.

33. The increasing Japanese penetration in Mexico's economy as well as the implications of this trend for U.S.-Mexican relations are the subject of the essay by Gabriel Székely and Donald Wyman, "Japón: Un nuevo factor en las relaciones México–Estados Unidos," in *México–Estados Unidos, 1985*, ed. Gabriel Székely (Mexico City: El Colegio de México, 1986).

34. "Declaracion conjunta de los presidentes de México y Venezuela," *Energéticos* 4, no. 10 (October 1980):27–28.

35. U.S. Department of Energy, *Monthly Energy Review*, various issues.

36. Francisco Labastida's diplomatic overtures to OPEC's leaders, with the approval of the president, had no precedent in Mexico. See Jaime Duran, "Conveniente la unión de exportadores de petróleo, sean o no de la OPEP," *Excélsior*, July 18, 1985; and Francisco Garfias, "Propuesta de México, Kuwait y Venezuela," *Excélsior*, June 27, 1985.

37. Samuel Berkstein has discussed this theme extensively, emphasizing the foreign policy challenges confronted by oil-exporting nations, in "Estrategia petrolera y política exterior," *Foro Internacional* 21, no. 1 (1980):65–82. Other analyses have endorsed more enthusiastically the idea that oil has already turned Mexico into a well-established regional power. See for example Bruce Bagley, "Mexico in the 1980s: A New Regional Power," *Current History* 80, no. 469 (November 1981):353–357.

38. For the complete text of López Portillo's speech, see "Los energéticos constituyen la responsabilidad compartida de toda la humanidad," *Tiempo*, October 8, 1979.

39. Henry R. Nau, "US Foreign Policy in the Energy Crisis," *Atlantic Quarterly* 12, no. 4 (Winter 1974-1975):426–439.

40. Roger D. Hansen, *Beyond the North-South Stalemate* (New York: McGraw-Hill, 1979); Robert L. Rothstein, *The Third World and U.S. Foreign Policy: Cooperation and Conflict in the 1980s* (Boulder, Colo.: Westview Press, 1981).

41. Independent Commission on International Development Issues, *North-South: A Programme for Survival* (Cambridge, Mass.: M.I.T. Press, 1980).

42. For further readings on Mexico's oil policy, see George W. Grayson, *The Politics of Mexican Oil* (Pittsburgh, Pa.: University of Pittsburgh Press, 1980); Gabriel Székely, "The 1976 Oil Export Decision: Effects of the Oil Boom on Mexico's Political Economy," Ph.D. dissertation, George Washington University, 1983; Gabriel Székely, "Recent Findings and Research Suggestions on Oil and Mexico's Development Process," *Latin American Research Review* 20, no.3 (1985):235–246; and George Baker's excellent review, which addresses the concerns of oil business groups interested in PEMEX, *Mexico's Petroleum Sector: Performance and Prospect* (Tulsa, Okla.: Penn Well Books, 1984).

8

Alternative Visions
of Mexican Development

This book has focused on the central features of the Mexican political system. We have tried to understand, analyze, and explain the causes and especially the legacies of its extraordinary stability. But political stability does not preclude change. Therefore, the book has also stressed the regime's flexibility in the face of evolving circumstances.

Since the mid-1930s, Mexico has transformed itself from a basically rural to a basically urban society, and the regime has incorporated into the political system the groups that have emerged from that transformation. The regime has also influenced the changing distribution of power in society. Even in those cases in which changes have not originated with it, the regime has proved capable of adapting to, and in due course attaining a degree of control over, many departures from the established order.

The Mexican political system has managed its continuity so adroitly that it has built institutions, procedures, understandings, and other bases formidable enough to have withstood enormous pressures in recent years and to have persuaded most observers (including us) of the likelihood of further stability. But the regime faces keen challenges to its stability, and even if it weathers them, stability is now accompanied by increasing change. Principally, the economic crisis has inflicted severe losses on a broad spectrum of the population. It has also triggered fundamental shifts in economic policy that carry not only further economic uncertainties but also unchartered political risks. In fact, economic volatility has been superimposed on a political system already in substantial flux. In that regard, we have analyzed political reform; some changing patterns of political socialization; the surge of the técnicos; the evolution and even decline of the PRI; the increased political role of the right and vocalness of some business leaders; and the acute left-right polarization over both domestic and foreign policy issues. And, of course, the regime's credibility has been jeopardized by the politically controversial options it has chosen to deal with the economic crisis.

Events in the second half of President de la Madrid's administration further complicated the future of the development model. Examples cited

255

in preceding chapters include increasing public demand for a drastic reduction of payments to service the foreign debt; the emergence within the PRI of leaders demanding party reform; and the coming together of leftist and rightist parties, business leaders, intellectuals, and civic organizations to demand that the regime respect electoral results. At a minimum, the consensus that contributed to stability for over fifty years came under scrutiny by a number of unusually active and vocal political forces.

Even prior to the economic crisis and political flux, when the regime was remarkably successful in molding economic and societal change to its own political ends, it did not prevent all other political actors from defining their own preferences regarding development policy. With crisis, flux, and the erosion of regime credibility, alternative development views—often at substantial odds with regime views—claim increased attention. Thus, we discuss the views of not only the regime but the business community, the nationalist left, and the Marxist left. Theirs are not the only alternatives that have been put forward, but they are the most developed. Therefore, the book concludes by analyzing the major competing programs and perspectives (at least those found within Mexico itself) on the future of Mexican development. This chapter is thus something of an epilogue rather than a summary presentation of our major arguments and conclusions; such summaries may be found at the end of each chapter.

THE REGIME'S VISIONS

To understand the regime's present and prospective development policies one should consider the recent past—especially the regime's development policies since the 1940s. This has been one of our primary concerns in previous chapters. Here, we merely reflect on how regime flexibility has translated itself into a constant search for new ways to adapt to emerging challenges and problems. In this respect, it could be argued that the regime has been involved in a trial-and-error process since 1970. On the political front, we have analyzed the regime's efforts to encourage greater political participation and to permit greater media freedom. President Echeverría responded to the crisis of dissent and repression with certain measures to open up the political system (e.g., eighteen-year-olds could exercise the right to vote by 1973). Similarly, President López Portillo responded to the crisis of legitimacy with further political reforms (e.g., most political parties that had for years sought legal status finally reached their goal as a result of the 1977 political and electoral reforms).

There have been some important exceptions to this flexibility, however. We have seen, for example, several cases in which the regime has forcibly limited its opening-up process (e.g., the elections in the mid-1980s). Moreover, the regime is still prepared to offer much less in terms of organizational than purely personal freedoms. And, of course, we see the continued use of co-optation and repression, which are mechanisms aimed at maintaining political control.[1] In sum, the regime's political reforms show a commitment to flexibility; at the same time, the restrictions on freedom show that the regime is ready to go only so far in implementing changes. Probably, it is somewhat undecided as to how far to go.

In the realm of socioeconomic policy, after discussing the dominant patterns prior to 1970, we suggested how the regime has tried since 1970 to respond to pressing problems, such as the neglect of the rural sector, insufficient health care and educational services, and income inequality. Reducing income inequality provides another illustration of an area in which the regime has been indecisive as to how far to go and in what ways. A manifestation of decisiveness, however, is the subordination of such social objectives to the perceived imperative of restored economic growth. In fact, regardless of how we ultimately assess recent policies concerning socioeconomic equality or political freedom, the regime has typically shown more confident resolve in how to pursue its three other historically and continually glorified goals—economic growth, political stability, and national independence. The regime has, for at least fifty years, made political stability paramount and has believed that with stability much is possible (including modifications and further improvements) and that without stability, much would be lost and little would be possible. It has stressed the strong reciprocal relationship between political stability and economic growth.

Nevertheless, within the regime itself there is not always a unified position regarding the appropriate orientation of the development model. In the first edition of this book, we discussed the two development plans elaborated under President López Portillo that represented competing views within the regime. The Industrial Plan (1979) advocated the continuation of policies very similar to those that had brought about remarkable economic growth and gradual social improvements in Mexico since the 1940s. Recognizing the drawbacks of the traditional model and the need for structural reform, the Global Plan (1980) called for the modernization of productive infrastructure and an increasing orientation toward world markets.[2] Although these planning and forecasting efforts constituted a welcome exercise, they gradually lost their value. The elaboration of those plans and of their modifications (under President de la Madrid) consumed too much time among government bureaucrats; plan provisions were often too vague and only indicative, not compulsory; ambitious goals were difficult to realize given the limited resources available in times of crisis; and the plans lacked credibility because they did not include responses to unfavorable scenarios like the collapse of oil prices.[3] The dominant economic view that emerged within de la Madrid's administration carried to its ultimate the logic of the Global Plan, in conjunction with a new National Development Plan (1983). Following often heated debate and infighting within the cabinet, the president directed Mexico toward what may be a largely irreversible process of greater integration into and exposure to international market forces. Thus, Mexico signed a trade agreement with the United States, substantially relaxed foreign investment regulations, entered GATT, and reached a new agreement with the IMF. Mexico would receive several billion dollars to continue honoring its foreign debt obligations; in turn, internally, Mexico proceeded to sell public enterprises and cut government subsidies (e.g., gasoline prices were raised to levels similar to those prevailing in the United States).

Whatever the division within the regime, the new economic policies were unusually clear-cut, forceful, and well defined. Not so the regime's political policies. Instead, we have seen variable, uncertain, unpredictable, and divided policies encompassing broadened toleration of dissent and a number of reform measures, on the one hand, but a persistence of authoritarian practices, including electoral restrictions, on the other. The more liberal or reformist elements associated with the regime (including prominent figures within the PRI itself) argue that democratization is normatively warranted, that it is required for a people to be free. Additionally, they make practical arguments concerning the regime's prospects for survival. Although democratization involves some risks, it might also bring handsome benefits in terms of political credibility, regime legitimacy, and citizen commitment to pursue solutions to Mexico's complex problems. In short, a new dedication to democratization could provide some counterbalance to the political threats engendered by economic crisis and despair over matters such as corruption and drugs. Moreover, persistent authoritarianism in the face of increased demands for liberalization could well lead to dangerously increased polarization and the further isolation of the regime. In this connection, it is notable that even business has not rallied behind the regime's hard-line political stances. On the contrary, it has increasingly criticized Mexico's lack of democracy. From this perspective, the participation of business and the PAN with leftist parties (PSUM, PMT, PRT) in a united opposition front (National Movement for Democracy) demanding fair elections may be a warning.[4]

Others within the regime, however, apparently believe that the fundamental economic changes cited above and the political risks that they entail require sustained political control and reassurances of domestic tranquility to quell potential fears by needed investors and lenders. The regime could continue negotiating with political oppositions and allowing some openness, but it must rely on the basic methods and structures that have insured political stability to the present. In short, even some officials who would ideally prefer to move toward democracy emphasize the risks, at least under present circumstances. Others simply prefer the political status quo to more liberal alternatives. Their preferences are sometimes based on the personal benefits that accrue to them in terms of power and money. For example, the leaders of organized labor, themselves often main sources of corruption, have repeatedly expressed opposition to political reform. Moreover, even some leaders of the reform group within the PRI had claimed just a few years ago, when *they* were holding government posts, that PRI and Mexican politics overall represented a model of democracy.[5] The point is that many questions remain about the depth of commitment to reform found in regime visions of development.

In part because the regimes's development plans depend largely on the behavior of the business community, in part because that community has increasingly articulated dissenting views, it is essential to consider its perspectives on development.

THE BUSINESS COMMUNITY'S VISIONS

It is feasible to talk of a relatively coordinated position within the business sector insofar as it has established an organization that tries to represent its views; that organization is the Coordinating Business Council, founded in 1975. Through the CCE, members of the business sector express positions that conflict with those of the regime. We have seen that this is not the first time that business has dissented from the regime. For example, many entrepreneurs opposed the 1938 oil nationalization, whereas others unsuccessfully pressured the government to withdraw its support of the Cuban regime in the early 1960s.[6] However, this is the first time that most major organizations of the business community have formulated their own perspectives on Mexican development in such a clear, explicit, and relatively unified manner.

It could be argued that business has advocated a different development model from that of the regime ever since the revolution. For much of the business sector, an ideal development model would be one with less public involvement in the economy, one in which private interests would assume control of many state firms. As Carlos Arriola puts it: "Businessmen have elaborated their own development project by seeking to put the state's political and economic resources at the service of private enterprise."[7] In such a model, credit would be more readily available and less tied to bargaining with the government. Mexican businessmen would engage in joint investment ventures with their counterparts in the United States and other nations, without having to face stiff government regulations or intensely critical public opinion. In this respect, great efforts would be made to change public perceptions, fed by the regime's rhetoric, of the business community as evil.[8] Additionally (with intriguing recent exceptions), tougher social and political control of popular dissent would be included in most such business-oriented models. In short, this model would be antithetical in many ways to the revolutionary and nationalistic rhetoric expounded by the regime.

Whatever the long-standing differences in views between business and the regime, considerable convergence has occurred under de la Madrid. In fact, the regime has apparently adopted certain perspectives that it traditionally dismissed as politically naive or ultimately self-defeating. Nonetheless, as Chapter 5 detailed, vocal articulation of business alternatives has increased. In fact, it seems that a new breed of business leaders is emerging in Mexico, and it is important to monitor its activities and views regarding development alternatives. This breed may be markedly distinct from the old guard that faded in part with the privately owned banks in 1982 (the *banqueros* were the unofficial yet perhaps most authoritative voices of the business community). An especially noteworthy role has been played by COPARMEX. Luis Bravo Mena depicts his organization as politically active even though it associates with no particular party and does not seek to seize power.[9] In addition to the now familiar calls for economic "modernization" (e.g., reduced government subsidies), Bravo emphasizes political modernization as well. This would include replacing mechanisms and structures of political control with an environment more conducive to open and independent political participation (e.g., free elections)—even given the risks that business would then have to face, such as negotiating with unions freed from governmental or other undemocratic control.

It is difficult to ascertain how much of the business sector and indeed the political-economic right is as ready for fundamental alternatives as COPARMEX claims to be. Evidence mounts of business's disenchantment with the regime and includes substantial agreement among major business groups. One might even go further and speculate about the possibility of "horizontal linkages" among rightist forces in society; these would encompass business groups, media, private universities, and the PAN. But differences exist among and within these units.[10] For example, the major television enterprise, Televisa, has apparently shown itself to be uninterested in antagonizing the regime while engaged in an ambitious program to internationalize its operations. New head Miguel Alemán (son of the late president) faced criticism from several groups for Televisa's coverage of the 1986 elections as well as protests about the allegedly fraudulent results. There have been divisions among some large and small organizations on such issues as the bank nationalization and the opening of the economy to further foreign penetration. Surely not all businesses stand ready to surrender the benefits associated with government political controls over most of the population. Others doubt whether austerity can bring about recovery and expansion, and they therefore favor increased government spending and higher wages for workers.[11] Furthermore, even when business is relatively united regarding desirable policies, it is often divided as to the proper political means to pursue them. Some leaders have fortified their ties to the PAN and have even become prominent PAN candidates (as in the 1986 Sinaloan gubernatorial race). But others use the PAN merely to pressure the PRI, and still others see their fate intertwined with PRI's, perhaps hoping to revamp the party some. Thus, businessmen were co-opted by the PRI to run for the governorships of Nuevo León and Chihuahua in 1985 and 1986 respectively. Meanwhile, other members of the business community seem uninterested in influencing national developments and have opted instead for capital flight, at least until the Mexican economy is put back on the right track. From our own perspective, what may be most interesting is the political debate within business circles and the attempts of some of their leaders to enhance communication and understanding with other civic associations and political organizations.

The increasing political activism of the business community has met with resistance not only from the regime but, naturally, from groups that advocate tougher policies toward, and controls over, the private sector. Those groups support a greater government role to help fulfill the goals of the

Mexican revolution and have criticized the conservative tendencies in the regime's development model, which include economic policies that contribute to the regime's isolation amid a polarizing political situation. We turn our attention to analyzing the position of the "nationalist left."

THE NATIONALIST LEFT'S VISIONS

What we call the "nationalist left" includes some members of the political elite as well as many intellectuals and certain activist elements of organized labor (e.g., electrical and telephone workers) affiliated with the CTM. It has been referred to in the past as "the left wing of the PRI" or "the left of the regime coalition." We believe the term "nationalist left" is more appropriate because many of its members are not part of the PRI or the regime.

A recent, and perhaps the most sophisticated, presentation of the nationalist left position can be attributed to former minister of programming and budget Carlos Tello and to National University economics professor Rolando Cordera.[12] Note that Tello was appointed head of the Banco de México immediately following the government takeover of private banks, whereas Cordera headed the congressional delegation of the PSUM from 1982 to 1985. The thrust of the Tello-Cordera argument is that only the fulfillment of the goals of the Mexican revolution—as embodied in the 1917 Constitution—could lead to the significant improvement of the dismal socioeconomic situation of the poor and thus to continued stability. Moreover, they have demanded that the government exercise full control over basic production. That is, a major priority should be to guarantee the nation's economic independence, and the government should resist the further internationalization of the economy as well as business-oriented proposals geared to a reprivatization of the economy. The nationalist left uses the experience under the Cárdenas administration as a historical reference point in advocating the strengthening of the old alliance between the regime and organized labor (CTM and other organizations in the Congress of Labor). Only then will the government be able to effect substantial economic and social reforms, despite resistance from domestic and foreign entrepreneurs.

This position includes but goes beyond what many would label "reformist." It reflects a well-founded concern that the regime increasingly has been unable (if not unwilling) to fulfill its *own* self-imposed revolutionary objectives. The regime has allegedly become less responsive over time to the aspirations of the working classes, thus undermining its own legitimacy. Instead, it has been responsive to the demands of foreign interests and a small economic elite that has not shared many of the costs of economic growth. The nationalist left fears that the continuation of this trend will lead either to instability or, should stability be maintained, to a far more authoritarian system accompanied by a horrible persistence or even aggravation of inequalities. Indeed, the nationalist left sees many of the challenges discussed in Chapter 1 as true threats to regime stability.

It is easier to find sympathizers with the positions of the nationalist left when seemingly radical acts of foreign policy, rather than domestic policy, are involved. There are many who might support the government's anti-U.S. rhetoric and its close ties with Cuba but who would be much more reserved in regard to domestic transformations. This parallels the juxtaposition of foreign policy leftism and domestic policy conservatism that characterizes the regime (see Chapter 6).

Perhaps the most telling criticism that can be made of the nationalist left is its excessive reliance on "either-or" propositions unaccompanied by sufficiently detailed elaborations of its own proposals. For example, it views a "neoliberal model" as the only alternative to its nationalistic development model. In the words of Tello and Cordera: "The neo-liberal project is a metropolitan project. It seeks a fundamental re-structuring of the international capitalist system according to the analysis and the perspectives of key financial and transnational centers. In the Mexican case, the neo-liberal vision would lead to an economy increasingly integrated to the U.S. economy . . . to a political congruence between the Mexican state and the United States."[13] Logically, the nationalist left associated the de la Madrid administration with this model. As we have noted, however, no concrete proposals have been forthcoming to solve, for example, the severe problems, such as excessive protectionism, that have contributed to undermining the financial health of the very actor the nationalist left wants to strengthen: the state. Rather, one could argue for the nationalist left's goals by arguing against its policy: The regime should force domestic producers to be more efficient and competitive, thereby making Mexico less dependent on foreign creditors to compensate for insufficient exports. Of course, a comprehensive fiscal reform—which the nationalist left supports—might be another significant means of improving the public sector's finances. The point is that a more consistent and specific approach is necessary if the nationalist left wants to propose viable alternatives to regime policies.

In any case, nationalist left positions appeared very isolated from actual policy during de la Madrid's administration. Previously, the regime was sometimes sympathetic to statements of the nationalist left, although it often regarded them as too naive, as unappreciative of the subtle but all-important bases of stability or the paramount need for stability. Increasingly, however, nationalist left and regime visions have formed stark contrasts. Even in foreign relations, Mexico softened certain independent approaches. In economic policy, moves such as joining GATT, opening up further to foreign investment and imports, imposing austerity measures while cutting subsidies to Mexican businesses and consumers (including the poor), selling public enterprises, and slashing the size of the bureaucracy all contradicted basic nationalist left visions of appropriate development. In terms of political formations, alliances with labor and progressive groups like intellectuals were weakened whereas ties to business and foreign interests were given priority, and técnicos rose in influence. Therefore, intellectuals became increasingly alienated from the regime (accelerating a process traceable to the government repression of 1968). Such alienation could undermine one of the sources of personnel, advice, and support that has for so long contributed to regime stability and legitimacy. More broadly, one wonders about the consequences of a sharpened cleavage between regime and nationalist left visions of development.

Obviously, nationalist left positions, particularly the reforms envisioned, have long been at odds (in most respects) with the business community's visions. In fact, the nationalist left has regarded domestic and foreign (U.S.) private entrepreneurs—not the Mexican regime—as Mexico's principal enemies. Thus, the nationalist left, whose views have perpetuated the image that the regime truly has revolutionary instincts and interests, has buttressed the regime's political legitimacy. Certainly, the nationalist left has generally fallen short of calling for a fundamental transformation of Mexico's socioeconomic and political systems. By contrast, the Marxist left has called for such changes. It is worried by problems that also concern the nationalist left, but it does not hope to handle these problems within the basic traditional framework of the regime and its successes in stability and growth. The Marxist left feels that stability and growth, as pursued by the regime, are incompatible with improved socioeconomic equality and true democratization. In the final analysis, the Marxist left may see the regime itself as the most important obstacle to building a new political and economic system. So the Marxist left may acknowledge that the regime has been right in its policies, although frightfully wrong in its goals and priorities. It does not like what the regime does, but it "gives the devil his due." The nationalist left, on the other hand, has been much more supportive of the regime regarding goals, but in a sense harsher regarding means and policies. The nationalist left has often tried to work with the regime by promoting its progressive tendencies. It might well be, then, that the regime pushes some members of the nationalist left toward the Marxist left when it pursues the sort of policies de la Madrid did. In any case, given the different perceptions of the regime held by the nationalist left and the Marxist left, it should not be surprising that these political forces often find themselves in conflict with one another. What are, in more specific terms, the perspectives and goals of the Marxist left?

THE MARXIST LEFT'S VISIONS

Mexico's Unified Socialist party (the former Mexican Communist party) occupies a prominent position within the Marxist left. However, the Marxist left also encompasses several small parties (such as Heberto Castillo's Mexican Workers party). It has the allegiance as well of several prestigious intellectuals (such as the former head of the National University, Pablo González Casanova).

The Marxist left seeks fundamental changes in Mexico's development model: the socialization of the economic means of production and a political regime that would not include the PRI. According to this view:

Socialism is the solution, particularly a socialism that would solve (as has been shown by the socialist countries themselves) not only the problems of insufficient employment, housing, health, and educational services; but a socialism that would also solve the problems of bureaucraticism and authoritarianism, objectives that are increasingly shared—with Cuba at the forefront—by all socialist and communist forces in the world.[14]

In order to build such a model of political and socioeconomic relations, emphasis is put upon the decisive and leading role of the working classes.[15] Here we can identify a very important difference between the nationalist left and the Marxist left. The former argues for an alliance between labor and the regime to implement certain reforms, whereas the latter advocates that the working class should pursue its interests independently. This does not mean that the Marxist left opposes the fiscal, social, and political reforms advocated by the nationalist left. What it means is that the Marxist left views such reforms with suspicion, as it views historical experiences such as the close alliance between the regime and labor during the Cárdenas years. It feels that these experiences did not result in a more just and democratic society. The main reason for predominant failure amid sporadic and limited success, the Marxist left argues, is that the regime is in fact generally responsive to domestic and foreign private interests, rather than to the demands of the poor.

Another significant contrast between the Marxist and nationalist left concerns dependency. Both groups see the impact of international political-economic forces as serious and largely negative. But whereas the nationalist left tries to persuade and help the regime to diminish Mexico's dependency, the Marxist left tends to emphasize the regime's comfortable and condemnable complicity with the international forces that deepen dependency.

The Marxist left favors a revolutionary transformation of society, but most of its followers do not expect to realize its goals immediately or violently. In fact, the Marxist left shares many objectives with the nationalist left in this respect. It favors nationalizations, comprehensive fiscal reform, more limited foreign investment, extension of medical care and educational services to all, expropriation of large landholdings, unemployment benefits for the people who do not find jobs, and so forth.[16]

Politically, the Marxist left claims to support the democratization and independence of labor unions, the independent organization of peasants, and freedom of dissent. It tends to view recent political and electoral reforms positively, although it would like to carry them much further. For example, because some members of the Marxist left now participate in Congress, they would like to strengthen the powers of the Chamber of Deputies and limit those of the president. The Marxists have proposed that the political parties, and not the Federal Electoral Commission dominated by the PRI regime, organize and supervise all aspects of the electoral process. Moreover, they have strongly denounced electoral fraud, even where such fraud has most directly affected the political right. Thus, the Marxist left's support for recent reforms by the regime is very qualified.

Obviously, the Marxist left's perspective on the development model is totally antagonistic to the perspective of the business community. Whereas socioeconomic business wants to reprivatize the economy, for example, the Marxists strive for the socialization of the means of production. Whereas business wants significantly reduced restrictions on foreign investment, the Marxists want more nationalizations. And whereas business generally benefits from the status quo, the Marxists want a revolution! Also obviously, the Marxist left opposed de la Madrid's austerity measures and basic political-economic policies, although it was divided as to what alliances to form with other opposition groups.

Critics of the Marxist left, including some who endorse its major goals, argue that revolutions usually involve very high political, economic, and human costs. Furthermore, many view skeptically the Marxist left's professed commitment to political democracy and freedoms, even though they may not question the sincerity of some Marxist leaders. Other critics add that a social revolution in Mexico is unrealistic because the Marxist left lacks a broad popular base of support. Finally, aside from all questions of cost, sincerity, and feasibility, many critics simply do not endorse the principles of the Marxist left.

CONCLUSIONS

Clearly, then, there have been major alternatives to the regime's visions of development. Additionally, the regime has retained substantial resources with which to modify its own development model, although this does not mean that the regime will succeed in revitalizing the model or that its policies will fail to take into account the interests of other political actors. To date, the regime has on balance been closer to business than to the nationalist left (let alone the Marxist left). But, significantly, the regime has been broad and fluid enough to avoid complete identification with either side and to allow for, indeed insist on, varying its own approaches. Thus, for example, after Echeverría drew unusually close to the nationalist left, López Portillo drew much closer to business (at least until his last year in office), and de la Madrid then turned further from the nationalist left and toward a different mix of business-oriented visions.

The Mexican regime has been politically strong and comparatively autonomous, although significant qualifications exist regarding both international and domestic constraints. It has also been flexible, effecting policies in response to pressures from international actors (such as the U.S. government and transnational corporations) and domestic actors (such as business and organized labor) and adapting to certain desires of traditional institutions (such as the church and the university). Indeed, change has continually been a tool to achieve stability. But the capacity of the regime to effect desired change may or may not prove adequate in the future. Among the several challenges to regime stability identified throughout this book, perhaps four stand out most prominently. Obviously, policies addressing one challenge may not address others or may even aggravate them. First, Mexico must generate more resources to improve the public sector's economic posture, fund social programs, and uphold national sovereignty. Second, Mexico must achieve economic recovery in a way that does not damage socioeconomic conditions to the point that organized and unorganized labor, both of which have already suffered greatly, would not tolerate. Third, however, the regime must also restore credibility with privileged groups including foreign interests, domestic business, and the middle class. Finally, there is the political challenge involved in maintaining legitimacy and support while not extending freedom and participation in a way that would risk a significant loss of regime control or regime ability to maintain stability.

Mexico's future development model, both in political and in economic terms, will be shaped to a very important degree by regime policies designed to deal with these and other problems. The model also will be shaped by the demands and responses of certain international actors and of an increasingly complex and vocal Mexican society.[17] We hope that our analysis has contributed to a better understanding of contemporary Mexico, of its problems and aspirations. Only time will tell the extent to which such problems will be solved and such aspirations will be fulfilled.

NOTES

1. José Luis Reyna has defined the objective of political control as "keeping the number of political demands limited and turning them into bureaucratic-administrative issues." See Reyna's *Control político, estabilidad y desarrollo en México,* Cuadernos del Centro de Estudios Sociológicos 3 (Mexico City: El Colegio de México, 1974), p. 25.

2. México, Secretaría de Programación y Presupuesto, *Plan global de desarrollo, 1980–1982* (Mexico City, 1980); and México, Secretaría de Patrimonio y Fomento Industrial, *Plan nacional de desarrollo industrial, 1979–1982* (Mexico City, 1979).

3. México, Secretaría de Programación y Presupuesto, *Plan Nacional de Desarrollo, 1983–1988* (Mexico City, 1983); see also Presidencia de la República, *Informe de ejecución del Plan Nacional de Desarrollo* (Mexico City, 1986). For a critic, see Eduardo González, "El Plan Nacional de Desarrollo logró todo lo imaginado," *Proceso,* April 7, 1986.

4. "Convocatoria nacional para el foro por el sufragio efectivo," *Proceso,* September 1, 1986.

5. Gonzalo Alvarez, "Se organiza en el PRI una corriente pro-democrática," *Uno Más Uno,* August 14, 1986. It seems that the leaders of this group of reformers within the PRI chose this Mexico City daily to systematically express their views. Beginning with the August 14 report, the reader will find interviews and relevant material in practically every edition of *Uno Más Uno* on the development of and the responses to the activities of this group. Some officials, such as Michoacán governor Cuauhtémoc Cárdenas, son of the former president, and Porfirio Muñoz Ledo, ex-cabinet minister and ex-head of the PRI, who advocate progressive political and economic policies, could be associated with the "nationalist left."

6. Well-documented case studies of business dissent include Lorenzo Meyer, *Mexico and the United States in the Oil Controversy, 1917–1942* (Austin: University of

Texas Press, 1977); and Olga Pellicer de Brody, *México y la revolución cubana* (Mexico City: El Colegio de México, 1972).

7. Carlos Arriola, *Las organizaciones empresariales y el estado* (Mexico City: Fondo de Cultura Económica, 1981), p. 126.

8. Consejo Coordinador Empresarial, "Declaración de Principios," and "Declaración sobre problemas nacionales," in Arriola, *Las organizaciones*, Appendix, pp. 168–204.

9. Luis Bravo Mena, "COPARMEX y la política mexicana," in *Government and Private Sector in Contemporary Mexico*, ed. Sylvia Maxfield and Ricardo Anzaldúa (La Jolla: Calif.: Center for U.S.-Mexican Studies, University of California, San Diego, 1987). Also relevant here is the speech by Alfredo Sandoval, president of the COPARMEX, during the forty-eighth annual meeting of that organization, "La modernización de México," (Mexico City, March 13, 1986), mimeo.

10. On the political views and activities of Mexican business see Chapter 5; and Dale Story, *Industry, the State, and Public Policy in Mexico* (Austin: University of Texas Press, 1986), pp. 106–124. On linkages and divisions on the right also see Daniel Levy, "The Political Consequences of Changing Socialization Patterns," in *Mexico's Political Stability: The Next Five Years*, ed. Roderic A. Camp (Boulder, Colo.: Westview Press, 1986), pp. 33–36. Additionally, the right continues to suffer from a lack of a strong intellectual base.

11. Juan A. Zúñiga, "La contracción de la inversión pública frenó producción y causó alto desempleo: Analistas," *El Financiero*, August 27, 1986.

12. Carlos Tello and Rolando Cordera, *Mexico: La disputa por la nación: Perspectivas y opciones del desarrollo* (Mexico City: Siglo XXI, 1981).

13. Ibid., p. 81.

14. See the introduction by editors Pablo González Casanova and Enrique Florescano to their *México, hoy* (Mexico City: Siglo XXI, 1979), p. 14.

15. Arnaldo Córdova, *La política de masas y el futuro de la izquierda en México* (Mexico City: Serie Popular Era, 1979).

16. See the document "Llamamiento del Partido Socialista Unificado en México," *Excélsior*, December 3, 1981.

17. For further reference, see Leopoldo Solís, *Alternativas para el desarrollo* (Mexico City: Cuadernos de Joaquín Mortiz, 1980); Miguel Basáñez, *La lucha por la hegemonía en México, 1968–1980* (Mexico City: Siglo XXI, 1981); Camp, ed., *Mexico's Political Stability*; Judith Gentleman, ed., *Mexican Politics in Transition* (Boulder, Colo.: Westview Press, 1986); John J. Bailey, *Governing Mexico, 1976–1988: The Statecraft of Crisis Management* (London: Macmillan, forthcoming).

Selected Bibliography

BOOKS AND ARTICLES

Alba, Francisco. *The Population of Mexico: Trends, Issues and Policies.* Trans. by Marjory Mattingly Urquidi. New Brunswick, N.J.: Transaction Press, 1982.

Alcázar, Mario. *Las organizaciones patronales en México.* Mexico City: El Colegio de México, 1970.

Alejo, Francisco Javier. "Demographic Patterns and Labor Market Trends in Mexico." In *Mexico's Economic Crisis: Challenges and Opportunities,* edited by Donald Wyman. La Jolla, Calif.: Center for U.S.-Mexican Studies, University of California, San Diego, 1983.

Alisky, Marvin. *Latin American Media: Guidance and Censorship.* Ames: Iowa State University Press, 1981.

Almeida, Vania, and Appendini, Kristen de. *Agricultura capitalista y agricultura campesina en México.* 2d ed. Mexico City: El Colegio de México, 1977.

Anguiano, Roberto E. *Las finanzas del sector público en México.* Mexico City: UNAM, 1968.

Arriola, Carlos. *Las organizaciones empresariales y el estado.* Mexico City: Fondo de Cultura Económica, 1981.

Aspra, L. Antonio. "Import Substitution in Mexico." *World Development* 5, nos. 1/2 (1977):111–124.

Bailey, David C. *Viva Cristo Rey!* Austin: University of Texas Press, 1973.

Bailey, John J. *Governing Mexico, 1976–1988: The Statecraft of Crisis Management.* London: Macmillan, forthcoming.

————. "The Impact of Major Groups on Policy-Making Trends in Government-Business Relations in Mexico." In *Mexico's Political Stability: The Next Five Years,* edited by Roderic A. Camp, pp. 119–142. Boulder, Colo.: Westview Press, 1986.

————. "What Explains the Decline of the PRI and Will It Continue?" In *Mexico's Political Stability: The Next Five Years,* edited by Roderic A. Camp, pp. 159–184. Boulder, Colo.: Westview Press, 1986.

Bailey, John J., and Baer, Delal. "Mexico's 1985 Midterm Elections: A Preliminary Assessment." *LASA Forum* 16, no. 3 (1985):4–10.

Baker, George. *Mexico's Petroleum Sector: Performance and Prospects.* Tulsa, Okla.: Penn Well Books, 1984.

Balassa, Bela. *The Newly Industrializing Countries in the World Economy.* New York: Pergamon Press, 1981.

Banco de Mexico. *Informe anual*. Various issues.

————. *Producto interno bruto y gasto, 1970–1978*. Mexico City, 1979.

Banco Nacional de Comercio Exterior. *México: La política económica del nuevo gobierno*. Mexico City, 1971.

Basáñez, Miguel. *La lucha por la hegemonía en México, 1968–1980*. Mexico City: Siglo XXI, 1981.

Benjamin, Thomas. "The Leviathan on the Zócalo: Recent Historiography of the Postrevolutionary Mexican State." *Latin American Research Review* 20, no. 3 (1985):195–217.

Bennett, Douglas C., and Sharpe, Kenneth. *Transnational Corporations Versus the State: The Political Economy of the Mexican Auto Industry*. Princeton, N.J.: Princeton University Press, 1985.

Bermúdez, Antonio J. *La política petrolera mexicana*. Mexico City: Cuadernos de Joaquín Mortiz, 1976.

Brandenburg, Frank. *The Making of Modern Mexico*. Englewood Cliffs, N.J.: Prentice-Hall, 1964.

Bueno, Gerardo. *Opciones de política económica en México: Después de la devaluación*. Mexico City: Técnos, 1977.

Bustamente, Jorge A. "El estudio de la zona fronteriza México–Estados Unidos." *Foro Internacional* 19, no. 1 (1979):471–516.

————. "Migración indocumentada." *Foro Internacional* 19, no. 2 (1978):317–325.

Calvert, Peter. "The Mexican Revolution: Theory or Fact." *Journal of Latin American Studies* 1, no. 1 (1969):51–68.

Camp, Roderic. *Intellectuals and the State in Twentieth-Century Mexico*. Austin: University of Texas Press, 1985.

————. *Mexico's Leaders: Their Education and Recruitment*. Tucson: University of Arizona Press, 1980.

————. "The Middle-Level Technocrat in Mexico." *Journal of Developing Areas* 6, no. 4 (July 1972):571–582.

————. "The Political-Technocrat in Mexico and the Survival of the Political System." *Latin American Research Review* 20, no. 1 (1985):97–118.

Camp, Roderic, ed. *Mexico's Political Stability: The Next Five Years*. Boulder, Colo.: Westview Press, 1986.

Cardoso, Fernando Henrique. "On the Characterization of Authoritarian Regimes in Latin America." In *The New Authoritarianism in Latin America*, edited by David Collier, pp. 33–57. Princeton, N.J.: Princeton University Press, 1979.

Castañeda, Jorge G. "Mexico at the Brink." *Foreign Affairs* 64 (Winter 1985-86):287–303.

Castillo, Heberto. *Necesario plan nacional de energéticos*. Mexico City: Servicios y Representaciones de Ingeniería, 1979.

Cline, Howard. *Mexico: Revolution to Evolution, 1940–60*. London: Oxford University Press, 1962.

Collier, David, ed. *The New Authoritarianism in Latin America*. Princeton, N.J.: Princeton University Press, 1979.

Comisión Federal Electoral. *Ley federal de organizaciones políticas y procesos electorales*. Mexico City, 1977.

Conklin, John. "Elite Studies: The Case of the Mexican Presidency." *Journal of Latin American Studies* 5, no. 2 (1973):247–269.

Connor, John M., and Mueller, Willard. *Market Power and Profitability of Multinational Corporations in Brazil and Mexico*. Washington, D.C.: Government Printing

Office, Report to the Subcommittee on Foreign Economic Policy of the Committee of Foreign Relations, U.S. Senate, April 1977.

Consejo Nacional de Ciencia y Tecnología, ed. *El petróleo en México y en el mundo.* Mexico City, 1979.

Cordero, Salvador, and Santín, Rafael. *Los grupos industriales: Una nueva organización económica en México.* Cuadernos del Centro de Estudios Sociológicos 23. Mexico City: El Colegio de México, 1977.

Córdova, Arnaldo. *La ideología de la revolución mexicana: La formación del nuevo régimen.* Mexico City: Era, 1973.

Cornelius, Wayne. "La migración ilegal mexicana a los Estados Unidos: Conclusiones de investigación recientes, implicaciones políticas y prioridades de investigación." *Foro Internacional* 18, no. 3 (1978):399–429.

————. "Nation-Building, Participation, and Distribution: The Politics of Social Reform Under Cárdenas." In *Crisis, Choice and Change: Historical Studies of Political Development,* edited by Gabriel A. Almond, Scott C. Flanagan, and Robert J. Mundt, pp. 392–498. Boston: Little, Brown and Co., 1973.

————. "Urbanization as an Agent of Latin American Political Stability: The Case of Mexico." *American Political Science Review* 63, no. 3(1969):833–857.

Corredor, Jaime. "Oil in Mexico." Mexico City: Office of Advisers to the President, November 1980.

Cosío Villegas, Daniel. *American Extremes.* Trans. by Américo Paredes. Austin: University of Texas Press, 1964.

————. *El sistema político mexicano: Las posibilidades de cambio.* Mexico City: Cuadernos de Joaquín Mortiz, 1974.

————. *La sucesión presidencial: Desenlace y perspectivas.* Mexico City: Cuadernos de Joaquín Mortiz, 1975.

Craig, Richard. "La Campaña Permanente: Mexico's Antidrug Campaign." *Journal of Interamerican Studies and World Affairs* 20, no. 2 (1978):107–132.

————. "Operation Condor." *Journal of Interamerican Studies and World Affairs* 22, no. 3 (1980):345–364.

de la Garza, Rodolfo O. "Demythologizing Chicano-Mexican Relations." In *Mexico-United States Relations,* edited by Susan Kaufman Purcell, pp. 88–96. New York: Academy of Political Science, 1981.

de la Garza, Rodolfo O., and Schmitt, Karl. "Texas Land Grants and Chicano-Mexican Relations: A Case Study." *Latin American Research Review* 21, no. 1 (1986):123–138.

Diamond, Larry, Linz, Juan, and Lipset, Seymour Martin, eds. *Democracy in Developing Countries* (Boulder, Colo.: Lynne Rienner Publishers, forthcoming).

Domínguez, Jorge, ed. *Mexico's Political Economy: Challenges at Home and Abroad.* Beverly Hills, Calif.: Sage Publications, 1982.

Eckstein, Shlomo et al. *Land Reform in Latin America: Bolivia, Chile, Mexico, Peru and Venezuela.* Staff Working Paper 275 (Washington, D.C.: World Bank, April 1978).

Erb, Guy F., and Thorup, Cathryn. *U.S.-Mexican Relations: The Issues Ahead.* Development Paper 35. Washington, D.C.: Overseas Development Council, 1984.

Erb, Richard D., and Ross, Stanley R., eds. *United States Relations with Mexico: Context and Content.* Washington, D.C.: American Enterprise Institute, 1981.

Fagen, Richard R., and Nau, Henry. "Mexican Gas: The Northern Connection." In *Capitalism and the State in U.S.-Latin American Relations,* edited by Richard Fagen, pp. 382–424. Stanford, Calif.: Stanford University Press, 1979.

Fagen, Richard R., and Tuohy, William S. *Politics and Privilege in a Mexican City.* Stanford, Calif.: Stanford University Press, 1972.

Feinberg, Richard E. "Bureaucratic Organization and U.S. Policy Toward Mexico." In *Mexico-United States Relations,* edited by Susan Kaufman Purcell, pp. 32–42. New York: Academy of Political Science, 1981.

Fernández Kelly, María Patricia. "The U.S.-Mexico Border: Recent Publications and the State of Current Research. *Latin American Research Review* 16, no. 3 (1981):250–267.

Fitzgerald, E.V.K. *Patterns of Public Sector Income and Expenditures in Mexico.* Austin: University of Texas, Institute of Latin American Studies, 1978.

————. "The State and Capital Accumulation in Mexico." *Journal of Latin American Studies* 10, no. 2 (1978):263–282.

Fuentes, Carlos. *The Death of Artemio Cruz.* Trans. by Sam Hileman. New York: Farrar, Straus, 1964.

Furtak, Robert K. *El partido de la revolución y la estabilidad política en México.* Mexico City: UNAM, 1978.

García y Griego, Manuel, and Vega, Gustavo, eds. *México–Estados Unidos, 1984.* Mexico City: El Colegio de México, 1985.

Gentleman, Judith, ed. *Mexican Politics in Transition.* Boulder, Colo.: Westview Press, 1986.

Gereffi, Gary. *The Pharmaceutical Industry and Dependency in the Third World.* Princeton, N.J.: Princeton University Press, 1983.

González Casanova, Pablo. *Democracy in Mexico.* Trans. by Danielle Salti. London: Oxford University Press, 1970.

González Casanova, Pablo, and Aguilar C., Héctor, eds. *México ante la crisis.* 2 vols. Mexico City: Siglo XXI, 1985.

González Casanova, Pablo, and Florescano, Enrique, eds. *México, hoy.* Mexico City: Siglo XXI, 1979.

Grabendorff, Wolf. "Mexico's Foreign Policy—Indeed a Foreign Policy?" *Journal of Interamerican Studies and World Affairs* 20, no. 1 (1978):87–88.

Grayson, George W. *The Politics of Mexican Oil.* Pittsburgh, Pa.: University of Pittsburgh Press, 1980.

————. *The United States and Mexico: Patterns of Influence.* New York: Praeger Publishers, 1984.

Green, Rosario. *El endeudamiento público en México, 1940–1973.* Mexico City: El Colegio de México, 1976.

————. "México: La política exterior del nuevo régimen." *Foro Internacional* 18, no. 1 (1977):1–9.

Grindle, Merilee. *Bureaucrats, Politicians, and the Peasantry in Mexico.* Berkeley: University of California Press, 1977.

————. "Power, Expertise and the 'Técnico': Suggestions from a Mexican Case Study." *Journal of Politics* 39, no. 2 (1977):399–426.

Hall, Linda B. "The United States–Mexican Border: Historical, Political, and Cultural Perspectives." *Latin American Research Review* 20, no. 2 (1985):223–229.

Hamilton, Nora. *The Limits of State Autonomy: Post-Revolutionary Mexico.* Princeton, N.J.: Princeton University Press, 1982.

Hansen, Roger D. "The Evolution of U.S.-Mexican Relations: A Socio-Political Perspective." In *United States Relations with Mexico: Context and Content,* edited by Richard D. Erb and Stanley R. Ross, pp. 39–48. Washington, D.C.: American Enterprise Institute, 1981.

_____. *The Politics of Mexican Development*. Baltimore, Md.: Johns Hopkins University Press, 1971.

Hellman, Judith Adler. *Mexico in Crisis*. 2d ed. London: Holmes and Meier, 1983.

Hewitt de Alcántara, Cynthia. *La modernización de la agricultura mexicana, 1940–1970*. Mexico City: Siglo XXI, 1978.

Hill, Kim Quaile, and Hurley, Patricia A. "Freedom of the Press in Latin America: A Thirty-Year Survey." *Latin American Research Review* 15, no. 2 (1980):212–218.

Huntington, Samuel P. *Political Order in Changing Societies*. New Haven, Conn: Yale University Press, 1968.

Independent Commission on International Development Issues. *North-South: A Programme for Survival*. Cambridge, Mass.: M.I.T. Press, 1980.

Inter-American Development Bank. *Economic and Social Progress in Latin America*. Washington, D.C.: IDB, various years.

Johnson, Kenneth F. *Mexican Democracy: A Critical View*. 3d ed. New York: Praeger Publishers, 1984.

Kaufman, Clifford. "Urbanization, Material Satisfaction and Mass Political Involvement: The Poor in Mexico City." *Comparative Political Studies* 4, no. 3 (1971):295–320.

Koslow, Lawrence E., and Murnane, Stephen P. "The Evolution of the Mexican Political System: A Paradigmatic Analysis." In *The Future of Mexico*, edited by Lawrence Koslow, pp. 47–98. Tempe: Arizone State University Press, 1979.

Krauze, Enrique. *Por una democracia sin adjetivos*. Mexico City: Joaquín Mortiz-Planeta, 1986.

Ladman, Jerry R. et al. *U.S.-Mexican Energy Relationships: Realities and Prospects*. Lexington, Mass.: Lexington Books, 1981.

Laichas, Thomas Michael. "Mexico in the U.S. Press: A Quantitative Study, 1972–1978." In *Statistical Abstract of Latin America*, edited by James W. Wilkie, Vol. 20, pp. 582–594. Los Angeles: UCLA Latin American Center Publications, 1980.

Lajous, V. Adrian. *Mexico: Energy Sector*. Mexico City: Secretaría de Patrimonio y Fomento Industrial, 1981.

Lajous de Solana, Roberta, and Jesús Velasco Márquez. "Visión de México en la prensa de Estados Unidos: 1984." In *México–Estados Unidos, 1984*, edited by Manuel García y Griego and Gustavo Vega, pp. 31–42. Mexico City: El Colegio de México, 1985.

Larin, Nicolás. *La rebelión de los cristeros (1926–1929)*. Trans. by Angel C. Tomás. Mexico City: Ediciones Era, 1968.

Leñero, Vicente. *Los periodistas*. Mexico City: Editorial Joaquín Mortiz, 1978.

León-Portilla, Miguel, ed. *Visión de los vencidos: Relaciones indígenas de la conquista*. 8th ed. Mexico City: UNAM, 1980.

Levy, Daniel. "Comparing Authoritarian Regimes in Latin America: Insights from Higher Education Policy." *Comparative Politics* 14, no. 1 (1981):31–52.

_____. *Higher Education and the State in Latin America: Private Challenges to Public Dominance*. Chicago: University of Chicago Press, 1986.

_____. "The Implications of Central American Conflicts for Mexican Politics." In *Mexico's Political Stability: The Next Five Years*, edited by Roderic A. Camp pp. 235–264. Boulder, Colo.: Westview Press, 1986.

_____. *University and Government in Mexico: Autonomy in an Authoritarian System*. New York: Praeger Publishers, 1980.

Levy, Daniel, and Székely, Gabriel. "Mexico: Challenges and Responses." *Current History* (January 1986):16–20, 37.

Lewis, Oscar. *Five Families.* New York: Basic Books, 1959.

Lieuwen, Edwin. *Mexican Militarism: The Political Rise and Fall of the Revolutionary Army, 1910–1940.* Albuquerque: University of New Mexico Press, 1968.

Lindblom, Charles E. *Politics and Markets.* New York: Basic Books, 1977.

Loaeza, Soledad. "La política del rumor: México, noviembre–diciembre 1976." *Foro Internacional* 17, no. 4 (1977):557–586.

Lomnitz, Larissa. *Networks and Marginality: Life in a Mexican Shantytown.* New York: Academic Press, 1977.

Looney, Robert E. *Mexico's Economy: A Policy Analysis with Forecasts to 1990.* Boulder, Colo.: Westview Press, 1978.

López Portillo, José. *Informe de gobierno.* Mexico City: Ministry of Planning and Budget, various issues.

Loyoza, Jorge Alberto. *El ejército mexicano (1911–1965).* Mexico City: El Colegio de México, 1970.

Luiselli, Cassio. *The Route to Food Self-Sufficiency in Mexico: Interactions with the U.S. Food System.* Monograph Series 17. La Jolla, Calif.: Center for U.S.-Mexican Studies, University of California, San Diego, 1985.

Lustig, Nora, ed. *Panorama y perspectivas de la economía mexicana.* Mexico City: El Colegio de México, 1980.

Mancke, Richard. *Mexican Oil and Natural Gas: Political, Economic and Strategic Implications.* New York: Praeger Publishers, 1979.

Marshall, F. Ray. "Economic Factors Influencing the International Migration of Workers." In *Views Across the Border: The United States and Mexico,* edited by Richard W. Weatherhead and Stanley R. Ross, pp. 163–182. Albuquerque: University of New Mexico Press, 1978.

Martínez Verdugo, Arnoldo. *Crisis política y alternativa comunista.* Mexico City: Ediciones de Cultura Popular, 1979.

Maxfield, Sylvia, and Ricardo Anzaldúa, eds. *The Government and Private Sector in Contemporary Mexico.* La Jolla, Calif.: Center for U.S.-Mexican Studies, University of California, San Diego, 1987.

México, Gabinete de Comercio Exterior, *El proceso de adhesión de México al acuerdo general sobre aranceles aduaneros y comercio (GATT).* Mexico City, 1986.

México, Oficina de Asesores del C. Presidente de la República. "Sistema alimentario mexicano." Mexico City, unpublished draft, 1980.

México, Proyectos Especiales de Desarrollo. "Programa de puertos industriales." Mexico City, unpublished draft, November/December 1979.

México, Secretaría de Gobernación. *Ley electoral mexicana, 1812–1973.* Mexico City, 1974.

———. "Ley de fomento agropecuario." In *Diario Oficial.* Mexico City, January 2, 1981.

México, Secretaría de Patrimonio y Fomento Industrial. *Plan nacional de desarrollo industrial, 1979–1982.* Mexico City, 1979.

———. *Programa de energía, metas a 1990 y proyecciones al año 2000.* Mexico City, 1981.

México, Secretaría de Programación y Presupuesto, *Estadísticas históricas nacionales.* 2 vols. Mexico City, 1985.

———. *Plan nacional de desarrollo, 1983–1988.* Mexico City, 1983.

———. *La industria petrolera en México.* Mexico City, 1979, 1985.

———. *Plan global de desarrollo, 1980–1982.* Mexico City, 1980.

México, Secretaría de Patrimonio Nacional. *Law to Promote Mexican Investment and to Regulate Foreign Investment.* Mexico City, 1973.

México, Secretaría del Trabajo y Previsión Social. *Proyecto: Plan nacional de empleo, 1980–1982.* Mexico City, November 1979.

Meyer, Lorenzo. "Historical Roots of the Authoritarian State in Mexico." In *Authoritarianism in Mexico,* edited by José Luis Reyna and Richard Weinert, pp. 3–22. Philadelphia, Pa.: Institute for the Study of Human Issues, 1977.

————. *Mexico and the United States in the Oil Controversy, 1917–1942.* Austin: University of Texas Press, 1977.

————. "México–Estados Unidos: Lo esencial de una relación." In *México–Estados Unidos, 1984,* edited by Manuel García y Griego and Gustavo Vega, pp. 15–30. Mexico City: El Colegio de México, 1985.

Meyer, Lorenzo et al. *Las empresas transnacionales en México.* Mexico City: El Colegio de México, 1974.

————. *Lecturas de política exterior mexicana.* Mexico City: El Colegio de México, 1979.

Meyer, Michael C., and Sherman, William L. *The Course of Mexican History.* New York: Oxford University Press, 1979.

Middlebrook, Kevin J. "Energy Security in U.S.-Mexican Relations." In *Energy and Security,* edited by David A. Deese and Joseph Nye, pp. 152–180. Cambridge, Mass.: Ballinger Publishing, 1980.

————. "Political Change in Mexico." In *Mexico–United States Relations,* edited by Susan Kaufman Purcell, pp. 55–66. New York: Academy of Political Science, 1981.

Mosk, Sanford. *Industrial Revolution in Mexico.* Berkeley: University of California Press, 1954.

Muller, Thomas, and Espenshade, Thomas J. *The Fourth Wave: California's Newest Immigrants.* Washington, D.C.: Urban Institute Press, 1985.

Nacional Financiera. *50 años de la revolución mexicana en cifras.* Mexico City, 1963.

————. *Statistics on the Mexican Economy.* Mexico City, 1977.

Nau, Henry R. "U.S.-Mexican Oil and Gas Relations: A Special Relationship?" In *United States Relations with Mexico: Context and Content,* edited by Richard D. Erb and Stanley R. Ross, pp. 195–211. Washington, D.C.: American Enterprise Institute, 1981.

Needler, Martin. *Mexican Politics: The Containment of Conflict.* New York: Praeger Publishers, 1982.

————. *Politics and Society in Mexico.* Albuquerque: University of New Mexico Press, 1971.

Ojeda, Mario. *Alcances y límites de la política exterior de México.* 2d ed. Mexico City: El Colegio de México, 1985.

————. "México ante los Estados Unidos en la coyuntura actual." *Foro Internacional* 18, no. 1 (1977):32–53.

————. *México: El surgimiento de una política exterior activa.* Mexico City: S.E.P., 1986.

Ojeda, Mario, ed. *Las relaciones de México con los países de América Central.* Mexico City: El Colegio de México, 1985.

Ojeda, Mario, and Herrera, René. *La política de México hacia Centroamérica, 1979–1982.* Mexico City: El Colegio de México, 1983.

Organization of American States. *Informes económicos de corto plazo. Mexico, 1980.* Washington, D.C.: OAS, August 18, 1980.

Oteyza, José Andrés. "México y el mercado internacional del petróleo." *Energéticos* 5, no. 6 (1981):27–28.
Padgett, L. Vincent. *The Mexican Political System*. 2d ed. Boston: Houghton Mifflin, 1976.
Padua, Jorge. *Educación, industrialización y progreso técnico en México*. Mexico City: El Colegio de México, 1984.
Paz, Octavio. *The Labyrinth of Solitude: Life and Thought in Mexico*. New York: Grove Press, 1961.
─────── . *The Other Mexico: Critique of the Pyramid*. Trans. by Lysander Kemp. New York: Grove Press, 1972.
─────── . "Reflections: Mexico and the United States." Trans. by Rachel Phillips. *New Yorker*, September 17, 1979, pp. 136–153.
Pellicer de Brody, Olga. "Cambios recientes en la política exterior mexicana." *Foro Internacional* 13, no. 2 (1972):139–154.
─────── . *México y la revolución cubana*. Mexico City: El Colegio de México, 1972.
─────── . "Veinte años de política exterior mexicana: 1960–1980." *Foro Internacional* 21, no. 2 (1980):152–159.
Peñaloza, Tomás. "La formulacion de la política exterior en los Estados Unidos de América y su impacto sobre México." *Foro Internacional* 18, no. 1 (1977).
Poulson, Barry W. "The Brain Drain from Mexico to the United States." In *U.S.-Mexico Economic Relations*, edited by Barry W. Poulson and Noel Osborn, pp. 245–260. Boulder, Colo.: Westview Press, 1979.
Purcell, John F.H., and Purcell, Susan Kaufman. "El estado y la empresa privada." *Nueva Política* 1, no. 2 (1976):229–250.
Purcell, Susan Kaufmann. "Business-Government Relations in Mexico: The Case of the Sugar Industry." *Comparative Politics* 13, no. 2 (1981):211–232.
─────── . *The Mexican Profit-Sharing Decision: Politics in an Authoritarian Regime*. Berkeley: University of California Press, 1975.
Purcell, Susan Kaufman, ed. *Mexico–United States Relations*. New York: Academy of Political Science, 1981.
Purcell, Susan, and Purcell, John F.H. "State and Society in Mexico: Must a Stable Polity Be Institutionalized?" *World Politics* 32, no. 2 (1980):194–227.
Reyna, José Luis. *Control político, estabilidad y desarrollo en México*. Cuadernos del Centro de Estudios Sociológicos 3. Mexico City: El Colegio de México, 1974.
Reyna, José Luis et al. *Tres estudios sobre el movimiento obrero en México*. Mexico City: El Colegio de México, 1976.
Reyna, José Luis, and Weinert, Richard. *Authoritarianism in Mexico*. Philadelphia, Pa.: Institute for the Study of Human Issues, 1977.
Reynolds, Clark. *The Mexican Economy: Twentieth Century Structure and Growth*. New Haven, Conn.: Yale University Press, 1970.
─────── . "Why Mexico's 'Stabilizing Development' Was Actually Destabilizing (with Some Implications for the Future)." *World Development* 6, no. 7-8 (July-August 1979):1005–1018.
Riding, Alan. *Distant Neighbors: Portrait of the Mexicans*. New York: Knopf, 1985.
Ríos-Bustamente, Antonio, ed. *Mexican Immigrant Workers in the U.S.* Los Angeles: UCLA, 1981.
Ronfeldt, David. *The Modern Mexican Military: A Reassessment*. Monograph Series 16. La Jolla, Calif.: Center for U.S.-Mexican Studies, University of California, San Diego, 1984.
Ronfeldt, David, Nehring, Richard, and Gandara, A. *Mexico's Petroleum and U.S. Policy: Implications for the 1980s*. Santa Monica, Calif.: Rand Corporation, June 1980.

Ross, Stanley, ed. *Is the Mexican Revolution Dead?* New York: Knopf, 1966.

Roxborough, Ian. *Unions and Politics in Mexico: The Case of the Automobile Industry.* New York: Cambridge University Press, 1984.

Safford, Frank. "Bases of Political Alignment in Early Republican Spanish America." In *New Approaches to Latin American History,* edited by Richard Graham and Peter H. Smith, pp. 71–111. Austin: University of Texas Press, 1974.

Sanderson, Steven E. *Agrarian Populism and the Mexican State: The Struggle for Land in Sonora.* Berkeley: University of California Press, 1981.

_____. *The Transformation of Mexican Agriculture: International Structure and the Politics of Rural Change.* Princeton, N.J.: Princeton University Press, 1986.

Sante, Angela M. Delli. "The Private Sector, Business Organizations, and International Influence: A Case Study of Mexico." In *Capitalism and the State in U.S.-Latin American Relations,* edited by Richard R. Fagen. Stanford, Calif.: Stanford University Press, 1979.

Schmitt, Karl M. *Mexico and the United States 1821–1973: Conflict and Coexistence.* New York: John Wiley, 1974.

Scott, Robert. *Mexican Government in Transition.* Urbana: University of Illinois Press, 1964.

Segovia, Rafael. *La politización del niño mexicano.* 2d ed. Mexico City: El Colegio de México, 1982.

Sepúlveda, Bernardo, and Chumacero, Antonio. *La inversión extranjera en México.* Mexico City: Fondo de Cultura Económica, 1973.

Shafer, Robert. *Mexican Business Organizations.* Syracuse, N.Y.: Syracuse University Press, 1973.

Shafer, Robert, and Mabry, Donald. *Neighbors—Mexico and the United States: Wetback's and Oil.* Chicago: Nelson-Hall, 1981.

Siglo XXI, eds. *El perfil de México en 1980.* 3 vols. Mexico City: Siglo XXI, 1970.

Silva Herzog, Jesús. *Trayectoria ideológica de la revolución mexicana.* Mexico City: S.E.P., 1973.

Smith, Peter. *The Labyrinths of Power: Political Recruitment in Twentieth Century Mexico.* Princeton, N.J.: Princeton University Press, 1979.

_____. "Leadership and Change, Intellectuals and Technocrats." In *Mexico's Political Stability: The Next Five Years,* edited by Roderic A. Camp, pp. 101–118. Boulder, Colo.: Westview Press, 1986.

Solís, Leopoldo. *Alternativas para el desarrollo.* Mexico City: Cuadernos de Joaquín Mortiz, 1980.

_____. *A Monetary Will-o-the-Wisp: Pursuit of Equity Through Deficit Spending.* Discussion Papers no. 77. Princeton, N.J.: Princeton University, 1977.

_____. *La realidad económica mexicana: Retrovisión y perspectivas.* 10th ed. Mexico City: Siglo XXI, 1980.

Spalding, Rose J. "State Power and Its Limits: Corporatism in Mexico." *Comparative Political Studies* 14, no. 2 (1981):139–161.

_____. "Welfare Policymaking: Theoretical Implications of a Mexican Case Study." *Comparative Politics* 12, no. 4 (1980):419–438.

Stevens, Evelyn. *Protest and Response in Mexico.* Cambridge, Mass.: M.I.T. Press, 1974.

Story, Dale. *Industry, the State and Public Policy in Mexico.* Austin: University of Texas Press, 1986.

_____. "Policy Cycles in Mexican Politics." *Latin American Research* 20, no. 3 (1985):139–161.

Székely, Gabriel. "The 1976 Oil Export Decision: Effects of the Oil Boom on Mexico's Political Economy." Ph.D. dissertation, George Washington University, 1983.

Székely, Gabriel, ed. *México-Estados Unidos, 1985.* Mexico City: El Colegio de México, 1986.

Tannenbaum, Frank. *The Struggle for Peace and Bread.* New York: Columbia University Press, 1950.

Tello, Carlos. *La nacionalización de la banca en México.* Mexico City: Siglo XXI, 1984.

Tello, Carlos, and Cordera, Rolando. *México: La disputa por la nación: Perspectivas y opciones del desarrollo.* Mexico City: Siglo XXI, 1981.

Tenenbaum, Barbara H. "Straightening Out Some of the Lumpen in the Development." *Latin American Perspectives* 2, no. 2 (1975):3–16.

Thorp, Rosemary, and Whitehead, Lawrence. *Inflation and Stabilization in Latin America.* New York: Holmes and Meier, 1979.

Turner, Frederick C. *The Dynamic of Mexican Nationalism.* Chapel Hill: University of North Carolina Press, 1968.

United Nations Economic Commission for Latin America. *México: Notas para el estudio económico de América Latina.* Washington, D.C.: UNECLA, 1979.

United Nations Educational, Scientific and Cultural Organization. *Statistical Yearbook 1977.* Paris: UNESCO, 1978.

U.S. Central Intelligence Agency. *The International Energy Situation: Outlook to 1985.* Washington, D.C., April 1977.

_____. *The World Oil Market in the Years Ahead.* Washington, D.C., August 1979.

U.S. Congress, Joint Economic Committee. *Recent Developments in Mexico and Their Economic Implications for the United States.* Hearings Before the Subcommittee on Inter-American Economic Relationships of the Joint Economic Committee, January 17 and 24, 1977. Washington, D.C., 1977.

U.S. Congressional Budget Office. *The World Oil Market in the 1980s: Implications for the United States.* Washington, D.C., May 1980.

U.S. Congressional Research Service. *Mexico's Oil and Gas Policy: An Analysis.* Washington, D.C., December 1978.

U.S. Council of Economic Advisors. *Economic Report of the President.* Washington, D.C.: Government Printing Office, various issues.

U.S. General Accounting Office. *Prospects for a Stronger U.S.-Mexico Energy Relationship.* Washington, D.C.: GAO, May 1, 1980.

U.S. House of Representatives. *Intelligence on the World Energy Outlook and Its Policy Implications.* Hearings Before the Subcommittee on Oversight of the Permanent Select Committee on Intelligence. Washington, D.C., 1980.

_____. *U.S.-Mexican Relations: An Update.* Hearings Before the Subcommittee of Inter-American Affairs of the Committee of Foreign Affairs. Washington, D.C., June 1981.

_____. *U.S.-Mexican Relations and the Energy Crisis.* Washington, D.C.: Committee on Foreign Affairs, June 1980.

U.S. House of Representatives, Committee on Science and Technology. *U.S.-Mexico Relations and Potentials Regarding Energy, Immigration, Scientific Cooperation and Technology Transfer.* Washington, D.C.: Government Printing Office, 1979.

U.S. Senate. *Mexico: The Promise and Problems of Petroleum.* Washington, D.C.: Committee on Energy and Natural Resources, March 1979.

_____. *The Western Hemisphere Energy System.* Hearings Before the Committee of Energy and Natural Resources. Washington, D.C., November 1979.

Vargas, Armando. "Coup at Excélsior." *Columbia Journalism Review* 15, no. 3 (1967):45–48.

Vasquez, Carlos, and García y Griego, Manuel, eds. *Mexican-U.S. Relations: Conflict and Convergence?* Los Angeles: UCLA, 1983.

Vaughan, Mary Kay. *The State, Education, and Social Class in Mexico, 1880–1928.* DeKalb: Northern Illinois University Press, 1982.

Vázquez, Josefina Zoraida, and Meyer, Lorenzo. *The United States and Mexico.* Chicago: University of Chicago Press, 1985.

Vernon, Raymond F. *The Dilemma of Mexico's Development: The Roles of the Private and Public Sectors.* Cambridge, Mass.: Harvard University Press, 1963.

Villarreal, René. "El petróleo como instrumento de desarrollo y de negociación internacional: México en los ochentas." *El Trimestre Económico* 48, no. 1 (1981):3–44.

————. "The Policy of Import-Substituting Industrialization, 1929–1975." In *Authoritarianism in Mexico,* edited by José Luis Reyna and Richard Weinert, pp. 67–107. Philadelphia, Pa.: Institute for the Study of Human Issues, 1977.

Weil, Thomas E. et al. *Area Handbook for Mexico.* Washington, D.C.: Government Printing Office, 1975.

Weintraub, Sidney. "Case Study of Economic Stabilization: Mexico." In *Economic Stabilization in Developing Countries,* edited by William R. Cline and Sidney Weintraub, pp. 271–296. Washington, D.C.: Brookings Institution, 1981.

Whitehead, Lawrence. *Mexico: From Bust to Boom: A Political Evaluation of the 1976–1979 Stabilization Program.* Latin American Program Working Paper no. 44. Washington, D.C.: Woodrow Wilson International Center for Scholars, June 1979.

Wilkie, James. *The Mexican Revolution: Federal Expenditures and Social Change Since 1910.* Berkeley: University of California Press, 1967.

Williams, Edward J. "The Implications of the Border for Mexican Policy and Mexican–United States Relations." In *Mexico's Political Stability: The Next Five Years,* edited by Roderic A. Camp, pp. 211–234. Boulder, Colo.: Westview Press, 1986.

Wionczek, Miguel. "On the Viability of a Policy for Science and Technology in Mexico." *Latin American Research Review* 16, no. 1 (1981):57–78.

————. *La sociedad mexicana: Presente y futuro.* Mexico City: Fondo de Cultura Económica, 1973.

Womack, John. *Zapata and the Mexican Revolution.* New York: Knopf, 1969.

Workshop on Alternative Energy Strategies. *Energy: Global Prospects, 1985–2000.* New York: McGraw-Hill, 1977.

World Bank. *Annual Report.* Washington, D.C., various issues.

————. *Energy in the Developing Countries.* Washington, D.C., August 1980.

————. *Mexico, Manufacturing Sector: Situation, Prospects and Policies.* Washington, D.C.: World Bank, March 1979.

————. *A Program to Accelerate Petroleum Production in the Developing Countries.* Washington, D.C., 1979.

————. *World Development Report.* Washington, D.C., various issues.

PRINCIPAL NEWSPAPERS AND MAGAZINES CONSULTED

Comercio Exterior
El Día
Diario Oficial
Energéticos
Excélsior

El Financiero
El Heraldo
La Jornada
Latin American Political Report
Latin American Weekly Report
New Yorker
New York Times
Novedades
Proceso
Razones
El Trimestre Económico
Uno Más Uno
Vuelta
Washington Post

Acronyms
and Abbreviations

bcfd	billion cubic feet per day
CANACINTRA	National Chamber of Manufacturing Industry
CCE	Coordinating Business Council
CCI	Independent Peasant Confederation
CNC	National Peasant Confederation
COCEP	Committee for Oil Exports
CONASUPO	National Staple Products Company
CONCAMIN	Confederation of Industrial Chambers
CONCANACO	Confederation of Chambers of Commerce of Mexico
COPARMEX	Confederation of Employers of the Mexican Republic
CROM	Mexican Regional Labor Confederation
CTM	Confederation of Mexican Workers
FSTSE	Federation of Unions of State Workers
GATT	General Agreement on Tariffs and Trade
GDP	gross domestic product
IEPES	Institute of Political, Economic, and Social Studies
IBM	International Business Machines
ISI	import substitution industrialization
mbd	million barrels per day
NAFINSA	National Development Bank
OAS	Organization of American States
OECD	Organization for Economic Cooperation and Development

OPEC	Organization of Petroleum-Exporting Countries
PAN	National Action party
PARM	Authentic Party of the Mexican Revolution
PCM	Mexican Communist party
PDM	Democratic Mexican party
PEMEX	Petróleos Mexicanos (Mexico's state oil company)
PIPSA	Producer and Importer of Paper
PMS	Mexican Socialist party
PMT	Mexican Workers party
PPS	Popular Socialist party
PRI	Institutionalized Revolutionary party
PRT	Revolutionary Party of the Workers
PSD	Social Democratic party
PST	Socialist Workers party
PSUM	Mexico's Unified Socialist party
SAM	Mexican Food System
SEP	Ministry of Public Education
UNCTAD	United Nations Conference on Trade and Development
UNESCO	United Nations Educational, Scientific and Cultural Organization
VAT	value added tax

Index